Retail Work

Critical Perspectives on Work and Employment

Series editors:
Irena Grugulis, Durham University, UK
Caroline Lloyd, School of Social Sciences, Cardiff University, UK
Chris Smith, Royal Holloway University of London School of Management, UK
Chris Warhurst, University of Strathclyde Business School, UK

Critical Perspectives on Work and Employment combines the best empirical research with leading edge, critical debate on key issues and developments in the field of work and employment. Extremely well regarded and popular, the series is linked to the highly successful *International Labour Process Conference*.

Formerly edited by David Knights, Hugh Willmott, Chris Smith and Paul Thompson, each volume in the series includes contributions from a range of disciplines, including the sociology of work and employment, business and management studies, human resource management, industrial relations and organisational analysis.

Further details of the *International Labour Process Conference* can be found at www.ilpc.org.uk.

Published:
Irena Grugulis and Ödül Bozkurt
RETAIL WORK

Paul Thompson and Chris Smith
WORKING LIFE

Maeve Houlihan and Sharon Bolton
WORK MATTERS

Alan McKinlay and Chris Smith
CREATIVE LABOUR

Chris Warhurst, Doris Ruth Eikhof and Axel Haunschild
WORK LESS, LIVE MORE?

Bill Harley, Jeff Hyman and Paul Thompson
PARTICIPATION AND DEMOCRACY AT WORK

Chris Warhurst, Ewart Keep and Irena Grugulis
THE SKILLS THAT MATTER

Andrew Sturdy, Irena Grugulis and Hugh Willmott
CUSTOMER SERVICE

Craig Prichard, Richard Hull, Mike Chumer and Hugh Willmott
MANAGING KNOWLEDGE

Alan Felstead and Nick Jewson
GLOBAL TRENDS IN FLEXIBLE LABOUR

Paul Thompson and Chris Warhurst
WORKPLACES OF THE FUTURE

More details of the publications in this series can be found at
http://www.palgrave.com/business/cpwe.asp

Critical Perspectives on Work and Employment Series

Series Standing Order ISBN 978-0230-23017-0

You can receive future titles in this series as they are published by placing a standing order. Please contact your bookseller or, in case of difficulty, write to us at the address below with your name and address, the title of the series and the ISBN quoted above.

Customer Services Department, Macmillan Distribution Ltd, Houndmills, Basingstoke, Hampshire RG21 6XS, England

Retail Work

Edited by
Irena Grugulis
Professor of Employment Studies,
Durham University, UK

and

Ödül Bozkurt
Lecturer, Department of Organisation
Work and Technology, Lancaster University
Management School, UK

palgrave
macmillan

First published 2011 by
PALGRAVE MACMILLAN

Palgrave Macmillan in the UK is an imprint of Macmillan Publishers Limited,
registered in England, company number 785998, of Houndmills, Basingstoke,
Hampshire RG21 6XS.

Palgrave Macmillan in the US is a division of St Martin's Press LLC,
175 Fifth Avenue, New York, NY 10010.

Palgrave Macmillan is the global academic imprint of the above companies
and has companies and representatives throughout the world.

Palgrave® and Macmillan® are registered trademarks in the United States,
the United Kingdom, Europe and other countries.

ISBN: 978–0–230–28357–2

This book is printed on paper suitable for recycling and made from fully
managed and sustained forest sources. Logging, pulping and manufacturing
processes are expected to conform to the environmental regulations of the
country of origin.

A catalogue record for this book is available from the British Library.

A catalog record for this book is available from the Library of Congress.

10 9 8 7 6 5 4 3 2 1
20 19 18 17 16 15 14 13 12 11

Printed and bound in Great Britain by
CPI Antony Rowe, Chippenham and Eastbourne

Contents

List of Illustrations

Tables

Figures

Acknowledgements

Chapter 10 was originally published by the ESRC Centre on Skills, Knowledge and Organisational Performance, Universities of Cardiff and Oxford as SKOPE Working Paper Number 91 http://www.skope.ox.ac.uk/. We are grateful for their permission to republish it here.

Every effort has been made to trace all copyright holders, but if any have been inadvertently overlooked the publishers will be pleased to make the necessary arrangements at the first opportunity.

Notes on Contributors

Thomas Andersson
Associate Professor in Management at the University of Skövde, Sweden. He is also a research fellow at the Gothenburg Research Institute in the programme 'Leadership, innovation and co-workership'. Following the completion of his doctoral thesis (2005), he was awarded the prestigious Wallander Grant to continue his research. He has published frequently in international journals including *International Studies of Management and Organization, International Journal of Retail and Distribution Management, Journal of Management Development, Qualitative Research in Accounting and Management, Journal of Health Organization and Management* and *Ephemera: Theory and Politics in Organization*.

Janis Bailey
Works in the Department of Employment Relations and Human Resources, Griffith University, Brisbane, Australia. Her research interests include union strategy and culture, the use of visual material in research and teaching, and vulnerable groups of workers. Her current projects include pay equity in the university sector, student part-time workers and innovative approaches to teaching 'capstone' courses in business programmes. She is a former union industrial officer, and is currently an office-holder in Australia's National Tertiary Education Union.

Ödül Bozkurt
Lecturer, Lancaster University Department of Organisation Work and Technology. She holds a PhD in Sociology from the University of California at Los Angeles. Her research interests include various aspects of the transformation of work within the context of globalization, particularly inside multinational corporations. Her work has been published in a number of

edited volumes and in academic journals including *Society* and *Gender Work and Organization*. Her most recent work focuses on issues of gender and management in a number of foreign-owned multinationals in Japan, including several global major retailers.

Françoise Carré
Research Director at the Center for Social Policy, University of Massachusetts Boston. Publications include *Non-standard Work: the Nature and Challenges of Changing Employment Arrangements* (2000) co-edited with M.A. Ferber, L. Golden and S. Herzenberg; 'Nonstandard work arrangements in France and the United States', in S. Houseman and M. Osawa (eds) *Non-standard Work Arrangements in Japan, Europe, and the United States* (2003); and 'Retail jobs in comparative perspective' (2010) co-authored with C. Tilly, M. vanKlaveren and D. Voss-Dahm in Jerôme Gautié and John Schmitt (eds) *Low-Wage Work in the Wealthy World*. Russell Sage Foundation.

Jeremy Clegg
Jean Monnet Professor of European Integration and International Business Management at Leeds University Business School, University of Leeds. His research interests include the impact of foreign-owned firms on the productivity and performance of firms in developing countries, particularly China. He is leading a project on outward foreign direct investment by Chinese firms in the UK and the EU, and has recently been working on an Engineering and Physical Sciences Research Council (EPSRC) research project on supermarkets and productivity. He served as Chair of the Academy of International Business, UK and Ireland Chapter, from 2001 to 2007.

Johanna Commander
Research Fellow at the Scottish Centre for Employment Research within the University of Strathclyde.

Asaf Darr
Studied Organizational Behaviour at the School of Industrial and Labour Relations, Cornell University. He is a Senior Lecturer in Organization Studies at the University of Haifa. In addition to many articles, he is the author of *Selling Technology: The Changing Shape of Sales in an Information Economy*, published in 2006 by Cornell University Press. Together with Nurit Bird-David, he published in 2009 the paper: 'Commodity, gift, and mass-gift: on gift-commodity hybrids in advanced mass consumption cultures' (*Economy and Society*). His current research is on the social fabric of advanced markets and on Jews and Palestinians in work organizations.

Alan Felstead
Research Professor at Cardiff School of Social Sciences, Cardiff University. His research focuses on: the quality of work; training, skills and learning;

non-standard employment; and the spaces and places of work. He has completed over 30 funded research projects (including 8 funded by the ESRC), produced 6 books, and written over 150 journal articles, chapter contributions and research reports. His recent books include: *Improving Working as Learning* (with Fuller, A., Jewson, N. and Unwin, L.), London: Routledge, 2009; and *Changing Places of Work* (with Jewson, N. and Walters, S.), London: Palgrave, 2005.

Alison Fuller

Professor of Education and Work and Head of the Lifelong and Work-Related Learning Research Centre in the School of Education, University of Southampton. Her research interests include: apprenticeship, changing patterns of participation in education, training and work; education – work transitions, and workplace learning. Alison has recently (with Alan Felstead, Lorna Unwin and Nick Jewson) co-authored the book *Improving Working as Learning* and has been appointed to the UK Commission on Employment and Skill's Expert Panel. She is also co-director of the multi-disciplinary Work Futures Research Centre at the University of Southampton and a researcher in the ESRC LLAKES Research Centre (www.llakes.org).

Mary Gatta

A Director, Gender and Workforce Policy at the Center for Women and Work, and on the faculty in the Department of Labor Studies and Employment Relations at Rutgers University. Her areas of expertise include gender and public policy, low-wage workers and service work. Dr Gatta has published several books, articles and policy papers. Her latest book, *Not Just Getting By: The New Era of Flexible Workforce Development* released from Lexington Press's imprint Press for Change, chronicles groundbreaking thinking and research on new and innovative workforce development initiatives that delivers skills training to single working poor mothers via the Internet.

Irena Grugulis

Professor of Employment Studies at Durham University, AIM/ESRC Services Fellow and an associate fellow of SKOPE. Her research focuses on all areas of skill, recent projects have covered the retail sector as well as work in film and TV and she is currently conducting an ethnography of work in computer games. Recent articles include 'Skill and performance' with Dimitrinka Stoyanova in the *British Journal of Industrial Relations*. Books include *Customer Service* with Andrew Sturdy and Hugh Willmott; *The Skills That Matter* with Chris Warhurst and Ewart Keep and *Skills, Training and Human Resource Development*, all published by Palgrave Macmillan.

Prue Huddleston

Professorial Fellow and Director of the Centre for Education and Industry, University of Warwick. Her research interests include work-related learning, vocational education and qualifications with a particular focus on 14–19 learners. She has recently completed an evaluation of the 14–19 Diploma Development process for DCSF and worked jointly on an ESRC funded project exploring the experiences and expectations of young people in 'Jobs without training'. She has published extensively on education/business partnership, in particular the role of employers in pupil work experience and on pupils' experience of part-time work.

Scott A. Hurrell

Lecturer in Work and Employment Studies in the Institute for Socio-Management at Stirling University. His research interests include skills and work organization, recruitment and selection and the work of front line service workers. Scott has published in international journals and has worked with policy bodies such as Futureskills Scotland the former Equal Opportunities Commission (Scotland), the Scottish Council for Voluntary Organisations and Scottish Government Departments.

Nick Jewson

Senior Research Fellow at the School of Social Sciences, Cardiff University. He is currently engaged in a large-scale research project, funded by the UK Commission for Employment and Skills and the Economic and Social Research Council, on the impact of the recession on training.

Laura K. Jordan

A doctoral candidate in Social Anthropology at the University of Manchester. An interest in researching themes of social injustice originally led her to shave her head and take temporary vows among Theravada Buddhist nuns in India and Burma, producing an award-winning BA thesis (Albion College, US) about these women's struggle for social legitimacy. The same interest subsequently took her to Mexico, where her master's research (CIESAS-Sureste) examined the social impacts of Coca-Cola's expansion in the Highlands of Chiapas. She is currently preparing a doctoral dissertation on the situation of hypermarket retail workers in the US.

Ali Kazemi

Associate Professor of Social Psychology at University of Skövde in Sweden. His research interests embrace different areas of basic and applied psychology and include well-being, decision making in social dilemmas, social justice, resource theory, traffic and transport behaviour, conflict management and human resource management. His research has been published in research volumes and scholarly journals. He has also edited the *Handbook of Social Resource Theory* in press by Springer; *A Theoretical Approach to Assess Road Safety Campaigns,* 2009 by the Belgian Road Safety Institute; and *Well-Being in Working Life,* 2009 by Studentlitteratur in Swedish.

Samantha Lynch

Lecturer in Employment Relations and Human Resource Management at the Kent Business School, University of Kent, UK. Dr Lynch is also the Director of the BA Employment Relations and Human Resource Management and Academic Lead for the MSc Human Resource Management. Dr Lynch lectures in human resource management to undergraduate and postgraduate students. Her main research interests include line managers and HRM, HRM and performance and employment in the retail industry.

Kate Mulholland

Kate Mulholland works in the department of Human Resource Management at the University of Strathclyde, Glasgow. She is presently researching the character of work and employment relations in distribution and retail. She has researched and published work on work organization in the privatized utilities, class, gender and family enterprise and work organization in call centres. Her book, *Class, Gender and the Family Business* (2003) was nominated for the BSA Philip Abrams Memorial Prize. She has taught employment relations at the University of the West of England and the Sociology of Work and Industry at the Queens University of Belfast and held research posts at Warwick Business School and Leicester University.

Dennis Nickson

Professor of Service Work and Employment and Head of the Department of Human Resource Management, University of Strathclyde. His main research and teaching interests are focussed in the broad area of human resource management in the interactive service sector. He has published widely in this and other areas, including articles in the *Human Resource Management Journal*, *International Journal of Human Resource Management* and *Work, Employment and Society*. Sole and co-authored books include *Human Resource Management for the Hospitality and Tourism Industries* (Butterworth Heinemann, 2007) and *Looking Good, Sounding Right* (Industrial Society, 2001).

Robin Price

Senior Lecturer in the School of Management at Queensland University of Technology. Robin has recently completed an Australia Research Council funded post-doctoral fellowship investigating secondary school students' experiences of part-time work. Her primary research interest is in service sector employment, particularly retail industry employment, where she spent many years before moving to academia.

Amanda Pyman

Senior Lecturer in Human Resource Management and Employment Relations in the Department of Management, Monash University, Melbourne Australia. Dr Pyman is also Deputy Director of the Monash MBA Program and an

Associate Fellow at Warwick Business School, University of Warwick, UK. Dr Pyman lectures in employment relations and human resource management to undergraduate and postgraduate students. Dr Pyman has published widely in national and international journals, and her main research interests include employee voice, labour market regulation, trade union strategy and effectiveness and privacy, monitoring and surveillance at work.

Steven Roberts

Lecturer in Lifelong and Work-related Learning at the School of Education, University of Southampton. Following several years in retail management, he took up a first degree Industrial Relations and Human Resource Management before moving into sociology as a graduate and, subsequently, a doctoral student at the University of Kent. This is reflected in his varied research interests, which include young people's experiences of and attitudes towards employment and post-compulsory education, the changing nature of the contemporary labour market, gender and class at work, and critical analyses of work-based training and skills development more generally.

Stefan Tengblad

Professor in Business Administration at University of Skövde, Sweden. His research interests concerns managerial work, organizational behaviour and Human Resource Management. He has published articles in *Journal of Management Studies, Organization Studies, Journal of Business Ethics, Scandinavian Journal of Management,* and *Qualitative Research in Accounting and Management,* and was the editor of *The Art of Science* (Copenhagen Business School Press 2005).

Chris Tilly

Professor of Urban Planning and Director of the Institute for Research on Labor and Employment at the University of California Los Angeles. Prof. Tilly is an economist specializing in labor, income distribution and local economic development, with research focusing on the US and Mexico. Tilly's books include *Half a Job: Bad and Good Part-Time Jobs in a Changing Labor Market, Glass Ceilings and Bottomless Pits: Women's Work, Women's Poverty, Work Under Capitalism, Stories Employers Tell: Race, Skill, and Hiring in America* and *The Gloves-Off Economy: Labor Standards at the Bottom of America's Labor Market.*

Lorna Unwin

Professor of Vocational Education at the Institute of Education, University of London and is also Deputy Director of the ESRC-funded LLAKES Research Centre. Her current research focuses on the ways in which employers and education and training providers are responding to and are affected by both the competitiveness and cohesion agendas within city-regions. This includes the changing nature of apprenticeship as both a model of learning and an instrument of State policy. Her recent books include *Improving Working for Learning*, 2009; and *Communities of Practice: Critical Perspectives*, 2008, both published by Routledge.

Maarten van Klaveren

Researcher at the Amsterdam Institute for Advanced Labour Studies (AIAS) at the University of Amsterdam and senior consultant at STZ consultancy and research, Eindhoven, the Netherlands. His research interests focus on the interrelations of work organization, wages and working conditions, in particular in multinational firms. Recent publications cover employment in retail and call centres, women's work and employment in 14 developing countries, trade union renewal, and the impact of foreign direct investment on wages and working conditions in EU countries.

Dorothea Voss-Dahm

Researcher at the Institute for Work, Skills and Training (IAQ) at the University of Duisburg-Essen, Germany. Her research interests cover social inequality in service work as well as the interplay between institutions and organizations. She is currently working on a larger project on vocational training systems in an international perspective and their influence on stability and flexibility in labour markets as well as on work relations in companies.

Chris Warhurst

Professor of Work and Organizational Studies at the University of Sydney. He is an editor of the *Critical Perspectives on Work and Employment* book series for Palgrave Macmillan and until the end of 2010 was co-editor of the journal *Work, Employment and Society*. He is co-editor of a number of books including *Work Less, Live More?* and *The Skills That Matter* (both Palgrave Macmillan). His research and teaching focus on labour process and labour market issues. Recent research has examined the gender pay gap in financial services, union learning funds and student financing. He has a particular interest in skill issues, providing advice to, amongst others, the UK and Scottish Governments and Skills Australia. His other main interest is aesthetic labour, with a book forthcoming for Sage.

Mikael Wickelgren

Assistant Professor in Management at the University of Skövde and a research fellow at the Gothenburg Research Institute where he is currently study-ing the criteria consumers use when buying new cars and risk strategies in bank management. His doctoral thesis *Engineering Emotion – Values as Means in Product Development* (2005) examined value-based product development projects in the Swedish auto industry.

Why Retail Work Demands a Closer Look

Ödül Bozkurt and Irena Grugulis

The cultishly popular film *The Big Lebowski* (1998) introduces the main character to the audience in a large, neon-lit supermarket, with generic piped music in the background and, judging by the deserted aisles, in the wee hours when night merges with morning. Our anti-hero, 'the man for his time and place' in the narrator's words, fumbles when asked for proof of ID as he tries to pay for his purchase by personal cheque, and then produces the only one he has: his 'Value Club Card' at this well-known Californian supermarket chain. Audience members recognize this sort of setting immediately – even if the subtext of the American 24-hour, constantly 'on' retail space is not exactly the same everywhere – it is a space we inhabit routinely. Part of the familiarity is engendered by others we have gotten used to encountering in these increasingly standardized settings. In fact, there are two other characters in the scene, neither of them as visible or as memorable as the errant consumer: a bored-looking, indifferent, fatigued checkout clerk whose experience at work is captured by her expressionless face as she has no option but to show patience with the tedious transaction, arms folded, and a Mexican call-out boy wearing a bright-coloured store uniform who carries the customer's ridiculously sparse purchase, a sole carton of milk, to his car in this intentionally ironic instance. Not only does the audience recognize this sort of space, but we also recognize these sorts of workers and these sorts of encounters with workers. In fact, many of us have *been* these workers, and recognize these sorts of customers.

Contemporary retail workplaces and workers figure prominently in shorthand popular cultural representations of the zeitgeist, because they are an integral part of how we live everyday life as consumers of an ever growing range of goods and services. And depictions that give us glimpses of retail jobs as downtrodden, thankless and rather hopeless certainly resonate far more immediately and strongly with most of us than the sort exulted by Sam Walton, the founder of Walmart, whose 'vigorous staff motivation and customer care program' included a pledge to be taken by workers: 'I solemnly promise and declare that every customer that comes within 10ft of me I will smile, look at them in the eye and greet them, so help me Sam' (McGoldrick, 2002: 500).

Indeed, there are grounds to argue that retail work is in many ways *the* new generic form of mass employment in the post-industrial socio-economic landscape. If the factory and the assembly line came to represent the quintessential workplace under industrialism, prompting much employment research (Beynon, 1985; Burawoy, 1979; Chinoy, 1955); technology-driven high-tech offices are conjured up by both celebrants and sceptics of the post-industrial economy in a similar manner. But a far more representative workplace of the post-industrial era may be Walmart, rather than Google. Certainly, Braverman (1974) anticipated the growing significance of retailing and observed the way in which retail employment demonstrated the worst impulses of service industries to replicate the extractive labour processes of industrialism, with increasing losses of discretion and autonomy on the job. He noted that 'a revolution is now being prepared which will make of retail workers, by and large, something closer to factory operatives than anyone had ever imagined possible'(371).

Yet while on the surface only all too familiar, retail work remains understudied. Despite a growing body of greatly insightful research exploring the dynamics of the transition from industrial to service-based economies over the past several decades, this specific area within services has not garnered much attention. While, for example, the fast food industry (Leidner, 1993; Ritzer, 1993) and call centres (Callaghan and Thompson, 2002; Taylor and Bain, 1999) have proved critical settings through which scholars have sought to challenge utopian statements about the purported change in the nature of jobs under post-industrialism, retail employment has not been privy to such sustained academic interest. This is particularly curious against a backdrop where both academic writing, mostly but not exclusively with a strategic thrust, and popular writing on retail *per se* has proliferated rapidly. There has been what could be called a 'boom' in such scholarship, inspirational books about exemplary businesses following a trajectory paralleling the rise and fall of different sectors over time, from automotives to software companies to now, perhaps, retailers (Bergdahl, 2006; Bevan, 2007; Brandes, 2004; Fishman, 2007; Lewis, 2005). Thus we are presented with surveys of the sector and assessments of what it takes to succeed in it (Berman, 2010; Randall and Seth, 2005), as well as studies looking at various aspects of retailing strategy such as internationalization (Dawson et al., 2006), marketing (McCormick, 2002) and logistics (Fernie and Sparks, 2009). Supermarkets have received the most attention in public debates on retail by a wide margin, several recent highly popular books investigating how they have had an impact on the way communities consume, work, and indeed, live (Bevan, 2006; Blythman, 2005; Seth and Randall, 2001; Simms, 2007; Spotts, 2006).

This growing interest in retailing is inextricably linked to the increasing significance of the sector as an economic, social, cultural and political force. In the post-war era, the retailing sector and consequently retail employment have undergone radical transformation, a process whose momentum has not diminished over time. As the large, multi-store format, especially in food retailing, came to dominate, retail businesses joined the ranks of the largest and most important companies. Major retailers' quarterly financial announcements now stand as much-heeded signs summarizing the direction and health of national economies and retail spending is taken as a clear indicator of consumer, and hence, of societal mood. The arrival of multinational retailers in new markets and the standardization of the line-up of high streets (and, of course, 'malls') around the world underscore how retail is globalizing, and in the process globalizing the world (Wrigley and Lowe, 2002). Large retailers also play a key role in what happens at the very local level, too, informing consumer choice in micro-geographies (Clarke et al., 2006) and routinely inciting 'community wars' against the arrival of supermarket chain stores in individual neighbourhoods. Yet, at the same time, a lack of major retailers often signals the death knell of the very same communities, and urban regeneration plans increasingly rely on participation by retail chains (Wrigley et al., 2002).

In most of this recent literature on retailing, employment issues figure as a chapter or even as footnotes. There is, however, an interesting development in the writing (and, one can only presume reading) about retail, and one that entails a much closer look at retail employment: the recent crop of books by retail workers themselves. Or, put differently, 'there is a new form of misery lit out there – and it goes bip!' (Long, 2009). Ahmad's *The Checkout Girl* (2009), based on the former investigative reporter's six months working at one of the largest supermarket chains in Britain, talks about the author's days spent trying to 'hit her bip target' and recounts experiences of dealing with customers with all sorts of idiosyncracies. In *Shelf Life* (2009), Simon Parke, a vicar of 20 years standing and the author of popular spirituality books, shares his experiences of seeking (and finding) the meaning of life on-the-job working in a supermarket. Anna Sam of France, a literary student who 'never planned to end up in a supermarket' but 'failed to find a job to match her qualification' (Sage, 2008), began writing a blog of her experiences after seven years working for a hypermarket (http://caissierenofutur.over-blog.com), attracting over 600,000 subscribers within the year. Her book, subsequently published in English under the title *A Life at the Tills* (2009), sold over 100,000 copies in France (Sage, 2009). Sam noted that everyone she ever worked with was at one time or another used as a cautionary tale by mothers urging their children to study by remarking, 'If you don't work hard at school, you'll end up like that lady behind the counter.' (Walden, 2009) and once she was asked by a six-year old if she was 'in prison'. While thoroughly engaging and highly in tune with the times, as evidenced by their popularity, these books make curiously little of the corporate policies behind the work practices their authors observe (and, indeed, suffer under) and instead focus far greater attention on the inconsiderate/rude/offensive customers. In failing to generate truly critical public debate about the nature of retail jobs, these books are narrowly missed opportunities. This is all the more regrettable given the availability of a precursor, an equally readable but infinitely more analytical account by academic/writer Barbara Ehrenreich, *Nickel and Dimed* (2001). Here, retail is afforded only one chapter in Ehrenreich's quest to find out if it is indeed possible to make ends meet through minimum-wage employment in the US, about her time at a Wal-Mart store in Minnesota, but it is one where the reader is given a vivid sense of how such grossly under-rewarded work can at the same time be compulsively engrossing for the workers who seek to experience *some* degree of authority and control over their labour and who have few alternative means of earning a living.

If retail work is understudied, then, perhaps this dearth of interest is warranted either by the fact that there is nothing that important to know about it or, relatedly, that we already know whatever there is to know about it. Although various studies on different aspects of employment have recently been carried out in the retail context, the most recent edited volume on the topic put together by academics remains Åkehurst and Alexander's *Retail Employment* from 1996. Is retail work trivial or self-evident to an extent to not warrant closer inspection, and do not studies on the service sector in general (such as Macdonald and Sirianni, 1996; Bosch and Lehndorff, 2005; Korczynski and Macdonald, 2009), or, for example, those on low-wage work (Carré et al., 2010), answer all the questions worth posing? Obviously, the motivation behind this edited volume is to argue that this is definitely not the case. The effort is based on the belief that retail work does deserve much closer and more focussed scholarly attention, because retail work is *significant, diverse* and *problematic*.

Retail work is significant

Retail work is significant in multiple ways. In sheer quantitative terms, as the chapters in this book detail, retail employment constitutes over 10 per cent of the total labour force in advanced economies. In the US, seven of the ten largest employers in 2004 were in food service and retail (Davis, 2009: 201). In the UK, 2.9 million people were employed in retail in December 2009, roughly equal to 11 per cent of the British workforce (British Retail Consortium, 2010). The implications of this include the importance of retailing to policy makers, employers, workers and academics alike. However, the frequent references to retail employment in public debates as the only or leading area of job growth, at least in the British context, often prove misleading. As the recent recession has shown, with 'heritage retailers' such as Woolworths declaring bankruptcy and going out of business, as well as the closure of many small independent retailers, leaving many British high streets all but deserted, retail work continues to be precarious. Over the last five years, employment in retailing in the UK has fallen by over 145,000 (British Retail Consortium, 2010). The share of retail employment in the entire British workforce was in fact one percent higher, at 12 per cent, in 2003 (Burt and Sparks, 2003). The impression that the share of the workforce employed in retail is constantly on the rise may therefore have more to do with the relative growth of retail jobs in comparison with traditional manufacturing jobs within the context of the overall shift of jobs from industry to services, and that from the perspective of individual workers, retail jobs often end up the only alternative against backdrops of declining job opportunities. In one trivial but telling example, in the recession-inspired reality show *The Fairy Jobmother* on British TV in the summer of 2010, in which a 'personal coach' prepares long-term unemployed families to get back into the labour market, at least one of the jobs one family member gets is inevitably in retail in each episode. Furthermore, while the numbers may not bear out such widespread portrayal of retail as (the only) growth area for jobs, the significance of the sector for employment needs to also take into account the different forms of employment generated across the entire supply chain and not only in the retail stores. Although rationalization has squeezed many jobs out of these retail linkage areas (Wright and Lund, 2003), the employment generated at the intersection points between retailers and suppliers does remains sizeable, if difficult to quantify.

Retail work is diverse

Despite the popular cultural shorthand used to depict retail workers as automatons who cannot wait to get out of these jobs if only the opportunities were there, retail work is widely diverse. The labour market spans a range from attractive, middle class dominated 'style' labour markets where workers enjoy heavy discounts on the latest fashions (Nickson et al., this volume; Warhurst and Nickson, 2007) to the poorly paid shift work offered by mass retailers (Bair and Bernstein, 2006). Retail work involves many different sub-sectors and many different types of workers in different age groups, in different stages of participation in the labour market. Furthermore, there are the visible and invisible sides of retail employment and not all work is confined to face-to-face service provision. There is work done on the shop floor but also in the entire supply chain that is involved in bringing the goods to the sites where consumers obtain them for subsequent consumption.

Retail work is diverse because, in the first instance, retail employers are diverse. They range from small 'boutique establishments' to global corporate giants, from ethnic businesses to family affairs, with immediate implications for the variability in the organization of work. In the UK, 9 per cent of all VAT-registered businesses were in retailing in 2010, with a total number of 192,600 retailers and, according to 2008 figures, 293,510 retail outlets (British Retail Consortium, 2010). These figures underscore the fact that although the giant supermarkets or the high-street stores selling brand-name products are the first to come to mind, they are by no means the only type of retail workplaces. In fact, often their very arrival in specific communities is ridden with conflict and disagreement precisely because of different views of how the corporate, large-scale, chain establishments will impact employment both quantitatively and qualitatively, at the expense of other types of retailers. One very widely debated issue has been, for example, whether the arrival of large supermarkets, and of course the 'queen' of them all, Walmart, actually creates or destroys jobs in the communities they move into (Basker, 2005). Neumark et al. (2008) find that each Walmart worker replaces approximately 1.4 retail workers (although while also noting that, given retail employment growth, this has meant a lower rate of growth in the number of jobs, rather than actual job losses). In the British context, community regeneration plans generally involve the discussion of plans to move in major retailers, which often spark heated debates between those who look at retail employment as the saviour of underprivileged, deprived communities (Percival, 2010) and those who argue that retail employment by large employers is created at the expense of small retailers (Simms, 2010).

Second, retail work is diverse because, as consumption patterns have changed, the products and services that retail workers need to deliver have become more diverse. Industry publications or practitioner conferences often make the point that despite the growth of the range of products retailers carry, the era of the 'one stop shop', even in the case of 'all under one roof' supermarkets, may be becoming obsolete, as consumers 'mix and match'. In the UK, Business Link, the government agency in place to provide support to businesses, lists ten categories within retail (and hire and repair), ranging from arts, antiques and second-hand goods retail to sports and recreation goods retail, and under these there are a further total of

60 subcategories (which actually make for an entertaining read) (Business Link, 2010).

Third, the skills demands in retail also vary dramatically. For soft skills these range from an insistence on middle class, attractive staff (Gatta and Nickson et al. both this volume) to differing levels of customer service (Sturdy, 2001; Macdonald and Siriani, 1996). McGauran (2001) observes the way that French customers insisted on high levels of product knowledge from the assistants who served them and Gamble's (2006) research into high-status multinational retailers in China reveals impressively knowledgeable and highly educated workers. This diversity is often linked to products. The recent Russell Sage project into low wage work has distinguished between male, full-time staff selling electrical goods and the predominantly female part-timers employed in supermarkets (Mason et al., 2008; see also Darr; and Price both this volume). But such differentials are not static and there seems to be more evidence of erosion in terms and conditions than in improvements (Van Klaveren and Voss-Dahm; Jordan both this volume; Kirsch et al., 2000).

Retail work is diverse because, the 'retail workforce', despite the flattening of hierarchies in store operations witnessed over the past two decades and the proliferation of increasingly isomorphic approaches to the utilization of labour (Grimshaw et al., 2001), remains comprised of different categories of workers. There is, first of all, a radical distinction between head office staff and store employees. Second, there is a distinction between managerial staff and shop floor workers in retail stores, particularly in the large multiples, which continues despite the context of disappearing middle ranks. Finally, one of the most visibly problematic aspects of diversity in this respect is the differences between part-time and full-time employment contracts, although this distinction is threatened as the former grows at seemingly unstoppable pace while the latter appears to be in irreversible entrenchment (Shackleton, 1998). In the US, food service and retail had the shortest tenures among employees among all sectors in 2004 (Davis, 2009: 201). This variability in the concrete employment forms also relates to the differences between workers who see and pursue retail as a job and those who view it as a career.

Retail employment is demographically diverse as well, despite being justifiably associated with women, youth and ethnic minority workers in most contexts. Admittedly, the gendered nature of retail employment (e.g., McGauran, 2001; McLaughlin, 1999) is critically linked with working-time arrangements that increasingly and heavily favour part-time contracts, as well as coincide in generating some of the grossest forms of inequality retail employment engenders. But the retail workforce is diverse among members of the same gender too, as well as being highly variable across a range of demographic divisions informed by the variable motivations behind individual workers taking up employment in the sector.

Finally, retail work is diverse because its particular forms and rewards remain variable across different market contexts and in different national employment systems. This is so despite the fact that national distinctions do appear to be eroding through the growing significance of globalization in retailing, and the diffusion of and convergence around various employment policies around 'of industry best practice' are increasingly defined in global terms. As Dawson and Mukoyama (2006: 1) note, 'international activity in retailing is evident in many ways: in the sourcing of goods for resale, the operation of shops, the use of foreign labour, the adoption of foreign ideas and the use of foreign capital'. Globalization impacts retailing and hence retail work in at least three, often overlapping ways. Perhaps the most concrete manifestation of how the retail sector is undergoing a transformation in line with the larger globalization of contemporary capitalism is the increasing transnationalization of the largest retailers (Wrigley et al., 2005). The world's largest retailer (and, incidentally, the world's biggest private employer), Walmart, is increasingly less of an 'all American' institution and more a global giant. Despite its high-profile failure in the German market, Walmart's global expansion continues especially into the populous emerging markets such as China and Brazil. Of the world's largest 100 retailers, the operations of only 29 were confined to their domestic markets in 2004 (Dawson, 2007: 37). These retailers play a hitherto understudied yet direct and significant role in the transfer and diffusion of a range of retail strategies, including those on employment, but the enactment of these strategies in different institutional contexts yields variable outcomes. A second way in which retail work is implicated in globalization is the diffusion not of the particular retail organizations but of the dominant forms of 'doing retail' around the world. The battles of the 'mom-and-pop shops'/ 'high-street independents' vs. the chainstore Goliaths unfold simultaneously in multiple country locations. Although such temporal coincidence of the conflicts underscores that consumption patterns, retailing strategies and consequently retail work are facing similar trajectories of transformation, institutional, legal, cultural, political and social differences between national contexts mean that similar dilemmas lead to diverse outcomes. Finally, globalization impacts retail employment even in the case of purely domestic retailers. In our research with one of the major British supermarket chains that only operates nationally, for example, a core change initiative and its specific prescriptions, most of them involving and in fact dictating changes in the management of workers, were formulated by a US-based retail consultancy that was contracted to bring in 'the state of the art' practices. Yet once again, we observed, the 'translation' of policies, the particular forms the practices took, and certainly the eventual impact of these on retail work were, though similar, still identifiably different than what has been observed in the American retailing context.

Retail work is problematic

The variability of and diversity in retail work are integral to the range of ways in which retail work is problematic. On the one hand, the problems pertaining to work and workers in different categories vary (e.g., across different types of retail employers, in different national contexts); on the other, some of the problems highlight or even stem from the inequalities engendered by the differences in the fortunes of different groups of workers (e.g., the confluence of female workers with part-time jobs and the disconnect between part-time jobs and career progression).

Underlining the diversity that also applies to the problems of retail work helps us make sense of some seemingly paradoxical elements in the discussion of 'the problems with retail jobs', such as the conflicting narratives of employers and workers about whether it is difficult to find 'good people for perfectly satisfying, challenging and rewarding jobs', or more difficult to find '[sufficiently] satisfying, challenging and rewarding jobs for good people'. Such oft-heard statements conflict directly, because they refer to different types of retail work and different groups of workers. For example, employers widely see high labour turnover (Booth and Hamer, 2007) in store operations as problematic, but tend to attribute this to the lack of motivation, engagement and commitment by workers. Since these qualities tend to be labelled 'soft skills', rather than reciprocal elements in a relationship in which employers play an active part (see Lafer, 2004) turnover is presented as a skills rather than a management issue. At another level, employers' difficulty in attracting graduates to retail employment (Andrews, 2009) is often traced back to unfavourable views of careers in retail among university students (Broadbridge, 2003), a general trend that does not appear to be changing radically despite the recent proliferation of retail-related university degree programmes and the number of students who undertake retail work while studying (see Huddleston, this volume).

For the vast majority of the retail workforce, as captured in the popular discourse about retail jobs, retail work is problematic because in many ways it brings together the worst of all worlds – it is low status because it is low-skilled, therefore low-paid, and being all of these things, it tends not to make for a desirable career. Even for those who do desire to make a career in retailing, the options are limited. The very same employer strategies that demand an increasingly more highly skilled workforce in head office functions also help jeopardise the quality and attractiveness of jobs in stores. A focus on generating margins, competitive advantages and hence profits within a context of constantly intensifying competition has increasingly forced retailers to rely on greater and faster innovation in head office functions while at the same time requiring rigorous rationalization of store operations. Such systemic polarization renders much of retail work problematic in a way that defies situational adjustments to try and improve the working conditions for individual workers.

The extreme rationalization of retail operations by the major employers not only makes retailing and hence retail employment by other types of (smaller) organizations more precarious, but also suppresses the potential for collective action by workers in their own ranks. The slicing up of working hours into bundles through advanced scheduling technology and techniques in an attempt to ever more closely match customer flows and product demands notoriously complicates the forging of group identities and hence the politics of workplace resistance. Several years after the film was released, the supermarket where *The Big Lebowski*'s opening scene took place was involved in one of the longest running and most widely supported union strikes in Californian, and indeed American, labour history. However the outcomes of the struggle were only partially satisfying for the union and its members. Garnering such high levels of participation and support appears, if anything, increasingly more difficult as retail work gets to be accepted as the sort of job where workers have no reason to expect anything better.

The book

This book is based on a stream that was run at the *International Labour Process Conference* in Edinburgh, 2009, with contributions from participants there as well as from others whose recent research addresses various aspects of employment in the retail context. It is revealing that, unlike, for example, assembly line workers, the caring professions, or even hospitality industry workers, there is to date no identifiable cluster of studies and networks of scholars engaged in investigating retail employment. This book attempts, as the conference stream did before it, to bring together researchers who have been carrying out work looking into retail and retailing but who are driven by a variety of theoretical interests and contribute to a range of different debates around employment. Some of us are primarily scholars of skills and the ways that labour markets demand, supply and reward them; some of us have a core interest in the link between education and jobs; some of us are keen to explore the micro-dynamics of various workplace practices such as teamwork or leadership as they are re-enacted in real life; some of us are concerned with issues of worker representation and equality. Exploring these themes together around the shared empirical object of retail should not only contribute to the debates on our respective themes, but also help to consolidate retail employment as a field of study where knowledge can be shared and accumulated.

The chapters are arranged under four themes that emerged from the contributions. These partially overlap with the points we have raised above, but do not and cannot fully circumscribe the lesson we learn from each chapter. Gender, for example, is an integral part of many of the chapters, but is taken up mostly in relation to other axes of inequality, like the distribution of part-time as opposed to full-time jobs. And some of the themes, such as skill and the way work is controlled, run throughout the book. The research contexts include a range of advanced capitalist countries, including the UK, the US, Germany, the Netherlands, Australia and Israel, providing us with the rewards of a comparative look at various core issues in retail work.

Part I: Work and skills

Skill is one of the four key areas of activity that The Employment Policy Action Group of the British Retail Consortium identified in 2010, the others being the national minimum wage, national insurance contributions and diversity. The organization claimed:

> The retail sector has an excellent record on training and upskilling its workforce. In 2008, 5,000 retail apprenticeships were completed and 63 per cent of all individuals in the sector were given training equivalent to 14 working days. The sector also provides employees with transferable skills which help them progress either within retail or other business sectors. (British Retail Consortium, 2010)

So at once a 'key target area' and one where claims of an 'excellent record' are made, skills is certainly a critical point of discussion for retail practitioners. In a key speech in 2010, the Chief Executive of the Institute of Grocery Distributors, currently the largest representative body for the food and grocery retailers in the UK, noted, 'We have great people in our industry, even though we're rarely front of mind when it comes to career planning or national skills assessments' (Denney-Finch, 2010). The industry's discourse around skills is certainly a rather confusing one. On the one hand, there are widespread (to the point of universal) claims that retailers do no recruit 'for' skills and employers state that they are equipped to train recruits in all the necessary skills themselves once on the job. On the other, references to a 'skills shortage', for example in terms of efforts to increase productivity in the retail sector in the UK, suggest otherwise (Hart et al., 2007). One of the most important areas in retail work that invite the attention of researchers is therefore that of skills.

Three of the chapters in this book address issues of skills and skilling in relation to retail work. Felstead, Fuller, Jewson and Unwin draw on some of the extensive data from their ESRC Teaching and Learning research to draw out skills and learning issues in supermarkets and sandwich retailing. Acknowledging that one of the principal weaknesses of HRM is that its analysis stops at the boundaries of the firm, the team have developed the 'Working as Learning Framework' (WALF) that uses data from the whole supply chain to set the context. In the two areas considered here influence is exerted at different points in this continuum. In supermarkets control is centralized at head office level and facilitated by in-store technologies (particularly the 'symbol gun'); while new product development in sandwich manufacturing varies according to clientele. It may be driven by the manufacturers themselves, as it is in firms that supply a number of small retail outlets, or by clients, when one powerful customer purchases the majority of output. These different pressure points and power relationships each have very different implications for work, learning and skills.

In Chapter 3 Gatta deals with a very different type of skill, the aesthetic and emotional ability to display the 'right personality' (and, in her own case, to be a 'Betsy's girl'). Focussing on distinctive and up-market retailers in New Jersey, USA she draws out the real skills employers recruit for and considers the implications of this for publicly funded training programmes that aim to bridge the gap between the skills employers desire and those potential workers possess. Store owners' emphasis on first impressions, the 'blink' moment when they 'just know' and the interpersonal skills that could not (in contrast to store-specific knowledge) be trained for. Yet, as Gatta points out, by emphasising this instead of, for example, retail experience, store owners can simply legitimise stereotypes and recruit by prejudice. There are actions that public workfare programmes can take in response to this, but there is also much they need to be wary of.

Nickson, Hurrell, Warhurst and Commander extend this discussion of soft skills with evidence from a survey of the Manchester 'style' labour market. This area, according to their respondents, is one of the most desirable in retailing with shops in which it is 'cool' to work. Here too, employers stressed appearance and personality, though were cautious on whether they selected on the basis of age, weight or height (perhaps because such an admission was more likely to attract legal action than a more general focus on 'appearance' or 'personality'). In contrast to Gatta's employers, the Manchester recruiters also valued product knowledge, but here too the emphasis on aesthetics may have been an easy proxy for discrimination.

In the last chapter in this section, Chapter 5, Robin Price shifts the focus away from sought after jobs in the 'style' labour markets and onto the more mundane face of retail work. She draws on detailed research into an Australian supermarket with all its corporate pressure to cut costs and centralize operations. This account allows us to see the deskilling at store level: as apprentice-trained butchers and bakers found that the extensive use of vacuum packed meats and premixed or par-baked breads and cakes result in the transfer of skills to workers at a different point in the supply chain; which skills were retained; and the impact of inflexible and fragmented staff budgets; and the skills that were retained. Grocery staff still needed to check the quality of produce, and butchers and bakers still baked and prepared meat in-store.

The picture that emerges most clearly from these four chapters is one of diversity. As noted above, retail employment is not homogeneous. At the 'high end' described by Gatta and Nickson et al., employer demands can be substantially different to those in the 'no frills' part of the sector yet interestingly, while technical skills and product knowledge are part of the work, all informants seemed happy to train staff themselves. Recruitment is focused on soft skills, aesthetics, glamour (and probably) class, race and gender. Away from these elite establishments the chapters by Felstead et al. and Price enable us to see both what skills are required of workers in supermarkets and sandwich manufacturers and the points in the supply chain at which influence is exerted. This is an important point since it provides both better explanations of the data, by not limiting analysis to the individual firm. Something which also has implications for policy should attempts be made to improve retail work.

Part II: Retail as a job versus retailing as a career

In the second part we consider the other dilemma that is oft posed about retail employment, that it is seen and experienced as transitory. In a study of university students, half of whom were in management/business degree programmes, Broadbridge found that only 2.6 per cent of the participants freely named retail as their first career choice, while 23.9 per cent indicated that they would definitely not consider such a career (2002:301). Although the subsequent recession together with the sudden contraction of the graduate job market in Britain provided opportunities for the likes of Sainsbury's graduate recruitment manager to claim that retail was 'attracting lots of graduates who might have otherwise applied to banks or other City firms' (CIPD, 2009), even the sector itself readily acknowledges that it is not a graduate 'destination'. For the majority of non-graduate workers in retail the key issue is the broader distinction between 'good' and 'bad' jobs, a distinction that often pivots on the material conditions of work: pay, prospects, scheduling and terms and conditions. Retailing is the site of much low-paid work with career prospects that are often limited to a minority of full-time staff (Mason et al., 2008) and scheduling to suit employers' rather than employees' needs (Arrowsmith and Sisson, 1999).

The complicated relationship between retail jobs and retail careers is explored in the three chapters in this second part of the book, each from a unique perspective and focusing on a particular aspect of this puzzle. Huddleston takes on the industry cries for lack of skilled personnel and poses the dilemmas of retention. Her study follows a small number of students over time, gathering data from them as they work part-time in retailing during their studies and observing whether and why they change jobs, within the sector, within a particular sub-sector and out of the sector. As she argues, there are growing numbers of students who do retail work as a part-time, stopgap means of earning money. This is a potentially unrivalled opportunity for employers to demonstrate the advantages of a longer-term career in retail yet few take advantage of this, the corollary perhaps of the deskilling and the gulf between managers and workers observed in other chapters. Huddleston questions how and why employers fail at converting the accumulated skills of these 'experienced' workers into long-term, permanent careers.

In Chapter 7 Roberts directs our attention to another understudied, unobserved group: that of 18–24-year-old men who work as part of a highly feminized workforce. These 'lost boys' are neglected by both researchers and policy makers. They are not unemployed, not students and not apprentices. As a result we know surprisingly little about them, their work experiences, expectations and prospects. Here, drawing on interviews with young men working in retail, Roberts observes a fascinating distinction between workers on full-time and part-time contracts. While the full-timers considered themselves established in retail, with clear and realistic ambitions for the future and pride in their work and work skills, the part-timers spoke slightingly of retail work and retail workers and their ambitions centred on attaining celebrity status, starring in a rock band or somehow making lots of money. It seems that here, the boundary between retail *work* and retail *careers* is both contractual and attitudinal.

Jordan, with an American example, has some depressing findings on the possibility of careers in retail. For her research, she worked in and interviewed workers from 'Hometown Market', a unionized US supermarket chain that prided itself on treating workers well. Wages were good for the sector, part-timers had ample opportunities to switch to full-time contracts if they wished to and fringe benefits included health insurance. But, since the 1990s, rationalizations have dramatically altered these 'good jobs', intensifying work, cutting employees' hours and limiting pay for new hires. Jordan observes that, perhaps in response to this, many of the staff see retail as a temporary stopgap with even long-serving workers desirous of avoiding being 'trapped' at Hometown. She argues that this re-framing of their experiences enables workers to cope with the indignities of low-paid, low-status work.

This focus on terms and conditions is a useful one and a good point on which to leave this section since the difference, at Hometown at least, between 'good' and 'bad' work was not one of skill or status in the labour market but pay and prospects. As Braverman (1974) observed, the romanticized accounts of many jobs that attribute more knowledge to them than they possess fail to note their pay slips in the process. These three chapters offer very different perspectives on retail work. For all it is a place which people are 'just passing through' and it is interesting to see the differences between those who stay, from the choices of Huddleston's graduates, to the realistic expectations of Roberts's lost boys to Jordan's constantly temporary workers.

Part III: The pressures of retail work

In the third section we look at some of the pressures and the structural factors behind the way retail employment is organized, from national, institutional frameworks to store-level human resource practices and the expectations and work of store managers. Klaveren and Voss-Dahm provide data from Germany and the Netherlands, collected as part of a wider, comparative study funded by Russell Sage. In their chapter, they reveal how these two countries, generally lauded as exemplars of good employment through regulation are making increasing use of 'loopholes' in the law to allow the quality and rewards of jobs to deteriorate. Here, the age-related national minimum wage in the Netherlands and the lower tax rates on part-time 'mini-jobs' in Germany have served to provide retail firms with cheap labour as young workers replace their older colleagues and tax breaks intended to advantage workers subsidize their employers instead.

In Chapter 10 Grugulis, Bozkurt and Clegg focus on supermarket store managers and contrast the language of leadership used in both stores and head office with the expectations and realities of work. Drawing on data from an EPSRC-funded study, they argue that managers were not inspirational visionaries but tightly controlled links in a chain who occasionally, and often illicitly, exercised small freedoms to change and improve the work of the store. Although all understood the nature of their work and their relative powerlessness they valued the leadership rhetoric. Its up-beat evangelism provided a much more aspirational account of work than the mundane realities of everyday life and helped them to mediate the human aspects of the work (as well as blaming them for every failing).

Mulholland's work on teamworking contrasts the cooperative image suggested by the term with practice in store. She argues that, in the supermarket she worked and researched in, teamworking took three forms: it was a rhetorical way of alluding to all staff; functionally organized groups of workers who were often used interchangeably between different jobs; and small work groups of four to five employees. Store rationalization, 'lean' working and 'lean' teams resulted in intensified work, demanding targets and team leaders allocated by management with managerial and supervisory responsibilities. Structurally the picture these chapters paint of retail work is a discouraging one. Pressure to perform, pressure to reduce labour costs and pressure to meet targets are combined with the use and abuse of legislative 'loopholes' to reduce staff costs.

Part IV: Negotiating 'good work' in retail

The confluence of low skills, low levels of discretion, low status and low pay, and the difficulties of forging a career, much less full-time employment, in much of the retailing sector for those who are willing to try despite all these disadvantages, account for why popular conceptions of retail work involve 'dead-ends' and 'dead beats'. Indeed, far from being misconceptions, much of the research in the area does underscore why such conceptions may not be ill-founded after all. Against this backdrop, is there indeed no room, and more importantly, no point in negotiating for 'good work' in retail? Is it a foregone conclusion that the conditions of retail employment around the world, especially by large retailers, is only to further deteriorate, with no recourse by individual workers and collective groups to resist, challenge or subvert the dictates of retail strategies of a 'race to the bottom'? The final section of the book begins an inquiry into such questions and provides three examples from three very different contexts of how retail work is negotiated at the individual, union and national employment system levels, in efforts to carve out spaces for and resurrect 'good work' in this notorious type of workplace.

Asaf Darr's chapter is taken from an ethnography of retail work, a rich and detailed account of this micro-market that forms one of the bulwarks of Capitalism. It is through retail after all that much of the buying and selling in markets takes place, so studying retail work in this way provides evidence on the way markets are enacted. As Darr's evidence shows, his Tel Aviv computer salespeople were not crudely rational economic actors, rather they saw themselves as participants in a moral economy. This morality took two forms: first, customers were expected to actually *be* customers and to purchase goods. Chatty grandmother 'Ruth', 'Michael Jackson' the moonwalker,

'Kramer' and 'David' who are regular visitors to the store but who never buy anything are the unknowing butts of jokes and mockery because of their failure in this regard. Second, customers are expected to know their place in the social order and to tailor their acquisitions accordingly so that they can make use of the goods that they buy. In the moral order 'good' salespeople do not push top-of-the-range systems on computer novices but equally computer novices do not invest in top-of-the-range systems and those who do are again the subject of humour.

Andersson, Kazemi, Tengblad and Wickelgren provide a more positive picture of the way institutional structures and varieties of Capitalism can alter retail work than that afforded by earlier chapters on the USA, Germany and the Netherlands. Reporting on an extensive survey of retail workers and managers in Sweden they find high levels of motivation, satisfaction and commitment and argue that this probably stems from the flat wage distribution. Interestingly, this was achieved not by upskilling workers but by simply paying decent wages and a general acceptance that wage dispersion should be narrow.

In the last chapter in this section, Lynch, Pyman, Bailey and Price focus on another way of negotiating good work, the role of the trade unions. They compare the organizing strategies of SDA and USDAW, the unions in Australia and the UK respectively. Despite the geographical distance these two unions face similar issues and approach them in similar ways. Both deal with feminized, youthful labour forces with low union densities and high numbers of part-time jobs. Both have to cope with high levels of turnover in their membership and both have adopted strategies of cooperation with management. The results of their campaigns and the influence of the Organizing Academies are considered here, together with the levels of bargaining coverage in the two countries.

Finally, in an incisive Endnote, Tilly and Carré offer an account of the perceptions and realities of retail work. Detailing seven widely held views they offer research-based answers which both praise and condemn retailers. They highlight the clear need for more research in this area, into retailing in general, as a means of illuminating the diversity of the various sub-sectors and through cross-national comparisons then conclude with some policy implications on retail recruitment and how to make retail jobs better.

Conclusions

So is retail work worthy of academic interest? It is in these micro-markets that the foundations of Capitalism are laid and in the presence and activities of customers that the employment relationship is structured and restructured.

Empirically retail accounts for a significant proportion of jobs (and particularly of women's jobs) and the sector encompasses a wide range of employment systems, conditions, skills and workers. We hope that this book, and the chapters within it, help to stimulate interest in the sector as a whole since we believe it is definitely worthy of further study.

REFERENCES

Ahmad, T. (2009) *The Check-out Girl*. London: Harper-Collins The Friday Project.

Åkehurst, G. and Alexander, N. (eds) (1996) *Retail Employment*. London: Frank Cass.

Andrews, C. (2009) 'Job that sounds simple but has many flavours', *The Times Careers Supplement*, June 17, 7.

Arrowsmith, J. and Sisson, K. (1999). 'Pay and working time: towards organisation-based systems?' *British Journal of Industrial Relations*, 37(1): 51–75.

Bair, J. and Bernstein, S. (2006) 'Labour and the Wal-Mart effect', in S.D. Brunn (ed.)*Wal-Mart World: The World's Biggest Corporation in the Global Economy*. London and New York: Routledge.

Basker, E. (2005) 'Job creation or destruction? Labor market effects of Wal-Mart expansion', *The Review of Economics and Statistics*, 87(1): 174–183.

Bergdahl, M. (2006) *What I Learned from Sam Walton: How to Compete and Thrive in a Wal-Mart World*. Hoboken, NJ: John Wiley and Sons.

Berman, B. (2010) 'Competing in Tough Times: The Best Practices of 10 World-Class Retailers', *Financial Times*, Prentice Hall.

Bevan, J. (2006) *Trolley Wars: The Battle of the Supermarkets*. London: Profile Books.

Bevan, J. (2007) The Rise and Fall of Marks and Spencer (and How It Rose Again). London: Profile Books.

Beynon. H. (1985) *Working for Ford*. Harmondsworth: Penguin.

Blythman, J. (2005) *Shopped: The Shocking Power of Britain's Supermarkets*. London: Harper Perennial.

Booth, S and Hamer, K. (2007), 'Labour turnover in the retail industry: predicting the role of individual, organisational and environmental factors', *International Journal of Retail and Distribution Management*, 35(4): 289–307.

Bosch, G. and Lehndorff, S. (eds) (2005) *Working in the Service Sector: Different Worlds*. Oxford: Routledge.

Brandes, D. (2004) *Bare Essentials: The Aldi Way to Retail Success*. London: Cyan/Campus Books.

Braverman, H. (1974) *Labor and Monopoly CapitalLabor and Monopoly Capital: The Degradation of Work in the Twentieth Century*. New York: Monthly Review Press.

▶

▶

British Retail Consortium (2010) *Retail Stats and Facts.* http://www.brc.org.uk/
    PressZone04.asp?iCat=277&sCat=RETAIL+STATS+AND+FACTS   (accessed
    30 June 2010).
Broadbridge, A. (2003) 'Student perceptions of retailing as a destination career',
    International Journal of Retail and Distribution Management, 31(6/7): 298–309.
Burt, S. and Sparks, L. (2003) *Competitive Analysis of the Retail Sector in the UK:
    Report submitted to the Department of Trade and Industry.* Stirling: Institute
    of Retail Studies.
Business Link. (2010) Your Type of Business – Site Map, http://www.businesslink.
    gov.uk/bdotg/action/sectorSiteMap (accessed 12 July 2010).
Callaghan, G. and Thompson, P. (2002) '"We recruit attitude": the selection
    and shaping of routine call centre labour', *Journal of Management Studies*,
    39(2), 233–254.
Carré, F., Tilly, C., Klaveren, M. and Voss-Dahm, D. (2010) 'Retail jobs in
    comparative perspective', in J. Gautié and J. Schmitt (eds) *Low Wage Work in
    the Wealthy World.* New York: Russell Sage Foundation.
Chartered Institute of Personnel Development (2009) http://www.cipd.co.uk/
    news/_articles/graduates-choose-retail-over-the-city.htm (accessed 13 July
    2010)
Chinoy, E. (1955) *Automobile Workers and the American Dream.* Garden City,
    NY: Doubleday.
Clarke, I., Hallsworth, A., Jackson, P., de Kervenoael, R. del Aguila, R.P. and
    Kirkup, M. (2006) 'Retail restructuring and consumer choice 1. Long-
    term local changes in consumer behaviour: Portsmouth, 1980–2002',
    Environment and Planning A, 38(1), 25–46.
Davis, G. F. (2009) *Managed by the Markets: How Finance Reshaped America.*
    Oxford: Oxford University Press.
Dawson, J. (2007) 'Scoping and contextualising retailer internationalisation',
    Journal of Economic Geography, 7: 373–397.
Dawson, J., Larke, R. and Mukoyama, M. (2006) *Strategic Issues in International
    Retailing.* London and New York: Routledge.
Denney-Finch, J. (2010) IGD Skills & Employment Summit – People and Skills
    for a Pivotal New Decade, 10 March 2010 http://www.igd.com/index.asp?i
    d=1&fid=6&sid=25&tid=162&cid=1462 (accessed 15 July 2010).
Ehrenreich, B. (2001) *Nickle and Dimed: On Not Getting by in America.* New
    York: Henry Holt and Company.
Fernie, J. and Sparks, L. (2009) *Logistics and Retail Management: Emerging Issues
    and New Challenges in the Retail Supply Chain.* London and Philadelphia:
    Kogan Page.
Fishman, C. (2007) *The Wal-Mart Effect: How an Out-of-town Superstore Became
    a Superpower.* London and New York: Penguin Books.
Gamble, J. (2006) 'Multinational retailers in China: proliferating 'McJobs' or
    developing skills?', *Journal of Management Studies*, 43(7):1463–1490.
Grimshaw, D., Ward, K.G., Rubery, J. and Beynon, H. (2001) 'Organisations
    and the transformation of the internal labour market', *Work, Employment
    and Society*, 15(1): 25–54.

▶

►

Hart, C., Stachow, G.B., Farrell, A.M. and Reed, G. (2007) 'Employer perceptions of skills gaps in retail: issues and implications for UK retailers', *International Journal of Retail and Distribution Management*, 35(4): 271–288.

Kirsch, J., Klein, M., Lehndorff, S., and Voss-Dahm, D. (2000). 'The organisation of working time in large German food retail firms', in C. Baret, S. Lehndorff and L. Sparks (eds) *Flexible Working in Food Retailing: a Comparison between France, Germany, the UK and Japan*. London and New York: Routledge.

Lafer, G. (2004). 'What is skill?', in C. Warhurst, I. Grugulis and E. Keep (eds) *The Skills That Matter*. Basingstoke: Palgrave Macmillan, 109–127.

Leidner, R. (1993) *Fast Food, Fast Talk*. Berkeley and Los Angeles: University of California Press.

Lewis, E. (2005) *Great Ikea! A Brand for All the People*. London: Cyan Communications.

Long, C. (2009) '*Checkout by Anna Sam/The Checkout Girl*, by Tazeen Ahmad', *The Sunday Times*, 16 August 2009 (accessed 2 July 2010).

Macdonald, C.L. and Sirianni, C. (eds) (1996) *Working in the Service Society*. Philadelphia: Temple University Press.

Mason, G., Mayhew, K., and Osborne, M. (2008). 'Low paid work in the United Kingdom: an overview', in C. Lloyd, G. Mason and K. Mayhew (eds) *Low Wage Work in the United Kingdom*. New York: Russell Sage Foundation.

McGauran, A. (2001) 'Masculine, feminine or neutral? In-company equal opportunities policies in Irish and French MNC retailing', *International Journal of Human Resource Management*, 12(5): 754–771.

McGoldrick, P. (2002) *Retail Marketing- 2nd Edition*. Maidenhead: McGraw-Hill Education.

McLaughlin, J. (1999) 'Gendering occupational identities and IT in the retail sector', *New Technology, Work and Employment*, 14(2): 143–156.

Neumark, D., Zhang, J. and Ciccarella, S. (2008) 'The effects of Wal-Mart on Local Labor Markets', *Journal of Urban Economics*, 63(2): 405–430.

Parke, S. (2009) *Shelf Life: How I Found the Meaning of Life Stacking Supermarket Shelves*. London: Rider.

Percival, J. (2010) 'Demos sees big role for supermarkets in regenerating poor communities', *Guardian*, 7 June, http://www.guardian.co.uk/uk/2010/jun/07/demos-supermarkets-poverty-regeneration-pride (accessed 12 July 2010).

Randall, G. and Seth, A. (2005) *Supermarket Wars: Global Strategies for Food Retailers*. New York: Palgrave Macmillan.

Ritzer, G. (1993) *The McDonaldization of Society: An Investigation into the Changing Character of Contemporary Social Life*. Newbury Park, CA: Pine Forge Press.

Sage, A. (2008) 'French checkout girl, Anna Sam's book takes revenge on rude shoppers' *The Sunday Times*, 7 June, http://entertainment.timesonline.co.uk/tol/arts_and_entertainment/books/article40833 58.ece (accessed 8 April 2010).

Sage, A. (2009) 'The checkout girl: abused, ignored and on a till near you', *The Times*, 6 March, http://women.timesonline.co.uk/tol/life_and_style/women/the_way_we_live/article58 53437.ece (accessed 8 April 2010).

►

▶

Sam, A. (2009) *A Life at the Tills, Reprint Edition.* London: Gallic Books.

Seth, A. and Randall, G. (2001) *The Grocers: The Rise and Rise of the Supermarket Chains.* London and Dover, NH: Kogan Page.

Shackleton, R. (1998) 'Part-time working in the 'super-service' era: labour force restructuring in the UK food retailing industry during the late 1980s and early 1990s', *Journal of Retailing and Consumer Services*, 5(4): 223–234.

Simms, A. (2007). *Tescopoly: How One Shop Came Out on Top and Why It Matters.* London: Constable.

Simms, A. (2010) 'Supermarkets don't regenerate communities – they hoover money out', *Guardian*, June 8, http://www.guardian.co.uk/commentisfree/2010/jun/08/supermarkets-regeneration (accessed July 15, 2010).

Spotts, G. and Greenwald, G. (2006) *Wal-Mart: The High Cost of Low Price.* Disinformation Company Ltd.

Sturdy, A. (2001). 'Servicing societies: colonisation, control, contradiction and contestation.', in A. Sturdy, I. Grugulis and H. Willmott (eds) *Customer Service: Empowerment and Entrapment.* Basingstoke: Palgrave.

Taylor, P. and Bain, P. (1999) ' "An assembly line in the head": work and employee relations in the call centre', *Industrial Relations Journal*, 30(2): 101–117.

Walden, C. (2009) 'How a checkout girl called Anna Sam bagged a best-seller', *Telegraph*, January 19, http://www.telegraph.co.uk/culture/4792402/How-a-checkout-girl-called-Anna-Sam-bagged-a-best-seller.html (accessed April 10, 2010).

Warhurst, C. and Nickson, D. (2007) 'A new labour aristocracy? Aesthetic labour and routine interactive service', *Work, Employment and Society*, 21(4): 785–798.

Wright, C. and Lund, J. (2003) 'Supply chain rationalization: retailer dominance and labour flexibility in the Australian food and grocery industry', *Work, Employment and Society*, 17(1): 137–157.

Wrigley, N., Coe, N.M. and Currah, A. (2005) 'Globalizing retail: conceptualizing the distribution-based transnational corporation (TNC)', *Progress in Human Geography*, 29(4): 437–457.

Wrigley, N., Guy, C. and Lowe, M. (2002) 'Urban regeneration, social inclusion and large store development: the Seacroft development in context', *Urban Studies*, 39(11): 2101–2114.

Wrigley, N. and Lowe, M. (2002) *Reading Retail: A Geographical Perspective on Retailing and Consumption Spaces.* Arnold, London and New York: Oxford University Press.

Work and Skills

Following the Retail Chain: Sandwiches, Supermarkets and the Potential for Workplace Learning

Alan Felstead, Alison Fuller, Nick Jewson and Lorna Unwin

Introduction

Supermarkets are frequently accused of abusing their growing market power. In the UK, grocery retailing is dominated by four supermarket chains which together account for two-thirds of sales (Competition Commission, 2008: Appendix 3.1). Similar market concentrations can be found in other parts of the industrialized world such as Australia, the US and in many parts of Europe. Supermarkets are alleged to use this dominance to force local shops out of business. This can result in the creation of so-called 'Tesco Towns', where the majority of money on food and drink is spent in Tesco (*Daily Telegraph*, 5 March 2009). Supermarkets are also accused of abusing their buying power by squeezing suppliers' margins unfairly and insisting on unreasonable delivery and service arrangements (*The Guardian*, 4 August 2009). However, how this effects workplace learning at store level and in the new product development departments of suppliers has rarely been the subject of investigation. This is the aim of this chapter.

By focusing on workplace learning in stores as well as in suppliers, the chapter has the additional aim of contributing to our understanding of how skills are developed at work beyond the world of retailing. This is a theme that has attracted considerable interest from policy makers who see the promotion of workplace learning as one of the key means of enhancing economic performance. Exhortations for improvements and enhancements to learning are now commonplace. Moreover, these calls are made more frequently, more widely and more loudly now than in the past. They can be heard in national and international policy debates, such as those that surround the International Labour Office's (ILO) campaign for 'Decent Work', the European Union's concern over the 'Quality of Work and Employment', and the OECD's interest in enhancing the skills of the workforce (ILO, 1999; European Foundation for the Improvement of Living and Working Conditions, 2002; OECD, 2005 and 2007).

A better understanding of learning at work – and the development of analytical, conceptual and methodological tools that can be applied and used in a variety of settings – is therefore urgently required across the industrialized world. Previous research has made forays into this complex field and has produced some valuable evidence and pioneering concepts. However, we are faced with many pieces of an incomplete jigsaw puzzle. This chapter summarizes our attempt to rise to this challenge by developing and applying a new framework that can be used conceptually and methodologically to research workplace learning. We illustrate this with evidence from the retail sector (see also Felstead et al., 2009).

The importance of such an endeavour has been further heightened by the severest economic recession in the industrialized world since the Great Depression in the 1930s (Chamberlin and Yueh, 2009). This has put businesses under intense pressure to cut costs in order to survive. Following the banking crisis that precipitated the recession, many governments are now having to squeeze public expenditure in order to balance their budgets. Individuals, too, are facing similar pressures as they cut back on non-essentials and scale back their spending. As a consequence, businesses, governments and individuals are all questioning their investment in *formal* training activities and, given the depth of this recession, it is not clear – as yet – whether this will have a significant effect on formal training volumes (Brunello, 2009; Shamash and Sims, 2009). However, learning that occurs as part of, and is situated in, the work process itself is likely to be more resilient to these economic pressures and may even prosper as businesses turn to forms of on-the-job learning.

While the economic climate is the most obvious constraint on and facilitator of workplace learning, there are others too. This chapter outlines a conceptual framework designed to give these features greater visibility and specificity than hitherto. The existing literature characterizes many of these features as forming the 'context' of workplace learning, but rarely is a conceptual framework outlined. In this chapter, we present the 'Working as Learning Framework' as a way of filling this conceptual gap, thereby illuminating the links between the macro-level forces that shape employment, the nature of work organization at the point of production, and the 'expansive' or 'restrictive' character of learning environments (Fuller and Unwin, 2003). The evidence is taken from firms in the UK, but the model itself should have a wider compass. The chapter, then, demonstrates the value of the framework by examining how it aids our understanding of workplace learning at two points in the retailing chain – in the product development departments of sandwich manufacturers and on the shop floor of supermarket chains. The empirical evidence for the former comes from: 29 interviews with 12 sandwich manufacturers; 3 interviews with suppliers of bread, chicken, flavourings and packaging; 13 interviews with retailers, both large and small; 3 interviews with stakeholders responsible for overseeing the industry by offering advice, providing training, disseminating best practice or verifying hygiene standards; and non-participant observation of the production process in 3 sandwich factories, product tasting sessions organized by manufacturers and the selling of sandwiches direct to the public. The supermarket evidence comes from: 31 store-level interviews with store managers, trading managers and stock management supervisors in 6 stores in the UK; 3 interviews with area managers; 2 interviews with staff at Head Office; and observation of retail workers carrying out their daily activities, including their use of the tools of stock control outlined below. The chapter ends by drawing out the implications of the research for studies of work in retailing and beyond.

Outlining the Working as Learning Framework (WALF)

It has long been recognized that workplace learning is, at worst, simply a by-product of what shops, factories and offices are primarily about. It may, however, be conceived more explicitly as one of the tools organizations can use to achieve their goals (Streeck 1989). In the private sector, profit is the ultimate driver of economic activity, while in the public sector meeting delivery targets – such as the number of patients treated or students taught – is the driving force. In each case, learning is a 'third-order' issue in meeting these goals. This puts it behind 'second-order' issues such as how work is organized and 'first-order' issues surrounding the nature of the product market served, the type of competition faced, and wider structures that impinge upon the ways in which products are made and services are delivered (Keep and Mayhew 1999; Keep et al., 2006). Exhortations to employers 'to change their ways' – and improve, enhance or increase workplace learning – without tackling these issues inevitably fall on deaf ears (Grimshaw et al., 2008).

Nevertheless, analytical progress has been made that illuminates some of the connections, especially those operating at the second-order level. Recent debates in human resource management and the sociology of work have begun to substantiate the suggestion that the quantity and quality of an employee's training and learning experience can, in part, be explained by the way in which work is organized. This is referred to using a variety of terms, such as 'high performance' or 'high involvement' work systems. These are based on four principles: employee involvement in decision-making about the completion of immediate work tasks; feedback on work performance and opportunities for development; rewarding performance and improving motivation; and sharing information and knowledge throughout the organization (Ashton and Sung, 2002; Hughes, 2008). Such principles are in stark contrast to Taylorist management techniques. Taylorism is exemplified by strict job demarcation, tight job descriptions, limited and firm-specific training, and minimal employee discretion exercised individually or as a team. A number of studies, based on survey evidence, suggest that 'high involvement' working and training are connected (Lynch and Black, 1995 and 1998; MacDuffie and Kochan, 1995; Whitfield, 2000; Felstead and Gallie, 2004). Furthermore, the way work is organized has a powerful effect not only on the incidence and intensity of training but also on its quality and the usefulness of workplace learning in general (Felstead et al., 2010).

Research that focuses on job design has started to highlight the wider context in which workplace learning takes place. However, such an analytical focus remains rooted in the workplace and fails to extend beyond the factory gates or shop floor. It, therefore, stops short of examining, in detail, how the commodities made or services delivered are influenced by the overall sequence of production and the wider forces of regulation at work. In other words, first-order issues remain largely unexplored. This chapter sets out how it is possible to research and connect these three 'orders' by examining workplace learning at different points in the retailing chain using what we refer to as the Working as Learning Framework (WALF). In so doing, the chapter hopes to equip other researchers with the conceptual and methodological tools with which to extend this approach to other sectors of the economy in the UK and beyond.

The Working as Learning Framework is built on three concepts: productive systems; work organization and learning environments. Our central argument is that in order to understand the extent to which learning environments at work are more or less 'expansive' or 'restrictive' (Fuller and Unwin, 2003), researchers need to examine how work is organized and how its organization is influenced by wider forces. The Framework specifies the links between the broad relationships that shape employment relations and the nature of workplace learning. This approach enables us to explore how these broader processes are played out in specific workplaces and in the narratives of people's working lives. This requires that research is carried out at a variety of levels at, and beyond, specific workplaces.

The concept of 'productive systems' provides the broadest perspective since it offers a holistic, relational model of economic activity that identifies interlocking levels of institutional practices and controls. This takes us beyond a workplace or even an organizational-level focus – typical of concepts such as 'high performance work systems' (Appelbaum et al., 2000). Instead, the notion of productive systems encompasses a multitude of stakeholders; customers, suppliers and sector bodies, as well as the employing organization. It refers to the totality of social relationships entailed in processes of commodity production and the provision of services, and which have horizontal and vertical dimensions. The horizontal dimension refers to the sequences in which raw materials are transformed into goods and services that are consumed by end-users, while the vertical refers to the regulation and control mechanisms that impinge on each stage of the production process (see Figures 2.1 and 2.2).

We use the concept of discretion to capture the degree of autonomy and responsibility exercised by workers in the labour processes in which they are engaged. The nature of the productive system may influence the latitude they are given as well as the level and nature of trust in the employment relationship. Managerial strategies may respond to the uncertainties inherent in complex productive systems by enhancing or by minimizing discretion and trust in the workplace.

Our prime focus is on learning environments, the networks of relationships within which learning takes place. Our analysis here draws on the concepts of 'expansive' and 'restrictive' learning environments (Fuller and Unwin, 2003) to offer a generative, transformative, process-conscious conception of learning. Moreover, the notions of expansive and restrictive extend to include the learning territories of individuals. This allows the expansive-restrictive model to link the organization of work in its broadest sense to the learning processes of individuals. Integrating the expansive-restrictive continuum with the productive systems perspective creates a conceptual framework (WALF) for understanding working as learning. WALF addresses systemic issues at the same time as illuminating the experiences of specific individuals. Moreover, it takes a dynamic view of these linkages, with an emphasis on process, change and development.

Figure 2.1   Stages of production

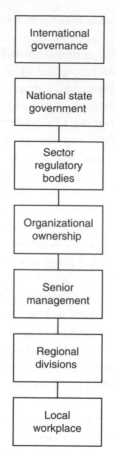

Figure 2.2   Structures of production

Applying WALF at two points in the retail chain

The analytical utility of WALF can best be illustrated by considering how it helps to shed light on the limits and opportunities for workplace learning in diverse organizational and sectoral contexts. In this chapter, we draw on evidence at two points in the retailing chain to exemplify the analytical utility of the Framework and the insights its application can generate. These two examples are the New Product Development (NPD) departments of sandwich manufacturers and the shop floor management of stock in supermarkets. The application of WALF in these two examples highlights the fact that the locus of control can shift in this analytical space. It may move backwards or forwards along the horizontal stages of production, and up or down the vertical structures of production. More specifically, the study of sandwich manufacturing shows that large retailers may exercise power backwards over those who develop and produce goods for sale, while within supermarket chains central managers may use stock control devices to reach down into stores. These backward and downward actions are shown to have consequences for the discretion levels exercised by workers and the nature of the learning environments they face.

Sandwich manufacturing

Like other processed foods, such as cook-chill meals (Glucksmann, 2008), the pre-packed sandwich was developed and launched by supermarkets. This, coupled with the huge numbers of products they sell, has given supermarkets an advantage over the manufacturers they contract to assemble, pack and deliver sandwiches. Supermarket chains continue to play a pivotal role in directing and overseeing sandwich manufacturers.

Sandwiches sold through retail outlets can be divided into two categories, generated by two different productive systems. We refer to those sandwiches that leave manufacturers' premises labelled with the supermarket's brand, rather than that of the manufacturer, as 'retailer label' sandwiches. The label printed on the container is emblematic of the power retailers have over their suppliers, and their suppliers' suppliers. This, in turn, determines the parameters within which producers operate and the learning environments within which innovation takes place. Production for supermarkets (and other large purchasers, such as coffee shop chains) is 'buyer-driven' (Gereffi, 1994 and 1999). However, although supermarkets sell huge volumes of sandwiches, there are other locations where consumers can buy sandwiches, such as corner shops, garages and small restaurants. These provide more numerous outlets, although their average sales volumes are far lower. They offer sandwich producers an alternative route to market and, moreover, opportunities to sell sandwiches under the brand of the manufacturer rather than the retailer. These we designate as 'manufacturer label' sandwiches. Where sandwiches take this route to market, there is a greater potentiality for the horizontal axis of the productive system to be 'producer-driven', with more push from the manufacturer and less pull from the retailer (Burch and Lawrence, 2005).

The two productive systems are defined by differences in the balance of power and locus of control. Where sandwiches carry the brand name of the retailer, the balance of power in the productive system as a whole is weighted towards retailers who impose stringent controls on manufacturers. We designate this variant as the Retailer Label Productive System or Retailer Label (RL). In contrast, where sandwiches carry the brand name of the manufacturer, not the retailer, the balance of power within the productive system is less heavily weighted towards retailers. Manufacturers typically have greater scope for independent action and innovation. Regulation of manufacturers is less likely to be under the direct control of a small number of retailers. We designate this variant of the productive system Manufacturer Label Productive System or, simply, Manufacturer Label (ML).

The overwhelming majority of sandwiches sold in supermarkets carry the retailers' label, not that of the manufacturer. They are RL products, manufactured in very large numbers and delivered to retailers on a daily basis. Manufacturers may produce sandwiches for more than one retailer, but the volumes demanded by supermarkets usually mean that manufacturers in this productive system are heavily committed to one or two retail chains. Supermarkets, in turn, develop a close working relationship with a limited number of manufacturers and play a significant part in the distribution process. The huge volumes of sandwiches required means that manufacturers are able to automate assembly lines. Relatively few manufacturers are of sufficient size and capital intensity to compete in this market.

The RL sandwiches sold by large retailers, such as supermarkets, are those with mass appeal. Although supermarkets often also carry a premium range, they tend to concentrate on a standard menu of predictable fillings and breads. This suits large-scale manufacturers who can automate, simplify and maintain long production runs. Where huge numbers of sandwiches are being produced and sold, marginal savings on time and resources are currently important to manufacturer and retailer alike. Thus, innovations in production processes and marginal cost savings may be as, if not more, significant as creating a new sandwich filling.

Within the RL productive system, the power balance favours retailers with the award of huge contracts that call for the production of tens of thousands of sandwiches each day. As dominant buyers, supermarkets are in a position to define product parameters, dictate terms and drive down margins. For their part, manufacturers are highly vulnerable to shifts in demand from the retailer as the following comments from our research indicate:

> The retailers are notorious for squeezing the suppliers as much as they possibly can because that's where they make their profit. (Howard, Senior Manager, Industry Regulation Authority)

> Everybody tends to say that we're very [supermarket name] driven, and that we're almost a slave to [supermarket name]...We are an extension of [supermarket name] really....We do a lot of liaising with them, you know, and obviously presenting new products to them as well. So they're very much heavily involved in the business. (Abigail, Senior HR Manager, RL Manufacturer B)

Retailers vary the amount of product they purchase on a daily basis and impose fines on manufacturers who fail to meet quotas. They demand rigorous standards in every aspect of manufacturers' factory operations, employment policies and product handling, enforced by a regime of rigorous in-house inspections. They frequently specify a limited and non-negotiable list of suppliers that manufacturers must use.

For their part, manufacturers in the RL productive system necessarily commit themselves to supplying products attuned to the needs and requirements of one or two retailers. They make efficiency savings by building large factories, investing in automated production and employing large workforces. Their plants become dependent on the business provided by just one or two purchasers as the following comment shows:

> Dedicated [supermarket name] facility. So we mould ourselves to what [supermarket name] want…we do a lot of work to try and make sure that [supermarket name] stay ahead of their competitors. Rather than us staying ahead of our competitors, we make sure [supermarket name] stay ahead of theirs. (Samantha, Financial Manager, RL Manufacturer B)

In practice, then, the RL productive system is confined to mass production of a limited range of products by a small number of manufacturers for a few national retail outlets. Retailers are mostly national supermarket chains with an established reputation for quality and service. Manufacturers catering for this market operate large plants producing high volumes of a standard range of popular products.

Sandwiches produced within the ML productive system, on the other hand, are sold under the brand name of the manufacturer, not the retail outlet. Packaging carries the name of the producer. ML producers are more varied and heterogeneous than RL producers in scale and character. At one extreme, there are many small producers, often operating out of cramped premises with a handful of staff, servicing the immediate geographical area. Their production rarely involves capital intensive methods. Frequently, firms such as these sell a high proportion of their stock directly to the public from peripatetic company-owned vans travelling between localities, such as industrial estates, where it is known that customers purchase snacks and lunchtime food. Small-scale ML producers also often seek to place sandwiches on the shelves of corner shops, newsagents, garages and similar outlets. Typically, their relationships with these retailers are informal, short-term and involve placing a few products in many different locations. There is often intense competition between small ML manufacturers over price and access to retail outlets, with rivals undercutting one another (see Fuller et al., 2006 and 2007).

Medium-sized and large-scale ML producers – with more staff, better premises and operating at a regional or even national level – are less likely to rely on van sales and more likely to sell their sandwiches through shops and restaurants. Some of these retail outlets are similar to those sought by small-scale ML firms; consequently, garages and corner shops may carry sandwich brands that are nationally known alongside those that are highly local. However, medium- and large-scale ML producers are also likely to seek formal contracts with larger, established retail outlets, such as universities or hospitals. Usually, such contractual arrangements tie a small number of ML sandwich manufacturers to the retailer over a number of years. Volumes purchased by retailers may vary over time, and shift between firms, but only contracted manufacturers will be used. However, to enter the competition for such contracts requires higher levels of external accreditation than is common among small-scale producers. The investment, expense and trouble involved in attaining and maintaining these accreditation standards restricts the numbers of ML producers who can compete for contracts of this kind.

Medium and large ML firms consciously adopt a policy of preserving their autonomy from retailers by maintaining a broad customer base, avoiding dependence on a few purchasers. These manufacturers do business with many retailers, each of whom represents a limited proportion of total sales, and so retailers are less able to dictate terms to them. The following comment is illustrative:

> We have always said as a company we'd never have a customer more than 10 per cent of our sales...if you have something like a supermarket, they'd be sort of 90 per cent of your sales. And they hold you over a barrel with prices. And it's just something we don't want to get into. (Julie, National Account Manager, large ML Manufacturer A)

Thus, within the ML productive system the balance of power is not so heavily weighted in favour of the retailer. In general, ML manufacturers enjoy a greater degree of discretion in their business activities and are less at the beck and call of retailers:

> The fact it is our brand allows us to do what we want...And the fact that we don't have our eggs in one basket also contributes to that. (Geraint, Senior Production Manager, large ML Manufacturer A)

> Everything we do is our decision. We decide we want to move in that direction, so we can do. Although some of our customers do lead us, it's still sort of our decision because it is our brand. (Ewan, Senior NPD Manager, large ML Manufacturer A)

ML producers are also freer to seek alternative suppliers, rather than those prescribed by the retailer. They are more able to develop products according to their own criteria, without having to seek authorization from monopsony retailers, and to find new and additional retail outlets. The corollary is that, within the ML productive system, each member of the supply chain is more likely to be responsible for due diligence with respect to their own specifications and standards. Greater autonomy is matched by greater accountability.

Thus, whereas the RL productive system is, in practice, fairly homogeneous, the ML productive system is more diverse and heterogeneous. ML manufacturers differ in the size of their output, workforce and range of products. Their sphere of operations varies from local through regional to national markets. There is also diversity in the way their products reach end consumers.

NPD specialists, in both RL and ML manufacturers, are in the business of innovation. They draw on a wide range of sources for new sandwiches. They monitor the products of competitors, attend trade fairs and professional venues, compete for industry awards, study culinary texts and seek inspiration from their personal experience of cooking, eating out and holidaying in exotic places. They are acutely interested in interpreting the direction of consumer tastes They liaise with retailers of their products and involve them in future developments. NPD personnel, then, enjoy opportunities for learning in the workplace that entail crossing boundaries between bodies of knowledge, skill and practice both within and outside the firm.

The NPD process involves strategic and regular changes in products offered to the market, often following a seasonal and/or annual cycle (Akgün and Lynn, 2002; van der Valk and Wynstra, 2005; Bakker et al., 2006; Mikkola and Skjøtt-Larsen, 2006). New sandwiches are introduced, existing products amended and established items 'delisted'. Regular and consistent NPD cycles may constitute a formal and explicit, or informal and implicit, condition of a contract with a retailer. RL manufacturers and larger ML producers employ specialist personnel engaged in NPD and their work constitutes a distinct business function within the organization. NPD work may lead to the development of products that have never before appeared on the shelves of retailers ('new to the market' products). However, it may also involve the development of products that have already proved popular in the marketplace, but that have not previously been offered by the firm ('new to the firm' products) (Tether, 2000). The latter approach is reactive; it involves identifying and matching market trends. The former is proactive; it generates products that create and lead market trends. Not least because of labelling regulations, it is difficult for manufacturers of 'new to the market' products to prevent other firms creating 'me too' products within relatively short time periods. Thus, NPD is a continuous and competitive process.

However, notwithstanding similarities between NPD personnel within the two variants of the productive system, there are important contrasts in their roles that have implications for their learning experiences. Differences in the structure of the RL and ML productive systems shape the direction, contents and form of their learning. NPD personnel within the RL productive system, for example, are constrained in their work by the technologies of production used by their employing organizations. Thus, profit maximization requires them to take advantage of the capital investment typical of RL firms. This directs them towards innovation at the high volume, low cost end of the market, where automated and mechanized assembly lines are most effective. These are unlikely to be 'new to the market' products.

The high degree of control that retailers exercise over the RL productive system also means that retailers play an active and directive role in the development of new products. NPD personnel often work to specifications generated by retailers that guide the direction and timetable of the innovation process. Initial suggestions for the development of new products may come, wholly or in part, from retailers. Retailers may set specifications for NPD initiatives and play a part in organizing the NPD process, within the manufacturing company. Signing off a new product typically requires agreement and approval of the retailer. In addition, retailers shape the NPD process through the controls they exercise over suppliers and primary producers located earlier in the stages of sandwich production. The following comments from two manufacturers make this point:

> That's the inhibiting thing is that, when you, sort of, develop a sandwich, you have to make sure you've got the right ingredients in it so that [supermarket name] have approved or meet their specs, their minimum specification. (Samantha, Financial Manager, RL Manufacturer B)

> So we don't have much of a choice in certain areas and so that does constrain us a little bit...It does narrow who you can work with. (Nigel, NPD Specialist, RL Manufacturer C)

In summary, then, new product development by sandwich manufacturers within the RL productive system is heavily influenced by relationships with monopsony retailers, who are involved in devising, developing and signing off new products. The NPD function within RL manufacturing organizations tends to be relatively specialized, differentiated and professionalized. The NPD process is often formalized and organized in a series of steps that involves retailers. There is a tendency to spot and follow emerging market trends rather than shape and lead the market, resulting in a focus on 'new to the firm' products. Hence, the learning environments of NPD personnel are likely to overlap with a wide range of aspects of the learning environments of specific retailers,

encourage the development of a broad awareness of industry-wide developments, facilitate the emergence of corporate-based team working with other
specialists, generate skills in negotiating formalized procedures, favour 'new to
the firm' innovations that match emerging trends in the market, and reward
cost-conscious use of mass production technologies.

In contrast to the RL productive system, many larger ML manufacturers
perceive profit maximization strategies to include the creation of unusual 'new
to the market' products at the premium end of the price range. Cheaper and
more predictable sandwiches do also appear in the portfolio of ML firms and
are a staple aspect of their offer. However, 'new to market' sandwiches are projected by ML manufacturers as a mark of the quality, added value and versatil-
ity of their products, reflected in higher prices. Such sandwiches enliven and
enrich the menus offered to retailers. Even when not sold in large numbers,
they are perceived as conveying to retailers and consumers a strong and valued
image. They also enable manufacturers to aim their menus at lucrative niche
markets, such as vegetarians and consumers of 'ethnic' foods:

> We have our core range of our regulars and our premiums... When you go
> with your sample set, it's always lovely to go and see a client and show
> them something they haven't seen before... It is definitely a USP of ours,
> you know, that we do innovate and we do try new things. (Olwen, NPD/
> Marketing Manager, large ML Manufacturer L)

Since unusual new items on the menu are seen as contributing to profitability, NPD personnel enjoy scope to develop a wide range of products,
encompassing not only the old favourites but also variations on standard
sandwiches and some items that incorporate unexpected ingredients and
taste sensations. As a result, large ML producers tend to have a broader
range of products on offer than RL firms, even though they produce some
of them in relatively small numbers. They are also likely to have a higher
proportion of their product range at the premium end of the market, where
consumers are more interested in unusual fillings. This approach to innovation is facilitated by the labour intensive modes of production often found
in medium- and large-size ML firms. Handcrafted production favours short
runs of speciality sandwiches.

It would certainly be wrong to suggest that NPD personnel in large ML
firms do not consult and liaise with retailers. They monitor patterns of
demand from retailers, seek retailers' advice before introducing new products
and maintain close contacts through occasions such as product tasting and
marketing events. Sales roles are often undertaken by national or regional
accounts managers who keep close relationships with retailers. Nevertheless,
in the ML productive system the initiative for new product development

is more firmly rooted in manufacturing firms themselves, rather than in retailers. Retailers expect ML manufacturers to take the lead in devising new sandwiches and launching new products on the market. This is reflected in a sense of independence and autonomy among NPD personnel in ML firms. Contact with retailers is confined to a limited range of activities that are specific to marketing. Extended partnership relations between retailers and manufacturers – widespread in the RL productive system and covering a broad range of employment policies and practices – are not typical of the ML productive system. Thus, NPD personnel in ML firms engage in more specialized and focused relationships with retailers than do those in RL. Whereas NPD specialists in RL firms cross boundaries with retailers, those in ML confine relationships with retailers to narrower channels. For example, the decision to launch a new product is typically signed off internally rather than approved by a larger retailer. Indeed, retailers within the RL productive system, such as supermarket chains, may even perceive ML manufacturers as potentially 'difficult', precisely because they are committed to acting independently:

> [ML firms] would look after their brand and would be more prescriptive about what they want to do…The branded people have quite a bit of power in terms of what they want to do…[ML] brands can be quite difficult because they just want to do it how they roughly want to do it. (Malcolm, Senior NPD Manager, National Supermarket Chain)

While large-scale ML firms frequently employ specialist NPD personnel, our research suggests that their NPD departments are often smaller, less specialized and less stratified than in RL firms. The NPD department may consist of just one or two individuals, often with experience across the business. As a result, NPD personnel within ML firms are more able to roam across all aspects of the product development process. They are also more likely to work informally with colleagues in other parts of the business, since the NPD process is less often divided into a series of fixed, discrete and bounded steps. Thus, for example, NPD managers are more likely to be responsible for taking the product right through the development and launch phases until it reaches the market. They are also likely to carry high levels of responsibility for all aspects of NPD within flattened organizational hierarchies, dealing directly in cross-functional communications with senior managers in other parts of the business that require rapid responses:

> We don't have massive tiers of management…Just go straight to the top really, you get the best results that way. (Julie, National account Manager, large ML Manufacturer A)

Wide-ranging professional roles and a lack of specialization mean that NPD personnel in large-scale ML firms are likely to develop work process knowledge that is specific to the firm and engage in opportunities to participate in multiple roles within the firm (cf. Boreham et al., 2002). Their learning environments cross boundaries within the firm, rather than outside the firm with retailers. A focus on 'new to the market' NPD allows ML firms to differentiate their wares from the standard products that dominate supermarket shelves. Unusual 'new to the market' products may not always sell in high numbers but serve to establish a perception of the firm as a high quality market leader.

In summary, then, new product development within the ML productive system is heavily influenced by profit maximizing strategies that prioritize 'new to the market' innovations at the premium, or top end, of the product range. There is a greater willingness to create market trends, rather simply follow them with 'me too' or 'new to the firm' products. A focus on premium sandwiches and less capital intensive production methods afford NPD personnel in larger ML firms greater scope to create unusual, pioneering and imaginative products. While consulting and liaising with retailers, NPD personnel enjoy a greater degree of autonomy, independence and initiative in devising and developing new products. The NPD function within ML manufacturers tends to be less specialized, differentiated and stratified. The NPD process is often less formalized. Hence, the learning environments of NPD personnel are less likely to overlap and meld with those of retailers, but may be more likely to offer opportunities to work fluidly and flexibly with colleagues inside the employing firm.

Supermarket retailing

Viewed from the perspective of the Working as Learning Framework, the study of sandwich manufacturing highlights the role that large retailers, in some circumstances, can play in exercising power *backwards* along the stages of production. As a result, those who develop sandwiches for sale do so with varying degrees of autonomy that has consequences for the ways and extent to which they themselves learn. Similarly, the facilitation of, and constraints on, the learning and development of retail workers has to be seen as a consequence of *downward* pressure from central management to influence the levels of discretion that can be exercised at store level and by individual workers. This is symbolized by the use of stock control devices by central managers to reach down into stores to control what is ordered and when (cf. Price, this volume).

Ordering and managing stock is a key function in retailing in general, and in food retailing in particular. As corporate management seeks ways to optimize performance, stock control in supermarket chains is increasingly being mediated and facilitated via information technology. From the perspective of Head Office, individual stores can be viewed as the transmitters of customer demands into the supply chain, thus enabling continuous replenishment of stock and feedback into purchasing strategy. According to some the use of computerized information systems in retailing 'begs for, and facilitates, more centralized management' (Kinsey and Ashman 2000: 86). An important artefact here is a device known as the 'symbol gun'. This electronic device is used in stores to check that the physical stock available on the shelves accords with what the computer states the store should have. This information is then used to replenish, collate and write off stock.

Initial interviews in supermarket retailing suggested that the use of computerized systems was centralizing the stock management function. This was having the effect of reducing local employees' involvement in the process and their ability to influence the range and quantity of products being ordered for their stores. Some longer-serving staff were concerned that having less personal and collective discretion to tailor stock requirements was having an adverse effect on the achievement of key performance indicators in the areas of sales, waste and availability. In addition, declining discretion was associated with less skill and, therefore, decreased job satisfaction by some employees. Some interviewees identified the 'symbol gun' as a key device in controlling the 'stock store management' system. As one observed:

These little guns obviously are controlling... Obviously we're putting all the information in to that, which takes it to the computers. So, I mean, without these in this store, we wouldn't know what our stock levels were and we'd be in a bit of a mess. We do rely on those. (Barbara, Systems Manager, Store A, The Supermarket)

Control over the management, ordering and presentation of stock was exercised through a range of technological tools, texts and mechanisms that were designed by Head Office with the aim of improving efficiency. These were linked most closely to ambient products, which have a relatively long shelf life and do not require refrigeration, and also to items that were on promotion in stores. Apart from occasional exceptions, stores could not adjust quantities ordered through this system. Similarly, through market research, the company identified 500 core items that were always in demand and thus must be available at all times to maximize sales. The orders for these items were 'locked down'; that is, they could not be adjusted by store staff. A centralizing approach to stock control was achieved by supervisors and managers following specified procedures to identify the reasons for, and subsequently to eliminate, gaps on the shelves. This strategy allowed the system to generate orders automatically, avoiding store interventions that might slow down stock replenishment and thus affect availability. Finally, precise instructions for the presentation of stock in stores were conveyed through 'planograms'. These documents depicted, through diagrams, the exact positioning and layout of merchandise by type of shelf, display cabinet and refrigerator. An updated planogram was issued to each store every two weeks by Head Office. From the perspective of senior management, located in the higher echelons of the company's productive system, a tightly controlled approach to stock management was justified by the performance gains to be made across what was described as the 'ordering through to sales process', and through the exercise of more tightly controlled and timely purchasing and throughput decisions.

Local store managers had more discretion to adjust fresh as opposed to ambient product orders as the scope for creating and reducing waste varied between these departments. Fresh food ordering was accomplished under a different system, which gave store and trading managers the opportunity to alter or cancel orders and to tailor the range and quantity of products they required for their particular store or department (Price, this volume, similarly highlights the variability of labour process control within stores). They were aided in this process by the availability of reports, which traced the sales and waste of each product in stock. A produce supervisor described this process as follows:

> Head Office, they track the sales of each product and they track the waste of each product and then every two weeks they send you a whole list out of this, broken down into departments...And you need, then, to decide...There's one there, Caesar Salad. The average sales weekly were £29.82 and the waste was £9.20. So we've wasted £9.20 but we sold nearly £30 worth. Now, I need to take a decision...is that really worth having it in the building because of the waste?' (Millie, Supervisor, Store C, The Supermarket)

Product ordering systems and devices, such as the symbol gun, resonate with the argument that order can be maintained through the deployment of texts, devices and trained people (Law, 1986). However, our evidence shows that artefacts were not only operating as tools of central control, but were also providing the means for local intervention, discretion and improvisation. Store-level decisions about whether to intervene in stock ordering were based, at least in part, on the context-specific or situated knowledge of staff (e.g., knowledge of local events and customer groups), but the means of executing this discretion relied on their ability to use the tools designed by Head Office. There was, however, tension and dynamism in the relationship between Head Office and stores that was indicative of the indeterminacy of productive systems and the different perspectives and priorities of groups located at different points in the vertical structures and horizontal stages of production.

Employees' compliance with the display specification set out in the planogram provided another example of control exercised from above in the structures of the productive system over staff behaviour, in this case, with reference to stock layout. As a Trading Manager remarked:

> Beforehand we used to be able to juggle it about a bit, but they don't want that anymore. They're telling you what they want in there and that's what you put in there [cabinet]. (Adam, Trading Manager, Store D, The Supermarket)

Store management, then, had limited discretion over the conception of their work, in that they were not in a position to specify the aims and objectives of their work process. However, they did have some discretion over how they executed their work tasks. Their ability to exercise this discretion draws on both tacit and codified sources of knowledge. In the following quotation, a trading manager points out that 'rough judgments', utilizing only on-the-job experience and tacit knowledge, could be inadequate:

> More or less it's done on judgment... We sort of, like, roughly judge how much we would need to get in compared to last week, whether we've sold enough of it... Doing that way has its pluses but it also has its minuses... It does need, I think, more analytical information to judge – to say, right, this is actually how much you've sold, this is what percentage you've done, you know. And then get more accurate figures to say, right, that is a good selling line let's get that in, that's a bad selling line, so let's get rid of it rather than keeping it on the shop floor. (Rachel, Trading Manager, Store B, The Supermarket)

Store managers had to combine their analytical skills with local 'know how'. Thus, making judgements in the course of dealing with specific tasks formed an important aspect of workplace learning. The evidence collected in this case study indicated that despite recent moves to further shift the locus of control of the stock management system upwards to Head Office, there was still scope for store employees to intervene in the process. Importantly, while the symbol gun was perceived as an artefact of control of the stock management function, it could also be used to adjust stock levels, particularly in relation to fresh produce. Fresh food could only be displayed for limited periods, so the scope for creating and reducing waste was high. In principle, orders for fresh products were automatically generated, but designated managers were given the opportunity to alter or cancel them using the symbol gun. The device enabled users to view the quantities of lines that were scheduled to come into the store, how much of these lines were currently in stock and their rate of sale (what quantities were usually sold). Based on this information, a local decision could be made to override the system, as this store manager's comment illustrates:

> So, what it's got on it [the symbol gun] is it's got your stock controls, your orders, availability, stock counting. They've all got various functions. The one we're going to use is 'view orders'. The majority of the time I don't need to amend it, but sometimes I do…Now, I've got 26 coming in, I've got 37 in stock and I'm selling roughly 35. So I would look to order, I would say, two of those. So to adjust the order, press Y. (Grace, Store Manager, Store B, The Supermarket)

Although the research data indicated that increasing centralization of stock management limits local managers' discretion, it also created potential learning opportunities. If store managers, for example, had the capacity to negotiate with Head Office, then it was possible for orders to be adjusted to meet local conditions even when the system was apparently inflexible. In the following extract, a trading manager explained that it was possible to arrange an alteration in an order relating to Minimum Presentation Levels (MPL) of bottled water – a product not usually available for adjustment – if he made a phone call to Head Office and explained why a change was needed:

> You can phone them up. You can tell them the reason why you're doing it and why you need it done, and they'll change it over the phone for you…They can do it instantly for you, just a flick of a switch…So you phone up head office, head office will send a message to your systems and say…increase the MPL, and then the next time your order generates, it will increase the order by well two-fold, three-fold, depending on what the MPL is. So, and then that'll send a message to the depot saying well they've ordered eight cases instead of four now, and then the depot will send you eight cases.' (Adam, Trading Manager, Store D, The Supermarket)

The capability to interact with Head Office in this way required: knowledge about which product orders can be adjusted; knowledge of what method to use and whom to call; and how to express the problem and provide convincing reasons why adjustment is needed. Put another way, tacit, analytical, negotiation and social skills were all needed. This example raises the questions of how consistently such skills were available amongst store management teams, and whether the company realized the extent of the knowledge and skills employees needed to identify and address stock problems effectively.

Our focus on workplace artefacts, such as the symbol gun and the planogram, has shed light on the extent to which employees are able to exercise discretion in relation to stock control and presentation. In relation to stock ordering, it emerged that discretion to adjust orders was available and was evidenced by the exercise of informed judgements by the relevant staff. It also emerged that lines normally perceived as non-adjustable could be changed if employees possessed sufficient knowledge about how the system worked and had the necessary interpersonal and negotiation skills. The symbol gun, then, was a Janus-like device that, on the one hand, acted as an instrument of Head Office control over stock management in local stores, but, on the other hand, could enable store managers to intervene in the system by using it to adjust orders of particular sorts of goods. In addition, the symbol gun acted as a boundary object, in the sense that the information it contained was utilized by two broad constituencies comprising, store and Head Office staff. In relation to stock presentation, on the other hand, there was little, if any, scope for staff to depart from the text as represented in the planogram and therefore little scope for officially sanctioned experiential learning. However, in the absence of a Head Office visit, minor changes to shelf layout were more likely to go unnoticed than changes to stock ordering which were recorded electronically and relayed to Head Office instantly (these are the 'small freedoms' discussed by Grugulis et al., this volume).

Conclusion

Our aim in incorporating the concepts of productive system, workplace organization and managerial strategies in our conceptualization of workplace learning is systematically to specify the contexts of learning. The resulting Working as Learning Framework not only highlights the links between the broadest system relationships that shape employment relations, but also enables us to explore how these broader processes are played out in specific workplaces and in the narratives of people's working lives. Elsewhere (see Felstead et al., 2009) the Framework has been used to understand the limits to and opportunities for workplace learning in ten further case study sectors that have different histories, trajectories, markets and driving forces.

This chapter has argued that a fuller understanding of learning in retailing needs to be embedded in a framework that considers the forces of production that lie beyond the point of sale. While the supply chains literature in manufacturing and construction has frequently made this point (see, e.g., Bishop et al., 2009), interest in the customer-worker interface can sometimes obscure its importance in retailing. The call centre literature has, for many years, had a similar preoccupation. However, recent research in this area has situated what goes on in call centres in a network of inter-connected economic activities that often stretch beyond national borders (see, Glucksmann, 2004; Taylor, 2010). It is our contention – and that of the Working as Learning Framework – that retailing researchers will find much value in pursuing a similar line of analytical inquiry. More importantly still, such a perspective highlights where in the retail chain most power and control is exercised, what effect it has on the labour process throughout the chain and where interventions can have greatest effect on the lives of those who work in different parts of the retailing chain. The market power of large supermarkets is central not only to how retail stores operate at the point of sale – which is justly the focus of many chapters in this volume – but also to how, why and through what means they are able to shape the labour process of the many suppliers who produce the products they sell. While the competition authorities have focused attention on the role large supermarkets play in crowding out competitors and squeezing suppliers, the consequences for those who work in supermarkets as well as in the supply chains that support them has received less attention by the competition authorities. However, as this chapter has shown, this is an additional consequence that cannot and should not be ignored.

Acknowledgements

The research reported in this chapter forms part of a larger project funded under the Economic and Social Research Council's Teaching and Learning Research Programme (RES-139-25-0110A) (for more details, see Felstead et al., 2009).

REFERENCES

Akgün, A.E. and Lynn, G.S. (2002) 'New product development team improvisation and speed-to-market: an extended model', *European Journal of Innovation Management*, 5(3): 117–129.
Appelbaum, E., Bailey, T., Berg, P. and Kalleberg, A. (2000) *Manufacturing Advantage: Why High-Performance Work Systems Pay Off.* Itacha: Cornell University Press.
Ashton, D. and Sung, J. (2002) *Supporting Learning for High Performance Working.* Geneva: International Labour Organization.

▶

►

Bakker, M., Leenders, R., Gabbay, S.M., Kratzer, J. and Van Engelen, J. (2006) 'Is trust really social capital? Knowledge sharing in product development projects', *The Learning Organization*, 13(6): 594–605.

Bishop, D., Felstead, A., Fuller, A., Jewson, N., Unwin, L. and Kakavelakis, K. (2009) 'Constructing learning: adversarial and collaborative working in the British construction industry', *Journal of Education and Work*, 22(4): 243–260.

Boreham, N., Samurçay, R. and Fischer, M. (2002) (eds) *Work Process Knowledge*. London: Routledge.

Brunello, G. (2009) 'The effect of economic downturns on apprenticeships and initial workplace training: a review of the evidence', paper prepared for the Education and Training Policy Division, OECD, Paris, June.

Burch, D. and Lawrence, G. (2005) 'Supermarket own brands, supply chains and the transformation of the agri-food system', *International Journal of Agriculture and Food*, 13(1): 1–18.

Chamberlin, G. and Yueh, L. (2009) 'Recession and recovery in the OECD', *Economic and Labour Market Review*, 3(10): 28–33.

Competition Commission (2008) *The Supply of Groceries in the UK: Market Investigation*. London: Competition Commission.

European Foundation for the Improvement of Living and Working Conditions (2002) *Quality of Work and Employment in Europe: Issues and Challenges*. Luxembourg: Office for Official Publications of the European Communities.

Felstead, A. and Gallie, D. (2004) 'For better or worse? Non-standard jobs and high involvement work systems', *International Journal of Human Resource Management*, 15(7): 1293–1316.

Felstead, A., Fuller, A., Jewson, N. and Unwin, L. (2009) *Improving Working as Learning*. London: Routledge.

Felstead, A., Gallie, D., Green, F. and Zhou, Y. (2010) 'Employee involvement, the quality of training and the learning environment: an individual-level analysis', *International Journal of Human Resource Management*, 21(10): 1667–1688.

Fuller, A. and Unwin, L. (2003) 'Learning as apprentices in the contemporary UK workplace: creating and managing expansive and restrictive participation', *Journal of Education and Work*, 16(4): 407–426.

Fuller, A., Unwin, L., Bishop, D., Felstead, A., Jewson, N., Kakavelakis, K. and Lee, T. (2006) 'Continuity, change and conflict: the role of knowing in different productive systems', *Learning as Work Research Paper No 7*. Cardiff: Cardiff School of Social Sciences, Cardiff University.

Fuller, A., Unwin, L., Felstead, A., Jewson, N. and Kakavelakis K. (2007) 'Creating and using knowledge: an analysis of the differential nature of workplace learning environments', *British Educational Research Journal*, 33(5): 743–759.

Gereffi, G. (1994) 'The organization of buy-driven global commodity chains: how US retailers shape overseas production networks', in M. Gereffi and M. Korzeniewicz (eds) *Commodity Chains and Global Capitalism*. Westport: Praeger.

►

▶
Gereffi, G. (1999) 'International trade and industrial upgrading in the apparel commodity chain', *Journal of International Economics*, 48: 37–70.

Glucksmann, M. (2008) 'Transformation of work: "ready-made" food and new international divisions of labour', paper presented at the Spring 2008 Seminar Series, Cardiff School of Social Sciences, Cardiff University, 1 May.

Glucksmann, M. (2004) 'Call configurations: varieties of call centre and divisions of labour', *Work, Employment and Society*, 18(4): 795–811.

Grimshaw, D., Lloyd, C. and Warhurst, C. (2008) 'Low-wage work in the United Kingdom: employment practices, institutional effects, and policy responses', in C. Lloyd, G. Mason and K. Mayhew (eds) *Low-Wage Work in the United Kingdom*. New York: Russell Sage Foundation.

Grugulis, I., Bozhurt, O. and Clegg, J. (2010) '"No place to hide"? The realities of leadership in UK supermarkets', in I. Grugulis (eds) *Retail Work*. London: Palgrave.

Hughes, J. (2008) 'The high-performance paradigm: a review and evaluation', *Learning as Work Research Paper No 16*. Cardiff: Cardiff School of Social Sciences, Cardiff University.

ILO (International Labour Reorganization) (1999) *Decent Work: Report of the Director-General*. London: International Labour Office.

Keep, E. and Mayhew, K. (1999) 'The assessment: knowledge, skills, and competitiveness', *Oxford Review of Economic Policy*, 15(1): 1–15.

Keep, E., Mayhew, K. and Payne, J. (2006) 'From skills revolution to productivity miracle – not as easy as it sounds?', *Oxford Review of Economic Policy*, 22(4): 539–559.

Kinsey J. and Ashman S. (2000) 'Information technology in the food supply industry', *Technology in Society*, 22(1): 83–96.

Law, J. (1986) 'On the methods of long-distance control: vessels, navigation and the Portuguese route to India', in J. Law (ed.) *Power, Action and Belief: A New Sociology of Knowledge?* London: Routledge and Kegan Paul.

Lynch, L.M. and Black, S.E. (1995) 'Beyond the incidence of training: evidence from a national employers survey', *National Bureau of Economic Research Working Paper No 5231*, August. Cambridge, MA: National Bureau of Economic Research.

Lynch, L.M. and Black, S.E. (1998) 'Beyond the incidence of employer-provided training', *Industrial and Labor Relations Review*, 52(1): 64–81.

MacDuffie, J.P. and Kochan, T.A. (1995) 'Do U.S. firms invest less in human resources? Training in the world auto industry', *Industrial Relations*, 34(2), April: 147–168.

Mikkola, J.H. and Skjøtt-Larsen, T. (2006) 'Platform management: implication for new product development and supply chain management', *European Business Review*, 18(3): 214–230.

OECD (2005) *Promoting Adult Learning*, Paris: Organisation for Economic Co-operation and Development.

OECD (2007) 'Lifelong learning and human capital', *OECD Policy Brief*, July. Paris: Organisation for Economic Co-operation and Development.

▶

▶

Price, R. (2010) 'Down the aisle: the effects of technological change on retail workers's skills', in I. Grugulis (eds) *Retail Work*. London: Palgrave.

Shamash, J. and Sims, C. (2009) 'Training in economic recessions', *City and Guilds Centre for Skills Development Briefing Note 18*, March.

Streeck, W. (1989) 'Skills and the limits of neo-liberalism: the enterprise of the future as the site for learning', *Work, Employment and Society*, 3(1): 89–104.

Taylor, P. (2010) ' "The missing link": analysing the Global Call Centre Value Chain', paper presented to the International Labour Process Conference, Rutgers State University of New Jersey, New Brunswick, 15–17 March.

Tether, B. (2000) 'Who co-operates for innovation within the supply-chain, and why? An analysis of the United Kingdom's Innovation Survey', *Centre for Research on Innovation and Competition, Discussion Paper No 35*. Manchester: University of Manchester.

van der Valk, W. and Wynstra, F. (2005) 'Supplier involvement in new product development in the food industry', *Industrial Marketing Management*, 34: 681–694.

Whitfield, K. (2000) 'High-performance workplaces, training, and the distribution of skills', *Industrial Relations*, 39(1), January: 1–25.

In the 'Blink' of an Eye – American High-End Small Retail Businesses and the Public Workforce System

3

Mary Gatta

During my last year of secondary school I held a part-time job at Betsy's[1] dress boutique. Betsy's was located on the New Jersey shoreline and specialized in high-end business attire, cocktail dresses and evening wear for women. When I applied for my job I was hired on the spot, despite the fact that I had no previous retail clothing experience. In fact at 17 years old my overall work experience was quite thin! Yet this lack of experience was not an employment barrier. Instead after an interview with the store manager, she told me I would make a great 'Betsy's girl', and I could start work just a few days later.

At 17 years old that hiring experience did not raise any flags for me. I just simply assumed that must be how they hire workers. Over twenty years later, with a sociological eye, I can see that my hiring was in great part predicated on how well I fit the 'Betsy's girl' image. I was a young, white, middle class woman who was friendly and energetic; would look good in the clothing sold in the boutique; and with whom customers would be comfortable soliciting fashion advice. These were the hiring criteria that mattered! While I did learn about different designers and fashion over my tenure at the dress shop, I did not have to bring those skills or technical knowledge to the job. Such a situation seems quite ironic, as the dress shop specialized in high-end designer clothing. One would think that a base knowledge in clothing would be a critical aspect of the hiring process. However it was not. I just had to be a 'Betsy's girl'.

Today many small retail firms continue to have their own version of 'Betsy's girls'. These are stores that specialize in higher-end goods, yet appear to make staff hiring decisions on other qualities and skills. However we know very little – from both a policy standpoint and scholarly perspective – how these small retail firms hire. In the US, often these firms are excluded from the local area workforce policy discussions and programmes headed up by state and county governments. The United States General Accounting Office (2001) has raised concerns regarding the lack of connection between small businesses and the public workforce system.[2] They note that small businesses are often ill-equipped to face the 'perplexing array of public and private employment and training services. In addition, the[se] businesses are often unaware of what assistance is available or whom to turn to help meet their workforce development requirements' (p.1). Tied to this is that many small retailers do not sit on the local workforce boards[3] that are charged with assessing and delivering public training opportunities in the US, nor do they have the personnel who can be dedicated to negotiating the public workforce system. This not only makes tailoring public training programmes to small firms difficult, but it also excludes these businesses from benefitting from potential workers who are trained by the public workforce system.

Yet while small firms are often excluded in *workforce policies* they are increasingly central parts of *economic development*, especially in smaller tourist cities. Many of the economic development policies, particularly in small and mid-size tourist destinations, centre on independently owned, distinctive retail and hospitality outlets. One of the main ways these areas distinguish themselves from larger retailers, and even more populated tourist destinations, is on the quality of customer service they can offer. Many smaller cities are reinventing themselves as tourist destinations that offer a small town, friendly feel, and then actively brand this to visitors. They fashion themselves as an escape from the larger cities and cookie cutter tourism of other American destinations such as Disneyland or Las Vegas. For example, an advertisement for Mystic, Connecticut notes:

Rediscover Mystic Country Connecticut where you will find yourself in one of the most beautiful spots in coastal New England. Witness untouched scenes and meet those charming personalities only this area holds for all of your Connecticut travel. (http://mysticcountry.com/)

The 'charming personalities' become part of the selling point to visit Mystic Connecticut. The economic development agenda and subsequent tourism frame is intentionally juxtaposed against the routinization and standardization with which other tourist attractions are typically associated. Most notable for my purposes is that tourism workers are often key players in that vision. As such the workers who staff the stores and restaurants become a *de facto* aspect of the tourism strategy. It then follows that the ways that workers get hired for these local jobs need to be explored. This is especially important as the job opportunities these stores offer are crucial employment possibilities for the local labour force. As such understanding the hiring framework within a local area's workforce development policy can better prepare potential workers – including the unemployed and underemployed.

In this chapter, I begin to explore ways to address this within the American context – highlighting the skills that matter in the hiring practices of US small retail boutiques and what this tells us about retail job opportunities and training. If the retail firms are a key part of the economic development strategy, how can the public workforce system help respond to the recruitment needs, provide job training and help facilitate access for more marginalized populations? This is particularly important in regard to notions of equity in job access and public workforce training programmes that are directed to help workers enter employment opportunities. Retail offers a potential entry point for many workers and can help them gain skills that can be transferred to other jobs. After reviewing the literature on worker skills and the style labour market, I then investigate the needs of employers in this area. Using original data from a survey of 25 independently owned small business in the style labour market, I begin this inquiry by addressing two main questions:

1. What are the criteria that employers/managers use to hire workers?
2. What can be the role of training in the public workforce system for these firms?

Methods

To investigate the skills demands of workers in independently owned small businesses, I conducted semi-structured interviews with 25 small business owners/managers in several upscale towns in Monmouth County, New Jersey- Red Bank, Long Branch and Monmouth Beach. These towns are small in population – with Long Branch being the largest with a population of 32,622 residents, followed by Red Bank and then Monmouth Beach, with populations of 11,600 and 3,500 residents respectively.[4] In addition, Monmouth County, located on the New Jersey shoreline, is one of the 'wealthier' counties in New Jersey. In 2007, the median household income was $79,633 (http://factfinder. census.gov/), as compared to the state median income of $66,509 and the national median of $50,007. The towns where I conducted my research have town centres hosting mostly high-end independently owned specialty stores and restaurants, catering not only to local residents but also to a large seasonal tourism cliental during the summer months.

Each respondent was the owner or manager of a retail goods shop (I excluded restaurants, bars and cafes) and had hiring discretion. Each establishment hired at least one employee. To gather my sample I 'pounded the pavement' and walked into stores, informed potential participants about my research project and asked if they would like to participate. Once they agreed, each participant was asked a series of questions regarding the skill needs at their establishment and the hiring criteria they used. Interviews ranged from 15 to 40 minutes. I took detailed notes during the interviews, and tape-recorded only those interviewees who would allow for that. I also provided subjects the opportunity to review the notes I took to be sure that I captured their responses accurately.

US Retail work and the style labour market

The service economy has received a great deal of attention from social scientists over the past decades. The shift from a manufacturing economy to a service one and its impacts on workers and broader economic and social trends has been a central part of the sociological studies of work. Yet while the shifts have led to a multitude of changes, our scholarship focus remains relatively myopic in terms of both the occupations and the labour processes studied. Studies of front-line workers in the service sector tend to cluster around flight attendants, call centre workers and restaurant workers. Moreover, guided by Arlie Russell Hochschild's (1983) influential work, the labour process of workers are typically framed around emotional labour, often ignoring or marginalizing other aspects of workers' attributes. In particular, discussions of skills involved in service work are quite scant (Gatta et al., 2009). As Marek Korczynski (2005) notes, 'debates on skills both within policy circles and academia have too often leapt from a focus on manufacturing to a focus informed by the all-embracing new paradigm of the knowledge economy. In this breathless journey, there is one notable segment of the workforce that tends to be left by the wayside – service workers, particularly those in direct contact with service recipients or customers' (p. 3). Korczynski and others (Bolton and Boyd, 2003; Brown et al., 2001) suggest that this exclusion is due, in large part, to a rigid definition of skills that, for too long, has been unable to grapple with job demands that are more intangibly based – those that define the service quality experienced by the customer.

Yet this gap in the literature is problematic, as retail service jobs represent a growing segment of the US economy. Retail is the US's largest industry (Carré and Tilly, 2008). Over 4.6 million workers are employed in retail sales jobs, and these jobs are expected to see a 12 per cent growth by 2016, equating to over a half a million new jobs created. Despite the fact that retail jobs represent a significant portion of the US job growth, retail work is rarely studied by American social scientists (Carré and Tilly, 2008; Williams, 2004 and Bernhardt, 1999 being exceptions). Moreover when researchers focus on retail work, these studies tend to be directed to large big-box employers – such as Wal-Mart and Home Depot. Such a focus is not surprising as the past few decades have seen a significant consolidation of the industry under big-box establishments, promoting Wal-Mart to the largest private employer in the US. When small retailers are studied the focus tends to be on entrepreneurship, especially that of women and minorities (see Light and Bonacich, 1991; Mirchandani, 1999). Often these studies will explore such factors as access to resources, success and barriers to success, use of networks, and individuals' motivations towards entrepreneurship. Yet a critical analysis of the employment and hiring implications of small independent retailers is left unexamined.

The marginalization of retail work is further concerning as retail occupations, like other interactive service work, require 'face-to-face' contact, which in many ways, ensures that they will be with us for a long while (Gatta et al., 2009). These jobs cannot easily be outsourced since they require service work, emotional labour and/or caring labour that the worker personally performs (Blinder, 2006; Gatta, 2002). Nor can they easily be replaced by technology because they require human labour, or, as Levy and Murnane (2005) note 'expert thinking' and 'complex communication skills.' In addition, they are predominately filled by women, minorities and immigrant workers who are not paid their 'comparable worth' compared to similarly skilled jobs held by male workers (Guy and Newman, 2004; England et.al, 2002)

Christine Williams (2004) suggests that the idea that technology and self-service will 'eliminate service workers is probably more of a retailers' fantasy than future...for many customers shopping is an interactive activity' (p.476). Yet for that experience to materialize retail firms need workers to be present onsite and be equipped to create such an experience. Besin-Cassino (2005) highlights in her ethnography of American coffeehouse work, that the need to create an 'experience' in the job starts right in the hiring process. She shares a job ad placed at the coffee bar that read: 'If you are looking for a fun place to work and to be part of a team, we offer a great work environment' (p. 63). Ironically, Besin-Cassino points out that the pay and skill requirements for the job are not even mentioned in the advertisement. Instead the idea of the work as an 'experience' is a central filter for prospective employees.

Besin-Cassino's coffeehouse represents the growing number of businesses that comprise what Nickson, Warhurst and Dutton (2004) refer to as the 'style labour market'– boutique hotels, designer retailers and style cafes, bars and restaurants (p. 3). Nickson et al. (2004), using Glasgow as an example, were among the first to notice that world cities have reinvented themselves as 'post-industrial' and in this process 'leisure shopping and a new café culture' have become central aspects of economic development. Indeed such trends appear to ring true in smaller, tourist US towns as these towns are redefining themselves as 'destinations' with higher-end shopping and dining. Such characterizations indicate that the service economy is evolving and heterogeneous. Yet despite its importance it is virtually ignored in the US. This gap in our knowledge not only prevents us from understanding the skills needs of workers in this marketplace, but also tends to force us to overgeneralize skills needs from studies of large big-box retailers and treats the service economy as a relatively homogenous sector.

Retailers in the style labour market tend to overtly distinguish themselves from the routinized, scripted and automated (Leidner, 1993, Ritzer, 1996) labour processes of the larger retailers. Nona Glazer (1993) traces how much of service work has progressively shifted from a full-service to self-service retail model. This 'work transfer' as she calls it forces the customer to help themselves, and whittles down service workers' jobs to the mundane core of stocking, cleaning, machine tending, script following and cashiering (Tannock, 2002). In contrast, small retail firms appear to distinctively advertise based on 'personalized service', emphasizing their workers are anything but mundane. Indeed, C. Wright Mills (1956) noted that a distinctive work feature of the salespeople in small/medium sized cities was the importance that these workers placed on their ability to personally know the customers they were serving. Mills reported workers were engaging in the 'handicraft methods of creating and maintaining the customer' (p.180). He juxtaposed this type of saleswork with large department store work where 'one knows the salesclerk not as a person, but as a commercial mask, a stereotyped greeting' (p. 182). Indeed Mills' observations of personalized service remain true today in many boutique retailers. An upscale women's clothing store on the New Jersey shore advertisement entices potential customers by noting:

> If you're tired of department store service, come to Coco Pari today to experience our 10,000 square foot, three level showroom in Red Bank, with consultants that were voted the best in the state. (www.cocopari.com)

Clearly pitting itself against the impersonal service of large department stores, Coco Pari is selling not just high-end clothing but also an experience. CoCo Pari's website further shares comments from clients highlighting the role the salespeople played in their experience, as in this example:

> I was greeted by a wonderful salesperson, Janine, who I found to be extremely personable and friendly. She made me feel as if I had been a long time customer. Never once did I feel rushed or pressured into buying anything. (www.cocopari.com)

Yet workers are not only expected to personalize their customer service, but they are also expected to look and act a certain way. Nickson et al. (2004) note that Glasgow's 'employers believed that having staff that look good and/ or sound right not only helped companies create a distinct image on the high street but also provided a business advantage for these companies in crowded retail and hospitality industries' (p. 10). The success of this business strategy is then based on the workers that small businesses employ. As such, having access to a well prepared labour pool, in addition to training opportunities, can be critical for small businesses.

However it is not only the retailers who highlight the distinction, local cities/towns do it as well. The personalized skilled service becomes part of the local economic development strategy. For instance, on the New Jersey shore, local towns are advertising at their visitor centres such draws as:

> Welcome to Red Bank – the gateway to the two-river area. Our town embodies the best of all worlds – fine arts and galleries, world class shopping, gourmet and casual dining, premier real estate properties both residential and commercial, theatres and performing arts, diverse cultures, the finest lodging and magnificent natural resources. What Red Bank also boasts are some of the most talented, hard working and energetic people one could ever hope to meet. (http://visit.redbank.com/)

The focus on personalized service and even the need for looking good and sounding right in retail is not new. Mills (1956) highlighted the salesperson he labelled the 'charmer' – who 'focuses the customer less upon her stock of goods than upon herself. She attracts the customer with modulated voice, artful attire and stance' (p. 175). Yet what is new is how business owners and cities/towns officials are able to capitalize on this retail work as part of a business and economic development strategy. It is then precisely the workers of the style labour market that are marketed by businesses and city tourism programmes. As part of the economic development agenda, the public workforce system must play a role in providing training and education opportunities to ensure not only that businesses have adequate labour pools, but also that job opportunities themselves can be democratized. It is up to researchers to begin to understand what this then means for the hiring strategies and criteria adopted by retailers, along with individuals' access to jobs.

As noted earlier, the growth of the style labour market demonstrates the increased demand for aesthetic skills in at least one sub-segment of retail employment (Nickson et al., 2004). Nickson et al. (2004) found that 99 per cent of Glasgow employers felt that social and interpersonal skills were of significant importance and 98 per cent of employers felt the same of self-presentation skills. Alternatively, 48 per cent of employers reported that technical skills were important for customer service staff (p. 22).[5] As Goffman (1959) informed us, this 'presentation of self' involves workers manipulating their clothing, hair and demeanour to present the specific kind of self that customers were expecting to encounter. Yet it is not just during the work tenure that workers are to 'present this self'; the potential workers were expected to present this self during the hiring process in the first place. At the job recruitment stage the right appearance and personality took precedence over technical qualifications of staff. Such work requires more than just technical and social skills, but also – aesthetic skills forcing workers to look good and sound right.

Thompson, Warhurst and Callaghan (2001) also highlighted the recruitment of employees who have the 'right' sort of disposition and appearance in Glasgow's style labour market. A hotel personnel manager, hiring staff for a café noted: 'we didn't actually look for people with experience...because we felt that wasn't particularly important. We wanted people that had a personality more than the skills because we felt we can train people to do the job' (p. 932).

Rachel Sherman's (2002, 2007) ethnographic account of luxury hotels in the US found that workers expanded upon the skills associated with caring labour to complete their work. Workers were expected to be able to personalize and customize the experiences of guests. To do this, workers needed to be able to (among other things) discern nuances of guests' interactions, gather and act on information about guest preferences, and create authentic and caring experiences for guests. Sherman found that these required both observational and active listening skills. She notes that at one of the hotels she studied during the employee training session, the human resources manager encouraged workers to use visual cues to provide guests with something they may need. Examples include when a guest comes to the hotel and appears tired, hotel staff should offer him/her a place to sit down; or if a guest arrives with a crying baby the staff should find a private space for the mother even if her room is not ready (p. 33).

Hotel front-line workers also must discern the needs of the customer based on subtle cues. Sherman provides the following example from concierge work:

> When a guest asks the concierge to recommend a restaurant, the concierge must (in addition to asking the guest about his tastes, of course) take into account factors such as where he is from, how old he is, and how sophisticated he appears, in order to increase the chances of making an appropriate choice. If the guest is older and appears unschooled in upscale dining, he may receive a reservation at a chain steakhouse; if a visitor from New York requests information on local entertainment, the concierge will not recommend the travelling version of the latest Broadway hit. (p. 33)

In addition to observation and listening skills such work also requires the skills to understand the nuances of cultural capital and how this is expressed in society. This requires a good working knowledge of cultures and how they manifest across social and economic class. It is also worthy of note that it requires creativity in personalizing the experience for each customer to his/her needs.

This is further supported by Lynne Pettinger's (2004) ethnographic study of the London retail service sector. In her study, which included participant observation (both as a worker and customer) along with interviews, she found that sales assistants are a critical part of the 'branding' of the retail store. She found that the social and aesthetic skills of the sales assistants were central to their success in the work. One of her interesting conclusions is that 'fashion-orientation is one facet of brand-strategy [used by the stores] and the ability to present a fashionable appearance is one of the skills needed by sales assistants in many stores' (p. 468).

David Wright (2005), drawing heavily on Bourdieu, further confirms how the bodies of workers become a significant factor in commercial success of retail firms. Wright finds that 'physical attractiveness, particular style of dress, and types of physical comportment all contribute to the production of the retail space as meaningful and ascetically pleasing to the customer' (p. 301). He goes on to suggest that the recruitment and management of workers for retail jobs then involves these aesthetic considerations. In particular in the context of the book shop, Wright finds that the recruitment also depends on a degree of judgement 'based upon the ability of potential recruits to articulate their enthusiasm for products in the right sort of way' (p. 305). In this particular case, it is evidenced as a 'love of books.' As one manager reported to Wright:

> People come into bookselling because they like books, and in my experience of interviewing several hundred people, the 'click' point in an interview is when you find out someone is genuinely passionate about reading or books on any level. It might be that they read, it might be they write or review or anything else, but they'll have an engagement and that's the people worth having. If they don't have that, they're not worth having in a bookshop. (pp. 305–306)

Moreover, how a worker interacts with the product being sold is increasingly recognized as important in service work and in the hiring process. As such, a growing area of inquiry is the relationship between the worker and product. Pettinger (2006) notes that it is the retail worker who is the individual who creates the shop, and the commodities in the shop as desirable consumer goods. Customer service, she suggests, is then used to sell particular material goods, and is not an end in and of itself. Instead the work of salespeople to facilitate customer service – cleaning, tidying, preparing and setting out stock – is essential to mediate between product and customer (p.54). This 'working on' of products by sales workers frames customer service and produces the consumption space.

Findings such as these, the authors posit, are critical as they suggest that management in the service industry is looking for a matrix of skills: aesthetic, social and technical. Yet the technical skills, employers report, can be developed via training once the employee is hired. Thus, at the point of recruitment, it is the social and aesthetic skills that were demanded by employers, and only once the person was employed are the technical skills and product knowledge addressed. As such, this presents significant challenges to our ability to prepare workers for these jobs, not to mention social equity in accessing this work. It is then necessary to look inside the work and capture how employers report they hire workers, in order to then inform public workforce development policies accordingly.

Hiring in the 'Blink' of an Eye?

Researching small, independent, high-end American retail employers highlighted that there were great similarities in how different employers evaluated and hired potential workers. Almost all retailers who were included in the study reported a two-stage approach to the hiring process. This approach consisted of a 'blink' moment and then more in-depth personal contact with the job-seeker. One employer summed up the entire process to screen applicants in her novelty gift shop in the following way:

> Usually people will fill out applications in our store. If I am there I'll take note of my impression of them. If they seem cheerful, fun, animated when speaking to me, full of personality, well spoken, I will take note of their name. I'll call these people first. If I didn't note anyone, I'll cold call based on the application process I listed and gauge the same qualities [as if they were here in person filling out an application]. When I meet with an applicant the most important part of the conversation is when I'm asking them to talk about themselves. They can recite their resume to me, but really being able to carry themselves as a person is more important to me.

So how did it work, and what was the importance of this approach in assessing potential employees? The employers spoke often of using 'blink' thinking as a key filter in the hiring process. In a recent bestseller, *Blink*,

Malcolm Gladwell (2005) talks about the non-conscious cognitive processes where individuals make 'two second blink' decisions. Gladwell argues that this 'thin-slicing' involves our ability to gauge what is important about a person, event or item with a limited amount of information and evidence. It is indeed a form of very rapid thinking from which individuals jump to a series of conclusions.

This blink moment is in line with Bourdieu's habitus: 'set of dispositions, reflexes and forms of behavior people acquire through acting in society' (2000, p. 19). Habitus, developed by internalizing the objective structures of the social world in the form of practices, is the unconscious schemata through which we perceive and judge our social world. In social interactions, habitus allows individuals to have a 'sense of the game' (1992, p. 21) that guides them. Bourdieu teaches us that human action is not an instantaneous reaction to immediate stimuli, and the slightest reaction of an individual to another is pregnant with the whole history of the persons and their relationships (p. 124).

The importance of the 'blink' moment was quite evident in employers' hiring decisions, and almost all employers reported that perspective workers had to pass a 'first impression' hurdle. Often this first test was unknown to the job-seeker, and in some cases performed when the job-seeker was filling out an application or even just asking for one. For example, a jewellery store owner told me: 'When an applicant walks in from the street we can tell in five minutes if someone will make it in our business'.

These rapid judgements were almost always based on a 'feeling' that the employer had of the applicant and were a significant determinant in whether the applicant would be even asked for a more in-depth application process. A gift shop owner states that she 'trusts [her] first impression when speaking to a potential employee.' And a manager of a bath and body store noted she went by 'gut feeling when meeting the applicant.' Like Gladwell's examples, retail employers noted that this 'blink' happened in those first few seconds of meeting someone, however unlike his examples, the retailers seem very conscious and open about using the 'blink' – indeed they attribute a certain legitimacy to their decision-making process. For them the 'blink' moment was the first (and perhaps the most important) employment screen, as it is often used to justify whether the potential worker will have a chance of being part of the store's retail sales team.

So what are the 'blink' moment characteristics that employers' screen on? Ironically, almost all the employers had a difficult time putting it into words. Similar to the bath and body store manager, many reported that they 'just knew when they met the person' or that they would 'feel it in their gut'. When pressed further they reported on aesthetic and personality cues from the applicant. A clothing store owner found it to be a 'high-end casual presentation, and sense of style.' Another noted 'youthful, fun, creative, spirited, unique'. The owner of a men's clothing store noted that what he looked for in that first impression was 'a clean appearance, style, accessories.' Indeed at some level, the employer is doing a trial run of the consumption experience. They imagine themselves as the potential customers of the retail store, and judge how likely they might be to buy from someone who looks and acts a certain way. And, they assume the customer is assessing the salesperson on is a 'blink' impression.

Yet that blink moment was only the first hurdle. After the first impression the next step in the hiring process was the interview. Here employers were clearer on what they were screening on. A pottery store manager said: 'Face to face meeting is that best way for us [to screen job applicants] ... [S]he told me that she looks for people who are 'energetic, responsible and outgoing.' This was reiterated by many of the employers. Several simply stated they looked for 'a people person' including, as one stated, 'the absolute priority is a high level of people/communication skills. This means outgoing, able to 'read' people, able to initiate conversation beyond product and transaction, and emotional intelligence'. In fact this owner stated that she requires 'lots of in person conversations, even prior to application and interview. I require candidates to come into the store and introduce themselves before I even give them an application.' She further noted that her hiring process often takes months because she is very selective.

A manager of a high-end cosmetics store noted that she looks for people who 'must be optimistic, excited to sell. They must be clean and put together in appearance.' A high-end clothing store cited 'strong work ethic, people skills, good salesmanship.'

Each of the store owners/managers I spoke with downplayed the importance of retail skills at the moment of hire. In fact, they made a clear categorical separation between what they saw as 'retail skills' and 'interpersonal skills', even though the personal skills they talk about include characteristics and even task-competencies directly informed by an ability to sell! As one stated, 'retail experience is helpful, but I have found that the retail aspect can be taught – the education and people skills can't.' Other felt that 'any skills needed to work retail can be acquired with training.' One woman explained: 'I'll often hire people with little or no retail experience, if that inexperienced person shows me they are excited to work here, positive, fun, communicative. I can't train a person to be sincere, honest, trustworthy and upbeat. And you can't fake it! It's obvious when you are!'

In addition to retail training, the employers also noted that they would train workers in the high-end products and services they provided to customers. In fact they did not expect their workers to come to them with the technical product knowledge needed for their store. A manager of an olive oil store said that 'all our workers need to know about the oils, vinegars, pottery and other products in the store, and we train them on it. We give them information on our products and have them shadow or work with someone while they learn the ropes.' Similarly, the manager of a high-end mattress store told me: 'Most new employees know nothing about DUX bed. We train so they have an in-depth knowledge of our products, as well as general idea of current trends in home décor and competitors' products'. To accomplish this she noted, 'we train by presenting the bed to the new employee as if they were a customer. The new employee will listen to the bed presentation and chime in when comfortable. They then will begin presentations to customers with the support of the 'trainer'.

Store owners/managers also report they train in store procedures including the technology and operations of the store. To accomplish this most of the employers I spoke with engage in a mix of presentations to the worker, and then shadowing with other workers. In fact, some of the employers that I surveyed continued to offer retail training, albeit not often, during a worker's tenure. 'Usually we have a store meeting twice a year (before the summer season and before Christmas season) to sharpen skills that may have softened.' Another noted that in her cosmetics store, 'Product lines come in to do training with the girls to introduce them to new products or teach new make-up techniques.' In addition to product knowledge another owner noted that 'the customer service/people skills is an ongoing process. We do constant training with printed materials, hands-on, role playing even shopping in other stores. We also have monthly one-hour staff meetings which are based around a theme, with training exercises and games. For example add-on sales training.'[6]

Emphatically, all the employers I spoke with were in close agreement on the ways they hire workers. They expected to train workers on retail skills, product and store procedures, and some were even willing to help develop and enhance the customer service skills of workers. They all felt that such training was part of what they could and should offer as employers. What they were less likely to provide training on were the basic customer service, aesthetic and emotion work demanded of retail work. They instead viewed this as something the prospective worker had or did not have, and was a prerequisite to hiring. Despite the need for customer service skills upon hiring, the criterion to evaluate whether a worker possessed them was less than concrete. None of the employers talked about certificates or other credentialed measures of customer service retail skills, and some even downplayed previous retail experience. Instead employers depended on feelings and assessment of workers, even at times when the workers were unaware they were being evaluated.

Workforce policy implications

My research with small high-end American retailers sheds light on important policy issues. In smaller and mid-sized tourist towns, these retail establishments can offer job opportunities for local residents. Yet, as the hiring procedure was described by many retailers, the process for securing such work is less than concrete. This creates challenges both in terms of equity in access to these jobs, and also the development and role of public workforce training programmes that can be vehicles for vulnerable workers to gain the training necessary to compete for such work.

First, in regard to equity in job access – the 'blink' hiring moment clearly provides significant barriers. Gladwell (2005) warns that 'our first impressions are generated by our experiences and our environment, which means that we can change our first impressions by changing the experiences that compromise those impressions' (p. 97-98). Interestingly, Gladwell (2005) building on research by Goldin and Rouse (2000), has even noted that 'blinding' prospective hiring managers, and thereby eliminating the blink moment – has successfully reduced sex bias in recruitment to philharmonic orchestras. Listening to prospective symphony members play, rather than *seeing* them play, significantly increased the number of women in the symphony. The blink moment then has the real potential of reproducing social inequality, as individuals can end up relying on cultural capital cues, stereotypes and prejudices. In many ways the blink moment can indeed be code for race and class bias. Nickson et al. (2003) has noted that the skills in personal presentation, self-confidence, grooming, deportment and accent required of Glasgow service workers are often linked to social class and educational background. As a result, many of these jobs would go to young college students and eliminate other workers. Qualities that are more concrete – such as retail training certifications, years of retail experience or product knowledge – are seen as less important in the hiring process, and these can disadvantage those workers who work in retail for entire careers, instead of as stopgap jobs en route to middle class professional employment.

This then presents significant challenges to the public workforce system. The employers I spoke with wanted potential workers to posses the customer service skills demanded in retail. This challenge is not new, as many larger retail and hospitality businesses have voiced similar concerns. In response to this American workforce boards have implemented training programmes, which include customer services and 'soft' skills demanded in the workplace. Pre-employment training initiatives can successfully deliver these skills in service occupations. Tom Barum (2002) observes that skill shortages in hospitality and other service occupations are increasingly seen in terms of generic rather than specific technical competencies. He notes that employers want workers trained in communications, people management and problem solving. This finding is similar to other work that has found that employers demand workers who possess the necessary social competencies and generic skills, and then the employers can train them in the technical skills and knowledge they need in the jobs. In addition, the National Retail Foundation and the public sector have collaborated on certification programmes in customer service.

Clearly then a role for the public workforce system can be to work with small retail employers to develop and deliver such training. To move in this direction real collaboration between retailers and training programmes must exist. Models already exist in the US with larger retail businesses partnering with public workforce system to develop retail skills centres in shopping malls throughout the country, focusing on retail and customer service skills. Engaging small retail owners can help not only ensure that the customer service skills needed in the high-end retail establishments are met, but can also help to develop certificates or other credentials that can measure a prospective employee's possession of such skills. Central to this is ensuring that small retails firms have 'buy-in' into the training. The small firms I spoke with proudly distinguished their customer service from those of the larger big-box stores. Therefore, existing customer service training programmes that are typically developed for larger retail businesses cannot simply be used for this type of customer service. Indeed customized customer service training programmes, along with industry accepted credentials can help reduce the reliance on a 'blink' moment and potentially open up job opportunities for more groups.

While training in customer service skills is increasingly seen as important via the public workforce system, training in aesthetic labour is not quite as straightforward. First, as Warhurst and Nickson (2009) have noted, much of the aesthetic labour is about style that an employer is looking for. As they point out, 'for employers, human capital, as indicated by qualifications, is not substitute for cultural capital, as manifest in deeply embodied dispositions (p. 10). Indeed, as Bourdieu (1984) has noted social class (among other things) manifested through aesthetics, with visual cues communicating information about a person's social class. The body, he suggests, is the physical capital that workers bring to employment. Warhurst and Nickson (2009) advocate training to improve aesthetic skills (which they see as appearance, visual and aural appeal). They do not view the training of workers as remaking the often working class/poor individual to a middle class mould, or as they call it the 'Eliza Doolittle Syndrome'; they instead advocate that training in aesthetic labour is 'an appeal for equity and pragmatism.' They argue that:

> twenty thousand people are unemployed in Glasgow but there exists 5,500 unfilled jobs. Our contention is that a proportion of those jobs are likely

to remain unfilled unless long-term unemployed people are equipped with aesthetic skills. Such jobs, such as hospitality, clearly demand employees to affect the appropriate role – required bodily dispositions, adopting 'masks for tasks' or simply 'surface acting', and the unemployed should be aware of this need. (p. 11)

Yet in the same ways that middle class aesthetic labour is embodied, so is poverty. For example, the lack of access of the poor to quality and affordable healthcare contributes to the physical scars of poverty – poor teeth, skin and impacts of a stressful life that go untreated when one does not have the healthcare to pay for it. Such indicators are difficult, if not impossible, to 'cover-up' or just 'mask for the task'. So while training in aesthetic labour can help enhance some opportunities, it will not eliminate the potential biases in the blink moment, nor will it alter the ways this labour market works.

In addition to training of potential workers, education and awareness of employers is also important, in helping to eliminate the 'blink' moment biases. In fact at some level it may be of paramount importance in providing job access. As Bourdieu (1992) reminds us: 'what depends on us is not the first move, but the second. It is difficult to control the first inclination of habitus, but reflexive analysis, which teaches us that we are the ones who endow the situation with part of the potency it has over us, allows us to alter our perceptions of the situation and thereby our reaction to it' (p. 136). Such reflexive attention can go a long way in not only recognizing this work and the skills associated, but also potentially open up job opportunities and diversify staff. Gladwell also acknowledges that it is only when we expose the biases of our 'blink' moments that we can get beyond them. Helping employers understand how the 'blink' moment impacts their hiring may help some of them see potential candidates in a different light.

The public workforce system can play a role to help move the hiring dialogue away from a focus on the 'blink' moment as 'you either have it or don't' to ways to instead work with employers to develop and credential these skills in prospective workers. Indeed as long as 'charming personalities' are part of the economic development system, it may very well behoove the public workforce system to work hand in hand with small retailers to improve such jobs and open up real opportunities throughout the retail industry.

Notes

I would like to thank Eileen Appelbaum for earlier comments on this chapter.

1 The name of the boutique has been changed.
2 This system is a network of federal, state and local offices charged with promoting economic growth and publically financed training of workers.
3 Workforce investment boards control the policy and programmes of the public workforce system in each state and local area. The boards consist of government agencies, businesses, community-based organizations and educational entities.
4 These are 2008 population estimates from www.city-data.com, accessed September 2009.
5 It is important to note that these data are compiled from the employers' perspectives on skills, and is of course dependent on who completes the survey (for example, direct managers, human resources directors, etc). Nevertheless it does provide insight into what employers are experiencing in service work.
6 The responses of the retailers also highlight how uneven training opportunities are for workers across small retail firms, further demonstrating the need for public workforce opportunities for workers.

REFERENCES

Besin-Cassino, Y. (2005) 'Consumption of production: part-time student employment in suburban united states', *Berkeley Journal of Sociology*, 49(1), Fall.
Blinder, A. (2006) 'Offshoring: the next industrial revolution', *Foreign Affairs*.
Bolton, S. and Boyd, C. (2003) 'Trolly dolly or skilled emotion manager? Moving on from hochschild's managed heart', *Work, Employment and Society* 17: 289–308.
Bourdieu, P. (1984) *Distinction: A Social Critique of the Judgment of Taste*. London: Routledge
Bourdieu, P. and Wacquant, L. (1992) *An Invitation to Reflexive Sociology*. U Chicago Press.
Bourdieu, P. (2000) 'The politics of protest. An interview by Kevin Ovenden', *Socialist Review Nr*, 242: 18–20.
Brown, P. et al. (2001) *High Skills: Globalisation, Competiitiveness, and Skill Formation*. Oxford: Oxford University Press.
Carré, F. and Tilly, C. (2008) 'America's biggest low-wage industry: Continuity and change in retail jobs', Institute for Research on Labor and Employment, UCLA.
England, P. et al. (2002) 'Wages of virtue: the relative pay of care work', *Social Problems*, 49: 455–473.

▶

▶

Gatta, M., Boushey, H. and Appelbaum, E. (2009) 'High touch and here to stay: future skills demands in US low wage service occupations', *Sociology*, 45: 968–989.

Gatta, M. (2002) *Juggling Food and Feelings: Emotional Balance in the Workplace*. Lanham, MD: Lexington Books.

Gladwell, M. (2005) *Blink: the Power of Thinking without Thinking*. New York: Little, Brown and Company.

Glazer, N. (1993) *Women's Paid and Unpaid Labor: The Work Transfer in Health Care and Retailing*. Philadelphia: Temple University Press.

Goldin, C. and Rouse, C. (2000). Orchestrating impartiality: The impact of 'blind' auditions on female musicians', *American Economic Review*, 90: 715–741.

Goffman, E. (1959) *The Presentation of Self in Everyday Life*. Harmondsworth: Penguin.

Guy, M. and Newman, M. (2004) 'Women's Jobs, Men's Jobs: Sex Segregation and Emotional Labor', *Public Administration Review*, 64: 289–298.

Hochschild, A. ([1983]2003). *The Second Shift*. New York: Penguin Books.

Korczynski, M. (2005) 'Service work and skills: an overview', *Human Resource Management Journal*, 15: 1–12.

Levy, F. and Murnane, R. (2005) 'How computer work and globalization shape human skill demands', paper prepared for Planning Meeting for 21st Century Skills, National Academy of the Sciences.

Leidner, R. (1993) *Fast Food, Fast Talk: Service Work and the Routinization of Everyday Life*. Berkeley, CA: University of California Press.

Light, I. and Bonacich, E. (1991) *Immigrant Entrepreneurs: Koreans in Los Angeles, 1965-1982*. Berkeley, CA: University of California Press.

Wright Mills, C. (1956) *White Collar: The American Middle Classes*. New York: Oxford University Press.

Mirchandani, K. (1999) 'Feminist insight on gendered work: new directions and research on women and entrepreneurship', *Gender Work and Organization*, 6: 224–235.

Nickson, D., Warhurst, C. and Dutton, E. (2004) 'Aesthetic labour and the policy-making agenda: time for a reappraisal of skills?' research Paper 48. SKOPE Publications: Warwick Business School, Coventry, England.

Pettinger, L. (2004) 'Brand culture and branded workers: service work and aesthetic labour in fashion retail', *Consumption, Markets and Culture*, 7: 165–184.

Pettinger, L. (2006) 'On the materiality of service work', *The Sociological Review*, 54: 48–65.

Ritzer, G. (1996) *The McDonaldization of Society*. Thousand Oaks, CA: Pine Forge Press.

Sherman, R. 2002. ' "Better Than Your Mother": Caring Labor in Luxury Hotels.' Working Paper No. 53, Center for Working Families, University of California, Berkeley. http://wfnetwork.bc.edu/berkeley/workingpapers.html

Sherman, R. (2007) *Class Acts: Service and Inequality in Luxury Hotels*. Berkeley: University of California Press.

▶

▶

Tannock, S. (2002) 'Why do working youth work where they do?' A Report of the Young Workers Project, Center for Labor Research and Education, UC Berkeley.

Thompson, P. et al. (2001) 'Ignorant theory and knowledgeable workers: interrogating the connections between knowledge skills and services', *Journal of Management Studies,* 38: 923–942.

Warhurst, C. and Nickson, D. (2009) 'Becoming a class act?: Reflections on aesthetic labor', http://www.hrm.strath.ac.uk/ILPC/2005/conf-papers/Warhurst-Nickson.pdf, accessed September 2009.

Williams, C. (2004) 'Inequality in the toy store', *Qualitative Sociology,* 27: 461–486.

Wright, D. (2005) 'Commodifying respectability: distinctions at work in the bookshop', *Journal of Consumer Culture,* 5: 295–314.

Labour Supply and Skills Demand in Fashion Retailing

4

Dennis Nickson, Scott A. Hurrell, Chris Warhurst and Johanna Commander

Introduction

If, as Adam Smith once famously suggested, Britain was a nation of shop-keepers then it is now a nation of shopworkers. Retail is a significant part of the UK economy, accounting for £256 billion in sales and one-third of all consumer spending (Skillsmart, 2007). It is the largest private sector employer in the UK, employing 3 million workers, or 1 in 10 of the working population. For future job creation in the UK economy retail is also similarly prominent and the sector is expected to create a further 250,000 jobs by 2014 (Skillsmart, 2007). The centrality of retail to economic success and job creation is apparent in other advanced economies. For example, in the US, retail sales is the occupation with the largest projected job growth in the period 2004–2014 (Gatta et al., 2009) and in Australia retail accounts for 1 in 6 workers (Buchanan et al., 2003). Within the UK these workers are employed in approximately 290,000 businesses, encompassing large and small organizations and also a number of sub-sectors. This variance suggests that retail should not be regarded as homogenous in its labour demands. Hart et al. (2007) note how skill requirements and the types of workers employed may differ across the sector. This chapter further opens up this point, providing an analysis of the labour supply and skills demands for the sub-sectors of clothing, footwear and leather goods, which are described by Skillsmart (2007: 48) as being 'significant categories in UK retailing'.

The chapter initially outlines the nature of the UK retail workforce and the skill issues facing the sector, focusing particularly on soft skills. Influenced by Hochschild (1983) these soft skills have mostly been conceived within the paradigm of emotional labour and equated with having the 'right' personality and attitude (e.g., Callaghan and Thompson, 2002). Consequently, much of the discussion surrounding soft skills has tended to concentrate on employees' social and interpersonal abilities and whether or not they are responsive, courteous and understanding with customers. However, this description of soft skills is partial. Whilst the importance of employee personality and attitude has been extensively discussed the issue of appearance has tended to be overlooked. Recent work has sought to rectify this oversight and has led to the development of what is termed 'aesthetic labour', involving the manner in which employees are expected to embody the product in industries such as retail and hospitality (see, e.g., Warhurst et al., 2000; Nickson et al., 2001; Warhurst and Nickson, 2007a). This labour refers to the hiring of people with corporeal capacities and attributes that favourably appeal to customers' senses and which are then organizationally mobilized, developed and commodified through training, management and regulation to produce an embodied style of service. As part of this process of embodiment, employees are expected to both demonstrate soft skills associated with personality and attitude and 'look good' or 'sound right'.

The chapter thus contributes to debates about the labour supply and skills demands in retail, reporting the findings of a survey of clothing, footwear and leather goods retailers in the Greater Manchester area in the UK. The chapter also offers insight into the variability of retail work, offering some support for the notion that fashion retail is different from other parts of the retail sector in the types of worker that it attracts, principally due to the soft skills demands of the sub-sector and the nature of the job.

The retail workforce and skills challenges

In the UK and elsewhere (Buchanan et al., 2003; Gatta et al., 2009) there are two main sources from which retail employers draw their labour: women and young workers. Although not as gendered as other industries, such as social care, retail still nevertheless has a predominance of women workers, with 60 per cent of the workforce in the UK being women, many of whom work part-time (Skillsmart, 2007). Scott (1994) has pointed to women being seen by retail employers as a source of cheap, flexible and high quality labour as their inherent 'feminine' skills are seen as being synonymous with the required soft skills. Equally, retail tends to be a young industry with a third of all workers under 25 years of age, a figure far higher than the economy as whole (Skillsmart, 2007). A large proportion of these young workers are students, such that they are now considered to be a structural part of the retail labour market (Huddleston and Hirst, 2004). As with women, students are deemed to be particularly attractive to retail employers due to their flexibility, cheapness and highly developed soft skills (see, e.g., Canny, 2002; Curtis and Lucas, 2001; Nickson et al., 2004).

For employers these soft skills centre on having the right personality, attitude and appearance, and are deemed to be important in delivering good customer service. In their survey of 147 retail and hospitality employers in Glasgow, Nickson et al. (2005) found that 93 per cent of their respondents attributed significant importance to the image of customer-facing staff. At the point of entry into the organization employers were much more concerned with the right personality and right appearance, which were considered important by virtually all respondents; while formal qualifications were regarded as important by only 20 per cent of respondents. Once in the organization, employers placed much greater emphasis on the importance of customer-facing employees' social and interpersonal and self-presentation skills (respectively 99 per cent and 98 per cent of respondents deemed these important) compared to technical skills, with 48 per cent of employers considering this aspect important. Bunt et al. (2005) also found that the skills demanded by retail employers in new recruits for sales and retail assistants, retail cashiers and checkout operator jobs centred on self-presentation, verbal communications and interpersonal and team work skills.

However, there are concerns about deficits in such skills, particularly in sales occupations, the largest occupational grouping in the retail workforce (Skillsmart, 2007). Hart et al. (2007) note that skills gaps in retailing are higher than the figure across the economy as a whole (26 per cent vs. 22 per cent) leading them to suggest that 'the adverse impact of these skills gaps for retailers can include difficulties in meeting customer needs, providing quality service and also increased organizational costs' (p. 272). This point is especially true when it is recognized that skills gaps are particularly acute for sales and elementary occupations and that customer handling skills are especially lacking (Skillsmart, 2007). As well as contending with skills gaps amongst existing employees, retail employers may also face labour and skill shortages, creating recruitment difficulties:

> While few organizations have difficulty recruiting sales assistants, attracting the right candidate is often difficult. A lack of people with the right 'attitude' has been seen as a major barrier to success...some retailers may be looking specifically for young people who 'look a certain way', this is especially important in some designer fashion retail outlets. (Huddleston and Hirst, 2004: 8)

In sum, across the retail sector as a whole there is evidence to suggest that employers face difficulties in recruiting employees with the appropriate soft skills and ensuring that existing employees are sufficiently skilled in customer service.

Appreciating the importance of sub-sectoral level analysis

Whilst the previous section offered a broad overview of the nature of the retail labour market and skills demands, it is also important to recognize the diversity within the sector. The 4-digit Standard Industrial Classification (SIC) descriptors list 24 sub-sectors in UK retail (Skillsmart, 2007). Thus there is the potential for significant differences between sub-sectors in terms of product and labour markets and the type of skills demanded.

In their work on food and electrical and electronic goods retailing, Mason and Osborne (2008) found significant differences regarding the type of labour and the skills demanded to get and do a job. Food retailing organizations relied on female part-timers, mostly with childcare responsibilities, and to a lesser extent students and older workers. These employees were expected to have a 'positive attitude', friendliness, communication skills and basic numeracy and literacy, in short customer service skills. Electrical retail firms differed markedly having mainly full-time male staff with pre-existing knowledge of electrical and electronic products. The greater emphasis on product knowledge meant that 'it was taken for granted that these selection criteria would lead to a predominately male workforce as a result of prevailing social attitudes towards electrical and electronic goods' (p. 152). Basic pay was also greater in electrical retail firms, sometimes supplemented by sales commissions. The provision of generally full-time employment, higher pay, greater emphasis on product knowledge and ongoing training lead Mason and Osborne to characterize electrical retailers as adopting a 'high road' approach to managing their employees. This approach contrasts with the 'low road' food retailers, with their reliance on low-paid, part-time, largely female employees who receive limited training.

As well as the differences in terms of people management practices there is also a further issue with regard to perceptions of retail work. More specifically, some sub-sectors appear more attractive to potential employees than others and potentially some brands may be deemed more attractive within those sub-sectors. The Retail E-Commerce Task Force (2002) surveyed 2,500 young people (11–19 year olds) on their perceptions of working in retail and found that certain sub-sectors were seen as more 'trendy' than others. Fifty eight per cent of 1,218 girls interviewed put fashion retailing as their first choice. For boys sportswear was most popular (23.8 per cent) followed by games and software (18.5 per cent) and music (14.8 per cent). Clearly there is also a gender dimension to this stratification and clothing, footwear and leather goods is more gendered than the retail sector as a whole. Pettinger (2005) notes how 72 per cent of the workforce in these sub-sectors is female, compared to 60 per cent across the sector as a whole.

There is also emergent work that suggests that there may be differences in workers' self-perception depending on the sub-sectors where they work. Wright (2005), for example, suggests that workers in the UK book trade see themselves as very different from, and superior to, other retail workers. Drawing on interviews with 30 managers and workers (including 15 shop floor workers) in 3 high street chain book retailers, Wright suggests that the appreciation of books and reading, which were deemed essential to getting jobs in the bookshops, are 'ascribed a certain value that places the trade in general in a hierarchal position over other trades and in particular in hierarchal positions over other workers' (p. 311). Thus even though bookshop workers, as with other retail workers, are low-paid, they see themselves as distinct because of the product they are selling and their personal attributes and characteristics. In terms of personal attributes, 27 of Wright's interviewees were graduates and they invested in their work a high degree of appreciation of the cultural goods being sold, which was dependent on the persona of a well read, cultivated self, built on appropriate cultural capital and 'middle classness'.

This sense of workers deriving status or cultural capital from their employment is also apparent in Johnston and Sandberg's (2008) ethnographic account of an 'exclusive' department store where the predominately female employees were recruited not only because of their physical attractiveness but also on the basis of their understandings of class and taste. In a similar vein, Walls (2008) in his ethnography of fashion retail found his co-workers would often contrast the 'coolness' of fashion retail to other retail jobs such as being a supermarket checkout operator. Leslie (2002) suggests that whilst fashion retail shares the low pay and part-time hours of the retail sector as a whole, the sub-sector is distinct from other forms of retail employment in: its prevalence of sales quotas for employees; its strict enforcement of image and presentation rules; and the blurring between employees' identities as consumer and workers, for example noting how many fashion retail workers seek a job as a means to procure a store discount to purchase goods, with evidence that top end fashion houses offer the highest reductions (Shedden, 2003).

Furthermore, within fashion retail there may be differences between product offerings, such that certain brands may well have greater cachet than others. Pettinger highlights differences between aspirational brands that are usually 'highly fashionable, designer intense and "cool"' (Pettinger, 2005: 469) and more prosaic brands. She describes an 'ideal' worker in the pseudonymous company, Fashion Junction, which offers expensive products in a highly designed environment:

The worker, wearing current stock and with appropriately fashionable hairstyle and make up, appears as a consumer as well as a worker, signalling what is fashionable to customers, and how they might look in the 'right' clothes. Workers at such stores are not only fashionably dressed, they are young, usually slim, with 'attractive' faces. (2004: 179)

Though the aestheticization of workers was particularly pronounced within Fashion Junction, a number of the other less fashionable brands still aimed for a certain 'style', with prescriptions on appearance and dress, seeking workers to embody that style. In the more design-led stores, such as Fashion Junction, employees would be expected to 'model' current stock, whilst in other more mass market companies' employees would wear a corporate uniform. Pettinger (2005) therefore argues the need to analyse a range of stores to allow for the development of a typology that can distinguish the different types of aesthetics required from designer outlets to less stringent mass market chains.

Recognizing differing employer requirements across several retail sub-sectors, Buchanan et al. (2003) develop a continuum that ranges from goods that 'sell themselves' to goods that require product knowledge or more advanced skills of workers in order to make sales. Supermarkets are positioned on one end of the continuum as representing goods that essentially sell themselves. The labour supply for sales assistants is characterized as being mature aged women returning to work and juniors still at school. The contrast is specialized book and music stores and fashion retail. Mirroring the findings in Wright's work, employers are seeking tertiary qualified workers with expertise in the product. The same is also true for fashion retail where labour supply was seen as being students and European mature women with wealthy husbands. Interestingly for specialized book and music and fashion retail Buchanan et al. suggest that labour and skills shortages are unlikely with employers able to source the required cultural capital from the external labour market. Supermarkets, however, struggled to attract quality labour. Clearly then it is useful to develop an analysis of labour supply and skills demands by sub-sector to appreciate why these differences may exist and what they may mean in terms of the employment opportunities available to different segments of the labour market.

Research methodology

The chapter draws on a postal survey of retail employers of clothing, footwear and leather goods (SIC codes 52.42 and 52.43) in the Greater Manchester area. This area is a major shopping destination in the North West of England with retail a key driver of its recent economic development (Skillsmart, 2004). The North West has the largest amount of new shops and stores being constructed in the UK (Skillsmart, 2007), with obvious implications for employment opportunities, including for the unemployed. Moreover in some of the shopping districts in Greater Manchester, clothing and footwear comprise nearly half of all retail business (BMG, 2005; 2006). Significantly, retailers in Greater Manchester have stated that a key reason for the existence of hard-to-fill vacancies for sales and customer service staff in general is the low number of applicants with the required soft skills (Skillsmart, 2004).

The survey was administered to a sample of 500 retailers. From the sample a final response rate of 35 per cent (n = 173) was achieved. The questionnaire was addressed to the store manager and included sections on recruitment and selection, skills demands, and skills shortages in potential recruits or skills gaps in the current workforce. Questions in these sections explored employer demand for aspects of emotional and aesthetic labour as well as qualifications and other job-related needs. Questions were also asked about organization's clothing and appearance policies and their approaches to training and appraisal. Using SPSS, results were first used to arrive at descriptive statistics and frequencies. Where differences were obtained between establishments the results were tested for statistical significance using chi square tests or one way analysis of variance (ANOVA) depending on the nature of the variable under investigation.

Research findings

Establishment and workforce characteristics

The vast majority of the establishments (73 per cent) that partook in the survey study were branches of multi-site chains. Such organizations may be realistically expected to have centralized practices in place regarding skills policies and also more formalized branding strategies. Participating establishments were relatively small with an average of 22 employees, although size varied considerably. All establishments in the sample catered for customers of a variety of ages and typically for both sexes. Quality and style were seen as more important to customers than cost by the respondents. Only 39 per cent of establishments rated cost as 'very important' or 'essential' to their customers, compared to 80 per cent for quality and 82 per cent for style.

Employers were asked about the demographics of their front line workers. On average, 74 per cent of staff in each establishment were female, supporting the view that fashion retailing is more gendered than the sector as a whole (Leslie, 2002; Pettinger, 2005). Front-line workers were typically young with, on average, almost 60 per cent of establishments' workforces aged between 16 and 25. Approximately 41 per cent of staff in each establishment were students and only 47 per cent of staff worked full-time, reflecting variable labour demand and that many staff were in education. Despite hiring many students, employers typically reported that staff needed either no or only basic education to get the job, reaffirming that front-line retail staff require little formal education. Additionally, very few staff had a specialist retail qualification.

Employer demand for employees getting and doing the job

Tables 4.1 and 4.2 examine the criteria stated by employers to be important for employees getting and doing the job. Employers were asked to rate these criteria on a five-point ascending scale from 'not at all important' to 'essential' (representing a minimum score of one and a maximum of 5).[1] The tables present frequencies of response and mean scores.

As shown in Table 4.1, reflecting the findings of Bunt et al. (2005), employers rated personality and appearance as the most important aspects when *selecting* front-line staff with 80 per cent suggesting that personality was either 'essential' or 'very important' and 68 per cent the 'right' appearance. Just over 41 per cent viewed previous experience as either essential or very important whilst only 5 per cent rated formal qualifications in this manner.

Factors that might be regarded as features of emotional labour were considered most important to employers in performing front-line work (see Table 4.2). A range of other factors were also considered 'very important' on average and reported as 'very important' or 'essential' by over 50 per cent of employers. These factors included but were not limited to technical skills, product knowledge and also one element of aesthetic labour; dress sense and style. Still 'fairly important' on average (with mean scores >2.5) were other aspects of aesthetic labour, such as voice and accent and overall physical appearance.

Table 4.1 Factors important in selection

	N	% reporting 'very important' or 'essential'	Range	Mean	Std. Dev.
Right personality	170	79.7	3–5	4.15	0.71
Right appearance	170	68.2	1–5	3.84	0.80
Previous experience	170	41.1	1–5	3.36	0.85
Qualifications	169	4.6	1–5	2.14	0.86

Table 4.2 Characteristics important in performing front-line work

	N	% reporting 'very important' or 'essential'	Range	Mean	Stan. Dev.
Ability to work with others	170	85.0	2–5	4.25	0.69
Ability to deal with customers	171	84.0	2–5	4.30	0.74
Availability and rostering	166	65.9	1–5	3.84	0.79
Product knowledge	170	65.5	1–5	3.86	0.88
Work ethic	166	63.0	1–5	3.68	1.03
Outgoing personality	169	60.2	1–5	3.72	0.83
Dress sense and style	168	57.2	1–5	3.68	0.88
Knowledge of store operations/ procedures	170	54.3	1–5	3.66	0.93
Ability to use equipment	169	48.0	1–5	3.47	1.00
Voice and accent	170	27.2	1–5	2.89	1.06
Previous job experience	166	28.3	1–5	3.07	0.84
Overall physical appearance	156	21.4	1–5	2.72	1.05
Formal education/qualifications	170	8.6	1–5	2.35	0.87
Age	164	7.4	1–5	2.07	0.92
Height	162	4.6	1–5	1.72	0.84
Weight	162	4.1	1–5	1.83	0.85

Other factors recognized as being 'fairly important' were job experience and the ability to use equipment. Aesthetic requirements of customer-facing work were thus related more to clothing and style than physical appearance per se, consistent with the importance that establishments believed customers placed on 'style'; and the workers that can best embody that style (Pettinger, 2004; 2005).

Formal education and qualifications clearly lack importance to employers, even though employers indicated that technical skills were important (see Table 4.2). Age, weight and height were also, apparently, not a great concern for employers. It may be that employers were aware of the delicacy of these potentially sensitive physical characteristics and were underplaying their importance in their response to the survey.

Recruitment and selection

As with other research findings on service industries (see, e.g., Lockyer and Scholarios, 2004) the survey results indicated that in Manchester retailing there was heavy reliance on informal recruitment methods, with the most popular being referrals from current staff (64 per cent) and window adverts

(60 per cent). The high figure for referrals also reflects that many retailers have incentive schemes in place for employees who refer potential recruits to the company. Two formal methods were the next most frequently reported categories; recruitment agencies and job centres (both 48 per cent) whilst 42 per cent used company websites. Other methods such as advertising in the local press, rehiring old staff and accepting casual callers were reported by 23 per cent to 32 per cent of establishments. The use of informal methods such as referrals suggests that employees may be recruited who 'fit' with employees already in the establishment and possibly, therefore, the establishment's brand. It is also the case that casual callers and those responding to window adverts typically present themselves in person which may be advantageous in allowing employers to screen for soft skills, especially those associated with aesthetics and appearance (Nickson et al., 2005).

Employers tended to use the 'classic trio' of application forms/CVs (60/78 per cent), interviews (71 per cent) and references (60 per cent) when selecting front-line staff. In addition, 24 per cent of the Manchester employers reported using role plays, 17 per cent product knowledge tests, 11 per cent requested photographs of applicants and 10 per cent used job simulations.

Employers were asked which selection methods were the most useful for selecting front-line staff. Almost two-thirds of respondents stated that interviews were the most useful method, giving a 'usefulness ratio' of 0.87 for those employers using interviews. The usefulness/use ratios for CVs, application forms and references were 0.40, 0.48 and 0.22 respectively. For role plays, however, the usefulness ratio was 0.58 suggesting that more employers could consider role plays, possibly at the expense of CVs, application forms and references. These findings indicate that employers prefer the opportunity to interact directly with potential employees, to allow them to make an immediate assessment of applicants' emotional and aesthetic labour potential.

Skills shortages

Managers were asked to rate the difficulty of recruiting for a range of job-related characteristics (see Table 4.3). Contrary to claims such as those of Huddleston and Hirst (2004) about skills shortages in applicants' attitudes and appearance, only a minority of employers in our survey had any significant difficulty in terms of the desired soft skills amongst potential employees. Where most difficulty did exist was in recruiting employees with the appropriate product or operational knowledge. It should be noted, however, that both knowledges can be very basic (Warhurst and Nickson, 2007a).

Aside from these most 'difficult' aspects, only four characteristics were reported as 'very difficult' or 'impossible' to recruit by over 10 per cent of establishments (previous job experience, availability and rostering, the ability

Table 4.3 Characteristics difficult to recruit

	N	% reporting 'very difficult' or 'impossible'	Range	Mean	Stan. Dev.
Product knowledge	169	26.0	1–5	3.01	0.82
Knowledge of store operations/ procedures	168	21.4	1–4	2.76	0.86
Work ethic	165	14.5	1–4	2.55	0.90
Ability to deal with customers	167	13.9	1–5	2.61	0.85
Availability and rostering	164	11	1–5	2.59	0.81
Previous job experience	166	10.4	1–5	2.50	0.84
Voice and accent	165	8.7	1–4	2.21	0.89
Formal education/qualifications	164	8.7	1–5	2.22	0.87
Outgoing personality	166	7.5	1–5	2.27	0.83
Ability to use equipment	166	4.6	1–4	2.19	0.69
Dress sense and style	166	4.1	1–5	2.23	0.75
Ability to work with others	167	2.9	1–5	2.21	0.67
Age	157	2.3	1–5	1.83	0.75
Weight	152	1.2	1–4	1.61	0.65
Physical appearance	156	1.2	1–4	1.74	0.61
Height	152	–	1–3	1.58	0.60

to deal with customers and work ethic). It was, therefore, 'harder' and more technical skills, abilities and knowledge that were perceived as causing skills shortages rather than factors such as personality, dress sense and style.

One explanation for this finding is that fashion retail has greater cachet than other types of retail. As noted earlier the Retail E-Commerce Task Force (2002) found that sub-sectors such as fashion, music/video, sport and software/games were seen as 'trendy' and the most appealing for potential young employees. Similarly, Walls (2008) found that amongst his co-workers (many of whom were students) fashion retail was often seen as part of an informal hierarchy, very different from working in a supermarket, for example. It is quite possible therefore that those applicants who possess the appropriate attitudes and appearance are more likely to be attracted to fashion retail leading to fewer skills shortages. This finding would also support the work of Leslie (2002) and Pettinger (2004; 2005) who recognize that many fashion retail workers already have a pre-existing identification with the brand as consumers; a process that is further reinforced when working in the store.

Importance of image and appearance

To further establish the importance of image and appearance the existence of, and reasons for, employers having clothing and appearance policies were explored. The vast majority of respondents (82 per cent) reported that their companies had standard rules or expectations relating to clothing worn at work. The most widely stated reasons for having clothing policies was for employees to fit the image or brand of the company (83 per cent) and to ensure that staff looked 'neat and presentable' (81 per cent). A smaller proportion of employers (50 per cent) reported that they used clothing policies to standardize the appearance of their staff. The emphasis on style and branding reflects earlier findings regarding the importance of the dress sense and style of front-line staff rather than physical appearance per se.

The importance of image or style was reiterated in employer responses to questions about the significance of certain factors in implementing clothing policies. Conformity to company brand/image stood out alone as, on average, 'very important'. Local manager's preference, customer preference and adherence to employment law were, however, on average, viewed as only 'fairly important'. These findings thus add further support to Leslie (2002) and Pettinger (2004; 2005) that organizations are concerned with the self-presentation and the aesthetics of individuals primarily as a means to convey brand image.

Clothing polices were also used for sales purposes. Fifty-five per cent of employers stated that clothing policies were used to 'model' current stock, with current stock the most popular source from which staff clothing was drawn (48 per cent of establishments with a clothing policy). The next most popular source of staff clothing (dedicated company clothing) was reported by less than a third of establishments with a clothing policy. The use of staff as 'models' indicates that employee appearance was used to sell products as well as to complement the image of the establishment (see also Leslie, 2002; Pettinger, 2004).

Employer appearance policies were also explored in the survey. Seventy-four per cent of establishments rated the appearance of customer-facing staff as either 'very important' or 'essential'. As with clothing, more than four out of five establishments had an appearance policy or standards. The most common subject covered was personal hygiene and general tidiness, reported by 91 per cent of establishments with an appearance policy. The next most commonly reported aspect, consistent with the results overall, was clothing style (76 per cent of those with a policy). Bodily adornment was also covered widely, with 55 per cent stating that make-up and personal grooming was included in the appearance policy, 50 per cent facial and bodily piercing, 49 per cent jewellery and 44 per cent visible tattoos. The aspects most rarely covered by appearance policies related to physiological characteristics and speech. Voice and accent was included in the policies of 7 per cent of workplaces, age in 5 per cent, weight in 4 per cent and height in 2 per cent. It is of course possible that not selecting employees on the basis of these physiological characteristics is seen as too straightforward to necessitate formal policy or are under reported in the survey due to concerns about legality and discrimination. With respect to weight for example, in their earlier piloting of aesthetic labour research in Glasgow, Warhurst and Nickson (2001) were told by one worker that her boutique fashion store employer screened out female job applicants with the larger dress sizes over size 16 as a matter of course.

As with the clothing policy, respondents were asked *why* they had an appearance policy, with conformity to company brand and image again the stand out factor, viewed as 'very important' or 'essential' by 60 per cent of establishments (see Table 4.4). Three other factors were rated on average as 'fairly important', namely, local manager's preference, customer preference and adherence to employment law. The importance of brand image to fashion retailers in implementing aesthetic labour policies is thus reinforced further still.

Differences between establishments were analysed to determine whether ownership structure (independent, chain or a franchise of a larger chain) or customer preferences affected the implementation of appearance and clothing policies. This analysis revealed that establishments that were part of a chain or franchised were approximately twice as likely to have clothing or appearance policies as independent stores, a finding that was statistically significant (see Table 4.5). This propensity may reflect the informality within independent shops or the fact that management is closer to the market and can personally communicate 'strategy' changes to staff without resorting to explicit policies. At the same time larger establishments are more likely to have explicit human resource policies, which will encompass rules for employee clothing and appearance. ANOVA analysis also revealed that chains were also statistically more likely to report that company brand/image was more important in the instigation of clothing policies.

Table 4.4 Organizations stated reasons for appearance policy

	N	% reporting 'very important' or 'essential'	Range	Mean	Stan. Dev.
Conformity to company brand/ image	146	59.5	1–5	3.84	1.13
Local manager's preference	148	41.8	1–5	3.24	1.15
Customer preference	138	31.2	1–5	3.06	1.15
Adherence to employment law	113	19	1–5	2.75	1.46

Table 4.5 Establishments (%) reporting rules/standards/expectations regarding...

	Independent single site operations	Independent franchised operation	Branch of a chain of shops	Chi square value
...the work clothing of customer-facing staff	48.1	100	92.9	35.28***
...the appearance of customer-facing staff	44.4	100	92.8	39.43***

*Note: *** statistically significant at p = 0.000.*

ANOVA analysis also revealed that where the customer base was concerned with style, an applicant's previous experience was deemed as more important in performing front-line work. Furthermore, the same analysis highlighted that where customers were reportedly more concerned with style, employer brand/image was deemed as more important in implementing appearance policies. Employers may, therefore, seek applicants' experience of the style-driven market and have employees who are more obviously style conscious where style matters more to their customers. The demands of a sector's customers may, therefore, impact upon the skills and other attributes that employers seek. Caution must be exercised with this finding however as only a small number of establishments reported that style was unimportant to their customers.

Training and appraisal

Despite the importance of workers' aesthetic and emotional capabilities, the most commonly provided types of training were related to 'technical' aspects such as product knowledge and company procedures. Training in 'soft skills' was, however, also widely reported. Ninety-two per cent of establishments provided training in product knowledge and 81 per cent did so in 'company systems and equipment'. Training in company clothing standards was, however, reported by 71 per cent of establishments whilst 43–44 per cent of establishments reported providing training in social/interpersonal skills or self-presentation/physical appearance.

Those employers providing presentation and physical appearance training were asked to elaborate on this training. The two most widely cited elements were dress sense and style and body language; both reported by 46 per cent of employers answering the question. In addition, 35 per cent provided training on what to say, 25 per cent in make-up and personal grooming and 8 per cent in voice and accent coaching. The fact that dress and style training was one of the two most widely reported subjects of physical appearance training supports the fact that it was the element of physical appearance viewed as the most important in carrying out customer-facing work.

Through assessing which elements of employees' work were appraised, the centrality of certain skills can be further established. As with training, the most commonly cited matter on which staff were appraised was product knowledge (reported by 71 per cent of employers). The second most popular subject of appraisal was use or knowledge of company systems/equipment, reported by 60 per cent of respondents. Soft skills were appraised, with 57 per cent of employers reporting that self-presentation and physical appearance were included in appraisal, 56 per cent that adherence to company clothing standards was included and 47 per cent social and interpersonal skills.

Whilst the correct appearance is important in getting customer-facing work, with certain elements also important in performing the work (especially dress sense and style), it is product knowledge that was the most useful performance indicator for these retail employers. Thus product knowledge was the area of appraisal highlighted as the 'most useful' (44 per cent of employers), followed by social and interpersonal skills (36 per cent) and then company systems and equipment. Only 17 per cent reported that self-presentation was the most useful element of appraisal and 14 per cent adherence to company clothing standards. Notwithstanding the usefulness of product knowledge in appraisal, when investigating the usefulness ratio (proportion reporting element was the most useful/proportion using the method) social and interpersonal skills had a ratio of 0.77 and product knowledge 0.62. These ratios suggest that more employers could consider the use of social and interpersonal skills as a means of appraisal, despite the increased demands for product knowledge in the clothing, footwear and leather goods sector.

Discussion and conclusion

The results from the Manchester survey affirm a number of the findings from survey evidence reported by Nickson et al. (2005) on the Glasgow retail and hospitality industries. In both surveys, employers were more concerned with the soft skills of applicants, such that having the 'right' personality, attitude and appearance was considered essential to do front-line work. Employers in both surveys were more likely to use informal recruitment methods. There was also evidence in both surveys of employers having prescriptions that outlined what constituted an acceptable appearance, through the use of appearance standards and dress codes. Training was also more likely to be offered with regards to harder technical aspects, such as product knowledge. Beyond these similarities there were also differences between the Glasgow and the more sectorally focused Manchester surveys. These differences raise a number of important issues.

A significant difference between the surveys was the issue of employer skills demands at the point of entry to the company, specifically in terms of how employers rated technical skills. Only 40 per cent of employers in the Glasgow survey rated technical skills as 'important' or 'critical'. By contrast, two-thirds of the Manchester employers rated product knowledge as very important or essential, alongside approximately 50 per cent who similarly rated the ability to use equipment and knowledge of store operations and procedures. Although product knowledge is not a 'skill' per se such requirements could conceivably fall within the technical skills category. As such this finding shows the relative importance of product knowledge in particular to retailers in the Manchester clothing, footwear and leather goods sub-sectors (a finding also contra to that of Gatta in this volume). Given that the products in the sub-sectors of the Manchester research are likely to be those requiring to be sold rather than sell themselves (Buchanan et al., 2003), there is likely to be a concomitant need for greater product knowledge amongst workers. Leslie (2002), for example, argues that employees in fashion retail are expected to have considerable knowledge of fashion and design and are expected to impart this knowledge in order to increase sales. This recognition of the relative importance of technical skills requires further analysis, an analysis that explores the nature of such 'skills'. For example, it might be simply knowledge of the latest stock or a combination of knowledge of stock and an ability to discern what suits a customer and how to sell it to them (as with a personal shopper).

There were also several noteworthy differences in the findings from Manchester and Glasgow with regard to some aspects of recruitment and selection, most notably the use of job centres. Employers in the broader Glasgow survey were 70 per cent more likely to report the use of job centres than their Manchester counterparts. This difference may be as a result of the skills that are being sought at the point of recruitment and selection, as many job centre recruits are from the unemployed or less privileged backgrounds. Employers may see any requirement for style and cultural capital as more forthcoming in students or workers from middle class backgrounds, and style was clearly an important factor in these establishments. This requirement for style may explain the substantially lower use of job centres among the more focused Manchester retail sub-sector. On the issue of skills shortages, Glasgow employers experienced more problems than Manchester employers in terms of whether applicants had the required interpersonal and social skills, rather than finding those who had the necessary technical skills. Manchester employers had less difficulty attracting the desired interpersonal and aesthetic skills, image or style. As we have previously argued the explanation for this finding could lie in the greater cachet ascribed to fashion retailing compared to other areas of retailing.

Recognising the above issues, Warhurst and Nickson (2007b) have recently sought to extend the debate about interactive service from a focus on work to workers. In particular, in arguing for a 'labour aristocracy' among certain groups of retail and hospitality workers they suggest that there may be different forms of service encounter than simply one of servility. A range of recent work (see, e.g., Johnston and Sandberg, 2008; Leslie, 2002; Pettinger, 2004; 2005; Wright, 2005) points to the manner in which some retail workers see themselves as distinct and not axiomatically redolent of the servile front line workers suggested in many accounts. In this regard there may be an argument that work in fashion retail is perceived to be glamorous work, done by glamorous people. This point has implications in terms of which qualities, related to soft skills are deemed to be important by fashion retail employers, and the potential for these to be proxied through signifiers such as class, gender and ethnicity.

Within the specific context of fashion retail recent accounts recognize that the feminine and masculine performativity required in doing the work is overwhelmingly middle class (Leslie, 2002; Walls, 2008). In this respect middle classness is being recast as a skill. A key implication is that the demand for soft skills may thus benefit the middle classes, including students, whilst disadvantaging other workers. Indeed, Warhurst and Nickson (2007a) suggest that there is a displacement effect in much service work, with students, who in the UK still tend to have middle class backgrounds, taking jobs that other types of workers, those from working class backgrounds and the long-term unemployed, may have been expected to fill. Certainly the relatively high level of student labour reported in the findings would be consistent with such an argument.

This point is particularly true, because as Witz et al. (2003: 41) note the 'embodied dispositions', or what can be perceived as aesthetic capacities and attributes that are recast as part of the soft skills demanded by employers in much interactive service work 'are not equally distributed socially'. As such many individuals may lack the required soft skills to access employment in the interactive service sector. This issue may be particularly pronounced in fashion retail, which attracts more students who are more likely to already possess the desired soft skills if these skills are really associated with middle classness.

In addition to class and gender there is also the issue of ethnicity. MacDonald and Merrill (2009) have recently attempted to consider the intersection of these social constructs in interactive service work, noting how workers' 'performance' has to align with certain customer and management expectations and in that sense, 'the service performance may be more or less aligned with the gender and ethnic identity of the worker' (p. 116). This latter point is also picked up by Leslie (2002) in her claim that the skills required in retail align with being white (see also Moss and Tilly, 1996). Whilst past research on the social construction of skill has tended to focus on the effect of gender, it is now clear that more research is required into the intersection of gender, class and ethnicity on the social construction of skills in retail. Moreover, and as Gatta also indicates in this volume, the construction of these skills also acts to create discrimination, with implications for access to retail jobs for workers deemed to be disadvantaged. In simple terms those who are unemployed, working class or from the 'wrong' ethnic background[2] are seemingly less likely to secure employment in fashion retail.

This chapter has set out to explore the potential variability in retail work through an analysis of the clothing, footwear and leather goods sub-sector. What this and other research points to is that there is clearly variability within retail work. Focusing on the labour supply and employer skills demands in this sub-sector, this variability clearly exists. The source of this variability stems from potential differences between different types of jobs, dependent on aspects such as the sub-sector, market niche, labour market from which employees are largely drawn and the required skills for getting and doing the job. The research also indicates that this variability manifests a hierarchy of jobs in retail as well, implying potential labour market discrimination. Further research is still required to explore the social practices and material conditions of a range of different retail jobs to allow for the development of richer accounts as to why these differences exist and how they impact on labour supply and skill demands.

Notes

1 The intervening points were 'not very important' (2), 'fairly important' (3) and 'very important' (4).

2 See, for example, Fleener (2005) for a discussion of the recent Abercrombie & Fitch case where the company agreed a near $50 million settlement with plaintiffs from a number of minority ethnic groupings, including African Americans, Latinos and Asian Americans. These plaintiffs either failed to get jobs or were excluded from sales floor positions as their natural physical features did not represent the company's conception of 'natural classic

American style'. It was argued by the plaintiffs that the 'A&F look' was 'virtually all white' and as Corbett (2007: 155) notes 'these plaintiffs succeeded when the attractive look the employer was seeking was not just pretty, but pretty and *white*' (emphasis in original).

REFERENCES

BMG (2005) 'Retail workforce development survey: the Arndale Centre', BMG Research Report.

BMG (2006) *Retail Workforce Development Survey: The Trafford Centre*, BMG Research Report.

Buchanan, J., Evesson, J. and Dawson, M. (2003) 'Chapter 6: Retail trade', in J. Buchanan and D. Hall (eds) *Beyond VET: The Changing Skill Needs of the Victorian Services Industries*. ACIRRT: University of Sydney.

Bunt, K., McAndrew, F. and A. Kuechel (2005) *Jobcentre Plus Employer (Market View) Survey 2004*, Norwich: HMSO.

Callaghan, G. and Thompson, P. (2002) ' "We recruit attitude": the selection and shaping of call centre labour', *Journal of Management Studies*, 39(2): 233–254.

Canny, A. (2002) 'Flexible labour? The growth of student employment in the UK', *Journal of Education and Work*, 15(3): 277–301.

Corbett, W. (2007) 'The ugly truth about appearance discrimination and the beauty of our employment discrimination law', *Duke Journal of Gender Law & Policy*, 14(1): 153–178.

Curtis, S. and Lucas, R. (2001) 'A coincidence of needs? Employers and full-time students', *Employee Relations*, 23(1): 38–54.

Fleener, H. (2005) 'Looks sell, but are they worth the cost? How tolerating looks-based discrimination leads to intolerable discrimination', *Washington University Law Quarterly*, 83(4): 1295–1330.

Gatta, M., Boushey, H. and Appelbaum, E. (2009) 'High-touch and here-to-stay: future skills demands in US low wage service occupations', *Sociology*, 43(5): 968–989.

Hart, C., Stachow, G., Farrell, A. and Reed, G. (2007) 'Employer perceptions of skills gaps in retail: issues and implications for UK retailers', *International Journal of Retail and Distribution Management*, 35(4): 271–288.

Huddleston, P. and Hirst, C. (2004) 'Are you being served? Skills gaps and training needs in the retail sector', SKOPE Research Paper No. 53, Universities of Oxford and Cardiff.

Johnston, A. and Sandberg, A. (2008) 'Controlling service work: an ambiguous accomplishment between employees, management and customers', *Journal of Consumer Culture*, 8(3): 389–417.

Leslie, D. (2002) 'Gender, retail employment and the clothing commodity chain', *Gender, Place and Culture*, 9(1): 61–76.

Lockyer, C. and Scholarios, D. (2004) 'Selecting hotel staff: why best practice does not always work', *International Journal of Contemporary Hospitality Management*, 16(2): 121–135.

▶

▶

Mason, J. and Osborne, M. (2008) 'Business strategies, work organization and low pay in United Kingdom retail', in C. Lloyd, G. Mason and K. Mayhew (eds) *Low Wage Work in the United Kingdom*. New York: Russell Sage Foundation.

MacDonald, C. L. and Merrill, D. (2009) 'Intersectionality in the emotional proletariat: a new lens on employment discrimination in service work', in M. Korczynski and C. L. MacDonald (eds) *Service Work: Critical Perspectives*. Abingdon: Taylor and Francis.

Moss, P. and Tilly, C. (1996) '"Soft" skills and race: an investigation of black men's employment problems', *Work and Occupations*, 23(3): 252–276.

Nickson, D., Warhurst, C. and Dutton, E. (2005) 'The importance of attitude and appearance in the service encounter in retail and hospitality', *Managing Service Quality*, 15(2): 195–208.

Nickson, D., Warhurst, C., Lockyer, C. and Dutton, E. (2004) 'Flexible friends? Lone parents and retail employment', *Employee Relations*, 26(4): 255–273.

Nickson, D., Warhurst, C., Witz, A. and Cullen, A.M. (2001) 'The importance of being aesthetic: work, employment and service organization', in A. Sturdy, I. Grugulis and H. Wilmott (eds) *Customer Service – Empowerment and Entrapment*. Basingstoke: Palgrave.

Pettinger, L. (2004) 'Brand culture and branded workers: service work and aesthetic labour in fashion retail', *Consumption, Market and Culture*, 7(2): 165–184.

Pettinger, L. (2005) 'Gendered work meets gendered goods: selling and service in clothing retail', *Gender, Work and Organization*, 12(5): 460–478.

Retail E-Commerce Task Force (2002) *Destination Retail: A Survey of Young People's Attitudes towards A Career in Retailing*. London: Foresight.

Scott, A. (1994) 'Gender segregation in the retail industry', in A. Scott (ed.) *Gender Segregation and Social Change*. Oxford: Oxford University Press.

Shedden, J. (2003) 'Never mind the salary…feel the discount', *Guardian (Jobs and Money Section)*, 29 November, 10–11.

Skillsmart (2007) *Sector Skills Agreement Stage One: Assessment of Current and Future Skills Needs*. London: Skillsmart.

Skillsmart (2004) *Manchester Enterprises ASP Sectoral Research: Retail Sector*. London: Skillsmart.

Walls, S. (2008) *'Are You Being Served?' Gendered Aesthetics Among Retail Workers*, Unpublished PhD, University of Durham.

Warhurst, C. and Nickson, D. (2001) *Looking Good and Sounding Right: Style Counselling and the Aesthetics of the New Economy*. London: Industrial Society.

Warhurst, C. and Nickson, D. (2007a) 'Employee experience of aesthetic labour in retail and hospitality', *Work, Employment and Society*, 21(1): 103–120.

Warhurst, C. and Nickson, D. (2007b) 'A new labour aristocracy? Aesthetic labour and routine interactive service', *Work, Employment and Society*, 21(4): 785–798.

Warhurst, C., Nickson, D., Witz, A. and Cullen, A. (2000) 'Aesthetic labour in interactive service work: some case study evidence from the "new" Glasgow', *Service Industries Journal*, 20(3): 1–18.

Wright, D. (2005) 'Commodifying respectability: distinctions at work in the bookshop', *Journal of Consumer Culture*, 5(3): 295–314.

Technological Change, Work Re-organization and Retail Workers' Skills in Production-Oriented Supermarket Departments

5

Robin Price

Re-configuration of corporate structures and the retailer–supplier interface in the retail industry have restructured product markets and supply chains, as well as supermarket employment, over the past two decades (du Gay, 1996; Baret et al., 2000; Wrigley and Lowe, 2002). Various studies have examined the consequent changes in labour usage practices within supermarkets and superstores (Dawson et al., 1986, 1987; Sparks, 1992; Penn and Wirth, 1993; Penn, 1995; Marchington, 1995; Baret et al., 2000). Commonly, this literature explores the interplay between shifts in the structure of the labour market, broader societal trends and retailers' employment strategies. However, while the types of labour usage and the drivers of changes to labour usage patterns have attracted significant academic attention, research has largely overlooked the ways in which the nature of supermarket work has evolved as a result of the impact of changing technology on managerial prerogative, and on the skill levels of workers in the industry (Marchington, 1995). Penn (1995) is a notable exception here, but his use of surveys disguises the nature of the skills involved because it involves self-reporting of overall impressions of skills.

Changes to the skills required of supermarket workers have occurred through various technological developments affecting products, packaging and people. Much has been written about the range of technologies available to the retailer, and how scanning technology – such as Universal Product Codes (UPC), electronic point of sale (EPOS) terminals and Electronic Data Interchange (EDI) – provides retailers with volumes of information about trading patterns, as well as information about customers and their purchasing preferences (Lansbury, 1983; Sparks et al., Smith, 2006). However, precisely how these innovations affect the skill levels of retail workers has attracted little attention (see Wong and Hendry, 1999, for an exception). This is not to say that the extant literature has ignored supermarket workers' skills. There is considerable debate in the literature about the effects on workers' skill levels of self-service food stores and other technologies. On the one hand, Sparks (1983) and Du Gay (1996) assert that most supermarket jobs have been deskilled while, on the other, Penn (1995) argues that technological changes within food retailing have increased skill levels, particularly for store management, but not for checkout staff. These differences in part reflect variations in methodology – Sparks (1983) conducts interviews and Penn (1995) includes questions about skill in surveys – but they are also a product of the limited empirical research into the nature of the supermarket labour process. This chapter argues for a more nuanced assessment of supermarket workers' skills, though on balance the evidence supports the deskilling thesis.

The data in this chapter, drawn from an extended study of supermarket employment practices, provides the empirical detail largely overlooked in existing debates. It extends the debate on retail work in two ways. First, it shows that retail formats are not homogenous, and that the tasks of employees working within different retail formats and different departments within a supermarket are distinct. Second, it examines the labour process within production-oriented departments of a supermarket to show how technology has accentuated the deskilling of workers, but in variable ways across departments. The first section of the chapter explores the literature on the labour process; specifically as it relates to skills in the service sector. Next, the methodology for the research project is briefly outlined. This is followed by a case study of a leading Australian supermarket retailer and its labour use practices. The analysis focuses on three production-focussed fresh food areas: the bakery, meat and fresh produce departments.

Skill and the labour process in retail work

Retailing is defined as 'the set of business activities involved in selling products and services to the ultimate (final) consumer' (Levy and Weitz, 1992: 6). Of particular note is the use of the words, 'goods and services'. As early as 1974, Braverman recognised the importance of both goods and services in a retail transaction, and the simultaneous production and consumption of labour as part of the retail process. Indeed, Braverman (1974: 360) argued that in service transactions 'the useful effects of labour become the commodity', hence labour had become commodified. In his seminal analysis of the labour process, he argued that 'capital wrested control from workers by expropriating their knowledge and skill and building it into systems of production and technology under management control' (Leidner 2006: 442). Although the inevitability of Braverman's deskilling thesis is much criticised (see Tinker, 2002), Braverman's argument was that the process of deskilling workers was inevitable, due to the nature of the capitalist process. Following Braverman, the commodification of labour in service industries has been the focus of other labour process scholars.

The very notion of skill has been contested. Braverman (1974: 443) defined skill as 'craft mastery' or 'the combination of knowledge of materials and processes with the practised manual dexterities required to carry on a specific branch of production'. While this definition of skill as 'craft mastery' may be historically contingent, in that early research into skills centres on manufacturing, Braverman's (1974: 444–445) assertion that 'the worker can regain mastery over collective and socialized production only by assuming the scientific, design and operational prerogatives of modern engineering' has broader resonance. As an extension of this, skill can be defined as 'largely based on knowledge, the unity of conception and execution, and the exercise of control by the workforce' (Thompson, 1989: 92). Skill, like knowledge, is a complex concept (Grugulis, 2007). For retail workers, the skills and knowledge required vary in accordance with the retail format adopted and to a lesser extent on the nature of the product being sold. The combination of a tangible good and an intangible service component is acknowledged in the services marketing (Levitt, 1972; Palmer, 1994) and retailing literature (Levy and Weitz, 1992). The labour process literature, however, tends towards generalizations about service and has only recently begun to differentiate between types of service. For example, Pettinger (2004) uses a labour process framework to identify different types of services associated with different fashion brands: self-service where there is a transfer of work from worker to consumer; routine service, such as processing sales and monitoring customers; and personal service, where interactions are personalised and the nature of the transaction fluctuates between service and selling. Pettinger (2004; 2006), not only recognizes the differences in the nature of the service component, but also argues that retail is as much about production as it is about service. Hence, she argues that in fashion retail outlets, work is: 'directed at producing consumption spaces' (Pettinger, 2006: 54). As such, Pettinger argues that retail is not simply a service industry, but involves production as well.

Hence when analysing service work, it is imperative not to assume that retail formats are homogeneous. Context matters: and this is clearly articulated within the retail industry literature (Winsor, Sheth and Manolis, 2004; Chabaud and Codron, 2005). The recent Russell Sage research into low wage work, for example, distinguishes between electrical white goods retailing, in which the mainly full-time staff received regular training from manufacturers and supermarket work where largely female part-timers were less well paid and trained (Mason and Osbourne, 2008, Van Klaveren and Voss-Dahm, this volume). Even within the same retail format, such as a supermarket, not all departments will have an equivalent 'goods and services mix' in their retail offering. In some cases, the nature of the labour process differs according to the nature of the product (Pettinger, 2004; Chabaud and Codron, 2005; Orlikowski, 2007), while in others, the product remains the same, but the nature of service is used by the firm to differentiate their retail brand in the marketplace (see Wright, 2005). The service component therefore differs both across and within retail formats. So too does the production process, and this has a direct effect on the nature of skills required. Accordingly, this chapter extends Pettinger's (2006) analysis by examining the previously ignored production focus within retail supermarkets.

Supermarket operation has changed over time. Supermarkets shifted towards a self-service offering after World War II in most developed countries (Kingston, 1994; du Gay, 1996; Humphrey, 1998). In the process, the skills and knowledge associated with selecting appropriate products passed from the retail worker to the customer (with the owner or manager retaining the skills associated with the selection of a product range). This skill transfer process, incorporating the deskilling of shop floor retail workers, was exacerbated by the advent of supermarket chains, where purchasing, storage and distribution decisions were centralised in head offices (Braverman, 1974; Kingston, 1994). Braverman noted the changing nature of work within supermarkets and drew direct comparisons with the deskilling in manufacturing:

> [the] 'skills' of store operations have long since been disassembled and in all decisive respects vested in management, a revolution is now being prepared which will make of retail workers, by and large, something closer to factory operatives than anyone had imagined possible. (Braverman, 1974: 371)

The attraction for retailers was 'reducing circulation costs' by reducing the labour or service component of the transaction (du Gay, 1996: 105). As customers took on more of the work and arguably acquired skill, the shop floor supermarket workers were deskilled (du Gay, 1996). Although, there were also positives as the shift to self-service potentially ended the 'servitude' of retail workers (du Gay, 2004: 159). Some 30 years later, it is accepted that retail managers' autonomy has been decreased due to the centralization of control to head office, at the same time as they have had an increase in responsibility for the financial performance of the store (Sparks, 1983; Christopherson, 1996; du Gay, 1996; Bailey and Bernhardt, 1997; Freathy and Sparks, 1997; Chabaud and Codron, 2005). However, other than assertions of deskilling, the ways in which the labour process has been transformed for store-level retail workers and the changes to their skills have rarely been subject to empirical examination (though see Felstead et al., this volume). This chapter helps to remedy this oversight by examining the skills of store-level workers across three departments within an Australian supermarket: meat, bakery and fresh produce. Each of these production-focussed departments has been subject to technological changes that have transformed the labour process for shop floor workers.

Methods

The data for this chapter are drawn from a larger project examining labour usage strategies within a leading Australian food retailer. Data collection involved: examination of organizational documents, including rosters and position descriptions; interviews with head office personnel, store management and employees; and non-participant observation during numerous visits to three supermarkets in Queensland over a three-year period. Thirty-three interviews with 22 members of store and head office management were conducted using a semi-structured interview schedule. Interviews were recorded, transcribed and manually analysed. The organization did not grant permission to talk to shop floor employees 'on company time' off the sales floor, therefore the researcher worked with employees while interviewing them. Interviews with one shop floor employee in each of ten departments were conducted. In-store background music, precluded the recording of interviews, but research notes were made immediately afterwards. While each of the stores had between eight and ten departments, depending on the store's product offering, only three production-focussed departments are discussed here.

'Supermarket Company' and its context

The Australian grocery market is dominated by two major food retailers, Coles and Woolworths, which together have over 70 per cent of the total grocery market (IBISWorld, 2008). Thus the Australian market reflects international trends in retail concentration (McGurr, 2002). Both companies have pursued business strategies designed to achieve economies of scale and reduce the cost of labour and logistics. In doing so, both companies mirror a global trend in reducing the cost of service transactions 'by adjusting staffing levels as tightly as possible to fluctuations in customer flows' (Baret et al., 2000: 167). Over the past decade, both organizations have successfully pursued cost reduction business strategies centred on improving the supply chain to reduce transport and handling costs, while at the same time minimising stock holdings and by improving the number of products 'in-stock' at all times (Coles, 2008; Woolworths, 2008), as retailers worldwide have done (Sparks et al., 2006). As part of these changes to business processes, both retailers have embraced technological change (Lansbury, 1983; Price, 2004). The case study organization discussed here, called Supermarket Company, is one of Australia's two major food retailing organizations, with over 700 stores, in excess of 110,000 employees and an annual turnover of $A36.6 billion in the 2007 financial year (IBISWorld, 2008).

Human resource practices and skill training within the organization were shaped by the nature of the internal labour market. While somewhat illogical (in that the internal labour market for all but skilled tradespeople starts from a base of casual part-time employment, which is hourly employment with no guarantee of ongoing work and thereby limits initial recruitment to those in the secondary labour market), promotion is internal and hence the organization consciously tried to inculcate its employees with its values and invests in employee skills training. All employees received register [till] training as part of their induction and all employees recruited for fresh food departments also received a three-hour food safety induction. This organization had adopted the Australian national retail training framework, adapting it to its needs, and was a registered training organization. Accreditation as a registered training organization (RTO) involved a stringent process of regular government accreditation of trainers, assessors and the training curriculum prescribed by the national framework. Formal accreditation allowed the organization to deliver nationally recognised training from the level 2 certificate in retail operations to the level 5 diploma in retail management. Not all employees had access to accredited training. Neither state nor federal government provided training assistance for casual employees, who comprised around 50 per cent of the organization's workforce. So, following Rainbird and Munro (2003: 30), training was neither available for all, nor necessarily 'enriching'. For employees aspiring to management positions, participation in accredited training was perceived as crucial: 'they would like to see you go in and do it, and if you don't do it, you don't get into anything' (Employee 8, male, grade 3, 30s). However, accredited training involved 'off-job' learning activities and this was seen as extending the working day for workers with other non-work commitments (Employee 8, male, grade 3, 30s). Hence, while the training systems in place nationally, and within the supermarket chain, recognized and articulated a set of 'skills' required in retail, and in supermarket retailing, the training was not available to all and, with the exception of management aspirants and the food safety induction, was not essential and operated independently of remuneration policies. Skilled tradespeople, such as qualified butchers and bakers, were recruited into full-time positions directly. Service assistants, identified as interested and capable, were placed on butchery and bakery apprenticeships to acquire the necessary skills.

Industrial relations arrangements broadly reflected notions of skill; but payment was linked to the job performed and ignored qualifications for all except qualified tradespeople. The organization's collective agreement listed five grades of employee. Grade 1 employees were new workers during their first four months of employment, cleaners and trolley collectors. Grade 2 employees included service assistants, pay office clerks and meat packers. Grade 3 employees were systems operators, pay roll clerks, service supervisors, stock hands, meat slicers and skilled bakery assistants. Grade 4 employees were non-salaried assistant department managers, while grade 5 employees included: non-salaried department managers, duty managers, qualified bakers, pastry cooks, and butchers. Most department and store managers were salaried and remunerated under individual contracts. While the collective agreement appeared to differentiate between employees on the basis of their skills, increments were not large, in January 2010, the margin between level 2 and level 3 employees was $A 47 cents per hour or 2.6 per cent and between level 2 service assistants and level 5 qualified tradespeople was $A 2.58 per hour or 14.3 per cent – this was primarily a differentiation on the basis of job role. The compression of relativities was not related to high pay rates for grade 2 employees either, as retail wages were the second lowest in the Australian labour market (ABS, 2009). Given that an apprenticeship to become a qualified butcher or baker took three years on 'apprentice' wages that were a percentage of adult rates, the financial return for qualifications was negligible. While the apprenticeship training included the full range of skills, assisted by off-job training in technical colleges, the range of skills used by butchers and bakers in stores was more limited and this exacerbated retention problems for the company. So, while skill was ostensibly recognized, both in the support for accredited training and in the collective agreement, there was a 'disconnect' between qualifications held by an individual worker, skills required for the job and the financial rewards for the employees who possess those skills.

Supermarket Company's business strategy emphasized cost minimisation and this actively drove labour usage strategies. Labour costs were one of only a few variables in the cost of doing business in stores, and the one most easily adjusted at store level. Within Supermarket Company rigid labour cost targets were set at less than ten per cent of sales. As a result, sales and variable costs, such as labour costs, were measured for each individual department, and formed one of the key performance indicators for store-level management. Labour hours were calculated on an 'average' cost of labour that distorted the labour costing process as juniors could earn as little as 50 per cent of the adult rate. There was a minimal recognition of differences in productivity between workers. The system 'makes allowances for an apprentice in meat and for the time taken to train them, but it doesn't make allowances for inexperienced people in say, dairy' (Manager 3, store manager, male, 50s). 'Learning allowances' were embedded in the labour allocation to cater for learning some jobs, but not all. Different departments had vastly different 'salaries to sales' percentages; with departments with high labour intensity where production occurred, such as the delicatessen and bakery, having a labour cost of 20 per cent of sales, while labour was less than two per cent of total sales at the checkouts. The need to adhere to departmental cost budgets militated against store-level functional flexibility and hence multi-skilling, and instead promoted the use of labour within a specific department. While it was possible for an employee to work across departments within the store, and the facility existed for transferring costs between departments, department managers were reluctant to do this, since it complicated the calculation of labour cost and 'requires some internal negotiation between managers, otherwise one manager will charge off an employee for 8 hours when they only actually worked six hours' (Manager 13, area HR, female, 40s). These practices reduced the potential for employees to experience a varied range of tasks and develop a broader range of skills. In order to understand the development of skills within departments, the following sections examine the nature of the labour process across several production-focussed departments, demonstrate differences in the nature of the labour process and explore how technological advancements have affected the labour process and workers' skills.

Premix ingredients and par-bake in the bakery

Bread products are perishable and need to be baked fresh daily, so supermarkets with an in-store bakery need tradespeople, namely bakers and pastry cooks, as well as apprentices engaged in learning the trade and other bakery assistants. Training as a baker or pastry cook required an accredited apprenticeship, nominally of three years' duration, but apprentices who could demonstrate competence earlier qualified earlier. During an apprenticeship, apprentices were required to demonstrate competence across a range of production skills, including the capacity to 'diagnose and respond to product and process faults' (Commonwealth of Australia, 2007a). As Chabaud and Codron (2005) acknowledge, these are complex skills. Producing bread products was expensive because it was skilled and labour intensive while the product itself is inexpensive and has a low profit margin.

Supermarket Company used various strategies to reduce the overall cost of, and reliance on, skilled labour. First, since bread products needed to be produced daily and early, workers in the bakery commenced their working day around 3.00 am; a time that attracted penalty payments under the collective agreement. In addition, because of the safety risks associated with large mixing machinery, two employees were required to be present at all times in case a worker was injured (Manager 11, bakery dept, female, 40s). Apprentices provided a cost effective 'second' worker, since they were paid significantly lower wages by virtue of their 'in training' status. Each store had at least one baking apprentice and some had two. Second, a shift towards different retail formats, such as smaller stores, meant there was insufficient floor space to house a bakery. For these sites, economies of scale were achieved by outsourcing the provision of bakery products to a larger neighbouring store and transporting products between stores. Third, techno-logical advancements have enabled food retailers to reduce their reliance on skilled labour, so that across the company, some stores have full-production bakeries and some 'warm spot bakeries that use premixed or frozen doughs' (BRI Australia, 2003). Technological innovations included: improvements to wheat; advances in premixed ingredients that improved ease of baking and enhance product shelf life; and the advent of frozen dough that required only defrosting and cooking; and par-baked products that just required heat-ing. One store manager, referring to these changes, asserted that minimal skill was now involved in bread-making:

> The stuff comes pre-mixed and you just add water. Most of the prepara-tion just involves adding water and stirring. We also get lots of stuff that's par-bake and we just have to heat it. There are economies of scale in doing that. It's much better for Sara Lee to make it, snap freeze it and all we have to do is defrost it. There is a lot less dependence on skill. (Manager 3, store manager, male, 50s)

While technological innovations reduced the required baking skills in stores with bakeries, Supermarket Company argued that it increases con-sumer variety.

A number of academic studies examine knowledge and 'skill' in bread-making (Nonaka, 1991; Gourlay, 2006; Ribeiro and Collins, 2007). These debate the construction of knowledge in the process of making bread. While the extent of this is contested, all recognise that bread-making contains some skill. This was also the case in supermarkets that produced baked products; some skill (factual and procedural knowledge acquired by remembering, applying and analysing [Anderson & Krathwohl, 2001]) remained, despite an overall reduction in the level of craft associated with baking due to the advent of premixes. Bakery workers still required some skill, strength and manual dexterity. Measurement of ingredients, mixing, apportioning and attention to baking times was required (Manager 11, bakery dept, female, 40s). In addi-tion, the mixing machinery was large and the bags of premixed ingredients were heavy, so physical strength was also required. The most skilled part of the task was planning the order of baking to produce the required products in a short space of time and in a small space, which required calculation and analysis. The use of par-baked products, where only heating was required, reduced the overall level of employee skill needed and this organization used trained bakery assistants, instead of qualified bakers, thereby saving over $A 2 per hour in labour costs. Bakery assistants also packaged products and iced cakes and donuts, although the bakery manager asserted that the skill required was limited as 'you can train people to decorate' (Manager 11, bakery manager, female, 40s). How long this training took was not divulged, although another informant claimed that you could train a bakery manager who had bakery assistant skills, plus management skills in 'two months of intensive training' (Manager 3, store manager, male, 50s).

In supermarket bakeries, bakers retained some skills. With the exception of par-bake products, the baker controlled conception, within the bounds of a given product range and expectations of the level of sales, as well as execution. It was the bakers who controlled the process of production of premixed products within the limits of the defined product range; while bakery assistants controlled packaging and presentation of stock and markdowns. There were clear lines of demarcation between workers in the bakery. Hence, while there has been some reduction in the overall level of required baker's skill in line with technological innovations, bakers still retained some skill and still required a qualification. Conversely, the bakery assistants, as service assistants with elementary in-house bakery training, had probably acquired some skill in slicing bread and cake icing, yet these were tasks for which no formal training was required. A similar process of demarcation of tasks, likewise enabled by technological innovations, was evident in the meat department.

Vacuum packing meat

Like bakers, butchers were skilled labours and were recognized as such in the collective agreement, receiving the same pay rate. Like bakers, butchers completed a three-year apprenticeship that qualified them to prepare meat, locate and assess cuts, calculate the yield from a carcass and 'value add' by preparing meat products (Commonwealth of Australia, 2007b). Again the nature of the in-store labour process separated the skilled tasks from the unskilled ones since, once butchered, the meat was packed by other workers, who were paid as 'meat packers'; the same rate as service assistants.

As with the bakery, however, the nature of the labour process for butchers has been transformed by technological changes. Food packaging processes, such as Cryovac® [vacuum packing], vacuum shrink bags, barrier trays (high impact polystyrene trays with corrugated bases) and oxygen-absorbing sachets, extended the longevity of meat and enabled off-site butchery and transportation. At the time this research was conducted, the form in which meat was delivered to stores varied, depending on whether the store had an in-house butcher or not. This reflected the size of the store and the nature of the retail format. In a large store with an in-house butcher, lamb and pigs were delivered hanging as a half beast, and butchery was required, yet beef arrived boxed. 'We'll get a carton of beef rumps all Cryovaced. It's all broken down into the various cuts' (Manager 3, store manager, male, 50s). But only a few of the very large stores maintained in-store butchery services. As a result, Supermarket Company established a distinct meat processing division, with specialization amongst butchers, which allowed for faster production. Meat was then delivered to stores, either as boxed beef to larger stores, or pre-packed and priced for smaller stores. In larger stores, butchers and packers were employed, while in smaller stores, cabinet attendants refilled the refrigerated cabinets and were paid as shop assistants. Again, as in the bakery, technological innovations resulted in a demarcation of skills between employees. Here, technology had not reduced the level of skill required, as meat still required butchery, but had allowed the skills associated with butchery to be re-located to a separate division. This reduced the skills required of in-store butchers and other meat department staff and moved the conception and most of the execution to the meat processing division. In the stores, store-level employees' skill levels were reduced to slicing and packing meat and re-stocking cabinets.

At the same time, these technological advancements have provided additional issues for management. In stores without butchers, careful monitoring of the shelf life of the product is required and the meat departments had a much reduced capacity to respond quickly to changes in patterns of customer demand and out-of-stock situations. Skills in these small stores revolved around re-ordering, refilling, checking use-by dates and marking down products near their use-by dates. In larger stores, the meat department remained production-focussed, with butchery of lamb, pork and slicing boxed veal and beef (Manager 10, meat dept, male, 40s). Here butchers deployed their skills to prepare and produce meat products, packers package the prepared meat cuts and the apprentice made the mince (Manager 10, meat dept, male, 40s). The arrival of beef and veal in boxes created another job, the meat slicer, and these workers simply slice the boxed meat products. In large stores, the butcher used their knowledge to conceive the cuts of meat and execute the process, but in the majority of stores the improved storage processes meant that meat was simply ordered from the meat processing division. For store-level workers in the smaller stores, there were no production-focussed skills involved and the opportunity to learn about butchery was much reduced. Skill requirements were limited to re-ordering and checking use-by dates. While these tasks required some skill, the skills differ from those required in butchery. The organization acknowledged this in its wage payment structures – meat packers were paid at grade 2, meat slicers at grade 3 and butchers at grade 5 – but also in the accredited training packages as meat packers received an elementary food safety induction, whereas butchers were required to complete a trade apprenticeship.

Universal product codes and pre-packaging fresh produce

Within fresh produce (i.e., fruit, vegetables and related items) changes in product identification and packaging have altered the in-store labour process. Corporate supermarkets largely eliminated the 'seasonality' of fresh foods, as cold storage and various treatments have extended storage periods, and global markets have developed (Humphrey, 1998: 156). Since computerised stock control systems are totally reliant on the accuracy of data input, and supermarkets were almost totally reliant on computerised stock control (see Felstead et al.'s chapter in this book), the introduction of Universal Product Codes (UPC) have delivered a means of improving data accuracy. Growers label produce with a sticker identifying varietal type and UPC. This practice transferred the cost of the labels to the growers and reduced the time taken to process sales, while improving sales accuracy. Store-level workers no longer needed to be able to identify different varieties of apples. However, some fresh produce does not lend itself to individual coding – for example, potatoes and rambutan (red Asian fruit with soft fleshy spikes). Supermarket Company pre-packaged fruit and vegetables so that packaging could carry UPCs as it does internationally (see Sparks et al., 2006). This improved data accuracy and minimized the spoilage created by customers and staff handling product. However, consumer tastes in Australia have prevented the pre-packaging of many items; Supermarket Company has trialled a number of pre-packed produce lines, but with some exceptions these have not been well received, in line with industry research that indicates that Australian consumers are not prepared to accept packaging of all produce and this may result in supermarkets losing custom to traditional fresh food producers (IBISWorld, 2008). Part of the problem is the co-location of supermarkets and green grocers within Australian shopping centres, so that an alternative retailer is readily available. Supermarkets are therefore limited in the extent to which pre-packaging can be introduced. To compensate for this, plastic crates with loose fresh product have been introduced into the supply chain, so that an entire plastic crate can be lifted out and replaced to reduce physical handling. Some products, such as cucumbers, have been shrink-wrapped so that a UPC can be adhered to the product, while for others, such as apples and avocados, the UPC is applied direct to the product. To improve sales data accuracy, pictures of each fresh produce were added to checkout software, but these were listed alphabetically, leading to problems if cashiers did not recognize the product.

A further problem was that fresh fruit and vegetables are perishable, and while stock on hand figures may accurately show quantity, they do not show quality. Human intervention is required to assess whether stock on hand is in saleable condition (see also Felstead et al., this volume). According to the retail literature, fresh produce departments have significant inefficiencies, which 'amount to between 2 and 4 per cent of the fresh produce department turnover' (Chabaud and Codron, 2005: 613). These costs relate to customer theft, losses due to unsaleable product and out-of-stock situations (Chabaud and Codron, 2005). Stock was also easily damaged by excessive handling; hence the labour process was designed to minimize stock handling (Manager 5, fresh produce dept, male, 40s) which also minimized labour costs. Tesco's response was to introduce strict temperature controls along the supply chain to extend the shelf life of fresh produce (Sparks et al., 2006), and Supermarket Company copied these innovations. The task of ensuring that produce was re-ordered and in saleable condition fell to department managers and assistant department managers and while they retained information and controlled ordering; ordering did not involve purchasing, but rather stock withdrawals from the distribution centre (Manager 5, fresh produce dept, male, 40s). Hence, fresh produce managers had no control over which growers or suppliers they dealt with or the products they stocked, they simply controlled quantities of a fixed product range required to maintain their sales.

The labour process in the fruit and vegetable department also involved the preparation and packaging of sale-ready goods:

> Slicing pumpkin, watermelon, rockmelon, pawpaw and pineapple; peeling excess layers off the onions; trimming stalks off the lettuce, removing the ugly outside leaves and bagging the lettuce; trimming the broccoli and cauliflower. (Manager 5, fresh produce dept, male, 40s)

This production process involved weighing the product, packing it and applying dated UPC labels. There was potential for this process to change, and for the cost and tasks to be transferred to suppliers. For example, since this research was conducted, the task of trimming and bagging of lettuce has been transferred to growers. Stringent food safety legislation, the limited size of the Australian market and geographical distance restrict the retailer's options for further cost savings, as shop floor workers within fresh produce require knowledge of types of fruit and vegetables and the skill to determine whether a product has perished, while managers require knowledge of sales patterns and local price competition. For shop floor workers, the daily tasks involved: price-checking competitors, organizing price tickets, refilling and rotating stock, removing bad stock, ordering, preparing fresh produce and maintaining hygiene standards (Manager 5, fresh produce dept, male, 40s). It was usually the manager or second-in-charge who was responsible for ordering, but service assistants performed all other tasks. While pre-packaging reduced the complexity – in that it was easier to stack containers than loose produce – it also increased the need for attention to detail, as one spoilt product in a pack could quickly spoil the remainder. The workers required knowledge of safe food handling and the life span of fresh produce, as well as a capacity to prepare fruit and vegetables for sale in the desired sizes and quantities. Thus the labour process demanded the ability to remember, understand and apply the knowledge of how to prepare products; but these were not considered higher order skills. The company provided no financial margin for skill in the fresh produce area, but did recognize that skill was required by including fresh produce modules in their accredited training programmes. It was not, however, essential that workers in fresh produce had any training beyond a three-hour food safety induction.

Discussion and conclusion

The literature argues that technological developments have been responsible for reducing the complexity and skill associated with much retail work (Sparks, 1983), shifting responsibility for control to the customer (du Gay, 1996), reducing the knowledge required by separating the conception from the execution of tasks, and increasing management and customer control over the way retail employees perform their work (Braverman, 1974; Freathy and Sparks, 1997; du Gay, 1996; Marchington, 1995). This chapter has explored the practices that have reduced the overall skill levels of employees by a cross-department comparison of production departments in supermarkets, thereby extending Pettinger's (2006) research on production in retailing to supermarkets. There are three main aspects to this deskilling process.

First, cost minimization business strategies exert a negative global effect on the skill levels of shop floor employees. Where it was possible to introduce a quicker, more cost effective practice, this organization did so. The evidence from this case therefore supports Braverman's (1974) argument regarding the inexorable nature of deskilling under the capitalist system and, more specifically, Sparks's argument about the reduction in the complexity of supermarket work (Sparks, 1983). The case also demonstrates that skill in retail has continued to decline since Sparks's research.

Second, the practice of dividing stores into separate cost centres, each with its own staffing budget, reduced the capacity for retail employees to develop a variety of skills and thereby exacerbated deskilling. The difficulties associated with transferring costs between departments meant that workers tended to be employed in one department, so their opportunities for multi-skilling were reduced, as were their opportunities for an extension of their (usually part-time) working hours. This practice was recognized and supported by the demarcation between jobs both in the collective agreement and in practice. In this organization, a shop floor worker employed as a meat packer must remain a meat packer, unless they undertook accredited training for a management role or re-located to another department. Thus skill levels have decreased not only due to technological developments but also in response to changes in work organization, recognizing that technology and work organization are intimately connected.

Third, and associated with the previous points, the technological innovations introduced across production-focussed departments have resulted in further deskilling of store-level workers. Here, there is evidence of a reduction in 'craft mastery' (Braverman, 1974: 443) or 'knowledge [and] the unity of conception and execution' (Thompson, 1989: 92) associated with baking and butchery. This had been achieved in the bakery by introducing premixed ingredients and par-baked products, which reduced the knowledge and skill associated with the baking trade. It has also encouraged a demarcation of labour, in which baking assistants performed many of the tasks, proving highly cost effective for the organization. The reduction in craft mastery had not been achieved to a similar extent in the area of meat production: rather, vacuum packing and other processes to extend shelf life meant that most butchery had been re-located to a specialized meat processing division and skilled jobs had largely disappeared from stores in the process. In the remaining large stores that retained a butcher, there was evidence of a reduction in skill with the introduction of boxed veal and beef that simply needed slicing and packing. Jobs were divided up so that the company could employ workers as meat slicers and packers and bakery assistants on lower wages than their fully trained colleagues. A policy of labour substitution (Rainbird and Munro, 2003). Within fresh produce, there is evidence of a reduction in skills associated with the move away from the sale of fresh produce selected by the consumer and towards pre-packaged UPC-labelled items; however, the extent of this is in the Australian context was limited by strong customer resistance. Since 'production' primarily involved slicing, trimming stalks, removing leaves and packaging, there was not a significant amount of skill associated with the labour process in this department.

While deskilling has been observed, all three of these departments still required workers with some skills. Given that all departments involved fresh food, all workers needed to have undertaken the food safety induction and to have passed the accompanying assessment. While this training is fairly elementary – clean fixtures properly, do not wear jewellery with stones, remove aged and perished product, avoid cross contamination – the effects of workers not adhering to the standards could have dire consequences for Supermarket Company. Skill was recognized in the form of accredited training packages that were portable across the retail industry, but not all workers were eligible and there was only a very small financial incentive to acquire skills, unless the worker aspired to a management position. Even for qualified tradespeople – butchers, bakers and pastry cooks – the payment for skill was marginal. Butchers and bakers as skilled tradespeople retain knowledge and some control over the labour process from production to execution, but in stores the breadth of tasks required had been reduced with the introduction of a meat processing division and premixed bread-making ingredients and the level of skill consequently reduced. Intermediate workers, such as meat slicers, meat packers and bakery assistants, also required some skill, mostly remembering, understanding and applying procedures. However, these workers did not demonstrate 'craft mastery' (Braverman, 1974: 443), as the skills required were elementary. For shop floor workers, the tasks revolved around refilling products, marking down aged product under strict guidelines and removing perished product. These workers simply needed to understand and apply instructions from their supervisors.

Based on the empirical evidence discussed in this chapter, some retail supermarket workers retain some 'skill', despite changes to the nature of the labour process brought about by technology and related changes in work organization. This was particularly the case in the bakery and butchery, but less so in stores without a butcher, and less so in fresh produce, which did not have a 'craft' tradition. Although the labour process had been simplified and rationalised, and a clear demarcation based on management or worker status and skills occurred in all departments, all departments nevertheless required employees to have some knowledge of products, production, placement or other processes. Such knowledge was predominantly simple remembering, understanding and applying knowledge acquired relatively quickly. This was reflected in the minimal allowances made by the organization for learning the skill and the financial rewards for skill under the collective agreement. Shop floor supermarket workers have been deskilled and despite investment in accredited training, this deskilling appears set to continue.

REFERENCES

Australian Bureau of Statistics (ABS) (2009) *Employee Earnings and Hours, Australia*, Aug 2008, catalogue 6306.0. Canberra: Australian Bureau of Statistics.

Bailey, T. and Bernhardt, A. (1997) In search of a high road in a low-wage industry, *Politics and Society*, 25(2): 179–201.

Baret, C., Lehndorff, S. and Sparks, L. (eds) (2000) *Flexible Working in Food Retailing: a Comparison between France, Germany, the United Kingdom and Japan.* Routledge, London.

Braverman, H. (1974) *Labor and Monopoly Capital: the Degradation of Work in the Twentieth Century.* New York: Monthly Review Press.

BRI Australia (2003) 'The Australian Baking Industry: a profile', report for the Department of Agriculture, Fisheries and Forestry, Canberra: Australian Government.

Chabaud, D. and Codron, J-M. (2005) 'How to integrate the specificities of some food departments into a retail store organization? Lessons and limits of the Aokian theory of the firm', *International Journal of Retail and Distribution Management*, 33(8): 597–617.

Christopherson, S. (1996) 'The production of consumption: retail restructuring and labour demand in the USA', in N. Wrigley and M. Lowe (eds) *Retailing, Consumption and Capital: towards the New Retail Geography.* Harlow: Addison Wesley Longman.

Coles (2008) Public submission to the Australian Competition and Consumer Commission Inquiry into the competitiveness of retail prices for standard groceries, March 2008, available from http://www.accc.gov.au/content/index.phtml/itemId/810417

Commonwealth of Australia (2007a) FDF03 Food Processing Industry Training Package (version 3). Canberra: Commonwealth of Australia.

Commonwealth of Australia (2007b) MTM07 Australian Meat Industry Training Package (version 2.00). Canberra: Commonwealth of Australia.

Dawson, J., Findlay, A. and Sparks, L. (1987) 'Employment in British superstores: summary of project findings', *Working Paper 8701*, Institute for Retail Studies. Stirling, Scotland: University of Stirling.

Dawson, J., Findlay, A. and Sparks, L. (1986) 'The importance of store operator on superstore employment levels', *The Service Industries Journal*, 6 (3): 349–361.

Du Gay, P. (2004) 'Self-service: retail, shopping and personhood', *Consumption, Markets and Culture*, 7(2): 149–163.

Du Gay, P. (1996) *Consumption and Identity at Work.* London: Sage.

Freathy, P. and Sparks, L. (1997) 'Working time in food retailing in the United Kingdom', National report on UK for DARES project, Institute for Retail Studies, Stirling, Scotland: University of Stirling.

Gourlay, S. (2006) 'Conceptualizing knowledge creation: A critique of Nonaka's theory', *Journal of Management Studies*, 43(7): 1415–1436.

Grugulis, I. (2007) *Skill, Training and Human Resource Development: A Critical Text.* Basingstoke: Palgrave Macmillan.

Hochschild, A. (1983) *The Managed Heart: The Commercialisation of Human Feeling.* Berkeley: University of California Press.

▶

▶

Humphrey, K. (1998) *Shelf Life: Supermarkets and the Changing Cultures of Consumption*. Cambridge: Cambridge University Press.

IBISWorld. (2008) *Supermarkets and Other Grocery Stores in Australia: G5111*. IBISWorld Industry Report, 18 September.

Kingston, B. (1994) *Basket, Bag and Trolley: A History of Shopping in Australia*. Melbourne: Oxford University Press.

Korczynski, M. (2002) *Human Resource Management in Service Work*. London: Palgrave.

Lansbury, R. (1983) 'Technological change and employee participation (in the Australian retail industry)', Employee participation research report no. 2. Canberra: Australian Government Publishing Service.

Leidner, R. (2006) 'Identity and work', in M. Korczynski, R. Hodson and P. Edwards (eds) *Social Theory at Work*. Oxford: Oxford University Press.

Levitt, T. (1972) 'Production line approach to service', *Harvard Business Review*, July–August: 45–56.

Levy, M. and Weitz, B. (1992) *Retailing Management*. Homewood, Ill: Irwin.

Marchington, M. (1995) 'Shopping down different aisles: a review of the literature on human resource management in large-scale food retailing', *Working Paper 9501*, UMIST, Manchester.

Mason, G. and M. Osborne. (2008). "Business strategies, work organisation and low pay in United Kingdom retailing." in *Low wage work in the United Kingdom*, edited by C. Lloyd, G. Mason, and K. Mayhew. New York: Russell Sage Foundation.

McGurr, P. (2002) 'The largest retail firms: a comparison of Asia-, Europe- and US-based retailers', *International Journal of Retail and Distribution Management*, 30(3): 145–150.

Nonaka, I. (1991) 'The knowledge- creating company', *Harvard Business Review*, November–December: 96–104.

Orlikowski, W. (2007) 'Sociomaterial practices: exploring technology at work', *Organization Studies*, 28(9): 1435–1448.

Palmer, A. (1994) *Principles of Services Marketing*. London: McGraw-Hill.

Penn, R. (1995) 'Flexibility, skill and technical change in UK retailing', *The Service Industries Journal*, 15 (3): 229–242.

Penn, R. and Wirth, B. (1993) 'Employment patterns in contemporary retailing: Gender and work in five supermarkets', *The Service Industries Journal*, 13(4): 252–266.

Pettinger, L. (2004) 'Brand culture and branded workers: Service work and aesthetic labour in fashion retail', *Consumption, Markets and Culture*, 7(2): 165–184.

Pettinger, L. (2006) 'On the materiality of service work', *The Sociological Review*, 54(1): 48–65.

Price, R. (2004) *Checking Out Supermarket Labour Usage: the Nature of Labour Usage and Employment Relations Consequences in a Food Retail Firm in Australia*, Unpublished PhD thesis, Griffith University, Brisbane, Australia.

Rainbird, H. and Munro, A. (2003) 'Workplace learning and the employment relationship in the public sector', *Human Resource Management Journal*, 13(2): 30–44.

▶

►

Ribeiro, R. and Collins, H. (2007) 'The bread-making machine: tacit knowledge and two types of action', *Organization Studies*, 28(9): 1417–1433.

Sparks, L. (1983) 'Employment characteristics of superstore retailing', *The Service Industries Journal*, 3(1): 63–78.

Sparks, L. (1992) 'Restructuring retail employment', *International Journal of Retail and Distribution Management*, 20(3): 12–19.

Sparks, L., Gustafsson, K., Jönson, G. and Smith, D. (2006) *Retailing Logistics and Fresh Food Packaging*. London: Kogan Page.

Thompson, P. (1989) *The Nature of Work: An Introduction to Debates on the Labour Process*, 2nd edition. Houndmills: Macmillan

Tinker, T. (2002) 'Spectres of Marx and Braverman in the twilight of Postmodernist labour process research', *Work, Employment and Society*, 16(2): 251–279.

Winsor, R., Sheth, J. and Manolis, C. (2004) 'Differentiating goods and services retailing using form and possession utilities', *Journal of Business Research*, 57(3): 249–255

Woolworths. (2008) Public submission to ACCC inquiry into the competitiveness of retail prices for standard groceries, available from http://www.accc.gov.au/content/index.phtml/itemId/810417

Wong, M. and Hendry, C. (1999) 'Employment strategy: comparing Japanese and British companies in Hong Kong', *Personnel Review*, 28(5/6): 474–490.

Wright, D. (2005) 'Mediating production and consumption: cultural capital and "cultural workers"', *British Journal of Sociology*, 56(1): 105–121.

Wrigley, N. and Lowe, M. (2002) *Reading Retail: A Geographical Perspective and Retailing and Consumption Spaces*. London: Arnold.

Retail as a Job versus Retailing as a Career

'It's All Right for Saturdays, But Not Forever.' The Employment of Part-Time Student Staff within the Retail Sector

6

Prue Huddleston

It has been demonstrated that students form a large and important labour pool for the retail sector and yet at the same time the sector complains about a lack of skilled labour and high labour turnover, an average of 40 per cent across the sector (Skillsmart, 2009). These messages appear contradictory given the large number of highly qualified, and presumably skilled, young people that at some time work within the sector. Anne Seaman, Chief Executive Skillsmart, suggests that:

> Retail is in the unique position of having nearly half a million students experiencing what it is like to work in the sector before they enter the world of full-time work. It is therefore a golden opportunity to show that the sector offers promising careers while young people are working in the industry during school, college and university. (Training Journal, 2008)

The last 20 years has witnessed a shift from a labour market in which student labour was marginal to one where it is a major feature (TUC, 2004). Whereas in the mid-1970s less than 30 per cent of 16–19 year olds studied full-time, and of those that did less than 5 per cent worked part-time. In contrast, by 2006 the percentage of full-time students in the labour force was 53 per cent. The majority of these young people work in the retail and hospitality sectors (People 1st, 2009: 3).

Engaging in employment while still in education is now an important experience for a substantial proportion of young people making the transition from school to work and blurs the boundary between school and work. Taken together pupil work experience as part of compulsory schooling, part-time employment, and work placement as part of a vocational programme, as in the new 14–19 Diploma qualifications, afford substantial experience of workplaces. It is no longer realistic to talk about young people as if they had no experience of the world beyond the classroom or the lecture theatre. Yet employer organizations have for the past 30 years talked of young people as if they were devoid of knowledge and experience of the world of work and of the necessary skills required to succeed in it (Huddleston and Keep, 1998; CBI 2007).

Such signals appear confusing, even contradictory, since retailers depend heavily upon youth labour to run their businesses. It is reasonable to assume that many of these young part-time workers are highly educated, well qualified undergraduates and sixth formers. Yet the sector reports skills shortages as a serious problem and, given that the sector is projected to grow despite the economic downturn, one that is likely to continue for the foreseeable future (Skillsmart, 2008). It appears that the sector is failing to capitalize on the 'captive' pool of part-time student labour and to convince it that the sector is worth considering as a possible future career. Moreover, many young, part-time workers are gaining valuable knowledge and skills through their engagement in the sector; skills that could be deployed in other employment sectors.

The retail sector provides, therefore, an interesting case study against which to test this view. It provides thousands of jobs for young people, both qualified and unqualified; young people who are seeking permanent work and those who are just passing through. The Sector Skills Council complains about the lack of skills in the sector, particularly the necessary 'people skills' including communication skills, customer handling skills, team working. Yet it provides a potentially fertile environment in which to develop such skills. The sector recognizes that it has for a long time suffered an image problem in that it is viewed as a sector characterized by low-skilled jobs, poor training, limited career prospects, unsocial hours and low pay (Harris and Church, 2002). However, it draws upon a large pool of labour, even if transitory, and could attempt to dispel some of the negativity surrounding retail working by indicating the opportunities available for skills development and career progression, even if these jobs are commonly viewed as 'jobs without training' (Maguire and Huddleston, 2009).

Intense market competition, including the proliferation of internet sales, coupled with economic downturn, has forced retailers to focus on reducing costs rather than raising prices. Attempts to reduce the wage bill have resulted in downsizing and even more intensive use of part-time and casual labour (Harris and Church, 2002, Simms, 2007). It is the use of part-time labour, in particular student labour – a significant labour pool for the retailer – that this chapter now turns.

Part-time employment and the shift to a student workforce

The sector is renowned for its part-time employment opportunities which many regard as a key component of its competitiveness. Just under a half (49 per cent) of all retail employees work part-time; the greatest proportion is female (71 per cent). Many young people work in the sector while studying, while retail's innate flexibility also offers opportunities for those seeking to balance childcare or other caring responsibilities, for those seeking to enhance retirement income and for career changers. (Skillsmart, 2010: 5)

In December 2009, the number of people in part-time employment in the UK was 7.7 million, of whom 1.86 million were male and 5.84 million female (IDS, 2008; ONS, 2009). Whilst not all these people are employed within the retail sector a large percentage is. The changing nature and patterns of retailing, with 24-hour trading across 365 days of the year, creates heavy dependence on a supply of flexible, part-time labour. Whilst this has always been the case, with seasonal trade variations, the situation has been intensified with changes in the patterns of trading and the growth of out-of-town shopping centres and online shopping. Internet sales have also increased the demand for associated retail employment, for example in despatch and customer service. Other related industries such as hospitality, leisure and tourism show similar patterns. For example, People 1st the Sector Skills Council for the hospitality, leisure, travel and tourism sector reports that:

The sector continues to be over-reliant on a shrinking pool of younger workers. 48 per cent of the sector's workforce is under the age of 30 compared to 18 per cent of the workforce across the whole economy. (People1st, 2009: 3).

The retail sector has traditionally been a significant employer of young people (16–25) to meet a wide range of employment demands. However, over the past two decades the retail sector has had to face a dramatic decline in young workers. Maguire and Maguire (1997) suggest that one of the many reasons for this has been employers' increased demand for non-standard forms of employment. This has brought about a shift in the nature and composition of retail sector employees. At the same time a rise in the participation of young people in further and higher education has resulted in more young people seeking part-time employment whilst undertaking full-time study; a situation exacerbated by student fees and increased living expenses.

Young retail workers are no longer just full-time sales assistants; they now include full-time students, youth trainees, including those undertaking retail apprenticeships, and 16–19 year olds classified as in 'jobs without training'. In other words this is a very heterogeneous group of young workers; although our knowledge of the current youth labour market remains patchy (Maguire and Huddleston, 2009). At one time, employment of students in shops, restaurants and pubs was considered 'casual'. This is no longer the case, roles have become more structured and they require specific skills, or employees may even need 'to look a certain way' (Warhurst and Nickson, 2001). Employers are also benefiting from this flexibility:

> The increasing 'casualization' of employee relations appears to have con-verged with many characteristics of the supply of student labour, such as the limited number of hours typically worked by individual students and the relative absence of domestic constraints. (Richardson, Evans and Gba-damosi, 2009: 320)

Retailers are capitalising on students' need for flexible, part-time work. Data provided in the report: *Post-16 Students and Part-Time Jobs: Patterns and Effects,* indicates that over two-fifths of full-time Year 12 students with jobs were in sales occupations (mostly sales assistants and checkout operators). Around a quarter were in unskilled manual occupations (mostly in sales and service, especially in catering and as shelf-fillers), and about a fifth were in personal and protective service occupations (mostly in catering occupations). Together, these three occupational groups made up more than 90 per cent of all student jobs in the 16–17 year age group (Payne, 2001). There is no reason to believe that the situation has changed markedly, only increased, since Payne's work because the numbers of young people remaining in full-time education post-16 has increased.

Hodgson and Spours (2001) support this finding suggesting that between 70 per cent and 80 per cent of 16–19 year olds in full-time education are also in paid employment. The picture is similar for those full-time students post-19, where, according to an NUS survey (NUS, 2008), 78 per cent of higher education students engage in part-time paid work whilst at university. According to the ONS, between August and October 2009 there were 916,000 young people between the ages of 16–24 who were reported as being in full-time education and in part-time employment (ONS, 2009). In addition, there were 276,000 young people reported to be in full-time education and seeking part-time work.

Students may be capturing jobs that traditionally unqualified young peo-ple entered, particularly in retailing, catering and tourism, but the nature of these jobs has also changed. Employers are aware of a ready pool of stu-dent labour willing to fill part-time and casual vacancies and they are also gaining the benefit of well qualified, or potentially qualified, recruits. The evidence of qualification, or willingness to pursue qualifications, may be used as a screening device when recruiting part-time employees, since in an employer's view 'it shows commitment' (Canny, 2002). However, it does not necessarily follow that such qualifications are valued per se (Maguire and Huddleston, 2009). While this points to over-qualification in the retail labour market for the types of 'shop floor' vacancies for which students are applying, it must be questioned the extent to which students are using these jobs as stepping-stones into higher-skilled jobs, or as a contribution to the, all important, CV. (Canny, 2002; Smith, 2009; Gracia, 2009; Richardson et.al., 2009). A recent article in the *Guardian* newspaper (*Guardian*, 6th July 2010) suggested that for new graduates:

> Any employment is better than no employment (even) if it's about flip-ping burgers or stacking shelves... there are lots of other skills required and valued, like people skills: you could be on a counter in a store. It's all about building up your skills base. (p. 1)

The retail industries state that they are keen to attract the brightest and best workers they can in an attempt to increase the number of graduates employed in managerial positions (BMG, 2007). But at another level, they also provide jobs for some of the more marginal workers that are excluded from other industries because of their lack of qualifications. To an increasing extent even these jobs are being filled by bright sixth formers and under-graduates on a part-time basis:

> Students are capturing a substantial proportion of employment which unqualified young people traditionally entered, particularly in retailing, catering and tourism. (Canny, 2002: 278)

At the management level, particularly within the largest High Street retailers, there is competition for access to graduate training programmes, and the rewards can be substantial. However, this by no means characterises the whole of the sector. Of all those sixth formers and undergraduates who experience working part-time in the retail environment, only a small pro-portion goes on to seek a career in retail. It would be useful for employers to know more about career expectations of these young people and what their aspirations are after graduation in order to develop policies and practice that are effective in attracting, motivating and training them (King, 2003). For the moment it appears that student labour is being used as an expedient to reduce costs and to redress the shortfall of young people previously employed in the sector (Huddleston and Hirst, 2004).

Skills shortages and skills gaps

Despite the heavy reliance on what might appear to be well educated and well qualified young people to fill part-time vacancies, the sector has consistently reported serious skills shortages, including customer handling and communication skills, team working, problem solving, planning and organizational skills, there are also reported deficits in the personal attributes, however conceived, of job applicants (Nickson et al., 2003; Huddleston and Hirst, 2004; Skillsmart, 2007). Skills shortages are reported both within sales occupations and at managerial level. In 2008, 51 per cent of retail staff were employed in sales and customer service occupations; 18 per cent as managers or senior officials (Skillsmart, 2008). There are recruitment difficulties and the retention of some types of staff is also an issue. However, these general concerns fail to reveal the diversity and complexity of the sector, which comprises both major high street retailers and small corner shops, with many variants in between.

Research conducted by ORC International (ORC International, 2009) for Skillsmart Retail covering 616 retailers across the UK identified that skills shortages and skills gaps have remained pretty constant over time and that the demand for soft skills continues to be viewed as important, if not more so than, technical and job-specific skills.

In 2009 Skillsmart hosted a conference for the sector entitled: 'Improving business performance through skills', at which it set out a vision for the industry not just to improve its skills levels but also the public perception of the sector as one which was unsupportive of training and development. Reports of skills shortages in the sector are not new, in 2002 Skillsmart announced:

> As retailers strive to delight their customers and to reduce their cost bases, a knowledgeable, skilled change oriented and highly productive workforce will be key to future success. (Skillsmart, 2002: 2)

With recurring frequency skills shortages have focused upon: customer service, basic literacy and numeracy, selling skills and product knowledge, communications. In addition certain personal attributes are cited as desirable, including willingness to take initiative, work in a team, act responsibly or be thrilled by *The River Island Experience* (Interview with store manager). Kingfisher group (2009) believes that improved qualification levels in general, and customer service in particular, will result in:

- Improved customer satisfaction scores and employee engagement
- Customer confidence in our 'friendly Expert staff'

- Improved retention rates for non-management staff'
- Support for wider social commitments around key skills, communication and pride in achievement.

Recruiting and retaining sales assistants is a major problem for many large and small to medium-sized enterprises (SMEs) in the retail sector. This problem is not new, over ten years ago, the *Trading Skills for Sales Assistants* report (Dench et al., 1997) suggested that these problems arise from skills gaps, concerning attitude, behaviour and personal characteristics.

While few organizations have difficulty recruiting sales assistants, attracting the right candidate is often difficult. A lack of people with the right 'attitude' has been seen as a major barrier to success. It is difficult to specify with any exactitude however, what this 'attitude' is (Huddleston and Hirst, 2004; ORC, 2009). Some retailers may be looking specifically for young people who 'look a certain way'. This is especially important in some designer fashion retail outlets, where even part-time employees are expected to purchase company merchandise to wear on the shop floor (interview with sales assistant Department Store chain). In some sports and leisure retail outlets, sales assistants are not only required to be knowledgeable about the products but they must also appear so:

> Like they do the sport themselves, for example, we've got people who are interested in skateboarding, cycling, climbing, that sort of thing, it's important like they are on the same wavelength as the customers; it's a lifestyle thing, and, of course, those are the sort of youngsters we get coming in here looking for jobs. (Sports store manager)

One of the primary reasons reported for skills gaps in the retail sector is the failure of companies to train and develop their staff and yet large retailers invest significant amounts of money in training. Many of the leading brand names have enviable training records; training is portable and has currency within the retail labour market. Smaller retailers cannot match, or afford, this.

Recruitment problems are the second reason given by 20 per cent of retail establishments. A high staff turnover (17 per cent of establishments) and a lack of motivation, interest and commitment (17 per cent) were other explanations offered for skills gaps. However, recruitment and retention issues, since the economic downturn, have been less acute than previously, according to a report published by CIPD (CIPD, 2009).

At the 'top end of the market' gaining employment, even part-time, within retail is not straightforward and it is competitive. Maguire and Huddleston (2009) highlight the significance for young people of 'dropping off CVs', 'knowing someone who works there', 'a relative having a word' in order to be considered for part-time work. There is clearly a 'pecking order' in what are perceived as 'desirable' and 'less desirable' part-time retail opportunities. One young person interviewed in the course of this research stated: 'Oh, I wouldn't want to work at the Co-op', another reported having 'traded up' by moving from a value brand supermarket to a 'high end' chain; also the staff discounts were seen as more favourable and 'his mother liked shopping there'. An interview with a manager in a High Street fashion chain indicated that she was overwhelmed by the number of young people who seek work in her store and who drop off speculative CVs; this is especially the case during the Christmas sales season.

A positive response to skills gaps is to provide further training, but there are deeper questions about the nature and duration of the training that need to be addressed, over and above the statutory requirements for health and safety and food hygiene. Delivery has to be customized and extremely flexible if it is to succeed, particularly if the recipients are part-time and working irregular shifts. The heterogeneous nature of part-time retail workers means that training has to speak to a very wide audience, including undergraduates and those with few formal qualifications. It is real mixed ability training. It must be attractive also to the significant number of workers in the retail sector that are not particularly interested in training, some of whom have basic skills needs:

> Quite frankly, I just want to get them through their books and to sign off the training; it's like sometimes I'm just begging people to come in and complete their tests. I just don't think they're interested. It's a nightmare really, I have to get so many through in order to get the funding. (Sheila, trainer, employed in a training organisation delivering government funded programmes for the retail sector)

Sheila had considerable experience within the sector (footwear) and had progressed from a shop floor assistant to sales supervisor, then to store management and finally into training (chiefly because of the opportunities it afforded to combine family commitments and employment). She was disappointed by the calibre of young people joining this government funded training programme and did not see them as having the necessary social skills to succeed within a retail environment. She recognised that her trainees would have difficulties if competing with students for part-time work within the sector. Yet the focus of the training scheme was to prepare these young unemployed people for jobs within the sector, even on a more permanent basis.

Retail footwear is a significant employer of part-time student labour. As long ago as 1999, the footwear retailer Schuh reported that 35.4 per cent of its part-time workforce was students (IDS, 1999). A glance at the company's website suggests that this trend has increased, the main job requirements: 'you do need to be dynamic, hardworking, fashion conscious and passionate about customer service. In return we offer a rewarding career in an exciting environment with great scope for personal initiative.' (Careers with Schuh, 2010)

Employees in the retail industry remain under qualified, compared with other industries. In the retail sector, 13 per cent have no nationally recognized qualifications, 24 per cent have such qualifications only to the equivalent of level 2, and 33 per cent have qualifications equivalent to level 3 or above (Skillsmart, 2009). However, this is not always seen as such a barrier to employers since many feel that adequate training can be given 'on the job' and that there is little need for formal qualifications; many also rate poorly qualifications offered by external providers (ORC, 2009), preferring 'in-house' provision.

As the retail industry attempts to re-define skills and provide suitable training how will this affect the current workforce? Will existing strategies be enough to change the situation, to improve customer service and move the industry forward? It appears amidst all this identification of skills shortages and skills gaps and the focus on training there is one important component that is being ignored. This is the shift in the retail workforce to part-time student employment, the majority of whom are 'just passing through'.

'Just passing through'

The following case studies reflect the experiences of a small, though not untypical, sample of young people who were interviewed during the course of several pieces of research, spanning over six years, undertaken by the author and that looked at skills gaps and training needs within the retail sector. Whilst generally these research studies were looking at broader issues than the employment of part-time student labour within the sector, they highlighted questions about the use of such labour and were felt to merit further investigation. They also raised important questions about the apparently contradictory attitudes of employers to school/college/university leavers, which the author has researched consistently for 20 years (see, e.g., Huddleston and Keep, 1998; Huddleston, 2000; Huddleston and Oh, 2004).

The case studies provide a more detailed analysis of these issues. They attempt to provide a lens through which to understand the motivations and eventual trajectories of those who, as students, experience part-time employment within the sector, and later reject it as a long-term career. They attempt to draw together common themes that have emerged during the course of several years work on the retail sector. One of these studies (Huddleston and Hirst, 2004) was made possible through a grant from SKOPE, the ESRC-funded research centre based at the Universities of Oxford and Cardiff. In addition, the findings from another ESRC-funded project: *Young People in Jobs without Training* (Maguire and Huddleston, 2009) have provided further insights into the ways in which young people engage with the labour market, either as full-time or part-time employees.

Because these findings draw upon several pieces of work that have been undertaken on the retail sector they provide consistent insights over time about the employment of part-time students within the sector. The garnering of subjects has been 'acquisitive' since once common patterns began to emerge further subjects were sought and added to the pool of possible interviewees. Subjects also self-referred when they heard that colleagues/friends were offering views ('snowball sampling'). Another source was a group of trainees on an initial teacher training programme who were found to have had significant experience as retail employees. A review of the CVs of a larger group of trainees confirmed that this was not untypical and provided further confirmation of the long-term and pervasive experience of part-time, retail employment.

Case studies are widely used across a range of social science research, they provide insights into particular 'lived experiences' that may help us to understand more about the wider group, or point to areas worthy of further investigation (Yin, 1994). The sample chosen to illustrate 'the student retail worker', whilst to some extent opportunistic in that they were all working in retail outlets based mainly in large urban High streets, or shopping centres, was regarded as 'typical' in the sense that they were all sixth form pupils, undergraduate students, or in the case of the trainees, postgraduates, though attending different schools and universities. Some of them moved from the former status to the latter during the course of the different pieces of research. All worked for well-known and ubiquitous High Street retailers and because these large companies have highly centralized processes and procedures it could be inferred that experiences regarding the terms and conditions of their employment, job roles and responsibilities, training and other workplace practices were representative of the experiences of other young people working in similar stores in other locations.

Individual students described here are illustrative of the larger group of possible subjects, but they are real subjects. I am indebted to Smith's (2009) study in helping to develop and reflect upon this approach, since she has constructed 'types' of young people based upon a range of subjects interviewed to develop hypothetical case studies. It was decided in the case of the study described here to use individual case studies because there was sufficient confidence that the subjects selected were representative of part-time student retail employees (there was a wider potential pool of subjects on which to draw in order to confirm selection).

The majority of these students worked, or had worked, continuously at the same store over considerable periods of time, others moved between different branches of the same retailer, two were able to continue to work for the same employer but switching between term-time and vacation time locations. This was viewed as a particular attraction of working for this retailer. One student switched between two competitor employers but within the same product sector. During the course of the research all remained in continuous part-time employment within retail. Typical patterns of work involved weekend working, including Sundays in some cases, in addition to some week night employment if required. This was more prevalent during the pre-Christmas period. During long vacation periods there were opportunities to provide holiday cover. Apart from the regular weekend commitment, other hours worked were arranged on an 'ad hoc' basis, often at very short notice. This did not appear to pose particular problems for the students and was welcomed by some since additional hours could be sought when extra cash was required.

A description of the sample is summarized in Table 6.1.

The range of jobs reported to have been undertaken by the respondents included:

customer sales assistant; check-out operative; fruit and vegetable assistant, shelf filling/re-stocking; merchandising; sales advisor; goods inwards handler; supervisor; shift manager; night team member; 'decorating the staff room'.

All the young people within the sample reported having been approached at some time about the possibility of joining the company on a permanent basis after completion of their studies; two remained, and one is still under pressure to consider a career with the company (a major food retailer) even though she is enrolled on a full-time teacher training course. One young person reported being urged to give up her studies in order to join the company on a full-time basis. When she failed to find employment in her chosen field at the end of her university course, she continued working for her retail employer until she eventually found work more aligned to her degree subject.

Part-time work within the retail sector can be 'dipped' in and out of as circumstances dictate:

Over Christmas, I'm planning on doubling my hours, which will double my pay. I don't mind working on Christmas Eve because all the customers are generally so excited buying their last minute supplies. (Graduate Saturday *Guardian* 10 October 2009; p. 11)

Table 6.1 Sample of part-time student employees

Name	Retail type	Length of employment	Starting age	Retained?	Current employment
Jack	Newsagents/ Stationers (A)	6 years	17	No	Interior designer
Peter	Newsagents/ Stationers (A)	6years	17	No	Graphic designer
Raj	Sports equipment and outfitters (B)	7 years	16	Yes	Sales supervisor at Company B
Lucy	Food retailer (C)	4 years	18	No	Animateur (museum education)
Lisa	Food retailer (C)	10 years	18	Yes	Regional manager, food hygiene and safety at Company C
Art	Food retailers (2x D and E)	5 years	16	No	Local authority planner
Jez	Food retailer (F)	7 years	16	Still undecided (remains part-time	Trainee teacher
Shazia	Fashion retailer (G)	4 years	20	Yes (part-time)	Trainee teacher

To date there has been a ready supply of such jobs, although the situation is competitive at the top end of the market.

The experiences of the young people in this study reflect those reported in Smith's (2009) work on young people and part-time work within the Australian labour market:

> The growth of service industries (particularly retail and fast food) that increasingly operate outside standard working hours has created a pool of part-time and actual jobs that are readily available to school students. (p. 431–432)

Like Smith's sample, the young people in this study 'had an intimate knowledge of the workplace', it was through the workplace that they found out 'about other options'. For example Art, changing from retailer D to E, found out about the vacancy through a friend. Jack found out about the job at retailer A through his friend Peter; Lucy is Lisa's sister. The retail sector relies upon these networks of young people to promote its vacancies. To some extent these networks act as a screening device providing access to a very specific pool of young labour – those who are committed, on the whole, to further and higher education and as such, it is hoped, are more likely to have acceptable standards of basic skills.

The young people's motivations for work were overwhelmingly, though not exclusively, financial. Whilst earning money was crucial other aspects of work were important, for example the social opportunities provided, the flexibility offered within the context of retail, the convenience of something '*in the area*'. For Shazia the opportunity to work in '*high end*' fashion (retailer G) was attractive, in particular the chance to buy designer clothes at discounted rates (up to 25 per cent). Art saw his move from retailer D to retailer E as a '*step up*'; here everything was better 'the products, the uniform, the discount'. It was as if by association some of this would rub off on to him.

Jack and Peter enjoyed the responsibility of 'being in charge at the end of the day', '*cashing up*', '*locking up*', although it could be argued that two part-time sixth formers should not have been given such responsibility, which also included tackling shoplifters and being in charge in the store during night time Christmas stock replenishment. Clearly, the sector expects a lot of its student labour.

The majority of the young people in this sample had no intention of making a full-time career in the sector. Their horizons were clearly defined by their current area of study and they could see no opportunity for its application within the retail sector. This is not surprising given that the tasks on which they were employed part-time were, in the main, low-skilled, repetitive, and shop floor focused. The hierarchical nature of employment within large retailers means that part-time shop floor personnel have little access to management or other company functions, so it is difficult to form a view of the scale of the total operation.

> We know when like the big boss man is coming in [regional manager] because the manager gets stressed and keeps talking about targets…we have to have a big tidy up, make sure everything's as it says on the plan. (Jack)

> We get scared if the temperature rises in the freezer cabinets, because we know that we'll really be in trouble if the health and safety people turn up. Other than that we just get on, clearing up the fruit and veg. making sure it looks good. (Lucy)

The majority of young people, who spend a significant proportion of their student lives working in retail, or in catering and hospitality, do not stay in the sector, and have no intention of doing so. The opportunities provided for balancing student and working lives, for earning money, for social network-ing and for working with products in which they might be interested are attractive, but they are not sufficient to keep them engaged as a long-term goal. They are a 'stop-gap' on the way to something else. As Jack put it: 'It's all right for Saturdays, but not forever.'

If Jack's view reflects those of a large proportion of students who work part-time in the retail sector, and if at the same time the sector continues to complain about skills shortages, what can the sector do to ameliorate the situation? It has potentially a large pool of well qualified and skilled people, with substantial experience of the sector, and yet it fails to capitalise on it. Moreover, the sector provides an opportunity for young people to develop a range of generic skills, allegedly much prized by employers:

> Customer-facing skills – like being polite when you really don't feel like it – are very, very useful and employers put an emphasis on these general skills when they are looking to recruit graduates. (Graduate Saturday *Guardian*, 10 October 2009, p. 11)

Changing the image of the retail sector

A report by the Retail E-Commerce Task Force (2002) suggested that the retail sector has been described as a 'Cinderella' industry in terms of its status and its inability to attract the best talents. Concerns over this poor perceived image have prompted Skillsmart to take steps to improve the sec-tor's image through media campaigns and opinion surveys of young people, their parents, careers advisors and other careers 'influencers'. (BMG, 2007). Whilst the situation is reported as having improved to some extent during successive waves of the survey in 2004, 2005, 2006, there remains a percep-tion that the sector is characterised by 'long unsocial hours and poor career prospects'. Opinions concerning 'the lack of challenge' associated with jobs in the sector is prevalent. More positively, the sector is viewed 'most favour-ably for developing skills useful in any workplace and for offering a wide range of opportunities for people of all ages.' (BMG, 2007: 7). Interviews with the young people in the foregoing section revealed how willing the sector is to give responsibility at an early age; for example, 'cashing up', being a 'key holder', 'approaching shoplifters', even 'standing in for the manager' for short periods.

The student sample reported that employment in retail was satisfactory as a student job; many retailers go out of their way to make it so (*Guardian* 10 October 2009) but it is still not seen as an ultimate career destination for the majority of young people who spend a fair proportion of their student lives working in shops. It could be argued that the majority of such part-time workers had no intention of seeking a long-term career in retail since their career intentions were probably formed when they embarked on an undergraduate programme. Since the BMG study confirms that 'respondents are most aware of frontline job roles' (BMG, 2007: 1) it is unlikely that they would know much about other opportunities within retail, for example in finance, marketing and supply-chain management. In small outlets this would certainly be the case.

The young people interviewed during the course of the research reported that when full-time opportunities had been raised with them these were mainly within the area of store management. Where there is no HR or training function present within the store – many HR and training personnel now work on a peripatetic basis across stores – then it is difficult to obtain a fuller picture of the types of opportunities that are available more widely in the company, particularly within head office functions. At retailer A, visits from HR tended to be about 'hiring and firing' issues; training was done either by 'watching someone else', or 'viewing a video or DVD' (Jack).

Of those young people in the sample who remained employed within the sector, one, Lisa, had found an opportunity directly related to her degree qualification, and Raj had been unsuccessful in his A level examinations and needed to find work quickly to support a family. He was able to remain in the same company and to eventually progress. Jez remains undecided and much will turn on her progress with teacher training. She reports that her store manager is still keen to recruit her to the graduate training scheme. Entry to graduate training programmes in this company is also highly competitive and she would be at a clear advantage as an experienced part-time employee of seven years.

Parents too have a significant role to play in forming young people's views of career opportunities; the BMG (2007) study revealed that parents' views on retailing could have a negative impact on the young people's perceptions. Although admittedly a small sample base, negative views about the sector as a job for their son or daughter included: 'poor career prospects', 'long unsocial hours', low salary/pay', 'lack of care/appreciation from employers' and 'little training available'. The survey does not make clear whether or not respondents had children working part-time, or full-time, within the sector and therefore on what basis they were making such judgements.

Like the young people in this chapter, those responding to the BMG survey had 'a favourable image of retailing as a friendly, open, accessible place of work, but as a part-time, or stop gap job, not as a career'. The financial rewards were acceptable as a student, but not as a full-time employee. Although part-time student employees may be unaware of the salaries available at the management level within retailing operations, they are not insubstantial and compare well with other graduate opportunities. Given that over 50 per cent of young people have their first work experience in stores it is strange that the sector does not actively encourage them to seek careers in the industry.

As the number of 20–39 year olds available for full-time employment decreases, the retail sector will continue to face difficulties in recruiting young people, other than as part-time student labour. The raising of the participation age, to 17 by 2013 and to 18 by 2015, will result in fewer young people being available for full-time employment and more of them seeking part-time work alongside their studies. Those young people who are in employment will perforce need to engage with some form of part-time education or training. This could be both an opportunity and a threat for the retail sector. Competition from other sectors for young workers could be fierce. The industry will need make itself attractive to a diverse group of young people, to demonstrate that there are opportunities for training, development and career progression for those who are 'passing through' as well as for those who have firmer career intentions in retail.

Conclusions

We have argued that the retail sector is the largest employer of part-time student labour and that this trend is likely to continue for the foreseeable future given the expansion of the sector and its requirement for flexible, part-time labour. Whilst it is a stopgap expedient for those who are 'passing through' and for the sector itself, it does not deal with the underlying challenges facing the sector in terms of its skills shortages and gaps, its perceived image and its need to attract and retain *'the brightest and best'*.

The sector is characterized by huge diversity in terms of the size of companies, the range and scale of operations, the workforce profile, and its willingness to engage in training and development, and its management approaches. This makes it difficult for the sector to speak with one voice and to develop strategies that will engage with such a complex agenda. Whilst there are concerns about the lack of basic skills levels, for example the sector provides jobs for marginal workers excluded from other employment because of lack of qualifications, it also recruits for part-time employment large numbers of potentially highly qualified young people. The majority of these, also those young people in the sample described here, do not wish to stay. Some of them had already decided this before they engaged in part-time work because the part-time retail job is a convenient means to an end. It provides necessary income, it is on the whole enjoyable, it is flexible and it is something one can do with one's friends.

Some students will decide to stay because they have identified opportunities within the company that are aligned to their career aspirations, as in the case of Lisa. Others will stay because they have to find work and they can expand their existing job into a full-time opportunity if the need arises, as Raj did. Some may be made aware of opportunities as they gain more knowledge of the company through extended involvement, for example in Jez's case.

The needs of the retail sector for attracting and developing a workforce that will be sustainable in the longer term will not be met simply by hiring and firing by the month. Whilst students provide a ready supply of flexible, presumably reasonably qualified, labour most of them are just passing through. The broader concerns of the sector, voiced by Skillsmart, are that the sector is characterised by poorly qualified, unskilled labour and that there is a need to put in place a thorough-going system of qualifications that allows for progression from trolley porter to store manager and beyond. Whilst students are displacing some of these young people it is difficult to see how such a comprehensive sector qualifications strategy can work. Are part-time students to be allowed access to this opportunity, or is it reserved for those who are full-time? How can the sector balance the training and development needs of part-time casual workers with those of more permanent full-time staff? Clearly, the two are very different.

If the sector is seen, and experienced, by students as a potential longer-term career possibility then it could be argued that the sector should do more to make their part-time student employees aware of the possibilities. The majority of this sample had sustained experience of the sector and certainly more than in their projected career destinations. For example, Jack and Peter had never worked part-time in design studios, Lucy had never worked within a museum or gallery context, Art had not undertaken a placement in a Planning Department. Such experiences were vicariously presented by University tutors and visiting lecturers.

It would seem that the retail sector is well placed to make the wider career opportunities available within the sector visible to young people in sixth forms, FE colleges and universities during their part-time employment experiences. If they fail to do this they are missing an opportunity to retain those who see the sector as 'all right for Saturdays but not forever.'

REFERENCES

BMG (2007) 'Quantifying perceptions of a career in retail – 2007', research report prepared for Skillsmart Retail. Birmingham: BMG Research.

▶

▶

Canny, Angela. (2002) 'Flexible labour? The growth of student employment in the UK', *Journal of Education and Work,* 15: 277–301.

CBI (2007) *Time Well Spent: Embedding Employability in Work Experience.* London: CBI

CIPD (2009) 'Recruitment, retention and turnover', Annual survey report 2009. London: CIPD.

Dench, S., Perryman, S. and Kodz, J. (1997) 'Trading skills for sales assistants', *IES Report 323.* Brighton: Institute for Employment Studies.

Gracia, L. (2009) 'Employability and higher education: contextualising female students' workplace experiences to enhance understanding of employability development', *Journal of Education and Work,* 22(4), September: 301–319.

Guardian (2009) 'Counter productive', *Graduate Saturday Guardian,* 10th October 2009.

Guardian (2010) 'Graduates warned of record 70 applicants for every job', *Guardian,* 6th July 2010.

Harris, F. and Church, C. (2002). *An Assessment of Skills Needs in the Retail and Related Industries.* London: Business Strategies, 1–131.

Hodgson, A., and Spours, K. (2001) 'Part-time work and full-time education in the UK: The emergence of a curriculum and policy issue', *Journal of Education and Work,* 14(3): 373–388.

Huddleston, P. and Keep, E. (1998) 'What do employers want; questions more easily asked than answered?' paper presented to International Partnership Conference, Trondheim, June.

Huddleston, P. (2000) 'Work placements for young people', in H. Rainbird (ed.) *Training in the Workplace.* Basingstoke: MacMillan Press Ltd, 210–227.

Huddleston, P. and Oh, S-A. (2004) 'The magic roundabout: work-related learning in the 14–19 curriculum', in *Oxford Review of Education,* 30(1), March, 81–100.

Huddleston, P. and Hirst, C. (2004) 'Are you being served? Skills gaps and training needs within the retail sector', research Paper 53 October, ESRC:SKOPE.

IDS (1999) *Students in Employment.* IDS Report 776. Income Data Services.

IDS (2008) Part-time workers. http://www.incomesdata.co.uk/studies/parttime.htm (accessed April 3, 2008).

King, Zella. (2003). 'New or traditional careers? A Study of UK Graduates' Preferences.' *Human Resource Management Journal* 13: 5–26.

Kingfisher plc (2009) Presentation given by Ian Cheshire, Group CEO, Kingfisher plc. Skillsmart Employer Conference 10th September 2009.

Maguire, M. and S. Maguire. (1997) 'Young people and the labour market', in R. MacDonald, *Youth, the 'Underclass' and Social Exclusion.* London: Routledge.

Maguire, S. and Huddleston, P. (2009) 'Where do young people work', in *Research in Post-Compulsory Education,* 14(4), December: 387–399.

Nickson, D., Warhurst, C., Cullen, A-M. and Watt, A. (2003) 'Bringing in the Excluded? Aesthetic labour, skills and training in the new economy', *Journal of Education and Work,* 16: 2.

▶

▶
NUS (2008) National Union of Students survey (funded by HSBC student research). http://www.nus.org.uk/en/Campaings/Higher-Education/National-student-Survey/.

ORC (2009) International, Skillsmart Retail Employer skills needs refresher survey. Autumn.

ONS (2009) Statistical Bulletin, Labour Market Statistics December 2009. London: ONS.

Payne, J. (2001) *Post-16 Students and Part-Time Jobs: Patterns and Effects.* London: Department for Education and Skills.

People 1st (2009) State of the Nation Executive Summary – 2009. People 1st.

Retail E-Commerce Task Force. (2002) *Destination Retail: A Survey of Young People's Attitudes towards a Career in Retailing.* London: Foresight, 1–34.

Richardson, M., Evans, C. and Gbadamosi, G. (2009) 'Funding full-time study through part-time work' in *Journal of Education and Work, 22(4), September: 319–334.*

Schuh (2010) http://www.schuh.co.uk/careers (accessed 8th July 2010).

Simms, A. (2007) *Tescopoloy.* London: Constable.

Skillsmart. (2002) Skillsmart *Business Plan 2002–2004.* London: Skillsmart Retail Ltd.

Skillsmart 2007) *Sector Skills Agreement Stage one Assessment of Current and Future Skills Needs.* London: Skillsmart Retail Ltd.

Skillsmart (2008) *Working Futures III.* London: Skillsmart Retail Ltd.

Skillsmart (2009) *Skillsmart Retail Analysis: current and future trends in U K retailing 2008–09.* London: Skillsmart Retail Ltd.

Skillsmart (2009) *Overview of the Current Retail Environment, 2009.* London: Skillsmart Retail Ltd.

Skillsmart (2010) *Skills Priorities for the Retail Sector in the UK and its Four Nations.* London: Skillsmart Retail Ltd.

Smith, E. (2009) 'New models of working and learning: how young people are shaping their futures differently', research in Post-Compulsory Education, 14(4), Dec. 429–441.

Training Journal (2008) http://www.trainingjournal.com.news/1585.html (accessed 30th October 2008).

TUC (2004) *TUC Case Study – Students at Work.* London: Trade Union Congress.

Warhurst, C. and Nickson, D. (2001) *Looking Good, Sounding Right.* London: Industrial Society.

Yin, R.K. (1994) *Case Study Research and Design and Methods.* 2nd ed. Thousand Oaks, CA: Sage Publications.

'The Lost Boys': An Overlooked Detail in Retail?

7

Steven Roberts

Introduction

The retail sector is second to none in regards to the number of jobs it provides for the UK economy (see below). Unsurprisingly, then, research interest in retail is growing and covers a wide range of topics including issues of strategy, logistics, branding and employment. Within the latter area, matters of motivation, skill development, promotion, and 'bridging' to retirement can all count retail as a suitable research site. In relation to such 'people issues', an overwhelming focus tends to be on the role gender plays in shaping such experiences; and often specifically the experience of women. This predominant interest in female employees is, of course, a valuable and legitimate concern, which enables researchers to reveal matters and methods of discrimination. However, whilst men continue to dominate the higher echelons and full-time positions in the sector, the retail industry also employs significant numbers of men, especially young men, in lower-level positions. Further, whilst the large concentration of young people in the industry is increasingly augmented by a growing number of students combining study and work, there is also a significant minority who seek permanent employment in retail. The experiences of young men in this category can easily be neglected and overlooked, yet an understanding of the work they do, the work they hope to do in the future and the way they form and manage their identities in this type of employment is worthwhile, particularly given the backdrop of increasingly higher-term rates of long-term unemployment for men than for women in the British context. This chapter is an effort to help us gain such an understanding and to fill an important gap in our knowledge about retail workers. This effort also has relevance for broader sociological and political debates. For example, the experiences of this group have also been overlooked by youth research more generally. Wallace (1987: 21–22) comments on a divide between the 'mainly employed' and the 'mainly unemployed', and employment-based research concerning young people has accordingly followed suit, primarily focussing on student employment (e.g., Canny, 2001), graduate careers (e.g., Kirton, 2009), apprenticeships (e.g., Lehmann, 2004; Taylor, 2008) or unemployment (e.g., Furlong and Cartmel, 2004) with little attention given to the prospects of those situated in the lower echelons of the labour market. While government policy is purported 'to improve the skills and fulfil the potential of all our young people and adults' (HM Treasury, 2004: 1), can such aims be achieved for those leaving education and entering the contemporary, less easily identifiable youth labour market? More specifically, can retail employment provide a basis for skills development? Whilst young adults often enter the labour market later than in previous generations, more British young people are in paid employment than compared with their European counterparts (Bynner, 2005), so such questions are highly pertinent.

In addition to being low-paid, the nature of the work young people engage in has been argued by many to be low-skill, low status and lacking in job security, when compared to more 'traditional' skilled jobs or even unskilled jobs in manufacturing (see, e.g., Furlong and Cartmel, 2007; Roberts, 1995; Talwar, 2002). A lack of provision in these areas leads to 'a cycle of in-work poverty, based on horizontal movements between short-term, low skilled jobs' (Lindsay and McQuaid, 2004: 301). Accordingly, the aim of this chapter is to highlight the importance of considering the employment experiences of this 'missing middle' of employment research. The 2007 Labour Force Survey is used to illustrate the importance of the retail sector as an employment destination for 18–24 year olds, both women and men. The dominant focus on the situation of women in retail is then briefly adumbrated before the chapter draws on a pilot study and the initial interviews from a qualitative research project with young men, employed in high street retail stores in the South-East of England, to offer some initial findings and insights. Dubbed the 'lost boys' here, they are those young men who are moderately qualified and who have work histories characterized by a series of sideways steps or fragmentation.

What do these 'lost boys' really think of retail jobs? What are their aspirations for work? What are their perceptions of the training on offer in the industry? Are these issues likely to be affected by full-/ part-time employment status? Such an investigation helps fill the gap noted by Nickson and Korczynski (2009: 298), who suggest that the actual experiences of men in front-line service work remain absent in comparison to attitudes towards taking up low-level service sector employment (e.g., Furlong and Cartmel, 2004; Nixon, 2009). In research on employee experiences within retail, non-students have often been overlooked or have had their views compounded with those of students (e.g., Warhurst and Nickson, 2007; Maguire et al., 2008).

Young workers: The detail in retail

Despite the public sector being the biggest UK employer, when Labour Force Survey sector collaborations are broken down into individual industry sections, section G, 'Wholesale, retail and motor trade' is the area that emerges as employing more than any other . Industry section G is a collaboration of three different trades brought together to form one industry section. Of these 3 trades, retail is by far the dominant employer, accounting for more than 11 per cent of the UK workforce, or around 3 million people (Skillsmart, 2007). More than half of the retail workforce is based in lower-level sales and customer service-related roles, another 18 per cent are classified as elementary or administrative roles, with around 17 per cent holding management positions. In terms of the distribution of part-time and full-time work, retail has the highest proportion of part-time workers within the UK economy, more than double the UK average of 25 per cent. Second, the workforce has a high proportion of young people, with a third of employees between 16 and 24 years old (Skillsmart, 2007).

As with the wider economy, part-time work is largely a female activity, with almost three quarters of such positions in retail occupied by women. The main points of concern here, given the large proportion of part-time workers are: (i) the long standing relationship between part-time jobs and a lack of opportunities for training at work (see, e.g., Arulampalam and Booth, 1998; Mason and Osborne, 2008; Skillsmart, 2007), (ii) the in-house, non-transferable nature of training that is available (Wheeler, 2006) and (iii) the high levels of 'churn' or movement between a series of low-level service sector jobs (Bentley and Gurumurthy, 1999; Furlong and Cartmel, 2004). Furthermore, retail is home to a workforce with the highest proportion of those qualified at level 2 or below on the UK's National Qualification framework (Skillsmart, 2007).

There is a significantly higher than average number of workers under 18 years of age within industry section G, making it a popular employment destination for young people in general (Skillsmart, 2007). Similarly, industry section G, and retail in particular, figures even more prominently in the employment of 18–24 year olds in relation to the labour force in general. Almost 1 in every 4 workers in this age group are employed in section G (Figure 7.1), nearly 2.5 times as many as the nearest sections 'Manufacturing' and 'Hotels and Restaurants'.

Retail gender split

The gender composition of the 18–24 age group in retail, specifically, is 45 per cent male and 55 per cent female (Figure 7.1). This is closer to equal than the average of the retail trade (40 per cent male), but is still marginally dominated by women. Closer analysis of the occupations that are held by these young people reveals an interesting finding in terms of the gender divide. There are, indeed, more young women employed in retail, and although a greater proportion takes up typically gendered positions in customer service roles, on the whole what they do is actually relatively similar in terms of occupational level to the roles undertaken by young men (see Table 7.1). The lower three occupations ('Sales and Customer Service', 'Process, Plant and Machine Operatives' and 'Elementary Occupations') combined account for 81.6 per cent of 18–24-year-old males and 83.1 per cent of the corresponding female cohort. So, despite leaning towards a gendered division of labour, 57.3 per cent of all 18–24-year-old men undertake customer service-related roles. Ultimately, we can be certain that the majority experience for both genders in this age group is employment in lower-level occupations.

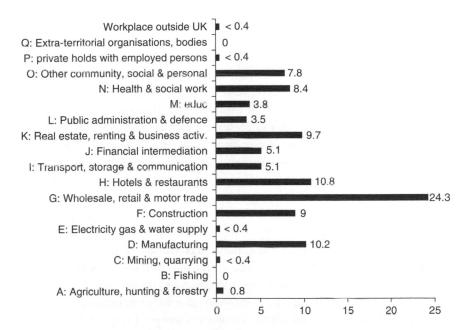

Figure 7.1 All 18–24 age group, industry distribution
Source: Quarterly LFS, July–September 2007.

Table 7.1 Occupation groups, 18–24 year olds in retail

Occupation / Sex	Male		Female		Total
	per cent within sex	per cent within occupation	per cent within sex	per cent within occupation	
1. Managers and senior professionals	7.7	54	5.4	46	6.5
2. Professional occupations	0.7	61.6	0.3	38.4	0.5
3. Associate professional and technical	3.2	34.7	4.9	65.3	4.1
4. Admin and secretarial	3	35.4	4.4	64.6	3.8
5. Skilled trades	3.9	70.3	1.3	29.7	2.5
6. Personal services	0	0	0.5	100	0.3
7. Sales and customer services	57.3	38	76.3	62	67.8
8. Process, plant and machine ops.	2.8	77.2	0.7	22.8	1.6
9. Elementary	21.5	74.1	6.1	25.9	13.1
Total	100	45	100	55	100

Source: Quarterly LFS, July–September 2007.

Full-time, part-time and gender

On the whole, 18–24 year olds are slightly more likely to be part-timers than retail employees. There is also a gendered element to part-time work in retail as the young women comprise 60 per cent of part-time staff for this age group (Table 7.1). This trend differs from that of the overall retail workforce, as women vastly dominate lower-level occupations and account for approximately 75 per cent of part-time positions (Skillsmart, 2007). The closer levels of part-time work between the young men and young women in retail roughly reflect the national trend where the largest group of men in part-time work are those under age 25 (EOC, 2003), and is compounded by the fact that the industry employs a large proportion of young people.

The high level of part-time employment among women is probably a barrier to career progression and development. Mason and Osborne (2008) found that job sharing, limited mobility and restricted availability of hours were highlighted by retailers as reasons for not considering part-time female staff for promotion. This is, however, tempered by the staff responses in the same study. Career progression for female employees seemed highly influenced by heteronormative attitudes, and the women in Mason and Osborne's study deemed their careers to be secondary to their domestic commitments (there is, however, debate as to whether such prioritising could be re-negotiated if childcare were more readily available and affordable. See Hakim (2000), Crompton and Lyonette (2005) for details). Full-time female workers pursuing careers in retail have also been shown to be hindered by a lack of role models as well as having childcare responsibilities (Foster et al., 2007) whilst furthermore suffering from the culture of male norms and values within the industry that reinforce the fact that, even though women dominate in numbers, they remain managed by men (Broadbridge, 2007b). While women do face such disadvantages, there are other potentially disadvantaged groups. In this case, 'moderately' qualified young men who have to date not received equivalent research focus – 'the lost boys'.

Young retail workers reasons for being in part-time work brings an interesting issue to the fore. Table 7.1 shows that the majority of 18–24 year olds employed on a part-time basis in retail are students. This is not much of a surprise because, as indicated by Canny (2001), having a job is now a majority experience for young people in education and retail lends itself to flexible hours of work around which students can fit their studies and social activities (see also NUS, 2008). Indeed, student recruitment often forms part of the employers' strategy of employing a flexible workforce that can complement fluctuating work patterns (Mason and Osborne, 2008; see also Huddleston, this volume).

Importantly though, a significant minority (17.5 per cent) of these young people work part-time because they cannot find full-time jobs. This desire for full-time employment among 18–24-year-old part-time staff in retail has an interesting gendered dimension. A third more young men than young women in this cohort are in part-time employment due to not being able to find a full-time position. Further, almost double the number of women actively choose part-time employment because they do not want a full-time position (See Table 7.2). This latter point is perhaps no surprise as the statistics reflect the mainstream gender binary that leads more women than men to fit work around domestic and familial responsibilities (Pfau-Effinger, 2004; James, 2008).

Whilst part-time work in Britain is often associated with women combining employment with childcare, it should not be assumed that this is the only group for whom full-time work could be considered undesirable due to other personal/ lifestyle choices. What is important, however, is to recognise the relationship between lower levels of qualifications and part-time employment (Fenton and Dermott, 2006) and the association of part-time work with low pay: 85 per cent of part-timers in retail earn less than two-thirds of the gross hourly wage of all employees (Mason and Osborne, 2008). Furthermore, this group of young men who are part-timers because they cannot find full-time work are of particular interest given the high levels of 'churn' between

Table 7.2 Reason for part-time job, 18–24 year olds in retail

Reason for PT job / Sex	in %	Male	Female	Total
Student or at school	within reason	39.3	60.7	100
	within sex	66.5	68.2	67.5
Ill or disabled	within reason	60.4	39.6	100
	within sex	1.1	0.5	0.7
Cant' find FT job	within reason	50.8	49.2	100
	within sex	22.4	14.4	17.5
Doesn't want FT job	within reason	28.1	71.9	100
	within sex	10	17	14.2

Source: Quarterly LFS, July–September 2007.

low-skill jobs and the low levels of training associated with the industry (Bentley and Gurumurthy, 1999; Furlong and Cartmel, 2004). This could, however, also apply to those in full-time positions, as being full-time does not necessarily result in the provision of adequate training; Skillsmart (2007) found that just one in five retail employees reported that they received training in the previous year and that one in three of all employees in the industry holds either basic or no qualifications (see also Mason and Osborne, 2008).

The relatively high proportion of part-time workers in the industry is a cause for concern for both sexes because part-time work is associated with decreased chances of obtaining work place training (Skillsmart, 2007), and whilst women make up the majority of part-time positions in retail, for this age group the gender split is much more even (as discussed above). To make matters worse, in a wide assessment of skills within retail, wholesale and related industries, Harris and Church (2002) found that training priorities were often in tension with training needs. Their research showed that where training was given, the majority of expenditure was channelled towards training those who were already the most able and/or the highest qualified staff.

'The Lost Boys': Another important detail in retail

Broadbridge (2007a) has noted that academic research into retail has focussed on a few dominant themes, (namely internationalisation, branding, logistics and fashion), whilst experiences of employment have tended to remain secondary. The remainder of the chapter, then, uses qualitative data drawn from an ongoing project to contribute to this void. The voices presented here give an insight into how these young men perceive their lives as retail workers, focussing specifically on the differences in attitude between full- and part-timers regarding the esteem in which they hold their job and their aspirations for work. Also of interest in this section is that the attitudes of young male full- and part-time staff converge on their evaluation of a lot of workplace training as being something that can only be gained through experience, and their rejection of any educational qualifications as a tool for progression within the industry.

Methods

The respondents for the study are 18–24-year-old males who are qualified up to the National Qualification Framework Level II. They live and work in the county of Kent, in the South-East of England, and are employed in front line, customer-facing roles by large retail chains with a national presence. The participants were recruited using a multi-level method to gain access to firms. Fifteen businesses were selected based on their national high street presence and numbers of staff, each having a minimum of 8,000 employees. Head offices were contacted for permission to enter stores at first, and where no response was obtained through this approach store managers in the research region were contacted individually.

In total, just two organizations gave carte-blanche access whilst a further three individual stores from other retailers granted access. However, because the young male workers that the study focuses on are very widely spread throughout the sector, this level of access garnered very few positive responses. Therefore, 'snowballing' via those respondents who had agreed to take part and other local contacts was utilized to deliver a full sample. The sample comprised of employees from eight retailers, all of whom were large, well known, organizations. There was some variation in unit size and product specialism, but this seemed to have very little discernable impact on the overarching emergent themes (see below).

The data discussed below is based on a focus group of five young retail workers and six individual interviews. The interviews, which lasted between 45 minutes and 2 hours, were biographical in nature and covered experiences of work and education to date as well as a discussion regarding aspirations in relation to both of these issues. The data generated has many parallels with the material in the oral histories elicited by Terkel (1974) and resembled the 'loosely structured but focussed discussions', outlined by Vickerstaff (2007: 335).

Given the limited numbers at this stage, these initial findings should be treated with some caution, but nevertheless they provide some interesting insights about a group that has, thus far, tended to be overlooked in the literature.

Initial findings

One young person's dead-end job is another's route out of a dead-end existence (Quinn et al., 2008). This is a theme that pervades the responses presented in this section and such positive or negative associations are in many ways epitomized by these contrasting comments from the focus group in response to the question 'what type of people work in retail?':

> Idiots [laughs]. Working at (Department Store), there's a load of people who work there, people with mortgages, people who are still at college, people who just had a kid and things like that. All totally different. It doesn't matter what sort of person you are, it is an easy job to do ... It is an easy job, you just have to stand there and lick people's arse, and that is all you have to do. (19 year old, part-time, Department Store)

> People who can deal with stress better than most people I think. Goes back to [the] diversity of the sector. If you wanna be a shelf stacker in Sainsbury's you can be a 15, 16 year old kid straight out of school, you can do it. Whereas if you wanna be a 'stock filler' or support somewhere you gotta have a bit of noggin [brains] about you. (24 year old, full-time, Car and Leisure store)

These extracts clearly show a differing degree of affiliation with the job. Where the first response has played down any significant skill requirements for all age groups and all personal situations for retail non-management staff, the latter response lends itself to Newman's (1999) contention that low-skill jobs can offer dignity and various opportunities for development given the right circumstance.

The young men who seemed the most at ease and the most accepting of their positions in retail were those who saw themselves in some way as 'more than a shelf stacker', and whose occupation was not immediately described as being typically associated with retail. For example, one interviewee, who works for a large car and leisure retailer, describes himself first and foremost as a 'bike mechanic', despite the fact that his job role also involves many of the elements of a more traditionally conceived sales assistant, including customer service-related issues. Similarly, a colleague in the same store describes his job in terms of the technical content of 'fitting audio equipment' before mentioning the name of the retailer he works for. Interestingly, he indicates that this is also something he has always aspired to do:

> [W]hen I was younger I always wanted to fit stereos in cars, like always reading 'max power' and stuff like that. And I was like, I love that, I wanna fit all that kind of stuff. But I've done loads of jobs to get where I am. I just thought that's what I wanted to do, so that's what I'm gonna do. (24 year old, full-time, Car and Leisure Store)

This reluctance to admit to being a retail employee in the first instance should not be interpreted as a rejection of the more typically retail elements of their job role. Many of the young men spoke very freely and positively about the service-related aspects in their job, embodied by this response from an interview:

> I get a buzz from helping people, especially customers. When they come to me and say 'I've got this problem'. And I can spend an hour with a customer and sort a problem out for them. When they go 'ah thanks' and shake your hand and say 'you've really helped me', it makes me feel so good. (24 year old, full-time, Car and Leisure Store)

This attitude was, however, more consistent with the responses of those who were full-time employees regardless of whether they were employed in some kind of specialist role. Part-timers tended to be a lot more negative in their responses about the job as a whole:

> If you not got anything (skills or qualifications) you gonna work in retail. You gonna sell something for somebody. You can't work for yourself. (24 year old, part-time, Outdoor pursuits Store)

> It's merry go round stuff. Every single week is the same ... if I was more qualified at something I enjoyed I wouldn't think that way because I would do something I enjoyed doing. Part time jobs are all the same. (20 year old, part-time, Supermarket)

In the focus group the divide was again sharp. The full-timers looked at their job, their occupation and their available choices far more positively:

> There is a lot more options for someone who is not skilled (these days), for unskilled workers. (21 year old, full-time, Car and Leisure store)

> But retail is a very diverse sector. Like (Car and Leisure store), is completely different to (Department Store) in terms of what you do. (24 year old, full-time, Car and Leisure store)

This is in stark contrast to the kinds of comments articulated by the part-timers:

> There's only, like, retail though. That's all there is. Different shops in retail (19 year old, part-time, Department Store)

This may in part stem from the embedded notion of hierarchy between full-time and part-time staff, something that the young men in the interviews and the focus group referred to quite prolifically:

> I've seen it from both sides having been a full-timer and a part-timer, when you are a part-timer, you get treated like shit, and when you are a full-timer you treat them [part-timers] like shit. A really crap job will come up and you get the part-timer to do it. (24 year old, full-time, Car and Leisure store)

> They [part-timers] don't put the hours into the week, whereas you are there all the time. That's the way it is there's ... like a hierarchy. (21 year old, full-time, Sportswear store)

> The full-timers have been at the place more and they know the run of the business more. And they've got the experience. It's a job, it's money ... They [the part-timers] don't wanna lose their job over something stupid so they'll do whatever is necessary ... You might not like doing it but that is life. (20 year old, part-time, Supermarket)

This divide is also represented in the aspirations that the young men had for both the medium and long term. The part-timers tended to either have what Devadason (2008: 1137) has referred to as 'blue sky plans' (i.e., hypothetical high-profile/ celebrity-style careers) without any real understanding or strategy in place for achieving them or hopes of a career elsewhere:

> I just wanna earn lots of money. That is all I wanna do. (19 year old, part-time, Fashion retailer)

> Something like sports journalism, so I can go to the game and write about it... (20 year old, part-time, Supermarket)

> I wanna be a train driver. An intense year of training. Then I get 40 grand a year! (24 year old, part-time, Department store)

> I'd like to be spotted by a scout and end up doing music, playing gigs and that. (20 year old, part-time, Fashion retailer)

In each case these aspirations represented what might be described as hopes or dreams rather than plans. This was different for the full-timers, who divulged much more grounded and planned visions of careers, including moving up the hierarchy in their current or other retail organizations, or even opening or owning their own retail store. This selection of quotes comes from full-timer responses to questions about future aspirations for work:

My aspirations change all the time, but one of the things I'd wanna do is to own my own cycle shop. (21 year old, full-timer Car and Leisure store)

Specifically for work as it is now, I wanna be the area trainer for in-car technology. (24 year old, full-timer Car and Leisure store)

I'd like to go to Australia for 6 months, work in a shop out there, see if it's any different. (22 year old, full-timer, Sportswear store)

I dunno if I can do it or not but basically I'd like to progress further up the ladder than I am now. (24 year old, full-timer, Department store)

These differences between the full-time and part-time staff demonstrated a distinct difference in the level of investment between the employees. The part-time staff did not necessarily see themselves as committed to a career in retail and often had dreams of something bigger, thinking it was perhaps just 'around the corner' (see Alheit, 1994). Yet they also conveyed a sense of being trapped because of their lack of a strategy for achieving their goals. The full-timers described their employment experiences and their aspirations in a more positive light, framed on the whole around a career in retail and they expressed more a sense of permanence. They did not see themselves as trapped, but instead indicated that they had made a choice, and that full-time work has set them on the path they are pursuing. At what point this distinction is made in the minds of these young people is in need of further investigation.

As well as these differences the young men's views converged around a couple of specific issues, namely: (i) their attitudes towards the way training can be conducted in the workplace and its attendant value and (ii) the lack of utility formal education holds for a career in retail. These points are now explored below.

During the focus group the issue of customer service skills was raised. The participants were asked to consider what kind of skills or qualifications this element of the job might include, and both full- and part-timers described this initially as being something that was inherent to the individual and not a particularly difficult task:

You just have to be happy and polite. (19 year old, part-time, Department store)

That is the main thing to be honest. If I was unhappy, if I looked like an absolute nob, covered in oil, not presentable, it does make a difference. (21 year old, full-time, Car and Leisure store)

They were pressed on whether you can learn these skills, if the employer might be able to train them in this respect, but the young men were all quite clear on this matter:

You don't get taught it, you more pick it up as you go along, talking to customers. Since I worked in (Car and leisure store) specifically, cos its a lot more interaction, I worked in [Supermarket] before, and you didn't really interact with customers very much. But when you interact with a customer a lot you sort of learn more how to talk to people, how to help them. You understand when they need help, when they just want ... you know you can have a customer come in and say I want 'this', or you can have one come in and say 'this is the problem'. (24 year old, full-time)

You learn to deal with the different moods of people. Like someone will come in and be really arrogant, they think they know everything so you learn to deal with them in the way they want to be dealt with. And someone can come in who is angry so you have to deal with them and diffuse their anger. (21 year old, full-time, Car and Leisure store)

It became clear that, for these young men, the key to developing this ability or skill is through experience, a 'learn through doing' approach more akin to vocational qualifications than something that can be mastered in a classroom, for instance. When asked again if employers provided training in matters of customer interaction, the responses were unanimous – formal training exists but it is not of any practical use:

[T]hey wanna encourage it. I mean you have a lot of like induction days or DVDs or something to watch. (19 year old, part-time, Department store)

We got training DVDs on how to deal with angry customers. I didn't really take anything from the DVD. I watched it and thought 'that's how they say' but until you get your first customer that is throwing a bike at you, which I have had, then you are really shoved in the deep end and you learn from each experience you have and how you deal with it. (24 year old, full-time, Car and Leisure store)

You can't have a video saying 'if a customer comes up doing this deal with them in this way' , because you just watching a video ... as soon as it happens you just deal with it in your own way. And deal with it in a responsible and respectful manner. (20 year old, part-time, Supermarket)

No, the way they do it is right but they can't put it in a real life situation – they can't really train you properly. (21 year old, full-time, Sportswear store)

The skills that can be trained in the eyes of these young men are specific skills relating to the technical aspects of a particular workplace:

I've done an IMI accreditation in installation of auxiliary electronics. (24 year old, full-time, Car and Leisure store)

Well, you can go to a key holder, that's the next step after a sales advisor, then you go into like a weekend supervisor then a FT supervisor and then management and you just work your way up. It takes, like, about 10 years to do it. (19 year old, part-time, Department store)

They train you how to do it (the job/ skill) at the place you work. (20 year old, part-time, part-time, fashion retailer)

This idea was important in stimulating questions of the value of educational qualifications for retail employment. Again, both the full- and part-time staff were agreed in renouncing the utility of anything learned at school for gaining a job in retail or indeed for transferring anything into the job itself, over and above 'the basics':

The value [of school] is learning your basics, with regards your maths, obviously and kind of your English skills. (21 year old, full-time, Car and Leisure store)

If you don't learn your English properly at school you can't communicate properly with the people in your job. So it sort of the basics ain't it. (24 year old, full-time, Car and Leisure store)

You just gotta be dumb enough to do it. If you are young ... (20 year old, part-time, Supermarket)

I've never had any interview where they have said 'so ... your qualifications ...' (24 year old, full-time, Fashion retailer)

My GCSEs were shit and I managed to get ... every time I applied for a retail job I got it (21 year old, FT, Sportswear store)

If education was important, it wouldn't be on the bottom of your CV. It would always be at the top, the first thing they read. So it's not that important at all. (19 year old, PT, Department store)

My last manager started as a part-time bloke with no qualifications, whatsoever, in three or four yrs from sales staff to manger. (22 year old, full-time, Fashion retailer)

Taken together, this rejection of the importance of previous educational achievements and the idea that one learns through experience and 'by doing' resonates with Hodkinson and Bloomer's (2002) concept of a 'learning career', marked by continuity and change. We can see that the dispositions towards learning that these young men demonstrate are, on the one hand, rooted in their habitus, evidenced by the rejection of qualifications as being significant for the job role. On the other hand, the action they take as learners in the context of work leads to a positive development of their intuitive disposition towards learning – albeit informal, uncertified learning.

Discussion and conclusion

The LFS data outlined here point to the fact that the retail sector is extremely significant for the 18–24-year-old cohort. Although retail employs a large group of students in this age range, a large number of young people who are not students are also part of the retail workforce in Britain. This age group shows a much more even gender split for both full- and part-time staff than for retail as a whole, which is predominantly occupied by female employees. The low level of the jobs is also quite evenly distributed with just over 80 per cent of both young men and young women employed in lower-level occupations. So, despite evidence indicating that women lose out in terms of career progression in retail (e.g., Broadbridge, 2007b; Mason and Osborne, 2008), there is also the question of which men and what characteristics succeed.

The accounts of 'the lost boys' raise important issues for employees, employers, policy makers and academics. This chapter has discussed the most salient points that emerged through these accounts. The first of these is the striking difference between the responses of the full-time and part-time young men in relation to their experiences of, feelings towards and hopes for future employment. Whilst the full-time core workers tended to have gained direction, some level of certainty, and have grounded their aspirations for work in relation to a career in retail, the peripheral part-timers' 'blue sky' plans remained speculative and largely unstructured. This may derive from the differences in the young men's intentions. For instance, the part-timers tended to indicate that their employment was transitory; a short-term side-step or interim position before either moving on to something more spectacular in work terms (along the lines of celebrity/ professional work) or for the purposes of funding their social lives through a longer period of 'emerging adulthood' (see Arnett, 2000) whilst they defer making career 'choices' and other responsibilities associated with adult responsibility such as independent living.

The full-timers were far more pragmatic about their career prospects and aspirations, but it is important to recognize several issues in this regard. First, the full-timers tended to have re-adjusted their work-related aspirations following a period of being in full-time work, having once displayed very similar 'transitory attitudes' when they were themselves part-time employees. The role of work in this respect could be argued to result in more realistic ambitions, yet on the other hand, it could also be argued to be a determining factor in abandoning other potential avenues. This divide is also partly bound up with issues of identity and the specificity of the product being sold. Without necessarily rejecting the selling and serving aspects of their role, the nature of the work was discernibly more bearable for full-timers who associated work in part with their out-of-work identity. As the 'boys' in the Car and Leisure store profess, rather than being retail assistants they labelled themselves 'audio specialists' or 'bike mechanics', in spite of their role seemingly being dominated by activities typically associated with retail sales assistants. In this respect, the organization utilizes and manages more than aesthetic (Warhurst and Nickson, 2007) and emotional (Hochschild, 1983) aspects of labour in the service encounter, and as such the product-enthusiast employee is complicit in becoming part of the commodity on offer. All of these issues appear to contribute to a greater acceptance of the nature of retail work on behalf of the full-time employees, whereas for the part-time staff the lack of identification with the product, their uncertain future ambitions (certain only in their intention not to remain in retail) and their understanding of their hierarchical position in relation to full-timers and (the 'shit jobs' such subordination consequently involves) all augment negative perceptions of the industry.

An important concern here is that, in regards to these more realistic ambitions, there did not appear to be any firm understanding of how few workers can actually realise their aspirations of store or area management roles, for example, or how limiting qualifications or external recruitment at graduate level can be. There is, of course, room for optimism because, as has been shown, men continue to do better than women in terms of gaining promotion to managerial positions in retail stores. In combination with the very real, and clearly inspirational, stories of the 'manager who started as a trolley boy/ part-timer' which permeated the discussions throughout the research, the fact that full-time positions are relatively scarce would suggest that promotion is not an easily achieved ambition. However, without wishing to prematurely dampen these aspirations it is important to offer a note of caution. Generally, the bond between occupational attainment and educational credentials has become tighter in recent decades (Roberts, 1995). The prevailing attitudes of all of the young men in this research towards training and education could lead them to struggle to obtain and maintain progressive employment in the sector – especially because of the recent and continuing turn towards graduate recruitment among retailers. It is not necessarily the case that managerial jobs now require graduates skills, because as Elias and Purcell (2003: 6) espouse 'employers may use job titles for graduate jobs that do not reflect changes in the nature and organization of the associated tasks'. However, graduate schemes are expanding, as too is graduate interest in what retail has to offer (see CIPD (2009) for evidence of this among supermarkets). This is perhaps partly to do with increases in student employment in part-time retail positions, and the experience and awareness of the industry's rewards, and contacts that such employees garner (See Huddleston, this volume). Upon graduation organizations are able, perhaps inclined, to offer work of a higher level (see Recruiter, 2009) and this is a potential barrier for both full- and part-time employees hoping for upward progression.

In addition to a lack of regard for formal education, training provision has also come under heavy scrutiny from both full- and part-time workers. These young men see training in retail as lacking both in quality and quantity as well as missing a sense of authenticity for the development of customer-facing skills. They feel, instead, that the 'learning by doing' approach that separates those who can 'handle the pressure' from those who cannot is the preferable method. This on-the-job learning raises questions about what exactly can be deemed to be a 'job without training', because whilst much of what these young men feel they learn is not certified at all, it is nonetheless classified by these individuals as something that is developed. It is perhaps a little speculative, but it could be argued that on occasions these jobs provide opportunities to learn as much, and as often, or more than some jobs with explicit training. The young men here are an excellent example of individuals who have benefited from the development of tacit skills, skills that are relevant to and developed through informal workplace learning. This is a positive step, and one that resonates with the experience of other employees in low-level work (e.g., Fuller and Unwin, 2002). Experiential learning can have wider potential benefits for the individual, such as developing social skills to utilize outside the workplace, and it could also deliver a means of putting the individual at the centre of the learning process, rather than the teacher, trainer or manager. However, the participant comments outlined in this chapter illustrate that a broadly conceived 'knowledge economy', requiring higher level skills than previous years, is somewhat of a fallacy (see Keep, 2000). Indeed, we might even question whether these young men are being 'upskilled' at all.

The final salient emergent finding is in relation to gendered responses to service work. The incompatible nature of jobs requiring deference, argued as being antithetical to typical working class masculinity (Willis, 1977; McDowell, 2003), is really challenged here. On the one hand typically masculine preferences for physical work are articulated, with a visible end result being favoured. Conversely, the protracted, pleasant service encounter is often embraced. Instead it is the routine till-point service encounter, with its monotonous Tayloristic associations, which is problematic to these young men. Part of the reason for this is that much of the contemporary research that pertains to retail and other service-related jobs focuses on the attitudes towards taking up such jobs (e.g., Furlong and Cartmel, 2004; McDowell, 2003; Nixon 2009). An exception might be Simpson (2004), who considered men's attitudes in female dominated occupations. Some of these, however, (e.g., teaching, nursing) require and attract vastly different educational and class profiles to the expanding service work in retail.

The present investigation into the experiences of young retail workers, then, reveals a different side to the story. Some of the issues that Leidner (1993: 199) identified as being 'incongruent with manliness' at McDonalds, such as an having to adopt an ingratiating manner, taking orders and holding one's tongue simply do not hold true for the 'lost boys'. Similarly, where Leidner found that managers and trainers at Combined Insurance re-framed typically female jobs to concentrate on qualities that allowed their male agents to consider their work as manly, such a construction was not necessary for these workers. There were times where the young men did admit to preferring to do physical work, but this was not at the expense of serving or selling. Their main gripe instead was the constrictions imposed by the required pace of getting the customer through the till and engaging in the scripted dialogue that supplements the task.

This variation in the importance of constructing masculinity at work may be related to age. It could be argued, therefore, that contemporary young men who work in service-based jobs do not necessarily deem work to be an essential site of the construction of masculinity in the way that was so apparent in studies by Willis (1977) and Sennett and Cobb (1972). This is, perhaps, a little controversial, but it is essential that we theorize this emerging difference. The facts are clear – manufacturing, mining and other traditional men's job have declined and been replaced by an increasing service sector over the last three decades. The current generation of 'lost boys', then, are working in industry sectors that employ the majority of workers, and retail in particular is a huge employer of young men as well as young women. The point of reference for these young men in regards to what a suitable job looks like, what it entails, has changed. Although the findings need to be treated tentatively, the responses here seem to verify this. Retail is seen as an acceptable job to these young men and one that is deemed, rightly or wrongly, to have the potential for upward career progression.

REFERENCES

Alheit, P. (1994) *Taking the Knocks: Youth Unemployment and Biography – A Qualitative Analysis*. Cassell: London.

Arnett, J.J. (2000) 'Emerging adulthood: a theory of development from the late teens through the twenties', *American Psychologist* , 55: 469–480.

Arulampalam, W. and Booth, A.L. (1998) 'Training and labour market flexibility: is there a trade off?', *British Journal of Industrial Relations*, 36(4): 521–536.

Bentley, T. and Gurumurthy, R. (1999) *Destination Unknown: Engaging with the Problem of Marginalised Youth*. London: Demos.

Broadbridge, A. (2007a) 'Editorial', *International Journal of Retail and Distribution Management*, 35(12).

Broadbridge, A. (2007b) 'Dominated by women: managed by men? The career development process of retail managers', *International Journal of Retail and Distribution Management*, 35(12): 956–974.

Bynner, J. (2005) 'Rethinking the youth phase of the life-course: the case for emerging adulthood?', *Journal of Youth Studies*, 8(4), December 2005: 367–384.

Canny, A. (2001) 'The transition from school to work: an Irish and English comparison', *Journal of Youth Studies*, 4(2): 133–154.

CIPD (2009) 'Graduates choose retail over city', *People Management*, 28th August 2009, Chartered Institute of Personnel and Development.

Crompton and Lyonette (2005) 'The new gender essentialism – domestic and family 'choices' and their relation to attitudes', *British Journal of Sociology*, 56(4): 601–620.

Devadason, R. (2008) 'To plan or not to plan? Young adult future orientations in two European cities', *Sociology*, 42(6): 1127–1145.

Elias, P. and Purcell, K. (2003) 'Measuring change in the graduate labour market', *Researching Graduate Careers Seven Years On*, Working Paper no. 1, University of Warwick.

EOC (2003) *Facts about Women and Men in Britain*. Manchester: Equal Opportunities Commission

Fenton, S. and Dermott, E. (2006) 'Fragmented careers? Winners and losers in young adult labour markets', *Work, Employment and Society*, 20(2): 205–221.

Foster, C., Whysall, P. and Harris, L. (2007) 'Female career progression in retailing', *International Journal of Retail and Distribution Management*, 35(12): 975–981.

Fuller, A. and Unwin, L. (2002) 'Developing pedagogies for the contemporary workplace', in K. Evans, P. Hodkinson and L. Unwin (eds) *Working to Learn*. London: Kogan Page.

Furlong, A. and Cartmel, F. (2004) *Vulnerable Young Men in Fragile Labour Markets: Employment, Unemployment and the Search for Long-term Security*. York: Joseph Rowntree Foundation.

Furlong, A. and Cartmel, F. (2007) *Young People and Social Change*, 2nd Edition. Maidenhead: Open University Press.

Gallie, D. and Paugam, S. (2002) *Social Precarity and Social Integration: Report for the European Commission Based on Eurobarometer 56.1*. Brussels: European Commission.

▶

►

Hakim, C. (2000) *Work Life-style Choices in the 21st Century.* Oxford University Press.

Harris, F. and Church, C. (2002) 'An assessment of skills needs in retail and related industries: May 2002', *Skills Dialogue Retail* 27-05-2002. London: Business Strategies.

HM Treasury (2004) 'Skills in the global economy', in *Pre-Budget Report*, December 2004, HMSO.

Hodkinson, P. and Bloomer, M. (2002) 'Learning careers: conceptualising lifelong work-based learning', in K. Evans, P. Hodkinson and L.Unwin (eds) *Working to Learn*, London: Kogan Page.

James, L. (2008) 'United by gender or divided by class? Women's work orientations and labour market behaviour', *Gender, Work and Organization*, 15(4): 394–412.

Keep, E. (2000) 'Learning organisations, lifelong learning and the mystery of vanishing employers', SKOPE Research Paper No. 8, Oxford and Warwick Universities.

Kirton, G. (2009) 'Career plans and aspirations of recent black and minority ethnic business graduates', *Work Employment and Society*, 23(1): 12–29.

Lehmann, W. (2004) '"For Some Reason, I Get a Little Scared": Structure, Agency, and Risk in School-Work Transitions', *Journal of Youth Studies, 7*(4): 379–396.

Leidner, R. (1993) *Fast Food, Fast Talk: Service Work and the Routinizations of Everyday Life.* Berkeley and Los Angeles: University of California Press.

Lindsay, C. and McQuaid, R.W. (2004) 'Avoiding the 'McJobs': unemployed job seekers and attitudes to service work', *Work Employment and Society*, 18(2): 297–319.

Maguire, S., Huddleston, P., Thompson, J. and Hirst, C. (2008) 'Young People in Jobs Without Training', ESRC Research Report June 2008, Centre for Education and Industry, Warwick University.

Mason, G. and Osborne, M. (2008) 'Business strategies, work organisation and low pay in United Kingdom retailing', in C. Lloyd, G. Mason, and K. Mayhew (eds) *Low Wage Work in the United Kingdom.* New York: Russell Sage Foundation, Chapter 4, pp. 131–168.

McDowell, L. (2003) *Redundant Masculinities? Employment Change and White Working Class Youth.* London: Blackwell.

Newman, K.S. (1999) *No Shame in My Game: The Working Poor in the Inner City.* New York: Russell Sage Foundation.

Nixon, D. (2009) 'I Can't put a smiley face on': working-class masculinity, emotional labour and service work in the 'new economy', *Gender Work and Organization*, 16(3): 300–322.

NUS (2008) *NUS Student Experience Report, 2008*, National Union of Students.

Pfau-Effinger, B. (2004) *Development of Culture, Welfare States and Women's Employment in Europe.* Surrey: Ashgate.

Quinn, J., Lawy, R. and Diment, K. (2008) 'Young People in Jobs without Training: Not just dead end kids in dead end jobs', Final Report, South West Observatory for Skills and Learning: University of Exeter.

►

▶

Recruiter (2009) 'Retail: graduates attracted by career variety', *Recruiter* (online) http://www.recruiter.co.uk/retail-graduates-attracted-by-career-variety/1000847.article (accessed 5th February 2010).

Roberts, K. (1995) *Youth and Unemployment in Modern Britain*. Oxford: Oxford University Press.

Sennett, R. and Cobb, J. (1972) *The Hidden Injuries of Class*. New York: Vintage Books.

Skillsmart (2007) 'Sector Skills Agreement, Stage One: Assessment of Current and Future Skills Needs', Skillsmart Retail, (online) http://www.skillsmartretail.com/pdfs/stage_one_report_skills_needs_assessment_final1.pdf (accessed 18th September 2008).

Taylor, A. (2008) ' "You have to have it in your nature": understanding the trajectories of youth apprentices', *Journal of Youth Studies*, 11(4): 393–411.

Talwar, J.P. (2002) *Fast Food, Fast Track: Immigrants, Big Business and the American Dream*. Boulder, CA: Westview.

Terkel, S. (1974) *Working*. New York: Pantheon.

Vickerstaff, S. (2007) ' "I was just the boy around the place": what made apprenticeships successful?', *Journal of Vocational Education and Training*, 59(3): 331–347.

Wallace, C. (1987) *for Richer, for Poorer: Growing Up in and Out of Work*. London: Tavistock.

Warhurst, C. and Nickson, D. (2007) 'Employee experience of aesthetic labour in retail and hospitality', *Work, Employment and Society*, 21(1): 103–120.

Wheeler, I. (2006) 'A qualified and trained workforce?: An analysis of Labour Force Survey data on levels of qualifications and training amongst those working in the retail sector' , research report for Skillsmart Retail.

Willis, P. (1977) *Learning to Labour: How Working Class Kids Get Working Class Jobs*. Farnborough: Saxon House.

Avoiding the 'Trap': Discursive Framing as a Means of Coping with Working Poverty

8

Laura K. Jordan

Introduction

The twin processes of deindustrialization and growing consumerism have brought retail to the fore of the US blue-collar jobs economy, eclipsing manufacturing as the defining sector. Nowhere is this fact more readily observable than in the American Midwest, where retail jobs have helped to fill at least part of the void left by the exodus of factory work.

This chapter draws on ethnographic and interview-based research conducted in 2009–2010 amongst workers at Hometown Market,[1] a prominent Midwestern hypermarket chain. It will begin by considering some of the ramifications that the shift from manufacturing to retail has for the so-called 'unskilled' jobs economy (Kusterer, 1978), and will then introduce the methodology and locus of the study. While retail jobs are typically portrayed in the literature as fundamentally part-time, low-wage and dead-end, this research indicates that this correlation is not inherent. The following section will therefore take a look at Hometown and its relatively recent move away from full-time, living-wage, career-material jobs and towards the lower-quality employment model that is more typically associated with retail. Ultimately, I argue that the job-market's shift from production to retail, coupled with the trend within retail towards a more flexible work-force, is creating a downward spiral for blue-collar employment in which retail is increasingly becoming a source of low-quality jobs that workers approach as temporary, wary of the danger of getting 'trapped' in them for the long term.

The transformation of the blue-collar jobscape

My father was one of your typical GM workers. (Pete, full-time, 22 years at Hometown)

My dad worked for GM for, like, ever … . He originally started out painting trucks, like right over here [pointing across the street], then he switched to watching a robot paint the trucks. (Wayne, part-time, ten years)

Michigan, where this study takes place – the heart of the so-called Midwestern 'rust belt' – is a particularly interesting context in which to study retail jobs, because it is a state whose economy has historically depended very heavily on manufacturing (Florida, 1996). From its zenith in 1979 until 2010, the absolute number of manufacturing jobs in the US has diminished by almost half, falling to 1941 levels (see Figure 8.1). Yet whereas from 1941 to 1979 manufacturing consistently represented about 20% of all U.S. jobs, by 2010 that proportion had fallen to only 8.2 per cent (US Bureau of Labor Statistics, 2010b; c).

At the same time, by 2008, 'retail salespersons' had become the single most populous occupational category in the US[2] (US Bureau of Labor Statistics, 2010a). The number of Americans working as salespersons, cashiers and stock clerks was comparable to the number in all production-related fields combined – including everything from butchers and bakers to lathe operators (US Bureau of Labor Statistics, 2010e). From a nation of producers, it is fair to say that the US had become a 'society of consumers' served by a nation of retail workers (Bauman, 2007: 52).

The job-market's shift in orientation from manufacturing to retail has several ramifications that are particularly relevant for a study situated in a region so traditionally dependent on industrial jobs as the American Midwest. First, it signals a significant rearrangement of the economic relationship between people and commodities: from production to consumption. No longer is *making* things the primary American activity; now the economic mainstage centres more precisely on the task of whetting and satisfying appetites for fashionable and economical goods (Baudrillard, 1981: 50; Shell, 2009), a task that primarily corresponds to retailers.

Of course, retail employees are themselves consumers. The young retail workers that Victoria Malkin (2004) observed in New York tended to value their job largely as a function of its capacity to fund self-expression through the consumption of fashionable stuff. In my own research I have found that for those workers who do not depend on the job for their 'bread and butter', retail work can indeed represent a practical way to fund 'extras': a teenager's

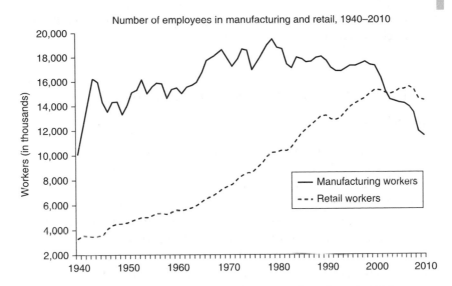

Figure 8.1   Number of employees in manufacturing and retail, 1940–2010

Note: While manufacturing jobs in the US have been in decline since 1979, retail employment has increased steadily throughout the last 70 years.

Source: (US Bureau of Labor Statistics, 2010c; f).

car, a retiree's trips to Arizona, a housewife's love of make-up. Yet a view of retail work as essentially a gateway to consumption of luxurious 'extras' fails to account for the legions of working poor in retail who do struggle on a bread-and-butter level.

The job prospects of blue-collar Michigan workers entering the labour market since the late 1980s have been radically affected by deindustrialization. For them, hourly-paid retail occupies the same crucial category that for previous generations was exemplified by entry-level manufacturing: it is a job that anyone can apply for, regardless of vocational or educational attainment. The checkout lane has thus succeeded the assembly line as the archetypal 'go-to' job for workers who may or may not come to the job-search with a certificate, diploma, or degree in hand.

Unfortunately for these workers, nonsupervisory retail work in the US pays an average of only 52 cents on the dollar of what nonsupervisory manufacturing did (U.S. Bureau of Labor Statistics, 2010c; f). When retail jobs become the only ones available, and when the pay and quality of those jobs goes down, this can create problems for workers who find themselves stuck in a job 'that may well be viewed as a long-term trap' (Kazis & Miller, 2001, 70). The remainder of this chapter will therefore consider how in one particular instance these changes have affected real workers' lives, and how these workers have sought to cope with increasingly adverse conditions, to improve clarity and flow.

The case of Hometown Market, Inc.

Methodology

With management's permission and my co-workers' foreknowledge, from December 2009 to March 2010, I worked as an hourly paid retail clerk at a Hometown Market store in Michigan for the purpose of research. This chapter incorporates insights from observations and informal conversations recorded in fieldnotes during this period, as well as from transcripts and notes from interviews with 36 retail workers, including 21 Hometown employees. Table 8.1 provides a summary profile of the Hometown workers interviewed.

Hometown Market, Inc. was an American discount hypermarket that originated as a small-town mom-and-pop store, and grew during the 1960s superstore boom that also saw the founding of many other major hypermarket chains, including Walmart, Target, Meijer, Kmart and Carrefour. Their stores sold everything from produce and prescription drugs to windshield wipers and potting soil, and each employed upwards of 800 workers.

While retail tends to be popularly characterized as a classic job for students or for women seeking to balance work with family obligations, the Hometown workforce did not reflect this stereotype. Many students did work at Hometown, but they did not represent a significant percentage of its labour force; in fact, while 3 of the 16 employees in my department were recent college graduates, none were actual students. For the most part, Hometown workers tended to range in age from their late 20s to early 60s. The same

Table 8.1 Classification, number and status of Hometown interviewees

Salaried		
Middle management	1	Full-time
Lower management	1	Full-time
Hourly		
General Merchandise	9	Part-time
Fashion	4	Part-time
Service	2	Part-time
Stocking Crew	1	Full-time
Media	1	Full-time
Produce	1	Full-time
Cashier	1	Part-time

held true for the 'housewife' cliché: only one worker in my department could be classified as such. Rather, Hometown workers' incomes went to support a variety of family arrangements, including single people living with their parents or on their own (with or without children), male and female heads of families, divorcées trying to make it on their own, retirees and others.

Whereas much literature to date has focused particularly closely on Walmart (Bernstein and Bivens, 2006; Ehrenreich, 2002; Fishman, 2006; Greenwald, 2005; Lichtenstein, 2006; 2010; Pierce, 2006) – and deservedly so, for that chain's impact has been enormous – Hometown presents a particularly interesting counterpoint for two reasons. First, Hometown is one of the few retailers that are (and have always been) unionized, as will presently be discussed in greater depth. Second, Hometown's history parallels Walmart's in an interesting way: both trace their origins to a frugal and beloved patriarch who nursed a small shop in the American heartland into a corporate empire. Both companies had recently seen their beloved patriarchs exit from the management of corporate affairs, albeit for different reasons. And both companies, in the wake of their respective founders' exits, embarked upon organizational change in ways that seemed detrimental to workers' interests, and – in veteran workers' perspectives – were widely interpreted as running counter to the spirit and wishes of the founder.

Hometown's principal point of interest as an object of study, however, lies in the fact that it both challenges the common assumption that retail cannot be a source of good jobs, and underscores the problematic nature of the 'race to the bottom' that is currently undermining job quality in that sector. While the literature often uncritically equates retail with part-time, low-wage, dead-end employment, my research indicates that this connection is not inherent. Hometown jobs used to offer workers good wages, good benefits, plentiful hours, their choice of full- or part-time status, and opportunities for career advancement – positive attributes that have all been undermined in the last decade. The following sections will describe the recent degradation of job quality at Hometown, and consider some ways in which workers have sought to cope.

The way Hometown 'used to be'

> [Hometown] used to be such a wonderful place to work. (Lena, full-time, 20 years)

Traditionally, Hometown was not your average big-box retailer. It was (and still is) a union shop, making it a statistical rarity: only 5.9 per cent of retail workers in the US have union representation.[3] The presence of the union meant several things for workers. First of all, under a union system, most privileges within the department – from choice of weekly schedule to dibs on full-time status – were conferred on the basis of seniority. Everyone knew everyone else's place in the pecking order, because that order was prominently displayed on the weekly schedule. The 'seniority-first' rule left little room for managerial favouritism in decisions about scheduling and other contentious matters, and thus Hometown managed to avoid some of the clientelism and bad blood that interviewees in other chains reported. And indeed, in the opinion of most Hometown informants, the relations between co-workers at the store tended to be harmonious. As James, a full-time department manager of 24 years put it,

> This store has always been really – everybody kind of watches [over] everybody, takes and keeps – you know – not back-stabbing like other stores that may be around here.

A second way in which work at Hometown traditionally differed from non-union retailers was job security. Under the union model, management did not have the right to fire anybody without clear and just cause, while employees had recourse to union representation and the grievance process if they felt they had been wronged. Some workers resented what they saw as a green light for lazy or irresponsible co-workers to 'get away with murder'. Others expressed appreciation for the peace of mind that came with knowing that their job could not be threatened unless they had done something to deserve it. One Hometown worker expressed an appreciation of union-based job security by contrasting his situation with that of a friend who worked at Walmart:

> When they don't have a union to protect them – the one lady that's a friend of mine, she has like 11 years, and she says there was another lady had eighteen, and another lady had like *twenty*, and [Walmart] let them [the latter two] go. And so she said, 'My eleven years don't mean *anything* if they're letting them go with eighteen or twenty.' (Pete, full-time, 22 years)

In sum, while the union's protection has its downsides, traditionally the inability of salaried managers to easily fire hourly employees at Hometown translated into a great deal of job security for the latter, and supported a more balanced power relationship between the two groups.

A third way in which the union shaped the experience of work at Hometown was through the contract, which was re-negotiated at least once every five years. One of the most important items in the contract were the hourly wage-scales, which progressed through a series of 'steps' that varied depending on the job. Each step represented a certain number of hours worked, and was tied to a small raise. The final step was known as the 'wage ceiling'. Ceiling wages at Hometown in the early 1980s often surpassed $30 an hour in 2010 dollars – an amount unheard of nowadays, when three quarters of employees in my department were 'topped out' at an average wage ceiling of $10.00 an hour. In the past, workers valued the meaningful progression toward a high wage as a tangible token of the company's appreciation of their experience, as an offset to inflation, and as material motivation to stay on for the long term. Indeed, in accordance with Ahmed and Wilder's (Ahmed & Wilder, 1995) findings that wages tend to be the primary determinant of turnover in retail, the long-time employees that I interviewed all recalled that high wages were an important part of what used to make the job 'too good to quit'.

Traditionally (but no longer in 2010), work at Hometown was based on a fifty-fifty ratio of part-time to full-time labour. The full-timers were primarily adults with seniority who had a long-term vision of their future at the store. In the past, this 'core' group was complemented by the part-timers, predominantly high school and college students, who were just 'passing through' (Kazis and Miller, 2001). Because full-time positions were an integral part of the work-structure, part-timers who were interested in becoming full-timers could be assured that opportunities would be available, should they stick around. In the meantime, part-timers interested in working more hours could easily find them, for as one of my co-workers said, in those days 'they gave out hours like candy' (Wayne).

In addition to plentiful hours and opportunities for full-time status, Hometown also traditionally offered its employees good prospects for career advancement, thanks to its large managerial staff. The abundance of managerial positions meant that ambitious hourly paid workers could reasonably aspire to promotion, which brought with it a guaranteed yearly salary with bonuses and periodic raises. The availability of both full-time and management positions made Hometown a good place for new hires to settle in for the long term.

Historically, it was not uncommon for workers to come to Hometown for the job, but stay for the health insurance. Indeed, access to health insurance has long been a prized thing in the US, and at the time of writing,[4] few part-time jobs offer this (Farber and Levy, 2000). But the benefits did not stop there. After completing their first year, Hometown employees were also eligible to enrol in a pension savings and investment plan, something that very few retailers offered. Together, these benefits made Hometown a practicable and attractive place for workers – even part-timers – to stay for the long-term. Lena's experience is a classic example:

> I got a divorce in 1988, I think that's about when it was. Had a job in a video store, and I wanted to go to school. And my boss said, 'You can't

go to school and be a manager at this video store.' So I quit the job at the video store, and got another job working in a cleaner's, and I went back to school. Well, the job didn't work out, so – I didn't have any health insurance benefits, so I applied here. And – *again*, this is the thing. Health insurance. They hired me *here*. I had *health insurance*. My parents were very relieved. And all of that's – that's how it is. So! I ah, I ended up staying here and workin' and goin' to school, and taking care of everybody and everything, and finally I said, 'I quit school. I'm gonna take my degree and go home.' I stayed *here*. It's a job; it's money. You know. Gotta be stupid to walk away from a job with health insurance. You're noticing that that's a big thing, isn't it? (Lena, full-time, 20 years; original emphasis)

Hometown jobs have traditionally offered a confluence of four necessary elements for building a career: opportunities for career advancement, good wages, a harmonious work environment and medical benefits. Because these characteristics made the job an attractive place to stay for the long term, it was fairly typical for new workers who initially came to Hometown for a 'temporary' stint to end up staying, becoming full-time, and having a twenty-plus year career at the store. However, unfortunately for Hometown workers, the end of the twentieth century would see an end not only to many of the attractive features of their jobs, but also to much of the viable alternative work in the area, effectively trapping them in declining wages and prospects for the future.

Cost-cutting and the decline of job quality

It's a big retail war that's ongoing right now, ... and it's like, you know, may the strongest survive. ... And if that means cutting hours, cutting back on personnel, and stuff like that, in order to be able to survive, then I think that's the thing that I've really been noticing as of the last three years. (Pete, full-time, 22 years)

Since the 1990s, Hometown's leadership had been engaged in a steady campaign to cut costs, partly as a response to trends in the US economy. Between 1996 and 2008, Americans' discretionary spending fell noticeably, which meant less business for retailers such as Hometown (US Bureau of Labor Statistics, 1996; 2008).

While Hometown's market was shrinking, competition was growing. Between 1994 and 2002, the local metropolitan area in which I carried out my study went from having three Hometowns and no Walmarts to having three Hometowns and three Walmarts (Yau, 2010). A similar story was unfolding throughout the company's territory. This, coupled with the rise of internet shopping, meant that the company was facing an unprecedented amount of competition from non-union sources. Hometown saw Walmart-style cost-cutting as the solution, and the union – limited by a no-strike agreement – was unable to prevent Hometown's subsumption into the 'Walmart effect'[5] (Fishman, 2006).

A third factor that may have contributed to the company's new direction was the leadership itself. Control of the company was passed on to the founder's children, who, according to the workers, lack their father's commitment to the company:

> You know, I don't think too much around the top, 'cause I just concentrate on what I've gotta do pretty much . ... But, um, the [founder's] kids have other things goin' on. Like I think one owns a winery, you know, one's in – so, you know, they've got things out there. I'm not sure that they're gonna wanna stay with [the retail business]. I don't know. They've got other sides – you know, other things to keep 'em busy. (Wendy, full-time, 24 years, department manager)

As a result, many employees felt that the heirs approached the push for efficiency with insufficient mindfulness of the impact that it would have on the workers and on customer service. As Pete commented about the point of customer service,

> [Since the cutbacks] there's maybe one person covering two departments. ... It's nothing new, because a lot of companies have been doing the same thing. I'm pretty sure you've been in different retailers [as a customer], with you being out there, and you're saying, 'Okay, I'm used to this. So I can't find anybody [to help me], so I'm gonna look for [the item I need] for myself.'

In the fall of 2003, Hometown laid off 15 per cent of its white-collar workforce; soon after, in early 2004, it announced the layoff of 2,000 more shop floor managers. My colleague Wayne recalled that the layoffs did not all happen at once, but gradually. As managers were offered severance packages, departments were combined until eventually a third of the store's floor space – containing products ranging from lipstick and windshield wipers to live fish and shrubbery – had administratively become one big department.

In all, about a third of the store's management positions were eliminated in the so-called 'shake-up', and those who remained saw their pay cut. One department manager related his experience of the turbulent period:

> You know, the hardest thing is, when they restructured, and cut a lot of management out, I went from, you know, [48 hours] to 40 hours, which

took like sixteen percent of my pay away. And at the same time, my wife had *lost* her job here. So yeah, there was a lot of stress – but at least I still had one [*laughs*]! (James, full-time, 24 years)

Once management positions became scarce, the backlog of aspirants meant that promotion was no longer a realistic option for most hourly paid clerks. Nevertheless, these long odds did not stop at least a third of the workers in my department from signing up to be considered, should a position become available.

Besides management, another casualty of the efficiency campaign was full-time status. As full-timers retired or left, their positions no longer got offered to the most. As a result, most areas of the store saw the number of full-timers dwindle, with many down to the last one. Taken together, the elimination of both management and full-time positions sealed off what used to be viable career paths. This dealt a great blow to the store's under-employed part-timers, who found themselves in what amounted to dead-end jobs.

As opportunities for career advancement vanished, workers also saw over-time[6] disappear and their hours slashed:

At the same time [as they were combining departments] they'd always, it seemed like, get rid of hours ... . Say *this* department has 40 hours, and *this* department has 40 hours. They would combine them, and the total of hours would only be 70 instead of 80. Ya know? So it seemed like they'd get rid of managers, then combine everything together, then cut the hours down ... [Then, as hourly workers quit,] I would say like for every four that were gone, they might try to hire one back in. (Wayne, part-time, ten years)

Yeah, the hours. Everybody's getting hours cut. Or *have* had their hours cut. And the only reason I get hours is because I'm full time, which is a blessing in disguise for me ... . If I went part time, they'd probably cut me down to 23 hours. (Lena, full-time, 20 years)

According to one former manager, the company used a lot of pressure and positive reinforcement to get managers to cut working hours down to a minimum:

Back when I was in management, one of the things they're more inter-ested in is man-hours: use the least amount of man-hours, that got you a pat on the back. Okay? Didn't matter how much money you were mak-ing [for the store]. But see, they were already thinking of the changing-process. Prime example, is the pet peeve with me, but they had a manager morning meeting, and they stood up in front of everybody. This one person made lots and lots of money [for the company]. She was really good at what she was doing, [but] she didn't get the praise. This *other* lady who used less man-hours but was $2,000 in the hole, they applauded her, because she used less man-hours. If you think about it, what they were trying to weed down was the fact that, 'We want to make money, but we want to make money with the least amount of hours.' (David, full-time, 23 years)

Just as the elimination of full-time and managerial positions severely limited underemployed part-timers' prospects for building a future in the store, the cutback in hours reduced their capacity to make a living in the present.

The reduction in working hours was not the only way in which the company sought to bring down the cost of labour. When a new labour contract was adopted in 2007, wages themselves took a hit. One aspect in particular that negatively affected compensation was a disparity in wage-scale structures between new-hire and old-hire workers. Because senior members were responsible for contract negotiations, the interests of those less senior were neglected   resulting in a deteriorated wage for newer generations of workers.

Another way in which Hometown wages took a hit in the 2007 contract was through inflation. In terms of brute dollars and cents, the average starting- and ceiling-wages of the 2007 contract appeared to enjoy a small increase over 2001 levels – of 7¢ and 48¢, respectively, – to $7.70 and $12.03 an hour. Yet when those figures are adjusted for inflation, under the 2007 contract, *real* starting- and ceiling-wages actually experienced a $1.26 and $1.53 per-hour drop, respectively – a loss of 12.7 per cent to 16.4 per cent of gross real income. The fall in real wages at Hometown between 2001 and 2007 is further illustrated when compared to the minimum wage. Over this period, the minimum wage in Michigan rose from $5.15 to $7.40. While the 2001 average Hometown starting wage stood a generous $2.28 above the minimum hourly wage, in 2007 it was only 30¢ above the minimum. Thus in many respects, the 2007 contract represented a significant erosion of hourly wages for Hometown workers.

Real wages fell, hours were cut and positions were eliminated, so that workers were stretched thinly over wider areas of the store. 350 employees were now tasked with servicing supercentres that were normally staffed by 850. General Merchandise employees might be simultaneously expected to greet everyone they passed, tend to customers that sought their attention both in person and over the portable phone they carried, keep up with their hourly 'returns' (the task of re-shelving returned and discarded items that belonged in their area), straighten all their shelves, price and stock merchandise, 'run' trash and cardboard from the back room to the compactor, clean up customer spills and messes, and cover for co-workers on breaks. While on slow days the steady stream of activity could be welcome, on busy days, it was not unusual for many (or even all) of these responsibilities to clamour for a worker's attention at the same time. During an interview, the irony of the situation was not lost on my co-worker Winston. Having recently witnessed Jerry, the department's only remaining full-timer, carrying five phones as he covered five departments, Winston asked rhetorically, 'What are you going to do with five phones?! You only have two ears.' You *can't* do it, he said; so you have to laugh. And indeed, refusing to take an impossible task seriously was one way that many workers routinely coped with the overwork of understaffing.

By obliging workers to cover a larger area of the store on their shifts at no extra pay, by weakening the wage-scale for incoming workers and by cutting real wages, Hometown managed to significantly reduce employee compensation. A part-time clerk who earned top wage and consistently worked 31.5 hours a week could take home up to $10,830 annually[7] – the federal poverty level for a single individual (Housing Works 2010). My co-worker Lena managed to support herself on her full-time wages, but said, 'I have no cushion;' life was paycheck-to-paycheck.

If earning a living at Hometown had become financially difficult for full-timers, it was impossible for part-timers. *All* of the part-timers at Hometown that I interviewed, and many full-timers, supplemented their wages with other sources of income. These might be government benefits, factory pensions, a partner's salary or alimony, parental support, a small business of their own, or a second job. Those who tried to manage, even on full-time wages, without other income sources were either barely staying afloat or in financial difficulties. Clearly, the level of pay available to workers became insufficient.

The push towards efficiency eliminated many of the things people valued most about their jobs, which in turn has had an alienating effect at the workplace. My colleague David, a full-timer of 23 years, explained:

[It's] the human element, I think. One time ... a person working felt like they were more important. Now it's more like a company, so the little guy doesn't feel as important ... . It's not the home-spun feel [anymore].

David's metaphor effectively underscores the negative impact that the so-called 'streamlining' has had on workers' feelings of connectedness to each other and to the workplace. As departments were shuffled around, positions and opportunities eliminated, and compensation cut, workers came to feel that 'the human element' had all but disappeared from workplace relations, and its place had been filled by 'the bottom line'.

A disturbing example of this was the pervasive conviction amongst highest-seniority workers who had 'topped out' the wage scale that instead of valuing their experience and expertise, the company would prefer to have them gone. Wayne explained why:

> [It's] because I'm topped out, I get health insurance, and I have three weeks' paid vacation and four personal days, paid. So if they can get rid of me, they can hire in another person, give them the same number of hours as me, pay him just over seven dollars an hour instead of just over ten dollars an hour, he won't have insurance, he won't have vacation, [and] he won't have personal days, so [they'll] never have to pay him for doing nothing.

These workers all perceived a definite change in the content of *what* the company valued. Whereas before the efficiency campaign the company had been willing to pay for experienced employees who had the expertise necessary to provide good customer service, after it preferred to save money with a high-turnover, part-time workforce. When experience becomes a liability, it can have a terrible effect on morale. Indeed, as Wayne recalled, 'people just got fed up with it, and a lot of people left.'

While many did leave to seek greener pastures (such as Home Depot or the armed forces), many stayed. Yet for the most part, these did not do so because they hoped to make a future there. One person I interviewed did indeed describe his job at Hometown as the answer to his prayers, but almost everyone else would have rather been somewhere else – ranging from Walmart to Florida. Despite this, people had different reasons for staying, which partly depended on their reason for working part-time. As Patrick Bollé notes, 'There is a fundamental distinction to be made between voluntary and involuntary part-time employment: whether people deliberately choose to work part time or accept reduced hours of work simply because they cannot find full-time employment' (Bollé, 2001: 220). Some of my interviewees were retirees, high schoolers, or spouses of professionals looking to earn some extra cash. Others were college students living at home and paying their own way through school. Yet many were actually trying to make a living. Why did *they* stay?

While reasons varied, after the efficiency-push, a Hometown job still offered workers a much-coveted boon: access to health insurance. Many workers reported that the *only* reason they continued to work at Hometown was because they could not afford to lose that insurance. But coverage did not come cheaply. Part-time employees who bought it through the company paid slightly over $50 a week for individual coverage; this could work out to a third of gross pay for employees at the lower end of the wage scale. Plans covering spouse and children were only available to full-timers, so the families of part-timers who were household breadwinners had to rely on Medicaid.[8] In addition, all incoming part-time employees had to wait six months before they were eligible for medical coverage. This is consistent with Farber and Levy's conclusion that private-sector employers 'are restricting access to health insurance by their peripheral short-term and part-time employees, so that the quality of core and peripheral jobs in this dimension is diverging' (Farber and Levy, 2000: 114).

In sum, since the late 1990s Hometown has experimented with various cost-cutting measures, including the phasing out of full-time positions, managerial layoffs and departmental amalgamations. This, together with a systematic cut in staff-hours, greatly diminished the opportunities for career advancement and intensified work, without giving workers any more pay for the additional responsibilities. On the contrary, as has been shown, real wages actually declined. In response to this, many workers quit. Many others, however, stayed. It is to them that this text will now turn its attention.

Facing the 'trap'

> I actually didn't even plan on plan on staying here this long, but ... it's hard to save up money when you hardly get any. (Sandra, part-time, three years)

> If you told me when I hired in that I would be there for ten years, I wouldn't believe you. But the people that have been there longer have so much more invested in it .... I didn't have my insurance through there for a long time, and didn't want to ... because I didn't want to feel like I was trapped. (Wayne, part-time, ten years)

The literature has conceptualized the notion of the 'trap' in low-status employment in two different ways. The first considers it to be a situation in which the low-wage job itself damages workers' possibilities for obtaining higher-paying work later in life (Cappellari, 2000; Dickens, 2000; Smith and Vavrichek, 1992). In this scenario, the stigma and lack of qualifications associated with low-wage work may frustrate workers' prospects for mobility into a better-paying sector. The 'mobility trap' is thus the likelihood that once one has gotten into low-wage work, one may not be able to get out. This instance resonates with the experience of my friend Ginny, a college-educated part-timer in Fashion who had been unable to find employment in her field after being laid off from her job at a hospital. While for her a Hometown job was exclusively a stopgap measure intended to provide income while she looked for another job, over time she began to despair that the longer she worked in retail, the more unattractive her résumé was becoming to prospective employers. As much as it despaired her, eventually she began to entertain the notion that perhaps she was indeed stuck there, and might remain in retail for the rest of her working life.

Part-time work may also prove a trap because a worker who is willing and able to work a full-time position cannot find one, and so has 'settled' for part-time (Bollé, 2001). The 'part-time trap' thus describes the frustration of having no choice but to work only 'half the job' (Tilly, 1996). Although both of these conceptualizations describe important phenomena affecting a significant number of Hometown workers, the state of being 'trapped' that most of my interviewees spoke of is closer to the second sense of the word.

However, the picture that emerges from their narrations is slightly 'messier' (Law, 2004) than the phenomenon that Bollé describes. He writes, 'From the worker's point of view, part-time employment can fulfil two main functions: ... [It] can facilitate entry into – or exit from – the labour market. It can [also] help workers reconcile employment with family, social and civic responsibilities' (Bollé, 2001: 226, 215). In almost all other cases, he argues, part-time work is involuntary, and therefore a trap (in his sense of the word). This may be true in many workplaces, but as has been demonstrated, before the push for efficiency, part-time jobs at Hometown were slightly different: through the seniority system, they could provide even involuntary part-timers with an appealing place to stay, a path into full time – in sum, a career. Thus it is fair to say that whilst few come to Hometown – or indeed any retailer (see Huddleston this volume) – with the intention of making a lifelong career, once there, many did choose to do just that.

Yet as this chapter has shown, that changed: wages went down, the possibilities for promotion and full time all but disappeared, hours were cut, and benefits remained as the only redeeming feature. It became a bad job, where the most workers could aspire to was to support themselves at the poverty line – if they were willing to wait several years to top out the wage scale. Hometown jobs, especially for new hires, virtually condemned a worker to reliance on the support of government, family or a second (or third) job – in other words, to poverty.

Speaking of class

For the working poor in the US, the economic problem of poverty is aggravated by the social stigma that surrounds it. As Sandra Morgen notes, neoliberal ideology casts poverty and reliance on others as a problem with moral roots, and 'devolves and privatizes the responsibility for support of poor families to those families themselves' (Morgen, 2001: 748). In light of the success that this ideology has had in placing a cultural premium on the notion of self-sufficiency, in the US it is widely seen as shameful for an able-bodied adult to rely on the government or family for material support.[9] In this way, chronically underemployed individuals may suffer doubly: not only from poverty itself, but also from stigma.

And indeed, some of the workers I interviewed readily identified and expressed pity for the poverty of those working around them:

> [People here are] even [below] poverty-level, I would say. 'Cause a lot of the young girls, cashiers, probably get food stamps, and stuff like that. And a lot of them have kids, *little* kids. Babies. Yeah. I've seen that. (Lena, full-time, 20 years)

> A lot of them have two jobs. I guess they can't make it on the wages. (Rafael, part-time, two years)

Yet when it came to the first person, there was no identification with the poverty of the wages. Instead, first-person narratives tended to project quite a different class identification:

> Most of us are middle class, here. (Lena)

> [I come from a] middle-class area. (Winston, part-time, ten years)

Initially this might appear to be a startling oxymoron. How can workers earning poverty wages claim to be 'middle class'? AFL-CIO[10] president Richard Trumka describes the American 'middle class' in this way:

> You're middle class … if you depend on your own personal skills to make a living. And, if you work hard, if you play by the rules, then you deserve a chance to own your own home, have a nice car, send your kids to college, and feel you've achieved something in this life. (quoted in Greenberg, 1996 [1995]: 322)

While his conceptualization invokes the notion of fairness by arguing that those who work hard *ought* to be able to materially support themselves and their family (and allow them to live the 'American dream' of self-sufficiency), it does little to clarify the ambiguity that appears to surround the term. One author exemplified this ambiguity in his very struggle to define it:

> The term 'middle class' has a broad meaning, … referring imperfectly to people who work for a living receive wages or salary but who do not own a business or play an executive role … . Although I do not attempt to impose

strict income brackets on the concept, I am thinking of people who fall in the bottom 60 percent of the income scale ... . But all of that is subject to a great deal of regional variation ... . Many of the voters meeting these criteria will think of themselves as 'middle class,' since almost half the populace (45 percent) does, but many will call themselves 'working class,' since an identical number ... choose that designation ... . But the term 'middle class' belongs to almost all these voters, even if they think of themselves as lower or working class. In that sense, *the term is an ideal* more than a firm group of people. (Greenberg, 1996 [1995]: 322, emphasis added)

Greenberg is not the only one who has been hard-pressed to pin down the colloquial meaning of the word. Indeed, in my fieldwork, I observed multiple group discussions amongst people of varied socio-economic backgrounds wherein the participants sought in vain to produce a satisfactory definition of what it meant to be 'middle class'. Anthropologist Bonnie Urciuoli sheds light on the confusion; in her semiotic analysis of the concept of 'skills', she concludes that the function of certain words lies in their vagueness. Their purpose is not to communicate a clear concept, but rather to signal alignment with a community's values (Urciuoli, 2008). I would argue that in my informants' discourses, the term 'middle class' behaved in a similar way. Rather being a descriptor of actual material circumstances or class sympathies, these workers described themselves as 'middle class' to discursively place themselves in congruity with broad cultural ideals that value self-sufficiency and stigmatize poverty as failure.

Temporariness and control

When workers spoke of not wanting to get 'trapped' in the job, what they found unpalatable was the prospect of spending the rest of their life there – and those with other aspirations dreaded someday making a personal investment in the job so great that exit would be indefinitely postponed:

> I specifically have told myself that I *will not put in* for management at [Hometown]. ... It's definitely along with getting trapped. I think if I move into management, that's one more thing. 'Cause I'll make more money, that's one more thing to just keep me there, and I never intended to be there for the ten years that I've been there. (Wayne, part-time, ten years)

Wariness of this outcome was often expressed in terms of temporariness – of being in the job only for the time being:

> I don't have a problem working here at [Hometown], but I wouldn't be here if I didn't need a car to get to school, and mainly, I don't want to

be working at [Hometown] for too long. Three years, to me, is too much. Obviously. And I plan on getting a Bachelor's degree, and after that I actually *plan* on working in my field, not just going to school. (Sandra, part-time, three years, Fashion)

Most of the people that work in retail … say, 'This is not my life … . I live two years down the road. I don't live here. This stupid blue vest that I wear, and putting this can of beans on the shelf, this isn't me. I'm better than this, and I'm going there.' (Derek, retail labour organiser)

Many did indeed move on to other things. Others simply had the genuine intention of moving on – some day. And yet many people did stay on, year after year. In fact, Hometown did not have nearly as high a turnover rate as might be predicted. Health insurance was an important factor in this, but there were other reasons. Some workers appreciated the union's protection. For others, exit was dependent on particular preconditions that might not have been satisfied yet – such as getting out of debt, graduating or having the next job lined up. Less positively, the depressed and deindustrialized state of the job market (with a local unemployment at nearly 30 per cent) meant that few alternative jobs were available. For a variety of reasons, workers frequently found themselves staying far longer than they would have hoped.

All of these exit-limiting factors were certainly present before Hometown's efficiency-push. Yet while workers still needed the job as much as always, the recent drop in wages and conditions backed them into a particularly tight corner. Estranged from the union and having no say in company policies, workers effectively found themselves with little structural power over their job's circumstances. However, powerlessness itself was not a dominant theme in the discourses I heard. On the contrary, informants were much more likely to articulate control they had over how hard they worked and their continued presence there:

A lot of us just get to the point where, 'I'm just gonna come in; I'm gonna do the minimal, I'm not gonna go overboard anymore … .' I can see attitude, and there are days when I feel it. And I just have to think, 'You know, at any time I can walk out of this job. I don't have to have it.' (Sue, part-time, three years)

In that vein, without doubting the genuineness of their intentions to eventually move on to better-paying, higher-status and/or more satisfying employment, I suggest that workers' verbal framings of their stay on the job as temporary can, in themselves, be means of asserting control over their own labour power, and reconciling personal dignity with relative structural powerlessness.

Discursive framing as a means of avoiding the 'trap'

'Middle class' identification and temporary framing are much more subtle processes than so-called 'false consciousness'. According to Stuart Hall (1986), the problem of false consciousness arises from a contradiction between an interpretation of Marx that sees 'correct' worker ideologies as deriving from the material circumstances of their own class experience, and Althusser's suggestion that workers rather tend to internalize bourgeois ideologies. The classically unsettling implication of this contradiction is that workers whose ideology does not correspond to their class position are ignorant, deluded or wrong, for it presumes that they have been duped into believing an untrue ideology designed to control them.

On the one hand, it does not seem to me that the Hometown's directors specifically designed the efficiency campaign to put workers in a tough situation. Yet there was no need for conspiracy or evil intent, as these things tend to happen on their own as a natural consequence of the directors' pursuit of their own and the company's interests. Similarly, the situation I observed did not seem to be a case of workers being duped into believing a lie. Rather, workers framed their situation in such a way as to resolve the contradiction between personal identity and dignity on the one hand, and their need, in the present, for the material support that the job provides.

In sum, I suggest that the prospect of getting 'trapped' inspires anxiety because to be trapped is to have lost control. The low wages and dead-end nature of the job stand at odds with both cultural ideals of self-sufficiency and workers' sense of self-worth. Rather than being a sign of workers' obliviousness to the contradiction, temporary framing and discursive identification with the middle class actually helped them to resolve it.

Conclusion

This chapter illustrates the cost that one company's push for greater efficiency has had on the sorts of jobs it offered, and on the workers themselves. It has discussed how they, in order to resolve the contradiction between the dignified self and the indignity of low status at work, sought to distance themselves discursively from the job – both with an eye to avoid getting 'trapped' in poverty wages for the long term, and as a means of avoiding identification with those wages.

While from a business perspective, some might argue that by cutting costs Hometown's leadership did exactly what it needed to do in order to survive, some might ask if the exact nature of the cuts was inevitable, and if they have not come at too great of a price. Hometown has gone from being a good place for workers to 'come for the job and stay for the career,' to purveying the sorts of jobs that many workers do not want to envision themselves in for the long term. Although it is not the sole cause, Walmart as a corporate actor played an important role in these events – both through rapid expansion that introduced an enormous amount of pressure on competitors in a brief span of time and by the fact that the effectiveness of Hometown's union has been limited by the fact that its competitors are not unionized. Workers, for their part, seem to have become cynically indifferent about the union's capacity to be an effective vehicle for their empowerment.

From the workers' perspective, lower wages are not a healthy direction for jobs to be taking. The US, and the Midwest in particular, has lost an enormous number of high-paying manufacturing jobs over recent decades. If retail is to be one of the industries that fill part of this gap, as its recent growth has positioned it to be, then there is a dire need for these to become good jobs, something that Hometown's history has shown to be realizable. Labour organizers have an important role to play in reconnecting with workers, and prove the latter's stake in labour movement through action. State actors must do a better job of protecting workers from employers who may not be primarily focused on the human ramifications of business decisions. Finally, employers must commit – either voluntarily, or through pressure by labor activists and government regulators – to guaranteeing a living wage, so that anyone who is willing and able can support him or herself without having to worry about getting 'trapped'.

Notes

1   Hometown Market is a pseudonym, as are all informant names used in the chapter.
2   This is according to the US Bureau of Labor Statistics' Occupational Employment Statistics (OES) programme (2010d), which tallies 821 distinct non-farm, non-household occupations.
3   Compared to 34.8 per cent of manufacturing workers in 1980 (Adams 1985: 26) and 11.9 per cent today (US Bureau of Labor Statistics, 2010c).
4   This is scheduled to change in 2014, when relevant sections of March 2010's Federal health insurance legislation take effect requiring most employers to offer health insurance.
5   The 'Walmart effect' is a phenomenon whereby a large, efficient company with monopsonic control of supplier prices (such as Walmart) embarks upon an aggressive campaign to further consolidate market share by

forcing suppliers and competitors alike to drastically slash costs or perish (Fishman, 2006).

6 Overtime work in the US is considered to be any hours worked beyond 40 hours per week. Each hour of overtime is compensated at 1.5 times the normal rate, making it a valuable and often coveted opportunity for accelerated earnings.

7 This calculation is based on a co-worker's paystub from the final week of January 2010 and includes deductions for taxes, union dues, short-term disability coverage and medical benefits.

8 Government medical insurance for the poor.

9 The characterization of the poor as morally deficient long predates neo-liberalism (Bigelow, 2005; Ross, 1991). However, the assumptions, values and ideals of the neoliberal model do maintain a special relationship with widespread attitudes towards poverty in US society.

10 American Federation of Labor and Congress of Industrial Organizations.

REFERENCES

Adams, L.T. (1985) 'Changing employment patterns of organized workers', *Monthly Labor Review*, 108 (2): 25–31.

Ahmed, Z.Z. and Wilder, P.S. (1995) 'Productivity in retail miscellaneous shopping goods stores', *Monthly Labor Review*, October.

Baudrillard, J. (1981) *For a Critique of the Political Economy of the Sign*. London: Telos.

Bauman, Z. (2007) *Consuming Life*. Cambridge: Polity.

Bernstein, J. and Bivens, L.J. (2006) *The Wal-Mart Debate: the False Choice between Prices and Wages*. Economic Policy Institute: Issue Brief #223 (June 15).

Bigelow, G. (2005) 'let there be markets: the evangelical roots of economics', *Harper's Magazine*, 310 (1860 [May]): 33 8.

Bollé, P. (2001) 'Part-time work: solution or trap?', in M.F. Loutfi (ed.) *Women, Gender and Work: What Is Equality and How Do We Get There?* Geneva: International Labour Office, 215-.

Cappellari, L. (2000) 'Low-wage mobility in the Italian labour market', *International Journal of Manpower*, 21(3/4): 264–290.

Dickens, R. (2000) 'Caught in a trap? Wage mobility in Great Britain: 1975–1994', *Economica*, 67(268): 477–498.

Ehrenreich, B. (2002) *Nickel and Dimed: Undercover in Low-Wage America*. New York: Granta.

Farber, H.S. and Levy, H. (2000) 'Recent trends in employer-sponsored health insurance coverage: are bad jobs getting worse?', *Journal of Health Economics*, 19(1): 93–119.

Fishman, C. (2006) *The Wal-Mart Effect: How the World's Most Powerful Company Really Works, and How It's Transforming the American Economy*. New York: Penguin.

▶

Florida, R. (1996) 'Regional Creative destruction: production organization, globalization, and the economic transformation of the midwest', *Economic Geography*, 72(3): 314–334.

Greenberg, S.B. (1996 [1995]) *Middle Class Dreams: the Politics and Power of the New American Majority*. New Haven, CT: Yale University Press.

Greenwald, R. (2005) *WAl-Mart: the High Cost of Low Price*. 98 mins.: Brave New Films.

Hall, S. (1986) 'The problem of ideology: Marxism without guarantees', *Journal of Communication Inquiry*, 10(2): 28–44.

Housing Works (2010) *2009 to 2010 Federal Poverty Guidelines*. Online: http://www.atdn.org/access/poverty.html (accessed 10th May 2010).

Huddleston, P. (this volume) '"It's all right for Saturdays, but not forever." The employment of part-time student staff within the retail sector. Just passing through'.

Kazis, R. and Miller, M. (2001) *Low-Wage Workers in the New Economy*. Washington, D.C.: The Urban Institute Press.

Kusterer, K.C. (1978) *Know-How on the Job: The Important Working Knowledge of 'Unskilled' Workers*. Boulder: Westview Press.

Law, J. (2004) *After Method: Mess in Social Science Research*. Abingdon (UK): Routledge.

Lichtenstein, N. (2006) 'Wal-Mart: a template for twenty-first-century capitalism', in N. Lichtenstein (ed.), *Wal-Mart: the Face of Twenty-First Century Capitalism*. New York: The New Press.

Lichtenstein, N. (2010) *The Retail Revolution: How Wal-Mart Created a Brave New World of Business*. New York: Picador.

Malkin, V. (2004) 'Who's behind the counter? Retail workers in New York City', in P. Kasinitz, J.H. Mollenkopf and M.C. Waters (eds) *Becoming New Yorkers: Ethnographies of the New Second Generation*. New York: Russell Sage Foundation.

Morgen, S. (2001) 'The agency of welfare workers: Negotiating devolution, privatization, and the meaning of self-sufficiency', *American Anthropologist*, 103(3): 747–761.

Pierce, J. (2006) *The Wal-Mart Way Not Sam's Way: An Associate View from Inside the Stores*. New York: Xlibris.

Ross, T. (1991) 'The rhetoric of poverty: their immorality, our helplessness', *Georgia Law Journal*, 79(5): 1499-.

Shell, E.R. (2009) *CHeap: the High Cost of Discount Culture*. New York: Penguin.

Smith, R.E. and Vavrichek, B. (1992) 'The wage mobility of minimum wage workers', *Industrial and Labor Relations Review*, 46(1): 82–88.

Tilly, C. (1996) *Half the Job: Bad and Good Part-Time Jobs in a Changing Labor Market*. Philadelphia: Temple University Press.

U.S. Bureau of Labor Statistics (1996) *Region of residence: Shares of average annual expenditures and source of income, Consumer Expenditure Survey*. Online: ftp://ftp.bls.gov/pub/special.requests/ce/share/1996/region.txt (accessed 13th May 2010).

► U.S. Bureau of Labor Statistics (2008) *Region of Residence: Shares of Average Annual Expenditures and Source of Income, Consumer Expenditure Survey.* Online: ftp://ftp.bls.gov/pub/special.requests/ce/share/2008/region.txt (accessed 13th May 2010).

U.S. Bureau of Labor Statistics (2010a) *Employment and Wages of the Largest Occupations, May 2008.* Online http://www.bls.gov/oes/current/largest_occs.htm (accessed 3 May 2010).

U.S. Bureau of Labor Statistics (2010b) *Employment status of the civilian noninstitutional population, 1940 to date.* Online http://www.bls.gov/cps/cpsaat1.pdf (accessed 5th May 2010).

U.S. Bureau of Labor Statistics (2010c) *Manufacturing: NAICS 31-33: Employment, all employees.* Online: http://www.bls.gov/iag/tgs/iag31-33.htm (accessed 5th May 2010).

U.S. Bureau of Labor Statistics (2010d) *Occupational Employment Statistics Frequently Asked Questions.* Online http://www.bls.gov/oes/oes_ques.htm#Ques24 (consulted 3 May 2010).

U.S. Bureau of Labor Statistics (2010e) *Production occupations.* Online http://www.bls.gov/oes/2008/may/oes510000.htm (accessed 4 May 2010).

U.S. Bureau of Labor Statistics (2010f) *Retail Trade: NAICS 44-45: Employment, all employees.* Online http://www.bls.gov/iag/tgs/iag44-45.htm (accessed 5th May 2010).

Urciuoli, D. (2008) 'Skills and selves in the new workplace', *American Ethnologist*, 35 (2): 211–228.

Yau, N. (2010) 'Watch the growth of Walmart and Sam's Club', *Flowing Data.* Online http://projects.flowingdata.com/walmart/ (accessed 9 May 2010).

The Pressures of Retail Work

Employers' 'Exit Options' and Low-Wage Retail Work: The Case of Supermarkets in the Netherlands and Germany

9

Maarten van Klaveren and Dorothea Voss-Dahm

Introduction

Work on the retail shop floor shares many commonalities across highly developed economies. Shop floor workers everywhere, and particularly in supermarkets, must take goods from the stockroom to the shop floor, replenish shelves, answer customer questions, ring up sales and receive payment. Another common feature of the retail trade in different countries is its high levels of dependency on fluctuating consumer footfall, almost invariably extending retailing hours beyond standard daytime shifts. Retail employers in Western Europe have responded to these fluctuations and non-standard operating hours by making substantial use of part-time labour. Combined with low hourly wages, on its own part-time retail employment hardly ever allows workers to maintain an adequate standard of living or a decent life (see Jordan, this volume).

It is often argued that such unfavourable outcomes for shop floor workers are the inevitable result of retail firms' search for numerical flexibility coupled with private consumers' quest for low-priced goods. This fragmentation of labour into part-time jobs can be regarded as a means to provide both services and direct customer contact flexibly and cheaply. However, in this chapter we argue that the search for flexible staffing only partially explains the employment patterns in Dutch and German retailing. Rather, such patterns are formed by interactions between firms and regulations, and particularly the *avoidance* of regulation. Taking the interrelations between firm strategies and country-specific institutional settings into account, we argue that retail firms in different national settings use various 'exit options'. Such options consist of loopholes in the national institutions' regulating pay, benefits and working conditions. As a consequence, even in a national regulatory context that in general protects workers by labour law or collective agreements a proliferation of low wages and precarious working-time arrangements can be observed (in marked contrast with the Swedish experience observed by Andersson et al., this volume). In this chapter we go into two 'exit options' in particular, the national minimum wage rate in the Netherlands and marginal part-time work in Germany. Both are subject to special regulation that retailers take extensive advantage of in their efforts to establish and maintain lower wages for part-time workers.

Our contribution draws on findings from a major research project on behalf of the Russell Sage Foundation (RSF) on low-wage work, analysing and comparing five sectors in five EU countries (Denmark, France, Germany, the Netherlands and the UK) and, ultimately, comparing these with the US. The retail trade was one of these five sectors. This contribution concentrates on supermarkets (food retail chains) in the Netherlands and Germany, in both countries the largest retail sub-sector and one of the two sub-sectors researched in the low-wage project (The other was consumer electronics retailing). We were responsible for the Dutch and German retail studies (Van Klaveren, 2008a; Voss-Dahm, 2008), including fieldwork in four supermarkets in each country in 2005–2006, and also carried out a comparison of retail jobs in the five European countries and the US, in cooperation with two colleagues from the US (Carré et al., 2010).

The chapter is structured as follows. Section 2 provides an overview of the employment structures in the retail trade in the Netherlands and Germany. We continue with two sections analysing dominant employment practices in food retail chains. In Section 3, 'lean retailing' is treated as a set of strategies adapting staffing levels to consumer streams, perfected through the use of advanced information and communication technologies (ICT). In Section 4, we discuss the country-specific exit options widely used by supermarket chains in their efforts to keep labour costs low, and show how these affect the composition and behaviour of the workforce. A final section presents conclusions.

Employment and wage structures in the Netherlands and Germany

The employment and wage structures of the retail trade in the Netherlands and Germany differ only minimally. Retail employment was a slightly smaller proportion of total employment in Germany (8.7 per cent) than in the Netherlands (9.0 per cent) in 2005, differences that were even more negligible when calculated in FTEs (full-time equivalents): 7.6 per cent in Germany and 7.7 per cent in the Netherlands (Van Klaveren et al., 2009).

Despite this similarity, private consumption patterns in both countries differ: private consumption constituted only 46 per cent of GDP (Gross Domestic Product) in 2006 in the Netherlands, against 55 per cent in Germany. Within Europe, the Netherlands has consistently had the lowest consumer-spending share of GDP, which reflects a consumer mindset that influences the way the retail trade operates: Low-consumption patterns seem to have pushed firms towards a greater focus on low prices and low costs and, in turn, low wages (Van Klaveren et al., 2009).

In the Netherlands supermarkets' share of retail employment is larger than in Germany. While in 2008 Dutch supermarkets had 223,100 employees, or 33.8 per cent of the retail total of 658,700 (HBD, 2009a, 2009b), the German equivalents for the same year were 741,400 employees in supermarkets and hypermarkets from a retail employment total of 2,953,300, or 25.1 per cent (Bundesagentur für Arbeit, 2009). Concentration in the food retail chains sub-sector is higher in the Netherlands, where the share of the top five food retailers in total sales in 2005–2006 was 88 per cent, against 69 per cent in Germany (Van Klaveren, 2010; Metro Group, 2006).

As we have already noted, a considerable share of retail workers in both the Netherlands and Germany are employed part-time; in the Netherlands part-timers even constitute the majority of workers in this sector. In 2008, 70 per cent of Dutch retail workers were part-timers, a figure rising to nearly 80 per cent in supermarkets (authors' calculations on data from Hoofdbedrijfschap Detailhandel (HBD)), a considerable proportion of whom were young workers. In the same year, 56 per cent of retail workers in Germany were part-timers and in German food retail chains 71 per cent worked part-time with nearly half of all part-timers (45 per cent) holding a so-called 'mini-job' with monthly earnings of Euro 400 or less. Because of this emphasis on part-timers, supermarkets in both countries have comparatively large numbers of employees. The German retail workforce is considerably more 'feminized', with nearly 72 per cent of women (head-count) in paid employment in 2008, against 63 per cent in the Netherlands. Moreover, while Dutch supermarkets actually employ a lower proportion of women than the retail sector as a whole, with 55 per cent in 2008 (Van Klaveren, 2010), in Germany women's share of the supermarket workforce was *higher* than the retail sector average, at 77 per cent (Bundesagentur für Arbeit, 2009). However, this lower proportion of women in the super-market workforce in the Netherlands was far more highly concentrated in front-line work. In the two jobs that we studied most closely, the cashiers (checkout operators) and the sales assistants mainly working at counters, 85 per cent were women workers in the Netherlands against 78 per cent in Germany – implying that in Dutch supermarkets very few women were employed in management and logistics functions.

Table 9.1 Employment structures in retailing in the Netherlands and Germany, 2008

	Employees in retailing (headcount)	Employees in food retail chains	Part-time in retailing	Part-time in food retailing	Female employment in retailing	Female employment in food retailing
	in % of all employees in retailing					
Netherlands	658,700	33.8	71	80	63	55
Germany	2,953,300	25.1	56	71	72	77

Sources: The Netherlands: calculations AIAS on data Hoofdbedrijfschap Detailhandel (HBD) and CBS (Statistics Netherlands); Germany: Employment Statistics of Federal Labour Office, special evaluation for IAQ (2009).

At first glance wage structures in the retail trade were similar in the two countries studied. Based on a large ongoing Internet survey, average gross hourly wages for workers aged 23 and over were also at similar levels in 2007–2008. In both countries the average wages of supermarket employees were higher than those in retailing at large, with a slightly larger gap in Germany at 12.66 versus 11.43 Euros, while the figures from the Netherlands were 11.87 versus 11.43 Euros (data: *WageIndicator*). For an analysis of working conditions at the margins of the labour market, the share of low-wage employment is important. According to international standards used by OECD and EU, low wages are defined as wages below the threshold of two-thirds of the median gross hourly wage in a country (Mason and Salverda, 2010). In 2003–2004 the low-wage share among retail workers was the highest among all industries in the Netherlands, while in Germany it was only surpassed by the hotel and restaurant sector (Van Klaveren, 2008b; Bosch and Kalina, 2008). For the same time period the share of low-paid employment in retail was slightly higher in the Netherlands, with 46 per cent of all retail employees, and 57 per cent of supermarket workers, earning below the low-pay threshold. In 2004, 42 per cent of all German retail employees remained below the low-pay threshold, while a year earlier 41 per cent of full-time sales assistants in food retailing were classified as low-paid (Van Klaveren, 2008a; Voss-Dahm, 2008).

More recently, the proportion of low-paid work in retailing and supermarkets seem to have stabilized in the Netherlands: according to *WageIndicator* data for 2007–2008, the respective shares of low-paid workers among those aged 23 and over were 48 per cent for supermarket staff and 51 per cent for retail as a whole. Figures for 2007 suggest that in German retailing the share of low-paid work has hardly changed in comparison with that three years earlier. While the low-pay threshold in that year was 9.19 Euros per hour, 37.5 per cent of all retail employees earned less than 9.00 Euros. It is also worth

Table 9.2 Wage structures in retailing in the Netherlands and Germany, 2003–2004 and 2007–2008

	Low-wage threshold (hourly gross wage in €)		Share of low-wage workers in retailing (in %)		Share of low-wage workers in food retailing (in %)	
Year	2004	2007	2003–2004	2007–2008	2003–2004	2007–2008
Netherlands	10.44	10.64	46	51 (>=age 23)	57	48 (>=age 23)
Germany	9.58 (West Germany) 6.97 (East Germany)	9.19 (Germany)	42	37.5 < 9€/hour	41 (only full-time sales assistants)	–

Sources: the Netherlands: 2003–2004: calculations AIAS on CBS microdata; 2007–2008: *WageIndicator* data; Germany: calculations IAQ on Socio Economic Panel (SOEP).

noting that the share of the *very* low-paid adults is larger in Germany than in the Netherlands. While in Germany nearly 15 per cent of all retail workers earned less than 6 Euros per hour in 2007, the share of adult retail workers in the Netherlands earning such low wages was negligible in 2007–2008 (Netherlands: *WageIndicator* data; Germany: own calculations IAQ based on Socio-Economic Panel (SOEP)).

Fragmentation of working time in the course of lean retailing

In general these figures confirm that for many retail workers fewer working hours are accompanied by low hourly wages – a combination that frustrates the possibility of obtaining a decent standard of living through retail employment alone. In our research project we raised the question of a possible interrelationship between the incidence of a low-wage–part-time pattern of employment and the ongoing intensification of the use of advanced ICT in labour processes. Accordingly, we studied whether ICT has an effect on employment practices in large retail firms.

'Lean retailing' is the catchword that encapsulates the technological challenge currently taking place in the retail trade and food retailing in particular (Abernathy et al., 2000; Christopherson, 2001). Its core logic dictates that production processes should be managed from the end of the supply chain, that is, from the point of sale, following the principle of just-in-time production. The ultimate aim of lean retailing is the maximization of economies of scale. Manufacturers and wholesalers are increasingly integrated into global supply chains governed and coordinated by large retailers (Swoboda,

Foscht and Cliquet, 2008), with large grocery retailers at the forefront of this development (Burt et al., 2008). Through efficient consumer response (ECR) systems, large retail firms enjoy privileged access to up-to-date information on consumers' purchasing behaviour (Bieber et al., 2004). Modern checkout systems constitute the technological core of these systems, since it is at the checkout that data on type and volume of products sold are recorded and passed on to manufacturers. A process that is likely to be faster and more efficient with the introduction of Radio Frequency Identification Device (RFID) technology since this technology, which can be used to track and monitor individual products through radio antennae, holds out the promise of quicker and more efficient distribution processes than can be achieved with current technologies like barcoding. When RFID replaces barcodes, customers will go through a gate and all the goods in their carts or baskets will be registered in a fraction of a second, allowing supermarkets to establish even more labour-saving strategies at checkouts than the self-scanning strategies already in place in large retail chains. For the time being technological problems and cost considerations hamper the large-scale implementation of RFID (cf. outcomes of the EU Bridge project). Nevertheless, it is clear that modern ICT has already considerably reduced work volumes in retailing and will most likely continue to do so.

In the course of our research we traced another and highly relevant impact of ICT, in the area of labour management in retail (cf. Wright and Lund, 2006). The large European food retailers have integrated the management of 'demand-led' logistic chains in stock management with labour management, through technologically advanced systems integrating the supply-chain management software with programmes supporting optimal-staffing strategies and personnel benchmarking. Optimal staff scheduling has become vitally important for both headquarters and store managers in their efforts to manage the gap between fluctuating workloads and individual pay, skills and working hours most efficiently. The basic principle underlying such computer-aided organization of working time is the exact adjustment of staffing levels to both fluctuating customer and stock flows. If well organized, this adjustment allows for the reduction of labour costs to the lowest possible levels while increasing numerical flexibility and preventing any idle hours (Voss-Dahm and Lehndorff, 2003).

With the growing importance of staffing and working-time policies in the context of rationalization, store management has become a central actor. 'Optimal staffing' from a managerial perspective may not coincide with optimal working hours (and pay) from a worker's perspective. The need for flexible staffing is fundamentally incompatible with rigid shift systems, as well as with fixed contractual working times agreed on an individual basis. Women working in mini-jobs and high school and university students in particular may have problems adjusting their working hours to changes in customer flows and may want to stick to regular work schedules because of family responsibilities and school or university schedules, respectively. In the Netherlands and Germany alike the duration of contractual working hours is increasingly just a basis for remuneration, whereas the distribution of actual working hours varies in accordance with workloads and individual availability. In fact, in a time bank system annual or monthly working-time accounts for individual workers are a standard feature of working-time management in retail in both countries. Particularly in Germany, employment contracts may only include the number of hours to be worked in a year. For instance, in a German supermarket the only contract offered to checkout operators stipulated 1,000 hours to be worked in a specific year.

We have to emphasize that staff scheduling and the distribution of working times varies between different work areas and functions. In the Netherlands as well as in Germany working-time arrangements on the full-service counters, where relatively few sales assistants are employed, are predominantly hybrid forms containing formal as well as informal elements. Here, the skilled employees are fully aware of time demands. They mostly arrange their own working times by agreement with colleagues, taking account of operational requirements. On the checkouts, staffed exclusively by part-timers, the main priority is to adjust working time to the variation in customer flows; for most Dutch and German supermarket chains queue-busting on the checkout is a cornerstone of customer service strategies. This flexible interchange between counter and checkout seems more common the smaller the store. To illustrate this, the manager of a medium-sized Dutch supermarket explained that:

> We maintain clear policies to keep lines short through the flexible opening of new checkouts. If necessary, we ask staff from counters and from the ranks of experienced shelf stackers to join. Yet we don't feel the need to formalize or reward these practices.

In the end, the 'institutionalized improvisation' of working times in combination with short-term planning of working times has its roots in short-term adjustments typical of customer-oriented service work, despite the elaborate computer-aided scheduling of working times. It is worth noting that in contrast to what is predominantly happening on the shop floor in both countries, works councils and unions have a formal say in scheduling, and co-determination laws require retail employers to negotiate scheduling with their works councils. In Germany, collective agreements in the retailing sector require employers to post schedules 26 weeks in advance. Representative bodies such as works councils in both countries have co-determination rights on collective working-time schedules, but the application of a post schedule 26 weeks in advance applies only in a relatively small number of establishments, most of which are warehouses. In most retail firms the working times of part-time workers follow managerial flexible staffing strategies – normally as an effect of an absent employee representation. The latter practice may well lead to frictions with employees' (working) time constraints, employee dissatisfaction and consequently high turnover and absenteeism. According to both our field research and the accounts of trade union officers in the sector, many supermarket workers in both countries complain of unilateral employer decisions concerning working times and days off.

Where does low-wage work come from?

Competitive pressures

In recent years, the diffusion of advanced IT systems for the management of global supply chains and for optimal staffing has set the stage for an intensification of price competition in retailing. A second main sectoral trend has been the spread of aggressive discount chains that take advantage of these logistical technologies to offer mass-consumption goods at permanently low prices. The US-based Wal-Mart is the best-known example of this model, but Germany's Aldi and Lidl are familiar to many Europeans. In their home country, these discounters captured 40 per cent of food sales in 2008 (ver.di, 2010). In both countries the political liberalization of zoning regulations has triggered an expansion of sales space, decreasing the productivity per square metre and lowering profit margins, especially in food retailing (for the Netherlands: HBD, 2009b; for Germany: EHI Retail Institute, 2009). Price wars, as in the case in the Netherlands where the major war started by Ahold's supermarket chain Albert Heijn in October 2003 which lasted three years, have been recurrent signs of fierce competition, within the context of declining disposable consumer incomes. Such wars act as catalysts for discounting the prices of goods, including those other than food. By the end of this supermarket price war in the Netherlands, the market share of food discounters had increased by 6 per cent points to 19 per cent, of which Aldi and Lidl took two-thirds (Van Klaveren, 2008a; 2010). In the course of the 1990s, under pressure from lean retailing and the spread of discounting and intensified competition, supermarket chains in both Germany and the Netherlands looked for opportunities to fragment volumes of work and to directly reduce hourly rates of pay. In both countries, the 'exit options', that is, loopholes in country-specific bargaining agreements or government regulations, provided relief to the employers.

The two exit options – statutory minimum wage rate in the Netherlands and marginal part-time employment arrangements in Germany – are highly adverted to part-time work. In both countries particular groups of part-time workers are treated differently because government regulations permit such discrimination. The ability of employers to take recourse to these exit options is especially problematic and worthy of attention since equal treatment of workers is anchored in employment law at both the national and the European level. In the Netherlands, a law passed in 1996 prohibited different arrangements in employment contracts based on working hours. This also includes contributions to the social security and tax systems: According to the so-called pro rata prescription the relation between income resp. working time and payroll deductions has to be the same (Tijdens, 2005). The requirement for the equal treatment of workers is laid down in a law on part-time and fixed-term contracts in Germany as well. Consequently in both countries wage penalties for part-timers could only be implemented via the strategic use of loopholes by retail employers.

The Netherlands: the youth minimum wage

The Netherlands has a long history of commitment to wage moderation, and in the last three decades the statutory minimum wage has been used to this effect with considerable success. Between 1945 and 1964, the government controlled wage negotiations between employers and trade unions. This phase that coincided with extensive economic growth, ended in 1964 under pressure from a tight labour market and concomitant strike activity. In that same year, the social partners agreed on a national minimum wage of 100 guilders a week for 'breadwinners'. In 1969 a statutory minimum wage was established, applicable to anyone over the age of 24. A few years later, the threshold for the adult minimum wage was lowered to the age of 23, and finally in 1974 a youth minimum wage was introduced for 15–22 year olds. Originally set at 40 per cent of the adult minimum wage (for 15 year olds), this rate was lowered to 30 per cent of the adult minimum wage in the employment crisis of the early 1980s, rising incrementally to 100 per cent of the adult wage at the age of 23. This scheme recalls the 1948-recommendations for youth wages by the Labour Foundation, the joint body of union confederations and employers' associations; whose reasoning was based on the presumed lower productivity and lower personal needs of younger workers (Bloemen and Brug, 1982; Salverda, Van Klaveren and Van der Meer, 2008). This regulation is still in existence. The 'long tail' has never been shortened : the minimum rate for a 15 year old currently is about Euro 2.90 an hour – so that in comparison with other EU countries the Netherlands has by far the lowest youth minimum wage and the highest age at which the full minimum wage starts to apply. This wage structure stimulates mutual wage competition between youths of different ages: and employers may feel tempted to reduce labour costs by substituting 'younger' for 'older' youths (cf. Salverda 2008).

From 1980 on, the Netherlands entered into a long period of wage moderation. The statutory minimum wages were lowered even in nominal terms by various 'freezes', lasting for a total of 13 years. As a result, the ratio of the adult minimum wage to the adult average wage fell from 62 per cent in 1979 to 45 per cent in 2004 (Van Klaveren et al., 2009). The steep decline in the minimum wage has stirred remarkably little public debate, neither about the situation of the working poor nor about the perspectives of young workers in industries such as retailing or hotels and restaurants. For quite some time, the leadership of the national trade unions seemed to go along with the productivity and lower personal needs arguments, neglecting the repeated demands of union youth groups to lower the threshold age for the adult minimum wage (gradually) to the age of 18. This state of affairs lasted until 2005, when the president of FNV, the largest union confederation, stood up for the 18-years' threshold – to date with no result (Jongerius, 2005). Thus, the combination of a relatively low adult minimum wage with very low youth rates was well situated to constitute an exit option for employers maintaining a low-wage orientation.

In 1994, the first Kok administration in the Netherlands announced broad plans for deregulation. Consequently, the large retail chains and wholesalers united in the Central Bureau Food Trade (CBL) and, led by Albert Heijn, lobbied intensively for an extension of shopping hours. This was opposed by federations of small- and medium-sized retailers. The CBL argued that the proposed changes would offer advantages such as greater sales volumes and better consumer service. Yet, when the 1996 Opening Hours (Shops) Act came into force, increasing maximum opening hours from 55 to 96 per week, two preconditions needed to be met before the large retailers could fully profit from the supply of young part-timers. First, they wanted a core of full-time employees to accept evening and Saturday work. Second, they argued for lower compensation levels for anti-social working hours in the two supermarket collective agreements. After tough negotiations with the unions, both goals were largely accomplished. In exchange for an extra one per cent wage increase, compensations for working on Saturdays and between six and eight pm were removed from the collective agreements between 1998 and 2000 (Tijdens, 1998, 2005). The re-organization processes that followed allowed the food chains to exploit the cost advantages of employing young workers exhaustively. They integrated order reception and replenishment or shelf-stacking into their regular work schedules, replacing adults with young workers in the process. Previously, shelf-stacking had been performed outside opening hours in overnight shifts by adult men and in evening shifts by adult men and women (Van Klaveren, 2010), work practices in the mid-2000s still reported from the UK (Mulholland, 2009 and this volume). However the expansion of opening hours was not very successful. After a high point in 1997–1998, most supermarkets backtracked and reduced their opening hours, partially because the newly targeted workers objected to late evening working hours. By 2004, evening sales had fallen below 10 per cent of total sales (HBD, 2005).

In Dutch retailing this widespread use of the low youth minimum wage rate cannot be separated from the increase in student labour during the last two decades, to an even higher extent than in the UK (cf. Huddleston in this volume), with the Netherlands – together with Denmark – topping the list of young people combining study and work in OECD countries. In 2005, 62 per cent of young people in the Netherlands and Denmark were in work, the highest employment-to-population (EPOP) rates of young people aged 15–24 in the OECD, while participation in education was about the same as elsewhere. (The EPOP rate for German 15-24-olds was 42 per cent – Mason and Salverda, 2010). In the Netherlands, the maximum earnings allowed in the national system of grants for students aged over 18 made employment for students increasingly attractive; in the 2000s earning levels rose rapidly to 70 per cent of the adult minimum wage. With 24 per cent of the working students aged 19–21 and 14 per cent of those aged 22–24 employed in stores in 2008, retailing continued to be students' favourite source of employment (Lok and Siermann, 2009). In retailing this facility to combine work and study distorted the youth labour market, effectively crowding out those who attempted to start a career (normally) after leaving school and need a full income, in favour of those who work while studying. This latter category amounted to about 60 per cent of all 15–19 year olds and 20 per cent of the 20–24 year olds employed in retail in 2005. Our case studies and other evidence suggest that many of those who turn to retail employment for a full income, particularly in urban areas, are young second-generation migrant workers (Van Klaveren, 2010). Currently they run a serious risk of getting stuck indefinitely in low-wage work.

In the heat of the food price wars Dutch retailers clearly preferred any young workers over adults, and particularly over adult women (The same shift in employment pattern is reported from food retailing in Denmark – cf. Esbjerg et al., 2008). In 2004, many adult female checkout operators in the Netherlands complained that they were 'bullied away' and replaced by cheaper youngsters. They reported that employers increasingly took unilateral decisions concerning days off and holidays, sometimes forcing them to give up their jobs. It is telling that between 2000 and 2005 the share of female workers in Dutch supermarkets fell by 4 percentage points, and has since remained at the new, lower level (Van Klaveren, 2010). In practice Dutch institutions favour recruiting those who combine work and subsidized study over other youngsters and adult women. It has to be noted that in recent years food retail employers in the Netherlands have started to recognize the causal relationships between low and age-specific minimum wages, the lack of monetary rewards for experience, and their own growing recruitment problems – with labour turnover for youth workers in some stores rising to over 100 per cent a year. As an initial attempt to tackle this, the collective agreement for supermarkets for 2008–2010 took a step towards implementing a form of experience rating for 18 and 19 year olds (Salverda, 2008).

Germany: the mini-jobs

In Germany, retailers use marginal part-time employment contracts, called mini-jobs, as an exit strategy that allows them to lower wages. Mini-jobs have been in existence since 1977 and were originally introduced as an opportunity for workers to be legally employed without paying taxes and social security contributions. In the 1970s and 1980s, when the German labour market was dominated by full-time male workers, marginal part-time only played a minor role. This changed in the course of the 1990s when employment forms other than the standard full-time employment relationship were regarded as a means to create more jobs (Sachverstaendigenrat, 2005). In 1998, under the first Social Democratic-Green government coalition, a reform of marginal part-time labour was passed that aimed to bring more employees into the social security system, including those who worked less than 15 hours a week and earned less than 325 Euros per month. For those mini-jobs employers have to pay a lump sum to the social security and tax systems, making a mini-job as expensive per hour as a regular job. By contrast, employees in a mini-job are exempted from paying taxes and social security contributions – making mini-jobs attractive in view of the fact that in Germany in a regular job about 23 per cent of gross wages have to be paid to the four pillars of social security system (pension, health, unemployment and long-term care insurance). Thus, at least in the short run, employees gained from a higher net wage in a mini-job compared to a regular job. In 2003, in the framework of the Hartz laws of the second Schroeder administration, the regulations changed again (Rudolph, 2003). First, the maximum exempted salary was raised to 400 Euros. Second, the working-time limit of 15 hours a week was removed. Third, the former addition of the income of a first (regular) and a second (mini)job was removed with regard to tax and social security contributions. Now also in a second job the mini-job is exempted from these contributions for employees. These changes, together with greater pressure from job centres on the unemployed to take up some form of paid employment and a steadily increasing female participation rate, have led to the sharp increase in the number of mini-jobs. While in 2000, 14 per cent of all employees in Germany worked in mini-jobs, by 2009 this share had increased to nearly 21 per cent.

The current arrangement provides specific groups in the labour market with incentives to work in a mini-job since it presumes the existence of a main (male) breadwinner. Students, pupils or pensioners are covered by the main household earner's status in the social security system, so they do not feel 'punished' by being excluded from the social security system in a mini-job and simply gain from a higher net wage because of the tax and social security exemption. The same is true for spouses with a partner working in a regular part-time or full-time job, since by status they gain from derived entitlements to the social security system. Although some changes in the general orientation of the country's family policy can be discerned (Bosch and Kalina, 2008: 90), the existing regulations serve to keep women's participation in paid-labour at low levels. Entitlements to social insurance benefits of married women are derived from the employment status of their husbands; the system of child care is underdeveloped; and the taxation system subjects any second household income to a high marginal tax rate. Women's average weekly working hours decreased from 30.2 in 2001 to 29.1 in 2006, as increasing numbers of women worked part-time or in mini-jobs (Kümmerling, Jansen and Lehndorff, 2008).

But how can mini-jobs be low-paid if wages have to be as high as in a regular job, with the only differences in total pay being reliant on different treatment in terms of tax and social security law? The lowering of wages takes place at the company level, where the net advantage of mini-jobs is taken away. As a manager of a large food retail company explained:

> We have a verbal agreement in our company on pay in mini-jobs. We pay them lower wages than those in regular jobs. It is not fair for those working only some hours a week to get a higher net hourly wage than those who have to pay taxes and social security contributions. In a way we don't disadvantage them, but we refuse to give them preferential treatment.

In view of the low margins in food retailing and the consequent pressure on personnel costs, food retail management has come to regard lower hourly wages in mini-jobs as a loophole since differences in tax and social security contributions for regular and mini-jobs are used to subsidize the employer rather than to benefit employees. This case is far from unique. In 2004, 87 per cent of those in mini-jobs working in retail earned hourly wages below the low-wage threshold (Voss-Dahm, 2008), a practice that has spread to other industries. Over time, nearly nine out of ten mini-jobbers (86 per cent in 2007) were continuously low-paid; in 2007 they made up nearly one in three (31 per cent) of all low-paid workers in Germany (Kalina and Weinkopf, 2009). Case studies have shown that mini-jobbers did not react against this and often were not even aware that their employers had such a wage policy. Something that is particularly true of the many women workers who do not expect to earn a substantial part of the household income in the first place, thereby keeping in line with the general principle of the conservative German welfare state on women's labour market participation (Esping-Andersen, 2000, Jany-Catrice and Lehndorff, 2005). Against this backdrop, retail employers experience hardly any difficulties in filling (small) part-time vacancies. The share of mini-jobs in retailing has increased steadily and one out of every three jobs in the sector was a mini-job in 2009 (Bundesagentur für Arbeit, 2009).

A special regulatory framework and its practice in companies favours mini-jobs over regular jobs, thereby crowding out those who work in retailing to gain a livelihood. Our case study revealed that it is common for management, reacting to decreasing sales, to ask female workers to reduce their working time in order to meet a required sales to personnel cost ratio. As a rule, in Western Germany the male dominated breadwinner model still appears to be strong as few women workers resist reductions in contractually agreed working hours, thereby perpetuating and even strengthening the social-conservative traits of the German employment model. Eastern Germany differs in this respect, with more pressure from women for larger part-time jobs (as in the Netherlands, with its officially sponsored movement for 'part-time work plus' or the so-called 'opplussen' of small part-time jobs). These developments illustrate how the self-reinforcing outcomes of the extensive use of exit options can result in a further deterioration of income opportunities for retail workers. As a result, part-time work in retailing hardly provides a decent living, at best just a modest second income.

Conclusion

Exit options, and the use that particular food retail chains make of them, instigate a race to the bottom intensifying wage pressures and excluding certain groups of workers from access to jobs with higher wages. Both the Dutch and the German examples show the impact of exit options on wage structures. Here, it is not just the consequences of deregulation at play, but the way exceptions are regulated by employment legislation that also provides incentives to large retail firms to lower wage rates. In both countries workers' representation remains a potential countervailing force, but in the retail industries – more than in nearly all other industries – the effectiveness of workers' representation is heavily constrained. In the Netherlands, coverage remains high at 98 per cent of the retail workforce partly due to the mandatory extension of collective bargaining, but clearly that is not, by itself, sufficient to yield a low incidence of low-wage work. In recent years the coverage rate of collective agreements has been rapidly decreasing in Germany and only about half of all retail employees were still covered by collective agreements in 2006 (Voss-Dahm, 2009). Unionization meets considerable difficulties in the retail industry. Based on a comparison of unionization efforts in Dutch, German and British retail firms, Dribbusch (2003) has argued that there is no specific resentment of unions among retail workers, but rather a lack of opportunity to join. Both the Dutch and German supermarket practices we studied confirm that union organizing meets structural constraints, especially the predominance of relatively small workplaces scattered over the country, and that of part-time work with the related workers' self-perceptions (see also Lynch et al., this volume). Union density in retail is low and decreasing in both countries, and is currently about 10–12 per cent. Under these conditions, workforces with weak bargaining power tend to bear the brunt of the sharp edge of cost-cutting management approaches, the more so where the enforcement of the essential elements in labour regulations is weak.

The high incidence of a low-wage–part-time pattern in retailing in the Netherlands and Germany shows that even in societies with strong corporatist traditions such additional regulation can lead to structural shifts in power relations between the negotiating partners; as a consequence, protective regulation for core workers may well be weakened too. Exit options can well be 'self-energizing' and grow into dominant institutions if firms follow cost-cutting strategies in reaction to fierce competition. Indeed, the use of these exit mechanisms in the Netherlands and Germany has extended beyond the retail industry, and this practice has been instrumental in the deterioration of the 'inclusiveness' of the respective national labour relations systems. This implies that the mechanisms included in these systems to extend wages, benefits and working conditions negotiated by workers in industries and occupations with strong bargaining power extends less to those with weak bargaining power than they have done until recently (Appelbaum et al., 2010). There is also a major danger that the expectations of newer cohorts of workers are ratcheted down. One example of this came from a participant in a focus group of checkout operators in one of the Dutch supermarket cases stated:

> Just look around, and you can see that working part-time is the normal state of affairs in this job . ... However, it's strange but it's quite difficult to build a decent living for yourself based on this work.

A large majority of retail workers will perceive part-time work as the standard employment relationship in the industry as particularly supermarkets in the Netherlands and Germany currently tend to offer mainly job opportunities for those who regard themselves as secondary earners. Such 'normalization' of the loopholes that benefit mostly employers' priorities for flexibility and low costs may in turn particularly impede the ambitions especially of minority workers who may regard such employment as a 'bridge' leading to other, more rewarding jobs.

REFERENCES

Abernathy, F.H., Dunlop, J.T., Hammond, J.H. and Weil, D. (2000) 'Retailing and supply chains in the information age', *Technology in Society*, 22(1): 5–31.

Appelbaum, E., Bosch, G., Gautié, J., Mason, G., Mayhew, K., Salverda, W., Schmitt, J. and N. Westergaard-Nielsen, N. (2010) 'Introduction and Overview', in J. Gautié and J. Schmitt (eds) *Low-Wage Work in the Wealthy World*. New York: Russell Sage Foundation, 1–32.

Bieber, D., Jacobsen, H., Naevecke, S., Schick, C. and Speer, F. (2004) *Innovation der Kooperation: Auf dem Weg zu einem neuen Verhaeltnis zwischen Industrie und Handel*. Berlin: Sigma.

Bloemen, E. and Brug, L. (1982) *Toevallig jong. Werkende jongeren na 1945 en de vakbeweging*. Nijmegen: SUN.

Bosch, G. and Kalina, T. (2008) 'Low-wage work in Germany: an overview', in G. Bosch and C. Weinkopf (eds) *Low-Wage Work in Germany*. New York: Russell Sage Foundation, 19–112.

Burt, S., Davies, K., Dawson, J. and Sparks, L. (2008) 'Categorizing patterns and processes in retail grocery internationalisation', *Journal of Retailing and Consumer Services*, 15: 78–92.

Carré, F., Tilly, M., van Klaveren, D., and Voss-Dahm (2010) 'Retail Jobs in Comparative Perspective', in J. Gautié and J. Schmitt (eds) *Low-Wage Work in the Wealthy World*. New York: Russell Sage Foundation, 211–268.

Christopherson, S. (2001) 'Lean retailing in marktliberalen und koordinierten Wirtschaften', in H. Rudolph (ed.) *Aldi oder Arkaden? Unternehmen und Arbeit im europaischen Einzelhandel*. Berlin: Sigma.

Dribbusch, H.(2003) *Gewerkschaftliche Mitgliedergewinnung im Dienstleistungssektor. Ein Drei-Laender-Vergleich im Einzelhandel*. Berlin: Sigma.

Esbjerg, L., Grunert, K.G., Buck, N. and Sonne Andersen, A.-M. (2008) 'Working in Danish retailing: Transitional workers going elsewhere, core employees going nowhere and career seekers striving to go somewhere', in N. Westergaard-Nielsen (ed.) *Low-Wage Work in Denmark*. New York: Russell Sage Foundation, 140–185.

Esping-Andersen, G. (2000) *Social Foundations of Postindustrial Economies*. Oxford: Oxford University Press.

▶

EHI Retail Institute (2009) *Handel aktuell.* Cologne.
European Union (EU) *Bridge project* (http://www.bridge-project.eu) (accessed 10 May 2010).
Hoofdbedrijfschap Detailhandel (HBD) (2005) *Branches in detail. Supermarkten.* The Hague.
HBD (2009a) *Werkgelegenheid in de detailhandel.* The Hague (www.hbd.nl).
HBD (2009b) *Jaarboek detailhandel 2009.* The Hague.
Jany-Catrice, F. and Lehndorff, S. (2005) 'Work organization and the importance of labour markets in the European retail trade', in G. Bosch, S. Lehndorff (eds) *Working in the Service Sector: A Tale from Different Worlds.* London: Routledge, 210–236.
Jongerius, A. (2005) 'FNV wil minimumloon vanaf 18 jaar', 19 September (http://www.nu.nl/economie/594626/fnv-wil-minimumloon-vanaf-18-jaar.html).
Kalina, T., C. Weinkopf (2009) *Niedriglohnbeschäftigung 2007 weiter gestiegen – zunehmende Bedeutung von Niedrigstlöhnen.* Universitaet Duisburg Essen: IAQ-Report 2009–2005.
Kümmerling, A., Jansen, A. and Lehndorff, S. (2008) *Immer mehr Frauen sind erwerbstätig ⊠ aber mit immer kürzeren Wochenarbeitszeiten.* Universitaet Duisburg Essen: IAQ-Report 2008–2004.
Lok, R. and Siermann, C. (2009) 'Student verdient gemiddeld ruim 5 duizend per jaar bij', *CBS webmagazine,* 17 August .
Metro-Group (2006) *Metro Handelslexikon 2006/2007.* Düsseldorf.
Mason, G. and Salverda, W. (2010) 'Low pay, working conditions, and living standards', in J. Gautié and J. Schmitt (eds) *Low-Wage Work in the Wealthy World.* New York: Russell Sage Foundation, 35–90.
Mulholland, K.(2009) 'Life on the supermarket floor: replenishment assistants and just-in-time systems', in S.C. Bolton and M. Houlihan (eds) *Work Matters. Critical Reflections on Contemporary Work.* Basingstoke: Palgrave Macmillan, 162–179.
Rudolph, H. (2003) *Geringfügige Beschaeftigung in neuem Outfit.* Nürnberg: IAB-Kurzbericht 6/2003.
Sachverstaendigenrat (2005) *Erfolge im Ausland – Herausforderungen im Inland. Jahresgutachten 2004/05.* Berlin.
Salverda, W. (2008) 'The Dutch minimum wage: radical reduction shifts main focus to part-time jobs', in D. Vaughan-Whitehead (ed.) *The Minimum Wage Revisited in the Enlarged EU: Issues and Challenges.* Geneva: International Labour Organisation, 291–330.
Salverda, W., van Klaveren, M. and van der Meer, M. (2008) 'The Debate in the Netherlands on Low Pay', in W. Salverda, M. van Klaveren and M. van der Meer (eds) *Low-Wage Work in the Netherlands.* New York: Russell Sage Foundation, 16–31.
Swoboda, B., Foscht, T. and Cliquet, G. (2008) 'International value chain processes by retailers and wholesalers – a general approach', *Journal of Retailing and Consumer Services,* 15: 63–77.
Tijdens, K. (1998) *Zeggenschap over arbeidstijden.* The Hague: Welboom.

▶

Tijdens, K.G. (2005) 'How important are institutional settings to prevent marginalisation of part-time employment?', in I. Marx and W. Salverda (eds) *Low-wage Employment in Europe*. Leuven / Voorburg: Acco, 81–99.

Van Klaveren, M. (2008a) 'Retail industry: the contrast of supermarkets and consumer electronics', in W. Salverda, M. van Klaveren and M. van der Meer (eds) *Low-Wage Work in the Netherlands*. New York: Russell Sage Foundation, 148–176.

Van Klaveren, M. (2008b) 'The position, design and methodology of the industry studies', in W. Salverda, M. van Klaveren and M. van der Meer (eds) *Low-Wage Work in the Netherlands*. New York: Russell Sage Foundation, 132–147.

Van Klaveren, M.(2010) *Low Wages in the Retail Industry in the Netherlands*. Amsterdam: AIAS-University of Amsterdam, Working Paper.

Van Klaveren, M., W. Salverda and K. Tijdens (2009) 'Retail jobs in the Netherlands: low pay in a context of long-term wage moderation', *International Labour Review*, 148(4): 413–438.

ver.di (2010) *Teilbranchenanalyse Lebensmitteleinzelhandel*. Berlin.

Voss-Dahm, D. (2008) 'Low-paid but committed to the industry: salespeople in the retail sector', in G. Bosch and C. Weinkopf (eds) *Low-Wage Work in Germany*. New York: Russell Sage Foundation, 253–287.

Voss-Dahm, D. (2009) 'Warum Simone auch zukünftig weniger verdient als Simon. Ursachen geschlechtsspezifischer Ungleichheit', in S. Lehndorff (ed.) *Abriss, Umbau, Renovierung? Studien zum Wandel des deutschen Kapitalismusmodells*. Hamburg: VSA-Verlag, 81–109.

Voss-Dahm, D. and Lehndorff, S. (2003) *Lust und Frust in moderner Verkaufsarbeit*. Gelsenkirchen: IAT.

Wright, C. and Lund, J. (2006) 'Variations on a lean theme: work restructuring in retail distribution', *New Technology, Work and Employment*, 21(1): 59–74.

'No Place to Hide'? The Realities of Leadership in UK Supermarkets

Irena Grugulis, Ödül Bozkurt and Jeremy Clegg

This article explores the realities of managerial work in two major British supermarket chains. While the prescriptive literature welcomes the displacement of bureaucratic management by rote with leadership (see, e.g., Zaleznik, 1992), empirical accounts of what managers and leaders actually do underscore how the purported tenets of 'leadership' tend to disappear upon closer inspection, even at the discursive level (Tengblad, 2004; Alvesson and Sveningsson, 2003a, 2003b; Meindl et al, 1985). Kelly (2008) has taken issue with the tendency in the leadership literature of discounting the ordinary everyday work activity of managers in lieu of a continued effort to theoretically pin down how leadership *really* ought to be conceptualized. He argues that the common terminology used by various writers conceals a wide diversity of practice and that leadership is locally produced. We join Kelly's contention that 'the apparently mundane practices that are made accountable and therefore observable remain unexplicated and actively ignored' (p. 774) and that this is regrettable. We diverge from his emphasis on the reification of leadership through language games, however, and focus, instead, on the dissonance between the salience of leadership in the popular and practitioner representations of management jobs and the actual limits to the discretion, initiative and control that managers are able to exercise in the concrete, routine and core practices associated with their roles. A dissonance that was actively exploited by the supermarkets' business models. Celebratory accounts of leadership were cascaded down the managerial hierarchy, from the corporate head office to the departmental managers, to spur managerial staff to greater efforts in routine work.

The empirical material we use to support these claims comes from a study of managers and managerial work in the stores of two of Britain's largest supermarkets. In the four store sites where research was carried out, the work of managers was heavily prescribed with ordering, product ranges, stock levels, store layouts, pricing, special offers and staffing policies all set out by respective functional divisions at head office. Their work was also closely monitored, and their personal performance assessed through the constant and close inspection of the sales, profit and customer service performance scores of the stores and departments they were responsible for. In line with Hales' (2005) observations, these managers were not entrepreneurial visionaries, but links in a chain with little real influence over policies and procedures. Their work was generally confined to striving to meet a range of very demanding performance targets over which they themselves had little, if any, control.

In both supermarket chains, leadership by managers in stores was considered vital for company performance, with 'the importance of people' to competing with rival chains and 'keeping customers satisfied' repeatedly stressed by the full range of interviewees. Yet this leadership was to be exercised in specific and specified ways. Both managers in charge of stores and those in charge of departments had little power over most aspects of their work but were expected to lead, inspire, motivate and monitor staff on customer service (in the widest sense). Head office executives and store-level managers themselves in both chains repeatedly stressed the charismatic and inspirational elements of leadership. In particular, this depiction of leadership required managers to mediate between the dual pressures of much service sector work, to minimize costs but maximize customer service (Korczynski, 2001, 2002; Taylor and Bain, 1999). In this context, leadership appeared to be a euphemism for the demand that managers mobilize their personal physical, emotional and social resources to make up for the discrepancies between targets and resources and be ardent pursuers of the employer's end of the wage-effort bargain. This type of contained leadership bears little resemblance to the celebratory accounts but it is probably a far closer reflection of the realities of workplace practice.

While the article stresses the mundane nature of managerial jobs in supermarket stores, it also highlights the way both individual managers and shop floor workers use the leadership rhetoric. This rhetoric was valued by the managers largely because of its unreality: while they ostensibly 'bought in' to the rhetoric, in practice most were adept at negotiating the dissonance between it and real work and none sought to put its wider tenets into practice. On the shop floor the dramatic language of leadership and transformation was used to legitimize managerial freedoms: these were trivial but they nevertheless proved an escape from scripting for people management and were deeply valued by the managers themselves. We elaborate on the constitutive parts of our arguments in the rest of this article. First, we provide a critical review of the popular ways of conceptualizing leadership in the literature and the way these are problematic in relation to managerial work in practice. Then we introduce the specific context of retail work and of our study to highlight the significance of both to an inquiry into the discrepancy between leadership rhetoric and managerial practice. This is followed by a discussion of the contradictions inherent in leadership on the supermarket shop floor and the nature of the spaces that remain for initiative and freedom.

Managers, leaders and 'real work'

It is popular to claim that managerial work is changing, that hidebound and bureaucratic managers who impede workplace performance are being (or should be) replaced with charismatic and visionary leaders who know when to subvert rules, inspire enthusiasm in their followers and contribute to corporate dynamism (Zaleznik, 1992; Alimo-Metcalfe and Alban-Metcalfe, 2005). Such claims, clearly, need to be tempered with caution (Storey, 2004a, 2004b). Students of business and management have long suffered from those thrills of novelty that set critical descriptions of the existing and unfashionable against enthusiastic predictions of what an ideal type of the latest fad might look like. An unfair but recurrent practice that, as Storey (2004a) notes, is being repeated for leadership.

This advocacy is rendered possible, at least in part, by the paucity of empirical accounts of who leaders are and what it is they actually do (see, e.g., Jackson and Parry, 2008). When data is available authors rarely write about transformational activities. Rather, they stress how ordinary leaders are and how mundane their work is (Tengblad, 2004; Alvesson and Sveningsson, 2003a, 2003b; Meindl et al., 1985; Carlson, 1951). Even charismatic leaders are not unfettered (Robinson and Kerr, 2009). Empirical enquiry strips leadership of its universal grandeur and helps depict a practice that is both contested (Collinson, 2005) and locally defined (Kelly, 2008). Bureaucratic forms of control are still going strong (Hales, 2002; Protherough and Pick, 2002; Power, 1997) and old-fashioned supervision rather than inspirational leadership is at the heart of most jobs (Hales, 2005; Delbridge and Lowe, 1997).

Kelly (2008), in his analysis of the nature of leadership and the various discourses that surround it, has argued that leadership as a practice is locally defined and here we propose one example of such local definition: in this study, the requirements of customer service did indeed shape the demand for leadership skills, but not quite in the way that the proponents of the spread of transformational leadership suggest. What was at stake was not an entrepreneurial transformation. On the contrary, managers' actions were tightly controlled and those controls were increasing. As well as following orders from head office, store and department managers were simultaneously required to inspire, enthuse and motivate the front-line staff they were responsible for. The positive connotations of the word leadership helped to motivate individual managers, as they in turn sought to motivate others (Etzioni, 1961). Here the dissonance between the leadership rhetoric and workplace realities was not an analytical lacuna but an important part of the process since images of leaders needed to be inspirational rather than accurate.

Retail work

Retail work accounts for a significant proportion of the working population, with 12 per cent of UK workers employed in retail (Burt and Sparks, 2003). While this work can be skilled, from the glamour of the 'style labour markets' (Nickson et al., 2001 and this volume), to the product knowledge of expert assistants in France (McGauran, 2000, 2001), the wide-ranging skills of apprentice-trained workers in Germany (Kirsch et al., 2000) or the impressive educational achievements of Chinese retail workers (Gamble, 2006), most British jobs are not (see also Price, this volume, for the Australian experience).

For the majority of British supermarkets, the main skills policy pursued is one that is 'tantamount to a personnel strategy based on zero competence', zero qualifications, zero training and zero career (Gadrey, 2000: 26). Margins are tight and the extensive centralization and standardization of supply chains and products (Baron et al., 2001) extends to work and work processes (Felstead et al., 2009 and this volume). Workers are valued for their presence and their temporal flexibility, not their skills, and presence and temporal flexibility are seldom highly paid. The retail sector accounts for 26 per cent of British low-paid workers (Mason et al., 2008) with 75 per cent of sales assistants and 80 per cent of checkout operators compensated at rates below the low-pay threshold (Mason and Osborne, 2008). Part-time and women workers, who dominate the sector (Arrowsmith and Sisson, 1999; Burt and Sparks, 2003) are particularly badly affected by this (see also van Klaveren and Voss-Dahm, this volume). Some stores deploy sophisticated HR management techniques such as psychometric tests (Freathy and Sparks, 2000) and merit-based pay but these are set against generally low wage rates, rigid control mechanisms and limited discretion (Arrowsmith and Sisson, 1999; Broadbridge, 2002; Burt and Sparks, 2003).

Against this backdrop, recent writing on retail employment from a strategic perspective has increasingly emphasized the role of management and managers in the overall performance of companies (Booth and Hamer, 2006; Hart et al., 2006). It argues that the link between managers' work and store (or firm) performance is through 'lay' workers, in one example, asserting that 'without strong management and leadership skills, store and employee productivity suffers together with lower staff motivation, ultimately leading to lower profits' (Hart et al., 2006:281–282) However, lists of actions such as 'providing good pay and benefits, praise and encouragement and support and training, or even at the most basic level, ensuring employees receive their correct rest periods at work' (Booth and Hamer, 2006: 299) do not accurately depict the real remit of managers in large-scale retail organizations.

Methods and methodology

This research was part of an EPSRC/AIM funded project on the organization and experience of employment in retailing. Since our main interest was in the processual aspects of work a multi-pronged, qualitative approach was adopted, as this was best suited to compare and contrast official organizational statements with real-life practices and experiences. Research was conducted in two of Britain's largest supermarket chains, here referred to as Retail 1 and Retail 2, respectively. Retail 1 had 356 stores and employed over 160,000 people. Retail 2's portfolio of stores included the convenience store format, which brought its total number of stores to 823, but it had slightly fewer employees at around 150,000. By and large their target clientele overlapped and they were direct competitors with similar market shares.

In each supermarket detailed interviews were conducted with head office staff who were responsible for determining strategies, setting policies and designing business processes. We were able to review a large amount and range of company material pertaining to company strategy, business models, performance indicators, human resource policies, recruitment and training programmes, and change initiatives. Interviews were carried out with top executives in strategy, human resources, training, marketing, accounting, customer services, profit/productivity/performance improvement departments. In addition to this, in each chain, two locations were selected for store-level research: store A and store B at Retail 1, store C and store D at Retail 2. In the stores interviews were conducted with the (general) store managers, who would be managing anywhere between 200 and 400 employees, the secondary tier of between 3 and 5 senior managers, had store-wide responsibility and supervised and coordinated the work of department managers and the managers of the 12–15 different departments such as produce, customer service, or bakery, ad well as well as a number of shop floor workers. All of the managers were salaried, while all of the shop floor workers were hourly paid. Store interviews with hourly paid workers were the most challenging. Our informants were welcoming and supportive but, owing to the tight margins and pressure on staff, few had time for interviews. The length of interviews with managers ranged from half an hour to multiple sessions of several hours, typically averaging an hour and a half to two hours. Some of the interviews with workers also lasted over an hour, but a number of them had to be interrupted shy of half an hour. All formal interviews were recorded, professionally transcribed and coded using NVivo Qualitative Data Analysis software. In total, 86 interviews were carried out: 46 in Retail 1, 34 in Retail 2, and the rest with a range of outside key informants including a top level executive of a third supermarket chain, industry experts based at the Institute of Grocery Distributors (IGD), and trade union representatives. In addition to the interviews, participant and non-participant observation was carried out by one of the research team at the Retail 1 head office and, more extensively, at one of the two Retail 1 stores included in the study (store A). In addition to observing recruitment group interviews, new employee induction sessions, and a range of daily activities in the store, the researcher also worked shifts of 10 to 15 hours a week for 6 weeks on the delicatessen, fish, rotisserie, pizza and ready-meal counters. A research diary was kept during this part of the fieldwork and transcribed.

'No place to hide'

Leadership was a 'quality' that was extensively referenced in the public presentations of managerial career paths in both supermarket chains. Retail 1's literature on career prospects described the training programme for shop floor workers who wished to become department managers as being 'built upon' their 'current leadership skills' through on-the-job training, while that for department managers with ambitions to be store managers or deputies was said to help them 'perfect their leadership style'. Retail 2's careers information on the company website directed those with some previous retail management experience and 'looking to grow into a leadership role' to the 'fast-track to Store Manager Development Program'. Hitting the link, interested parties were informed that nobody played a more important role in the supermarket's everyday operations (turnaround) than the managers in the stores, whose leadership 'inspires our people to deliver a great everyday customer experience'. Retail 2's recruitment process for senior managers included psychometric tests that were, among other qualities, designed to pick up leadership skills and potential. Retail 1's programmes for management development included selection hurdles such as role play sessions where future managers were expected to stand out from among their peers by displaying the desired abilities, with 'leadership' prominent among these.

While leadership skills and qualities were presented as core to the work of everyone and as particularly central for progression into managerial roles, in stores almost every aspect of work for every kind of employee, from shop floor workers during their training period all the way to the general store manager, was set out, standardized and occasionally scripted by the experts at head office. Buyers sourced goods and set prices at the head offices, with computer networks monitoring sales in stores and re-ordering supplies. The corporate HR department set wages and provided clear targets for store managers in terms of staffing, leaving stores with a balancing act between resources and targets. Checkout tills used electronic scanning, shelf-stackers followed planograms that provided detailed layout plans for displays, price guns printed out price tags, including reductions, as decided by head office software depending on the time of day. According to long-serving informants, limits on discretion were increasing. The remaining specialist departments, such as the delicatessen counter (which included meats, cheeses and fish) and the bakery were coming under increasing levels of central control. A trained butcher (now the manager of a non-food department) revealed that most meats were now cut and packaged before arrival in store. The same was true for cheeses. In the smaller stores bakeries worked entirely from deliveries of frozen goods that they re-heated, and in larger stores there was a mix of supplier-packed, frozen, ambient and chilled products, and goods baked in store. But even breads baked in store arrived ready made up with instructions on times for mixing, proving and baking. The only formally accredited staff in stores were pharmacists employed in special stand-alone units on some sites. Such a policy of standardization was deliberate and referred to with pride. The wage planning manager in the Business Improvement Group at Retail 1 head office summarized the challenge as 'how lazy we can make it... make the process easy for them so it becomes a natural habit'.

This close prescription and standardization of work tasks was not a surprising observation to make of hourly paid workers, or in the context of retail employment, traditionally known for its reliance on low skills and low wages. What was unusual was that the same restrictions applied to managers. In fact, the managers were under far greater surveillance in terms of observable results. Because performance and productivity measurements were taken at both department and store level, which were then linked back and traceable to individual managers, their performance evaluation was quantified and routinized. There was no comparable performance evaluation of individual shop floor workers except for those at the tills, although Retail 2 had just introduced a new performance enhancement programme to track the performance of individual workers. Yet these practices, too, only increased the number of indicators by which managers' performance could be monitored, as the ultimate responsibility for meeting unit-based targets, as well as ensuring that individual workers showed the head-office dictated levels of performance still lay with the managers.

An executive in the productivity improvement division of Retail 2's head office operations, who had risen through the ranks, observed that the role of store managers had changed considerably over the last 20 years:

> I think what we probably lost was a bit of the entrepreneurial or trades-manship of the store manager to say, 'Oh next week that's going on offer, I want 200 of them next week'. Because they were good traders, and experienced. And they knew how they were going to present it. Honestly when I joined... the store manager where I trained was a bit of a wide boy I suppose, but he would do things like – well he made me do it – Saturday afternoon if we were overstocked, I remember him saying 'We're overstocked on lettuces. [Name] go to the front door and stand there and sell your lettuces!' And you'd do things like say 'Come on, here's your lettuce! Get one for the rabbit! Half price!' And you'd literally drop them in people's baskets as they walked through the door so they almost got no choice but to have your lettuce. (Productivity Improvement Manager, Retail 2, Head Office)

But in the current arrangements, because of the focus on what Pye (1968) terms the 'workmanship of certainty', the emphasis in store for both managers and workers was on obedience to instruction. In fact, much of a manager's work was about ensuring such obedience:

> [The parent company] is very much about... they use a word quite a lot called compliance and there is a lot of compliance and the phrase they used... was 'there is no place to hide' [*Was that like an official thing?*] No it was kind of like – you know with all the systems, their systems monitor everything, they monitor everything. Every little thing is monitored so there is no place to hide. I am not saying in terms of hiding things that are wrong but they see everything. (Senior Manager, Retail 1, Store B)

A policy backed up by the motto 'comply then complain', which had clear implications for the way work was conducted:

> [I]f the company says to you 9 am Monday morning stand on one leg in the foyer, I want you to do it, at 9 am and if that's all of you, I want you to do it but then you'll all stand there thinking why on God's earth are we doing this, then ask the question, why do we need to do this? What benefit am I getting from it? But do it in the first place before you even

complain about it, because until you've tried it you don't know what it's going to do, but it's driving that culture. (General Store Manager, Retail 1, Store A)

This approach was generally greeted with enthusiasm:

I love this comply and then complain. You know because you put it right, you do it the way they want you to do it and then if it is not right you feed back what is wrong with it so you complain after you have had a go at it at putting it right. And I think that is absolutely vital. You know we have a duty to feed back and give that feedback but you know we don't have that right until we have had a go at it…. the right way first. (Training Manager, Retail 1, Training Store)

Unsurprisingly, such an approach influenced the skills expected of both workers and managers as well as leaving little space for transformational leadership. Skill levels were low and product knowledge in particular was a welcome, but almost optional part of work. Several of our informants did possess expertise and boasted strong personal interests in electronics or fish or experience in bakeries, but while this might allow front-line workers to develop a personal pride in aspects of their work, it was not a job requirement and was rarely shared by the senior management team in stores, whose career progression was based on obligatory movement between different departments. Head office executives spoke of promoting people with an interest in a particular area of work, a 'passion about food' or 'a personal interest', and management training did provide product information as part of the process, but the demand for and emphasis on specialist knowledge was limited. Mason and Osborne's (2008) comparison of supermarkets with electrical retailers reveals that the (often supplier provided) training in product knowledge that characterized electrical goods had few parallels in supermarkets, while Gamble's (2006) research into Chinese retailers showed a well educated workforce and a highly demanding customer base not reflected in our study. In these supermarkets workers could apply for entry-level managerial posts as soon as their twelve weeks of initial training were complete (although the graduate training schemes in both supermarkets were rather different).

Graduates were more noticeable in the head offices and in certain specialisms (3 of the 4 store-based HR managers we spoke to were graduates, compared to 3 of the 23 managers in Retail 1 Store A). But while one of the HR managers thought that having a degree was useful for 'the analytical side of what (managers) need to do', in general formal qualifications were not a significant criteria for managerial posts. The vast majority of managers had come up from the ranks of hourly paid shop floor workers. Interestingly, the non-graduate managers all spoke of the encouragement they had received from their managers to embark on management training. In the absence of universal demand for specialist training or knowledge, leadership, both demonstrated and potential, was presented as the key element in selection decisions for such career progression:

> I mean, when I interview managers to join my team, I'm not necessarily looking for 'Do they know what baked beans and yoghurts are?' and 'Have they filled them before?' . I'm looking for attitude, I'm looking for personal resilience and I'm looking for a track record. What have they done before? What have they done in the past? But it doesn't necessarily mean that if I've got a grocery manager position I want a grocery manager from another store. Because it's about managing people, it's about managing hearts and minds really. (General Store Manager, Retail 1, Store A)

But while store language focused on obedience and hearts and minds, the structural features of promotion ensured that, in practice, most managers and leaders were men. Moving between departments was an integral part of career mobility in both supermarkets. Promotion, even for the first foray into managerial duties, involved a switch of departments, while subsequent expansions of responsibility meant managers would be moved to increasingly larger departments in the stores. For general store managers, and for the second tier of senior management, geographical mobility was required and managers were expected to move between different stores in the same 'regional cluster' (generally between 15 to 25 stores, depending on the region).

Interestingly, managerial informants stressed how lenient their superiors were when imposing these travel requirements. Annual performance appraisals distinguished between preferences for a thirty-minute or a one-hour commute, Retail 2 store managers were told by their regional bosses to prioritize their families and the general manager of store B asserted proudly that he would not be despatched to the other end of the country against his will. But, while all managers seemed to accept that mobility was required, for others the geographical differences between managerial and front-line worker posts discouraged progression and helped to account for the fact that, while the lower ranks of supermarket workers were dominated by women, the managers were predominately male. Many of the workers we interviewed were attracted to retail by the fact that it was part-time: women with caring responsibilities, students, young people and older workers dominated the workforce. People worked in their local stores and their limited hours often suited their other responsibilities or desire for education. Managerial posts, by contrast, were almost universally full-time. And this despite the fact that, given the length opening hours (24 hours for Retail 1 and 8 am to 10 pm for Retail 2) no one manager would be able to control their store continually (see Moss-Kanter, 1977; Dalton, 1966). We did meet a two women managers in shared posts but these were rare and had been specifically created to accommodate these informants' demands for job sharing (see also Mason and Osborne, 2008).

Small freedoms

Unlike the transformational visionaries of the leadership literature, the freedoms enjoyed by the supermarket managers in this study were generally minor and illicit. Despite the recurrent official emphasis on 'comply then complain' most created their own small discretionary spaces. The most commonly cited example was in store, counter or shelf layout. Detailed specifications were sent down from head office dictating the number and placement of products. But these were based on national averages of other stores in that category with little sensitivity for local geography, tastes or customer base. Accordingly, in practice local knowledge, personal interest and the desire to personalize space often triumphed over the formal specifications. It was, of course, possible to protest against layouts officially. The general manager of Retail 1 Store A had done so when he wished to re-site the movie and video booth in his city centre store, taking it out of the foyer where it was vulnerable to repeated thefts and switching it with a sandwich booth that would have benefited from being more readily accessible. His request involved developing a detailed business case and visits from senior management but was eventually turned down (or indefinitely postponed pending a fuller refurbishment to include a pharmacy). Other were less regulation bound:

> I just did it, I got told to do it. They put trust in me to change the layout in the store of Home and Leisure, to move products around if I believed it would gain sales. And for example all the Home section wasn't together, DIY and water was with pots and pans, party ranges weren't with disposable paper tableware, so I put a new shop-floor plan together to move it all around and we did that.... [A]t [names other store] I'd gone through a couple of revamps where I'd actually changed over 200 bays in [other store] because we went through revamps to get bigger and better ranges in so I'd done a lot of work in the past on how a department should flow and how it should look and how we get the best out of the ranges and stuff like that so putting that experience into here and grouping the departments

together .... [*Did you have to negotiate with Head Office?*] No we just did it. (Senior Manager, Retail 1, Store B)

Occasionally re-siting compensated for inadequacies in the briefing documents. One manager liked to get experienced staff to adapt official shelving briefs to suit the store:

They know if they've been doing that for a couple of years, they know what will sell and what won't. Now [if] it's a novice then they wouldn't, so I'd need them to do it in space flexing which will tell them the quantity. The plan would tell them how many facings so, say, it was like that it wanted a capacity of 70 on four facings but you can fit that 70 on two facings I would expect you to do it to two facings. And that's where you gain space as well on the plan if you needed to open up on something else because it wasn't lasting on the shop. [*So you've got to play around quite a bit?*] Yes you've got to play around with it, yes. Everything's not as easy as black and white on paper. (General Merchandise Manager, Retail 1 Store B)

Occasionally individuals also needed to override the computer systems to overcome limitations. The demand for hot dog rolls on bonfire night, more salads and fresh vegetables for barbecues on unexpectedly hot days, and ensuring that local tastes were provided for through particular fish or flavours of roast chicken were matters of relative individual discretion.

But most of these practices were heavily discouraged officially and many were formally denied. One manager of a Retail 2 supermarket during a first interview and guided tour of his store was enthusiastic about the way Retail 2's head office experts designed and laid out the shelf space. An enthusiasm that lasted until one of the researchers took out a camera to photograph the excellent layout. He was immediately asked not to take photographs, since the manager had exercised his own discretion and did not want news of this individuality to get back to head office.

People and leadership

Amidst the widespread use of regulation, standardization and constraint there was one area where managers were both encouraged and expected to use their own discretion and, in the rhetoric of their head offices, exercise 'leadership'. This was in the area of people management. The structural means for doing this was very limited. Wages, staffing levels and worker tasks were all pre-set by head office, although some local adjustments were possible. Store managers who recruited staff would be told how many 'hours' they could hire, but it was up to them to decide how to divide this up, so, for example, 20 hours might translate into 3 new part-timers working distinctive shifts. This often proved difficult to implement, since computer staffing levels did not always translate into viable recruitment:

> The Personnel Manager, she cares a lot, but [for] the company [it's] all about its process, [it's] not really about the people. And so the process is sort of disguised as this 'caring' – but it's not. So these people, they just expect you to do more and more, and we take more and more sales but we don't necessarily get the hours. Produce was given 20 extra hours for quarter three in line with sales and things, but I can't recruit for these 20 hours because all that'll happen is they'll get taken away after Christmas or the sales won't be there so I'll never see them anyway. You know they're not tangible, I can't take them and use them. (Produce Manager, Retail 1, Store A)

Much of this was work intensification. Head office staff expected local managers to know to whom they could allocate particular tasks to save a few hours on the timesheet and this was considered excellence in leadership:

> [S]o we're looking for the managers to not be creative in the ways they do their processes, I want them to follow the processes exactly how the systems define them...I want them to lay the store out how the system devises and I want them to fill the shelves how it says on the tin, if you like, but then absolutely be as creative as possible in the way you service the customers. More the way we would be going. (Business Improvement Director, Retail 1, Head Office)

This 'creativity' was also set down in systems and structures of the stores. The performance of their departments or stores in terms of customer service was assessed through monthly 'mystery shopper' visits, while regular staff meetings provided managers with an opportunity to motivate. The morning shifts in both supermarkets began with caucus-style meetings, held in a central location on the shop floor in Retail 1 and in a staff area in Retail 2, between the store manager, the upper management team and all the departmental managers who were on shift. Department managers held the same sort of 'getting the day started' meetings with their respective department staff. News about how the store or unit was doing in terms of the performance criteria was often a major theme, good performance was usually emphasized as a reason to feel good and underperformance as grave and in need of immediate attention. In the briefing templates handed down from the head offices, spots were allocated for events to note, improve or celebrate. Managers' motivational role (whether through generating pride or alarm) was possibly most necessary during these meetings, as announcements, for example, about the roll-out of new uniforms could be rendered exciting, or a letter of appreciation from a customer as emotionally touching, through their performative skills.

Performance related pay was extensively used. For general store managers it could amount to as much as 40 per cent of salary and even hourly paid workers might earn over £100. Individual performance was supposed to be assessed separately, as one informant noted: 'sometimes you can have a department which hasn't performed well on paper but what that manager's contributed to that maybe it's a total different story'. But in practice greatest weight was placed on store and overall company performance in a given trading year. Both supermarkets used some version of recognition schemes where small monetary awards from £10 to £50 could be given out, and this was largely at managers' discretion to 'celebrate success', as there was 'a lot of pressure on everybody to perform all the time' (bakery manager, Retail 2). But managers appreciated that the effectiveness of such schemes was limited:

> [A] lot is spending time with them and motivating them. You know if you motivate them they work far better than – [*How can you motivate them? What do you have at your disposal to motivate them?*] You don't really have any financial really, apart from you've got the yearly bonus, you know colleagues get a yearly bonus. So you've got the bonus to aim for. I don't know really...I think everyone is motivated by doing a good job and job satisfaction and spending time with people and I think a lot of it as well is getting to know colleagues, I know just about everyone by their first name and things like that. (Senior Manager, Retail 1 Store A)

The financial outcomes of managers' work was assessed through daily checks and monitoring of sales, waste, loss of products and the profits their departments or stores generated. Many were factors over which they had little control. Describing her Key Result Areas, which included absences, sales, labour turnover, waste, and the customer service score the HR manager (Retail 1, Store A) commented, '[s]o all my key result areas are linked with everybody else's, so it's my influencing skills that are really being looked at for that....As a manager, you're paid to manage; you're not paid to fill the shop necessarily'.

This confidence was widespread. But as the store managers pointed out structural conditions, including local labour markets, might be ignored in head office plans but heavily influenced how effective such work intensification could be. One, who was responsible for staffing a city centre store in a University town spoke with envy of a friend who managed a rural outlet. If workers in the city centre felt unfairly treated they had a choice of part-time service sector jobs to move to. Their rural counterparts, in the absence of other local job opportunities, stayed in post (many had been there since the store opened). Yet this was the area over which managers were deemed to have most control and many seemed to accept this. When our informants spoke about leadership, their most common reaction was to emphasize the difference that they, as individuals, could make. A graduate departmental manager in his early 20s noted that he needed to 'work on leadership and people skills'. It was not that these managers did not appreciate the impact that computer breakdowns, local labour markets, employee turnover, stock levels and the weather could have. They did, and dealt with such problems every day. But they also saw them as excuses for a lack of leadership. It was the managers' job to enthuse and inspire others, even when policies and practices had not been explained to them and even if they disagreed with head office decisions (see also Smith, 1990; Watson, 1994). According to three of our informants:

the depot might have been short of people and deliveries haven't turned up on time. That could throw things off. Or promotional stuff hasn't turned up. But there's nothing in a store that we can't fix, and it's all about driving the right attitude in the management teams. Because if you drive that attitude well, you can fix anything. (General Store Manager, Retail 1, Store A)

At the end of the day we've got to be the leader...I think there's a difference between being a manager and being a leader and we have to become leaders and...we need to keep a real positive approach, because if we turn round to staff and say yes, what we may think in our heart of hearts is one thing, but when we go out there we're out on stage, we've got to perform and say, 'OK, it's tough, but however if we all do this that and the other and get stuck in, we're going to win this'. And you've somehow got to inspire your people out there, you know, so you've got to leave that at the door, because we can't do anything about that. Somehow what you have got to do is deal with the colleagues you have got, to ensure that they're motivated, trained, they're quick to do the job, and hyped up, and they're going to go out there and deliver it. (Senior Manager A, Retail 2, Store C)

OK, if I'm in store today and we get the [mystery shopper] man and I get 90 per cent, then that's on my watch so was I here, was I up in the office looking at the PC or was I downstairs driving the availability, saying,

'Where are those cauliflowers, where's that, where's that, where's that?' Or did I allow there to be nobody on produce because both the departments' managers... are on the same day off, and when they came in there was no cauliflower or lettuce because the person down there was actually on the till and I didn't actually know.... Yes so if I'm going to be running a store tomorrow, for instance, I should really know who's in what's going on and any problems. (Senior Manager B, Retail 2, Store C)

Leadership in these supermarkets was very specific and very detailed. Formal HR practices, meeting templates and detailed systems were in place. Informants gave examples that included monitoring work to ensure people were achieving their targets, retraining those who were not; monitoring stock levels; and being present on the shop floor. However ultimately encounters with people, whether employees or customers, could not be scripted. The leadership rhetoric, because of its lack of links to the reality of daily work, was used as a motivational tool to persuade managers to work more intensively themselves and encourage others to extra effort.

Discussion and conclusions

This article has presented an empirically based discussion of leadership in British supermarkets. The managers we observed were constrained by extensive regulation. Their experience of deskilling and discretion, consent and control bears little resemblance to the entrepreneurial visionaries described by writers on leadership. Yet despite that, most of our informants described aspects of what they did as leadership, maintaining proudly, and often in defiance of the evidence, the difference that they, as individuals could make.

Evidence from elsewhere confirms the impact that line managers have (Rainbird and Munro, 2003) but, this impact is not without limits. Here, head office systems, computerized schedules, pre-packaged and automatically ordered goods, design planograms and set hours and pay rates provided internal constraints just as location, labour market and the local economy supplied external ones. Our informants needed to accept the leadership rhetoric enough to assert that they could make a difference, but not so much that that difference was extended to questioning the constraints on them; a difference accepted in practice by most.

This leads us to two conclusions. First, that leadership was a small freedom rather than a radical transformation (see also Rosenthal et al., 1997 on empowerment; Edwards and Collinson, 2002). It affected only the minutiae of the work but even this trivial level of discretion made a great deal of difference to the individual managers. The illicit freedoms of revising store layouts and adjusting stock orders, which managers engaged in to make their mark on work and improve store performance, were matched by official and acceptable areas of freedom in the unscriptable areas of people management.

These trivial freedoms lead us to our second conclusion, on the implications for academic analysis. Leadership is, at least in part, what leaders do, how they do it and who they are. If, as here, mainly male managers worked to pre-set routines with tightly monitored targets then this needs to feature in our understanding of leadership. Yet to date, most accounts have neglected the mundane aspects of work, the very elements highlighted as core in this study. The leadership rhetoric, valued for its emotive qualities and its unreality, was used by managers and their superiors to value, inspire and intensify their input. And managers showed a sophistication missing from many academic writings in their ability to distinguish between rhetorical flourishes and real-world job design. Given this we suggest that future research may wish to focus more clearly on the unexciting, hackneyed and everyday aspects of work and to consider the form the language of leadership really takes on the shop floor. The unrealities of leadership are important but they have already absorbed too much academic attention and need to be clearly distinguished from the realities. Future studies, developed through empirical evidence, need to provide a nuanced, local and empirically based understanding of what really happens.

REFERENCES

Alimo-Metcalfe, B. and Alban-Metcalfe, J. (2005) 'Leadership: time for a new direction?' *Leadership,* 1(1): 51–71.
Alvesson, M. and Sveningsson, S. (2003a) 'The great disappearance act: difficulties in doing leadership', *Leadership Quarterly,* 14: 359–381.
Alvesson, M. and Sveningsson, S. (2003b) 'Managers doing leadership: the extra ordinarization of the mundane', *Human Relations,* 56(12):1435–1459.
Arrowsmith, J. and Sisson, K. (1999) 'Pay and working time: towards organisation-based systems?' *British Journal of Industrial Relations,* 37(1): 51–75.
Baron, S., Harris, K., Leaver, D. and Oldfield, B.M. (2001) 'Beyond convenience: the future for independent food and grocery retailers in the UK', *The International Review of Retail, Distribution and Consumer Research,* 11(4): 395–414.
Booth, S. and Hamer, K. (2006) 'Labour turnover in the retail industry: predicting the role of individual, organisational and environmental factors', *International Journal of Retail and Distribution Management,* 35(4): 289–307.

▶

Broadbridge, A. (2002) 'Rationalising retail employment: a view from the outside looking in', *International Journal of Retail and Distribution Management,* 30(11): 536–543.

Burt, S. and Sparks, L. (2003) 'Department of trade and industry: competitive analysis of the retail sector in the UK.'

Carlson, S. (1951) *Executive Behaviour: a study of the workload and the working methods of managing directors.* Stockholm: Stromberg.

Collinson, D. (2005) 'Dialectics of leadership.' *Human Relations* 58(11): 1419–1442.

Dalton, M. (1966) *Men who Manage.* New York and London: Wiley.

Delbridge, R. and Lowe, J. (1997) 'Manufacturing control: supervisory systems on the 'new' shopfloor', *Sociology,* 31(3): 409–426.

Edwards, P. and Collinson, M. (2002) 'Empowerment and Managerial Labour Strategies: Pragmatism Regained.' *Work and Occupations,* 29(3): 272–299.

Etzioni, A. (1961) *A Comparative Analysis of Complex Organisations.* New York: Free Press.

Felstead, A., Fuller, A., Jewson, N. and Unwin, L. (2009) *Improving Working as Learning.* London: Routledge.

Freathy, P. and Sparks, L. (2000) 'The organisation of working time in large UK food retail firms', in C. Baret, S. Lehndorff and L. Sparks (eds) *Flexible Working Time in Food Retailing: A Comparison between France, Germany the UK and Japan.* London and New York: Routledge.

Gadrey, J. (2000) 'Working time configurations: theory, methods and assumptions for an international comparison', in C. Baret, S. Lehndorff and L. Sparks (eds) *Flexible Working in Food Retailing: A Comparison between France, Germany, the UK and Japan.* London and New York: Routledge.

Gamble, J. (2006) 'Multinational retailers in China: proliferating 'McJobs' or developing skills?' *Journal of Management Studies,* 43(7): 1463–1490.

Hales, C. (2002) ' "Bureaucracy-lite" and Continuities in Managerial Work', *British Journal of Management,* 13(1): 51–66.

Hales, C. (2005) 'Rooted in supervision, branching into management: continuity and change in the role of first-line manager', *Journal of Management Studies,* 42(3): 471–506.

Hart, C., Stachow, G.B., Grazyna, B., Farrell, A.M. and Reed, G. (2006) 'Employer perceptions of skills gaps in retail: issues and implications for UK retailers', *International Journal of Retail and Distribution Management,* 35(4): 271–288.

Jackson, B. and Parry, K. (2008) *A Very Short, Fairly Interesting and Reasonably Cheap Book about Studying Leadership.* London: Sage.

Kelly, S. (2008) 'Leadership: a categorical mistake?' *Human Relations,* 61(6): 763–782.

Kirsch, J., Klein, M., Lehndorff, S. and Voss-Dahm, D. (2000). 'The organisation of working time in large German food retail firms', in C. Baret, S. Lehndorff and L. Sparks (eds) *Flexible Working in Food Retailing: A Comparison between France, Germany, the UK and Japan.* London and New York: Routledge.

▶

Korczynski, M. (2001) 'The contradictions of service work: call centre as customer-oriented bureaucracy', in A. Sturdy, I. Grugulis, and H. Willmott (eds) *Customer Service: Empowerment and Entrapment*. Basingstoke: Palgrave, 79–101.

Korczynski, M. (2002) *Human Resource Management in Service Work*. Basingstoke: Palgrave.

Mason, G., Mayhew, K. and Osborne, M. (2008) 'Low paid work in the United Kingdom: an overview', in C. Lloyd, G. Mason and K. Mayhew (eds) *Low wage work in the United Kingdom*. New York: Russell Sage Foundation.

Mason, G. and Osborne, M. (2008) 'Business strategies, work organisation and low pay in United Kingdom retailing', in C. Lloyd, G. Mason, and K. Mayhew (eds) *Low wage work in the United Kingdom*. New York: Russell Sage Foundation.

McGauran, A.-M. (2000) 'Vive la différence: the gendering of occupational structures in a case study of Irish and French retailing', *Women's Studies International Forum* 23(5): 613–627.

McGauran, A.-M. (2001) 'Masculine, feminine or neutral? In-company equal opportunities policies in Irish and French MNC retailing', *International Journal of Human Resource Management*, 12(5): 754–771.

Meindl, J.R., Ehrlich, S.B. and Dukerich, J.M. (1985) 'The romance of leadership', *Administrative Science Quarterly*, 30(1): 78–102.

Moss-Kanter, R. (1977) *Men and Women of the Corporation*. New York: Basic Books.

Nickson, D., Warhurst, C., Witz, A. and Cullen, A.-M. (2001) 'The importance of being aesthetic: work, employment and service organisation', in A. Sturdy, I. Grugulis, and H. Willmott (eds) *Customer Service: Empowerment and Entrapment*. Basingstoke: Palgrave.

Power, M. (1997) *The Audit Society*. Oxford: Oxford University Press.

Protherough, R. and Pick, J. (2002) *Managing Britannia*. Exeter: Imprint Academic.

Pye, D. (1968). *The Nature and Art of Workmanship*. Cambridge: Cambridge University Press.

Rainbird, H. and Munro, A. (2003). 'Workplace learning and the employment relationship in the public sector', *Human Resource Management Journal*, 13(2): 30–44.

Robinson, S.K. and Kerr, R. (2009). 'The symbolic violence of leadership: a critical hermeneutic study of leadership and succession in a British organisation in the post-Soviet context', *Human Relations*, 62(6): 875–903.

Rosenthal, P., Hill, S. and Peccei, R. (1997). 'Checking out service: evaluating excellence, HRM and TQM in retailing', *Work, Employment and Society*, 11(3): 481–503.

Smith, V. (1990) *Managing in the Corporate Interest: Control and Resistance in An American Bank*. Berkley, Los Angeles and Oxford: University of California Press.

▶

Storey, J. (2004a) 'Changing theories of leadership and leadership development', in J. Storey (ed.) *Leadership in Organizations: Current Issues and Future Trends*. London: Routledge.

Storey, J. (2004b) 'Signs of change: "damned rascals" and beyond', in J. Storey (ed.) *Leadership in Organizations: Current Issues and Key Trends*. London: Routledge.

Taylor, P. and Bain, P. (1999) 'An assembly line in the head: work and employee relations in the call centre', *Industrial Relations Journal,* 30(2): 101–117.

Tengblad, S. (2004) 'Expectations of alignment: examining the link between financial markets and managerial work', *Organization Studies* 25(4): 583–606.

Watson, T.J. (1994) *In Search of Management*. London: Routledge.

Zaleznik, A. (1992) 'Managers and leaders: are they different?' *Harvard Business Review,* 70(2): 126–135.

'In Search of Teamworking in a Major Supermarket: A Fig-Leaf for Flexibility?'

11

Kate Mulholland

This chapter explores the management approach to teamwork in the aftermath of the introduction of lean production in a major supermarket. Informal group working was dissolved and lean teamwork imposed accompanied by further standardization and task individualization. Senior workers who acted informally as team leaders, were replaced with new team leaders. The new 'lean team' takes three forms. First, rooted in a unitary managerial perspective, the team is company-wide and is portrayed as a collaborative partnership between management and labour, conveyed in the notion of the 'team spirit' (Proctor and Mueller, 2000; Rinehart et al., 1997). Second, teams are organized around core functions such as checkout and replenishment, where team members are required to work flexibly. Third, aside from butchers and bakers there is a minority of tacitly skilled code checkers and merchandisers organized in small groups who do not work flexibly. This chapter will explore how lean production, a new management system initiated changes to work practices that set the scene for lean teamwork. In examining the character of the new lean teamwork in replenishment and checkout functions and including the Night Shift, Grocery and Checkout teams, the chapter will argue that the primary purpose of the lean teamwork is to accommodate numerical flexibility and the deployment of staff across jobs.

The teamworking debate

Over the last two decades the widespread diffusion of teamwork as a feature of work organization has generated much debate including a wide range of studies in sectors and organizations, such as vehicle manufacture (Rinehart et al., 1997; Danford, 1999), the service sector (Proctor and Mueller, 2000), pharmaceuticals (Lloyd and Newell, 2000), the Royal Mail (Martinez Lucio et al., 2000), public information call centres (Mulholland, 2002) and more recently NHS call centres (Smith et al., 2008). What is clear from these studies is while they report the spread of teamwork beyond the manufacturing sector, they also raise critical questions over how the influence of lean production has changed the character of teamwork from a model based on socio-technical systems and variations of autonomous group work.

Womack, Roos and Jones (1990) advocate of the lean team, argue that teamwork is at the heart of lean work, and claim that team members are autonomous, make decisions and utilize skill and knowledge in problem solving. A departure from the strictures of the Fordist approach, the lean team organization nurtures a workplace culture that is inherently innovative and efficient, where, having abandoned trade union allegiance committed members deliver higher productivity, This then suggests major change mechanisms, namely, work redesign that includes a unified, but autonomous workplace culture, which purportedly can be applied universally.

This claim has been widely challenged. Rinehart et al. (1997) amongst others argue that Womack's neat recipe is inherently contradictory. On the question of autonomy, the authors point out that this is in fact associated with the earlier socio-economic model of teamwork, while the lean team is increasingly defined in line with management priorities, suggestive of a top–down workplace culture. Proctor and Mueller (2000) argue that the current wave of teamworking is distinguished particularly by the relationship between organizational strategic intent and performance informing how work is structured and managed. They argue that the new teamwork ties value with performance, which Mueller (1994) sees as demonstrative of a change in the managerial purpose of lean teamworking, as a shift from social to economic concerns in workplace organization. Danford's (1999) extensive survey of Japanese management techniques – the precursor of lean production – has identified the design mechanisms that have accompanied teamwork including the maximum use of labour, the minimization of idle work time, the erosion of traditional skill demarcations, task fragmentation and job enlargement underpinned by flexibility. It seems that the principal rationale for the lean team is economic and Rinehart et al.'s (1997) study of a Japanese transplant in Canada argues that the lean team is more a product of social engineering rather than a fundamental re-organization of work.

Shifting to the service sector Mulholland's (2002) research in public information call centres found that line management drew on team organization to generate a 'fun culture', where, the intended effect was to mask a fundamentally Tayloristic work structure and productivity. Smith et al.'s (2008) study of teamworking amongst nurses in a fragmented NHS call centre add another interesting twist to the debate, when they suggest that teams served an administrative function, while tacitly sustaining an ideological role by presenting a view of public sector management as modern.

It is surprising that although retail work in supermarkets has been growing for several decades, teamwork in this context has only recently begun to attract the attention of researchers. For instance, Mulholland's (2008; 2009) study of organizational change in a major supermarket shows that parallel with the introduction of lean production and the just-in-time system in the organization of work, teamwork was transformed from a variation of group work, that was critical to worker autonomy, to a management-driven activity. In the lean team, performance was individualized and target-driven leaving little room for the development of shop floor interaction. Given that teamwork conjures up notions of the collective which may plausibly be based on worker interdependence and cooperation, the new team configuration seems at odds with expectations.

Methodology

This chapter is based on qualitative research in two branches of a major British supermarket chain over two different phases. In the first phase the researcher used covert participant observation to explore the dynamics of the work experience and employment relations of front-line workers. In order to overcome initial difficulties with gaining access to the hourly paid workforce, the researcher took a part-time job as a Replenishment Assistant on an evening shift from 2005 to 2006. This was an excellent opportunity to directly experience the labour process and to share the realities of doing the job alongside the other workers. Becoming just another worker brought into focus the meaning of doing a low-paid, low-trust service job in a labour process that was underpinned by work pacing and incessant managerial demands for increased productivity. The strength of this particular approach was that it provided a deeper insight into how worker groups engage in monotonous, tedious, boring and physically hard jobs, but also continually struggle to retain some control over work organization. This phase of the research reported on the way such major organizational change re-configured teamwork (Mulholland, 2009).

However, the pace of work and the covert nature of the research approach limited the ways in which the managerial logic behind work organization and teamwork could be explored. In the second phase of the research, I redefined the research agenda and openly negotiated access to a second supermarket of a similar size in the same chain and carried out interviews with store management. The focus of this phase was the managerial reasoning for changes in work organization and the re-organization teamwork. Using a semi-structured and open-ended interview schedule 10 members of the management team were interviewed, including the store manager, one deputy store manager, four departmental managers and four team leaders. Observations were also recorded during team meetings.

Work organization at ShopCo

The two stores included in this study were of a similar size of about 50, 000 sq. ft and each one employed approximately 400 predominantly part-time workers including management. With the exception of management, staff were hourly paid and pay rates were set slightly above the minimum wage with small increments for unsocial hours and a bonus contingent on business performance. Other lean initiatives, such as pay harmonization and single status had eliminated some grades, and resulted in a new pay banding based on two grades. With the exception of a few specialized tasks, most of the hourly paid staff were on Grade 2, while newly established team leaders received slightly higher pay and were on Grade 3. The corresponding wages for the grade 2 groups were between £5.50 for staff and £7 per hour for team leaders. Marginally higher than the National Minimum Wage, this finding is consistent with Mason et al.'s (2008) study of low pay in food retailing. *In the store* only bakers received better pay, because their skills were scarce.

The new management structure was three-tiered and consisted of store manager, deputy store manager and departmental managers. A recent horizontal restructuring had reduced managerial jobs from 26 to 20 as a consequence of the merging of sections, the re-composition of tasks and the redistribution of responsibility. This re-organization had led to the formalization of the job of 'Team Leader'. The merging of sections resulted in an enlarged role for the departmental managers who were responsible for a wider range of tasks in larger sections (see Grugulis et al., this volume). Although these managers had overall responsibility for departments such as Fresh Produce, many of the day-to-day operations were delegated to the newly established team leader positions.

Change initiatives at ShopCo

The research conducted at ShopCo found that the management embrace of the lean team was prefaced by a series of re-organizations coined 'Leanway', implemented by a 'simplification team'. This team consisted of a group of managers from different sections and functions given responsibility for the diffusion and practice of the lean model. One of the departmental managers spelled out the purposes of the lean method and explained how it was filtered down to the shop floor:

> We are in a constant state of change, and we have had Leanway that has been focused on the colleagues on the shop-floor. It incorporates a number of different procedures, where we simplify the daily routines, and make the jobs simpler, so that the jobs can be done quicker and more efficiently. A lot of what we were doing was outdated. (Departmental Manager, Checkout)

This clearly stated that lean was a management technique that was ultimately concerned with simplifying and increasing work speed on the shop floor, and was reminiscent of traditional Taylorism. At ShopCo this was initiated by developments in information technologies and the subsequent synchronization of the labour processes in food production, distribution and consumption. The linking of three sections helped establish Just-in-Time (JIT) systems. These new technologies did not initiate a change in the form or structure of traditional group work, rather they provided management with an opportunity to re-organize work. As Mulholland (2009) reports there was a re-focus on performance and all jobs were timed using time and motion studies. This resulted in the establishment of productivity targets, and a very a noticeable increase in the intensity and pace of work. The fairness and accuracy of such work measurement has been questioned by Wright and Lund (1996) in their very extensive research into the Australian and American food distribution sector. Alongside these changes to the labour process, JIT also brought about a 90 per cent reduction in stock inventories, the numerical handing of goods, the removal of buffers and some reduction in the overall employee headcount. The significance of the re-organised delivery system was that it gave a new urgency to how quickly goods were received and shelved in ways that impinged on established work patterns and practices within the store.

Once the lean method had been initiated managers focused on patterns of work organization amongst both semi-skilled and tacitly skilled teams:

> In this company, people used to work in 'silos', and if they worked in the meat room, they were butchers and that was all they did. In some ways that was a very good way of working. They were close knit teams. But at the end of the day, it is all about the overall results. (Store Manager)

The reference to 'silos' suggest that issues at the heart of this comment are job demarcation and performance. Although these work teams were not necessarily skilled, they were able to differentiate themselves from other store workers. While the strengths of the close-knit character of group work are acknowledged, this comment asserts that such workplace solidarity failed to achieve results, since it hindered productivity, a goal of the lean method.

In this context, the question of worker autonomy, however limited, also became an issue of central concern. For instance, when referring to the replenishing task, where shelf stackers had limited discretion over how they allocated and organized daily routines, the store manager said:

> Some elements of the work can be done where we organize them in groups or in pairs. We did that for a long time. We would have four working down an aisle. They had their own methods, but they also had a chat and a laugh and we didn't get enough of work out of them.

The store manager typified a concern with output when workers with discretion take liberties and slack to restrict productivity. But while managers regarded laughter and talk as a diversion from work, for team members it was a means of coping with a physically hard, tiring and stressful job (Mulholland, 2009). The lean method also led to questioning the efficiency of job ownership. According to one of the deputy store managers:

> Lean has come in and labour has been cut. I mean there were people in jobs in the past that didn't exist, and now because of profitability, people have no option but to be flexible. It's not necessarily because they want to, it's just that they have to.

The issue of flexibility was at the heart of these terse comments. Workers in small groups negotiated the allocation of jobs within the team, and negotiated with line managers when they occasionally helped other teams. By contrast, workers in the newly organized teams were deployed at the discretion of management. This flexibility was not established consensually. Indeed, Mulholland (2009) argues that despite the absence of trade union organization in the day-to-day operations, there was tacit resistance to flexibility reminiscent of misbehaviour (Ackroyd and Thompson, 1999). Staff wanted to remain in the jobs they knew and so restricted output to the standard norm. Through flexibility workers also lost the support and solidarity of established team membership. The fact that Leanway defined flexibility from the viewpoint of management was another indication of how its introduction involved a shift of power to management in defining and driving worker productivity, rendering the deployment of labour non-negotiable.

Another critical change brought about by the lean method was the reconfiguration of the team leader role. Prior to the introduction of the lean method this job did not exist, and senior workers managed the routine operations of work groups. Team leaders, by contrast, were selected by management on the basis of work experience and corporate commitment, and their role was invested with some institutional power in the monitoring, surveillance and disciplining of team members. Unlike the senior workers, they engaged in work pacing and could use disciplinary power to enforce performance and productivity. While senior managers claimed that traditional authoritarian managerial styles had been abandoned, Mulholland (2009) found only very patchy evidence for this, and argues that whenever productivity is paramount, line management resort to terse tough language. This concurs with Rinehart et al. (1997), who argue that the new team concept and the disappearance of the foreman role did not necessarily generate a more democratic workplace culture with the establishment of the team leader role.

In explaining the rationale for such re-organization, the store manager said:

> We are driven by the bottom line, aren't we? That is sales and profits and what comes in between is cost that needs to be controlled.

Changes to working patterns and team re-configurations were underpinned by the need to cut costs, a development that parallels a wider shift from social to economic priorities in contemporary organizations (Proctor and Mueller, 2000).

The single company-wide team

In the new team configuration the single company-wide team (Benders, 1999) incorporated the whole workforce consisting of approximately 400 staff including 20 managers. In this context the team was portrayed by management as a collaborative partnership between management and labour. This particular team had no tangible structure, in the sense that there was no opportunity for the whole store to meet and interact as a team. However, some sense of how the company perceived the team was conveyed by the Store Manager:

> The team stems from the bottom line, that means getting committed and motivated people working towards the same common goals of sales and profits.

In this context the team was a communications network for the dispersal of corporate goals concerned with commitment and performance, and management expected staff to share a belief in achieving better sales and profits.

Core Teams, the Night Shift and productivity

Teams were tangibly structured around particular core functions (Proctor and Mueller, 2000), such as the Replenishment Team on the Night Shift, Checkout and Grocery. While each of these sections was recognized as a team, the labour process was fragmented, and there was very little opportunity for interaction between team members *within* their particular team. However, there is more managed interaction *between* teams and members of the Grocery Team shifted to other sections in times of need.

One example of the core team was the night shift. The team consisted of approximately 50 replenishers, whose task was to ensure that all the nightly scheduled deliveries were received, processed and shelved by the end of the shift. The importance of this team was highlighted by the store manager:

> The night shift is an area where productivity is incredibly important. If you haven't got great productivity on the night shift, you sink as a business.

This comment should be understood within the remit of the company's business plan, where the profitability of the company hinged on the productivity of the night shift. In the case of the night team, the hard business message was continually conveyed to the staff at the 'Huddle', a term that is suggestive of something cosy, close and convivial, however, this research revealed an authoritarian structure, in which the managers appraised workers on their progress towards daily targets and productivity. Workers were then allocated to jobs on particular aisles, some with specifically timed schedules under continual supervision. Discipline was scheduled into the night manager's time table, and issues relating to worker absence, productivity and conduct were addressed on a daily basis, suggesting a rather unforgiving managerial regime. Explaining the routine:

> I have a slot from 10 o'clock until 7am to get all the deliveries out and on the shelves ready for the doors opening. This includes the merchandising and tidying up. We have a 15 minute Huddle, and I put people on the aisles. I am supposed to do a check on them every 15 minutes, this depends on all the other stuff I have to get through. I have to do disciplinaries and 'back to work interviews,' but I rely a lot on my team leaders to get the stuff out. There is no let up. A lot of people don't hack it, and they leave for one reason or another. No excuse is acceptable everyone has to pull their weight. (Night Shift Manager, Replenishment Team)

This comment concurred with that of the store manager, in that the productivity on the night shift was critical. What the managers did not say was that the twilight replenishing shift was cut during the re-organization, and this placed additional pressure on the night workers. Moreover, there was no scope for the night team to leave deliveries unfinished, since the overall job design did not make any allocation for this work to be transferred to day replenishment. The Grocery Team, who stacked the shelves during the day had to be available to work in other sections, such as checkout, if necessary.

There were additional organizational problems inherent in the model. It portrayed the synchronization of labour allocation and scheduled deliveries as a smooth seamless operation, but in practice it was very difficult to finely tune the labour process to such precisely targeted productivity. In particular, it did not sufficiently account for organizational hitches, such as late deliveries and incorrect product sorting. This was spelled out by one of the night team leaders:

To be honest I am not very impressed. Everything is coming in very mixed. This makes my job very complicated, because me and my team have to do the sorting. Then we have late deliveries. We then have to get the productivity out on top of that. I mean some people can achieve it, but not everybody can work at a super-human speed for 10 hours. So I don't think it works. But I know some of the managers who very much stick to it.

She disputed whether just-in-time improved the job from an organizational perspective, since deliveries were often late and not correctly sorted. Then, in describing the expected pace of work as 'super-human' she argued that not all her team could keep up with the company performance standard for a whole 10-hour shift. Her concern was with work measurement, echoing Wright and Lund (1996) who argue that the industrial engineering measurement of jobs in this sector is inaccurate. Unlike traditional workplaces where the timing of work was often negotiated with trade unions, peoples' performance and jobs in supermarkets were timed and established solely by management. The impact this had on operational managers was such that, when confronting productivity pressures, many abandoned the human resource approach and adopted an authoritarian style, as one of the senior managers frankly admitted:

It does depend on the personality of the team leaders and managers, and I have done a lot of work with the overnight shift. The temptation is there when you are a manager at night you have to be a workhorse. Whipping all the time. "Come on, get down, and you should have done that by now." You see that often across our business. This happens all the time, and it is a real slog overnight. The people over-night have to put out 51 cases per hour for 10 hours. So there is a temptation there to keep driving. They (workers) are really worked on. Its 'Can you work a bit faster and get that on'. They have to go from the minute they arrive to the minute they leave. It's hard to keep people working at that rate.

Most managers drew on the scientificism associated with work measurement to justify their uncompromising approach to worker performance:

If there are new starters, well you have to take that into account. And you go and coach them or you might get someone to buddy up with them. But there is no reason why they can't keep up, because with Leanway every job is scientifically assessed. So it can be done. (Night Manager, Replenishment Team)

This manager's overall responsibility for the night shift's productivity probably explained his defense of productivity measurement. By contrast, one of the night team leaders disputed the validity of scientific measurement:

I apply this productivity tool only very loosely. I can tell by looking at somebody how they are getting on. If somebody is working well, I don't use that tool.

Researcher: Why not?

It does not take into account a lot of the work, the amount of stock, that comes in from the warehouse. You also never know what state the shelves are going to be in. Then sorting and dressing is supposed to be taken into account, but isn't.

Aspects of the shelving process such as the preparation of the shelves and aisles and final presentation of the shelf were not sufficiently accounted for in the measurements, aside from the problem of late deliveries. Only core features of the task were measured and it is the absence of elemental aspects of the job amongst other things in the measurement of such work that concern Wright and Lund (1996).

Additionally, another team leader points out that poor ergonomic features of the job and particularly the cold conditions made the work more difficult to endure.

The biggest challenge on nights is to keep everybody motivated. Because 10 hours is a very long time, and after lunch at 3.30 am everyone is at their very lowest point. They get very cold and tired and it's impossible to keep productivity up. The cold comes straight from the chillers and goes down the back of the neck. If they look blue I send them into the toilets to stand under the hand dryers to get warm. Some people just can't take it, and this job is most unpopular. (Linda Team Leader Night)

This suggests that first line managers had some very limited discretion in terms of how far they pursued their targets. However, this team differed from the 'new team' and resembled traditional group working. It consisted of four specialized code checkers and a team leader, who were collectively responsible for ensuring that the quality of chilled products in the fridges adhered to the standards set down by safety guidelines. Moreover, the group were very close and the team leader worked alongside them in a capacity that was similar to the former senior worker's job. While this might seem a diversion from the dominant productivist organizational culture, it was clear from the interviews with senior management that this format was a necessary compromise for getting the work done. As one commented:

Linda on nights, she struggles a bit, it is very hard for her to keep the team going. It's very, very cold and they are heroes on that team.

The importance of the job, combined with its unpopularity proved to be a bargaining tool for the team to gain a small concession from management. This job requires much attention to detail and accuracy as the freshness of the each item was checked and items were appropriately rotated. Given that the company depended on the quality of the night team's work for its reputation, allowing the members to defrost under hand dryers was perhaps a small price to pay to get the job done.

Core teams: The Checkout: *'items per minute'* and a *'willingness to serve'*

The biggest core team at ShopCo was the Checkout Team. It consisted of approximately 100 full- and part-time workers. Organizationally it was difficult to call it a team, because work done by checkout assistants was solitary, with each worker operating a specific till in the continuous throughput of customers. The design of the checkout station was not conducive to worker interaction, because the layout was fragmented resembling an assembly line. The team was then imposed on this structure. Unlike the Night Team, the checkout team consisted of numerous staggered shifts, making it very difficult for management to hold a pre-shift meeting. The departmental manager said:

Checkout is a very difficult team to run because of the size of it, and because of the nature of the job. I can't have a 'Huddle' because we have so many shifts and colleagues starting at different times. There is never a given point, where I could say, 'Stop and have a chat' to my team as a single group, which is very frustrating for me as a manager. (Checkout Manager)

This manager complained that the size of the team, the particular work patterns and the character of the task operated to the detriment of team building. He also pointed out that the work design afforded no opportunity for better communication between himself and team members either collectively or individually. He desired more team cohesiveness, but weighed this up against productivity demands.

It is very important for us to run the checkout operation efficiently, and on as few hours as we can, working with as few operatives as is viable, but working to the maximum. The main target for the cashiers is basically how fast they can scan. We aim for 19 items per minute, which is perfectly reasonable and achievable. (Checkout Manager)

However, managerial logic was frequently contradictory and in this instance team cohesion was sacrificed on the altar of productivity, a reflection of the low cost logic of the lean model that took pride in doing more for less, in this case with fewer staff.

In exploring how the managers trained the checkout assistants to manage the demands of speed and customer service, the departmental manager said:

Well, I would like you (the checkout assistant) to take this on and try and do this job in this way not for any extra money, or for a promise of the next pay rise. We do this through coaching and feedback.

This human resource management discourse was firmly backed by punitive lean measures that included routine close monitoring and discipline. Operational managers relied on the first line management, the team leaders, for the day-to-day management of the team. The new team leader jobs were invested with sufficient authority to define the fate of the operatives at ShopCo. One of the checkout team leaders explained how this was played out:

A major part of my job is doing 'observations' and investigating 'items per minute' (IPM) and 'tracking". I give them a Pass, or a Fail, and this is based on three other things, Greeting, Interaction, and the Mystery Shopper and this tells how much they show an interest in the customer and whether they offer to help with packing. Whether they keep eye contact, and showing a willingness to serve. (Team Leader, Checkout)

The duty of the team leader was to check and enforce the barrage of employee monitoring and measuring devices that pertained to both productivity and customer service. Resurrecting nineteenth-century domestic servitude checkout supermarket assistants were expected to show due deference to the customers, including appropriate eye contact and offers of help. At the same time, they must develop the duplicitous technique of rushing the customer through, while feigning politeness. This is where the power of the team leader was enhanced. The individual operative's pace of work was closely monitored, recorded and assessed on a pass/fail grading system on a monthly basis by the team leader. Checkout assistants were also individually assessed on service quality that included a greeting formula and particular customer interaction, although in the middle of the checkout process, they were allowed to drop the eye contact and accelerate the throughput of items. Additionally, they were required to pass the Mystery Shopper Test, which meant that checkout staff were surreptitiously monitored by an independent organization, or a pseudo customer. The scores were duly monitored by the team leader. Overall, the team leader's job was to ensure that checkout assistants conformed to company protocol.

In exploring the different ways management encouraged the checkout assistants to be part of 'the team', one of the managers said:

> Well, it is very difficult for me to relate to that. But I would like to think that they feel part of the team, and I can understand if they didn't, especially on a busy day such as last Saturday. You work eight hours until someone comes to give you a break. That might be the only colleague they will see all day. (Checkout Manager)

This manager conceded that management had little conception of the team as a unit of work organization, nor was the team a network of cooperative and interacting relationships. Checkout work was individualized, staff had little opportunity to engage with each other, and that it is reasonable for them not to feel part of the team. Another manager commented:

> The cashiers' main role is to be outgoing and chatty. Now moral support is not necessary and they don't need it. I mean each colleague understands that another colleague can't come off her/his till to support him they can't act as "spare parts. (Checkout Manager)

The reality was that checkout was one of the most fragmented sections, and jobs were designed to foster a degree of perfunctory and momentary interactions between assistants and customers, as opposed to interaction between team members.

Core teams: the grocery team: job flexibility versus job ownership

The grocery team was large with approximately 100 staff divided into subsections, such as Chilled Food, Dry Grocery, Wines and Spirits and Fresh Food. The management structure consisted of one departmental manager assisted by team leaders. While the key function of this department was ongoing replenishing and merchandising, it differed from other teams in that it was regarded as a labour resource for other departments. The staff were called to help with emergencies and to fill in wherever additional labour was required. The Grocery department was a perfect example of how stress and tension underpinned work design in the store, since workers were put under pressure by the organization's demand for high levels of productivity on their allocated jobs, while being instantly available to deploy to other departments. Since the Checkout function took priority over other work, such as day replenishment, the deployment of the replenishment assistants was a perfect example of how functional flexibility operated in a low cost, low trust, tightly controlled labour regime.

> If you work here, you have to be prepared to work anywhere. It is wherever you are needed at any particular time. But you still have your own work. (Deputy Manager)

This labour regime was premised on the assumption that there was sufficient porosity in the working day for the grocery replenishers to be deployed elsewhere, whilst also meeting their own productivity requirements.
Managers did realize the effect this had on employees:

> Yes the colleagues do mind working around. They get attached to their own jobs, and if they can't fulfill that job role, they get frustrated, because that is what they are targeted to do. (Grocery Manager)

Staff greatly resented the idea of flexibility and tried to protect established working patterns (Mulholland, 2009). However, this manager empathized with the team members over the difficulties caused by flexibility in fulfilling their set jobs. But managers also attempted to go beyond the formal targets. One of the team leaders said:

> I do 'Smart Targets' which means I can say to one the colleagues, 'Fill that gap'. For example, I give them 10 minutes to shelf 10 cases of kitchen rolls, if they take more time, I 'coach' them, and if they still don't get it. Well...(Team Leader Groceries)

Productivity for the 'smart target' was calculated to exceed the standard time that was set at 51 cases per hour, and provided an example of how the sweating of labour was built into the new teamwork. Referring to deployed staff as 'Shock Troops', this team leader commented on the manner in which she was able to call a greater number of team members from other crisis situations.

Using flexibility as a means of addressing labour shortages on a routine basis created problems not only for team members but also for the operational managers.

> Obviously the guys from other teams will not do an excellent job on the checkout. To them the checkout job is another role and not theirs. To them it is just an annoyance. (Customer Services Manager)

From this manager's perspective staff from other teams performed comparatively less well, and this research shows that staff are not trained to be interchangeable between different functions.

While flexibility between teams as a means of managing staff shortages posed problems for the workers, it tended to encourage managers to compete with each other for staff. As one said:

> There is often a very heated argument between me and other managers over taking their staff. I can fully understand that, they have their work to do no matter what. And it is [a] very difficult thing for the colleagues too. They will say to me, 'I have 30 cases to put out, and I go home in half an hour. If I go on the till I will not finish my work'. Of course, their line manager will later take them to task, when they haven't reached their target. (Checkout Manager)

This indicated the pressure that workers and managers experienced under lean production. Although, managers were hardly sanguine about the organizational problems posed by the new approach, they were unlikely to challenge it, since they were incentivized through bonus payments to ensure it endured. Nevertheless, this illustrates how the stresses and tensions are played out in a work organization premised on too few workers (Parker and Slaughter, 1988).

This research found that while senior management waxed lyrical about the new team concept, the departmental and first line management found it increasingly difficult to explain how they fostered a team culture amongst the staff. The customer services manager said:

> Well, I don't get the time to build the team. But it's about the language we use, such as, 'We are doing it this way'. But if we had more labour and

fewer targets, although there would be more people I could communicate better. Whatever hours and labour we get, it's all used on the tills. More labour would free me up and take the pressure off them, so they could be more relaxed in their role.

He speculated how he would foster the team spirit, if only he had more staff. His vision of the team was set in a more relaxed environment for team members and included more time for communication. It seemed that for this manager, the inclusive language characteristic of the company-wide team was not sufficient and that something more tangible and concrete was required to generate team cohesion.

In summing up the new lean team, the store manager said:

I would say the new team has more value for the business, than it does for the quality of working life for the colleagues. This is a very hard business and the company gets its pound of flesh from everybody and the team helps us with that.

There was no equivocation in this comment that the lean team has led to the creation of profit for the business, while it does not improve the working life of team members. It goes on to say that in a tough business environment the lean team is a management instrument for the creation of value.

Conclusions

In conclusion, this research suggests that this new form of teamworking was rooted in wider organizational restructuring premised on lean production (Womack et al., 1990). Resonant with Proctor and Mueller's (2000) examination of what they describe as second wave teamworking, or Japanization, this new teamwork was management-driven and underpinned by an economic rational. Here, it is argued that teamworking took three forms, a company-wide team, teams structured by their operational functions, and group work, a throwback to traditional practices.

This chapter argues that the company-wide team was not identifiable in any tangible form, but rather existed as discourse that management drew on to foster a notion of unity. The usefulness of such imagery was that it created an invisible thread in the diffusion of the corporate message from senior management to the shop floor.

The second form of teamworking was that of the functionally based team. For management the central function of this team was to re-allocate staff with a view to using the least number of work hours and team members with the highest levels of effectiveness. The functional teams consisted of 50 to 100 members and were imposed on a fragmented Tayloristic labour process, where most workers remained unskilled and were thus easily disposable and interchangeable across jobs (Rinehart et al., 1997). Under the new lean teamworking, management directed staff to jobs on a daily basis, with some qualification. First, checkout staff were allowed to remain on particular tills, since this accommodated monitoring, financial scrutiny and accountability. Second, training and skill also defined the limits of flexibility, and trained checkout teams were less likely to be deployed to replenishing tasks. However, in practice, some replenishing teams were used as buffers, when members were deployed to alleviate staff shortages in other sections. The deployment of team members to other tasks led to the sweating of labour, for instance the use of 'smart targets', when team leaders resorted to increasing the pace of work by setting targets above the standard measure.

The third type of team formation resembled traditional group work, and was restricted to particular functions. These were small teams of 4 to 5 semi-skilled workers such as code checkers and bakers, who were headed by a new team leader. While these teams were not functionally flexible, they shared the same fragmented and standardized labour process and pay rates of other team members. Posed against the socio-technical team model, it is very difficult to argue that any of these formations, with the exception of the semi-skilled groups, bear much resemblance to the notion of a team.

Ironically, this research revealed that operational problems provided the conditions for a kind of teamworking, which in some ways chimes with Van der Broek et al.'s (2004) findings. On these occasions, staff left their individualized tasks and till stations and worked cooperatively to solve problems. Nevertheless, it was clear that this could be equally achieved without the presence of team organization. The lean team was not about enhancing the worker experience as Womack et al. (1990) believe, for this study shows that despite managers' team talk, they insisted that team members stood alone and performed. There was in fact little encouragement for co-worker support, rather, the team had become a managerial tool that could be used in a variety of ways and for different purposes.

It has also been argued that the new team leader role that replaced the senior worker enhanced the control of work in this supermarket, and incorporated some of the middle management tasks in terms of day-to-day surveillance. In most instances, team leaders followed bureaucratic protocol enforcing performance, with one exception. In one instance, one of the team leaders managing one of the small teams used more imagination and rapport with her team members in efforts to reach productivity targets. This team leader also questioned the fairness of performance measurement.

This chapter has argued that management drew on 'team discourse', an ideological device, in order to disseminate the idea of the company as a teamworking towards the common goal of productivity and profit. The interviews with managers showed that while they were honest about the demands the work made on team members, they nevertheless adopted a narrative of 'we are enduring this together' in their interactions with shop floor staff, despite the disparities in pay, power and benefits. The company-wide team played an ideological role in facilitating this. However, Mulholland (2008; 2009) questions whether staff were any more committed to the business post lean team organization. Rather they greatly resented changes to their work practices, and resisted them as best they could in an organization with weak trade union organization. It seems that the new lean team has been a managerial vehicle for the implementation of flexibility and increases in the pace of work, features of Tayloristic work organization that could be as easily achieved without 'new teamwork'.

REFERENCES

Ackroyd, S. and Thompson, P. (1999) *Organisational Misbehaviour.* London: Sage Publications.

Benders, J. and Van Hootegem, G. (1999) 'Teams and their contexts: moving the team discussion beyond existing dichotomies', *Journal of Management Studies,* 36(5): 609–628.

Bolton, S. and Houlihan, M. (eds) *Work Matters: Critical Reflections on Contemporary Work.* London: Palgrave.

Danford, A. (1999) *Japanese Management Techniques and British Workers.* Mansell.

Lloyd, C., Mason, G. and Mayhew, K. (eds) (2008) *Low Wage Work in the United Kingdom.* New York: Russell Sage Foundation.

Lloyd, C. and Newell, H. (2000) 'Selling teams to the salesforce: teamworking in the UK pharmaceutical industry', in S. Proctor and F. Mueller(eds) *Teamworking.* Basingstoke: Macmillan Business, 183–202.

Martinez Lucio, M., Jenkins, S. and Noon, M. (2000) 'Management Strategy: union identity and oppositionalism: teamwork in the Royal Mail', in S. Proctor, and F. Mueller (eds) Basingstoke: Macmillan Business, 262–279.

Mason, G. and Osborne, M. (2008) 'Business strategies, work organisation and low pay in United Kingdom retailing', in C. Lloyd, G. Mason and K. Mayhew (eds) *Low Wage Work in the United Kingdom.* New York: Russell Sage Foundation, 131–168.

Mueller, F. (1994) 'Team between hierarchy and commitment: change strategies and the internal "environment", *Journal of Management Studies,* 31(3): 383–403.

▶

▶

Mulholland, K. (2002) 'gender, emotional labour and teamworking in a call centre', *Personnel Review*, 31(3): 283–303.

Mulholland, K. (2009) 'Life on the supermarket floor: the impact of just–in-time systems and supermarket work organisation for replenishment assistants', in S. Bolton and M. Houlihan (eds) *Work Matters: Critical Reflections on Contemporary Work*. London: Palgrave.

Parker, M. and Slaughter, J. (1988) *Choosing Sides: Unions and the Team Concept*. Boston: South End Press.

Procter, S. and Mueller, F. (eds) (2000) *Teamworking*, Basingstoke: Macmillan Business, 262–279.

Rinehart, J., Huxley, C. and Robinson, D. (1997) *Just Another Car Factory? Lean Production and its Discontents*. Ithaca and London: ILP Press, Cornell University Press.

Smith, C., Wise, S., Valseechi, R. and Mueller, F. (2008) 'It's teamwork but not as we know it': the discourse and practice of teamwork in health industry call centres in the UK', International Labour Process Conference 18th –20th March, 2008, University College, Dublin.

Van der Broek, D., Callaghan, G. and Thompson, P. (2004) 'Teams without teamwork? Explaining the call centre', *Paradox Economic and Industrial Democracy*, 25(2): 197–218.

Womack, J. P., Jones, D.T. and Roos, D. (1990) *The Machine that Changed the World*. London: Simon & Schuster.

Wright, C. and Lund, J. (1996) 'Best-practice Taylorism: yankee speed-up in Australian grocery distribution', *Journal of Industrial Relations Journal*, 38(2): 196–212.

Negotiating 'Good Work' in Retail

Humour in Retail Work: Jokes Salespeople Tell about Their Clients

12

Asaf Darr

Introduction

A defining feature of our era is the rapid growth of the information and service economy. This infrastructural shift has changed the way we produce and consume. It has also changed the occupational landscape, bringing knowledge and service work to centre stage. For example, Hecker (2005. 71) analysing Bureau of Labour Statistics employment projection for 2004 2014 in the US labour force states: 'Among the 10 major occupational groups, employment in the two largest in 2004 – professional and related occupations and service occupations – is projected to increase the fastest and add the most jobs [*in the USA*] from 2004 to 2014.'

The transition from an industrial to a service oriented economy has been accompanied and assisted by many factors, including an ideological shift, emphasizing customer satisfaction rather than an efficient production process. The dictum 'the customer is always right' has successfully spread around the globe, fostered by technological innovations such as global computer networks and also by the rapid growth of the geographical reach of multinational firms. As the client has become the focus of firms' attention, those organizations that fail to integrate service-oriented structures and processes are expected to lose their competitive edge (Dupuy, 1999). Retail work is a central part of this client oriented economy, and it deserves increasing research attention.

To be sure, the emerging service economy has not gone unnoticed by the research community, although not all see its consequences in the same light. Some researchers describe the shift from inflexible and unfriendly bureaucracies to more flexible customer oriented organizational structures as a great triumph and a liberating force for both firms and the larger public (Dupuy,

1999). Other scholars depict the client-centred culture more critically and see it as an emerging, and more subtle, control mechanism designed to further the subjugation and deskilling of service and retail workers (Bolton, 2005; Darr, 2003, 2006; Leidner, 1993). Regardless of the difference in approach, both streams of thought highlight the greater centrality of the clients in service employment, and seem to agree that service orientation has become influential in structuring the contemporary world of work.

Within the more critical research stream about the client centred culture of the contemporary economy, Labour Process Theory (LPT) has loomed large in contributing to our understanding of the changing nature of service and retail work. Shifting the focus from the production line to the service floor, however, has required LPT scholars to make a number of theoretical adjustments, an important one of these being the inclusion of the customer within the traditional management–worker framework (Bolton, 2005; Korczinsky, 2005; Leidner, 1993).

The constitution of the service triangle, composed of workers, managers and customers, has been accompanied by a debate among critical sociologists of work over the exact role of customers in the emerging service and retail sectors. Some researchers depict the customer in this arrangement simply as an emerging control mechanism over the quality of service, utilized by employers, for example, through client surveys (Darr, 2003; Fuller and Smith, 1996; Rosenthal et al., 2001). Other scholars ascribe customers with greater social agency, and argue that they could actually influence and even manipulate the service encounter by using their market power as clients and the ideology of customer sovereignty. Some of these researchers portray a more complex web of interests, one that sometimes creates surprising coalitions between salespeople and clients, against management and the dominant discourse of enterprise (Bolton, 2005; Korczynski, 2005; Lopez, 1996).

While the inclusion of the customer in LPT analysis has been an important move forward, the analysis of interactions between service providers and customers, empirically explored mainly in call centres, is still largely confined to the theoretical focus on the management control apparatus and various forms of workers' resistance. This chapter acknowledges the importance of the management–workers cleavage. For example, the frustration and anger of salespeople towards customers, which we will see below, is partly the result of management's design of retail work. Here, the source of management's pressure on retail workers is obscured and the customers become their control agents. Yet, this chapter also argues that it is important to view some aspects of the retail encounter independently of management–workers relationship. More specifically, this chapter will describe some aspects of the moral economy that is constituted between sellers and buyers on the retail floor.

Moral economy is defined by Grint (1998: 328) as 'the pattern of work relationships that are rooted in social, moral, and symbolic norms and traditions, in contrast to the "market economy" where relationships are presumed to be based wholly on individual rational evaluations of efforts, cost and reward.' Employing role theory within an interactionist framework, and inspired by Goffman (1963; 1969), this study will examine the set of roles and behavioural scripts retail salespeople ascribe to themselves and to the clients with whom they interact. More specifically, this chapter will depict the moral economy of retail sales work through an analysis of the jokes that salespeople tell about their clients.

As this chapter demonstrates, the system of meaning on the retail floor as seen from the salespeople's point of view is a system based on moral perceptions of the social roles of sellers and buyers in economic exchange. This moral economy is obviously anchored in the 'real economy', and is based on reciprocity and on the mutual obligation of sellers and buyers to adhere to their social roles in the process of economic exchange.

The salespeople discussed in this chapter worked in a retail computer store. They generally accepted the ethos of good service to clients as a fundamental part of their work and of their occupational identity. For example, one salesperson explained why he wanted to work for this computer chain as follows: 'One reason I like working here is that we really have customer service, I like to give client service, to help as much as possible.' A different salesperson working in the store tried to explain why customers tend to return to the store and then ask for her assistance: 'They [my customers] tell me that I'm very reliable, I listen to them, I really try to direct them to the product they actually need rather than push products on them.' Yet, as the front-line workers of a capitalist firm, they were also strongly oriented towards selling and closing deals. The incentive plans offered by the employer to the salespeople as well as the occupational sense of what constitutes professional sales work were both based on a direct emphasis on the client. In fact, most of the work-related tensions cited by the salespeople interviewed for this study were reported to arise from the salespeople's interactions with their customers, and not from those with management. This fact obviously also serves the interests of management. For example, the built-in tension between service quality and volume of sales is fundamental to many service encounters, as numerous studies of call centres have already noted (for a short review, see Sturdy et al., 2001: 7–8). The salespeople in this study also attempted to optimize their efforts so that as many encounters as possible would yield a sale. Yet, while their counterparts in call centres are said to feel caught up in the midst of often contradictory management demands that cause moral and emotional distress, the salespeople in the computer store studied here appeared to have developed a local moral economy directed at the customers, which helps them cope with customer-related tensions. Even though basically accepting the need to service clients well and generally motivated by their employer's commission system, these retail workers also had a strong awareness to what they perceived as the social roles of clients. They viewed customers as also having obligations in the sales interaction, namely to show a serious attitude and a basic willingness to buy. Thus, the ethos of 'the customer is always right' was transformed by the salespeople into a more balanced view of the sales interaction, in which each party in the transaction had to abide by certain rules of engagement, defined by a distinct role and a distinct set of social obligations (for a similar case of situated and mutual obligations in economic exchange see Geertz, 1978).

In the interviews the salespeople seldom expressed frustration towards customers who acted as control agents for management by complaining about bad service, probably since they perceived such complaints as legitimate. Yet, they did often express frustration and anger towards clients who engaged them in long sales encounters but eventually failed to buy. The frustration of the salespeople over customers' violation of their role as potential buyers was captured in jokes and humorous stories they shared with other members of their occupational community.

In the following pages I will focus on these jokes and humorous stories. The data were collected through in-depth interviews with salespeople and direct observations in the computer store where research was carried out for 15 months. In this analysis jokes are used as a diagnostic tool. Jokes are perceived in Western cultures and within the Israeli society as a legitimate venue for expressing ambiguity, anger, frustration and hostility. In the context of this study they provided a powerful means of identifying social undercurrents and the fundamental yet hidden tensions salespeople experience when dealing with clients on the retail shop floor. Jokes shared within the occupational community assisted in creating and sustaining a shared identity anchored in similar experiences at work. They were as such also part of occupational socialization; signalling normative boundaries and helping pass on valuable knowledge to new salespeople on how to manage emotional labour on the retail floor. Young salespeople listened to workplace jokes, from which they learned about different types of clients and about how to handle them, as well as deal with the frustration and anger they could sometimes cause. All these aspects of joke telling will be discussed below. But before presenting the research findings, this chapter offers a short review of the recent literature on sales work and also about jokes in work organizations.

Literature review

Retail and more specifically sales work has for decades been a neglected area of study in the sociology of work, presumably due to the low occupational status attributed to salespeople. Sociologists of work have traditionally focused on the more privileged segments of the occupational structure, particularly the professions on the one hand and on industrial work on the other hand. But with the emergence of a service economy, driven partly by the information revolution, researchers have begun paying closer attention to an important segment of the new economy – service and service work (see Bolton, 2005; Korczynski, 2005; Lopez, 1996). In fact, in the emerging economy service and sales work have often been meshed together, for example in call centres.

Most recent studies on service and sales work focus on call centres that represent a prototypical work organization in the emerging economy. These studies tend to emphasise the complex control apparatus being implemented in call centres and the diverse ways in which workers express their limited autonomy by resisting the intentions of management (Fernie and Metcalf, 1998; For a critique and an emphasis on workers' resistance, see Bain and Taylor, 2000), Another body of literature on retail work has tried to contextualise the customer-centred culture, by providing case studies showing the control apparatus exercised by management over the work of salespeople. Here, the sales floor is depicted as the location where the built-in tensions and paradoxes of capitalism are played out (Bolton, 2005; Callaghan and Thompson, 2002; Korczynski, 2005; Leidner, 1996; Lopez, 1996). While the recent attention to service work in call centre informs some important scholarly contributions, there is also a pressing need to go beyond the call centre and to enhance our understanding of other more mundane, yet prevalent types of retail work, especially those involving face-to-face interactions on the sales floor.

A study of retail sales provides important insights into how markets operate in practice. After all, it is the salespeople and customers, going about their daily endeavours, who produce and reproduce 'the market' as a social institution. A study of retail sales also brings face-to-face sales encounters, which have been largely neglected in the literature, to centre stage. Finally, the focus on interactive sales encounters highlights the significance of the material setting of the interactions and the qualities of the products being traded in a way that existing literature has so far not attempted to do.

The scant empirical research of sales interactions on the retail floor (See Bourdieu, 2005: 148–184; Clark and Pinch, 1995; Leidner, 1993, 1996 for a few important exceptions) obscures the important domain of the micro-foundations of markets, and prevents a fuller understanding of markets in action. Generally speaking, an empirical examination of sales interactions would assist in refuting unsubstantiated assumptions as to the knowledge structures and social processes in advanced retail markets. For example, economists as well as economic anthropologists often assume that advanced markets allow symmetric distributions of knowledge of the product offered for sale. As a consequence, buyers in a mass market are expected to engage in an extensive information search about products' quality and cost. They are said to seek additional offers to one already received (Geertz, 1978: 31), and to engage in short and focused retail encounters. Furthermore, an analysis of face-to-face sales interactions can help identify the local social mechanisms designed to bridge the information gap between sellers and buyers. These mechanisms, like the use of a local Mafioso in a Sicilian horse markets or the use of auctions in cases where value is difficult to assess, which tend to be culture-specific, are central to any understanding of market structures and processes, as some sociological and anthropological research about craft markets has clearly demonstrated (For the case of Sicily, see Gambetta, 1990; Herrmann, 1997; Sherry, 1983; Sherry and McGrath, 1989; For the case of auctions see Smith, 1990).

Two main gaps can be identified in the research literature on retail work. The first is the insufficient attention given to the study of mass retail markets from a sociological perspective. The second is the general neglect of retail work and face-to-face sales interactions, and more generally the micro-foundations of markets, as an object of study. This chapter offers a modest contribution towards closing these gaps. In this study the sales floor is depicted as a social arena in which sellers and buyers play their social roles within a well defined moral economy. As this chapter will demonstrate, some of the tension inherent in sales work is expressed in jokes and humorous stories salespeople tell about their clients. To understand how jokes can become a diagnostic tool in the sociology of work, I offer in the next few pages a brief review of the literature about joke telling in work organizations.

Humour and Jokes in organizational studies

The use of humour and joke telling is part and parcel of organizational life, and has attracted vast research attention over the past few decades. For example, Coser (1956: 63–64) in his seminal study, highlights the impact of humour on group identity and group cohesiveness. According to him, humour allows the expression of hostility while maintaining intimacy within the inner group. Humour can also support a sense of consciousness of kind and of difference among social groups. Following the anthropologist Radcliffe-Brown (1952), Coser depicts joking relationships between teams as a form of alliance. Jokes also signal a group's moral boundaries (Janes and Olson, 2000), since they often refer to unacceptable or absurd forms of behaviour.

Workplace joking behaviour is also depicted in the research literature as a coping strategy. An example is a study of the members of a group of trades people in Australia entering a training programme to become secondary school teachers, who feel their occupational identity is threatened and cope with this situation by engaging in joke telling (Robert, 1989). Workplace joking, including the subjective perceptions of potentially offensive jokes, is examined in relation to gender and ethnic differences (Mechling and Mechling, 1985; Smeltzer and Leap, 1988; Watts, 2007); as a pillar of group and organizational cultures (Collinson, 1988; Linstead, 1985); and, in a study that compares the types of humour used by different status groups in the workplace and looks at how status groups become part of distinct joking networks, as a practice which fosters in-group distinction (Duncan, 1985).

More recently, Romero and Pescosolido (2008) have presented a comprehensive model of the impact of humour on team effectiveness. These scholars join previous researchers, who have effectively integrated humour studies into managerial thinking and ideology (e.g., Caudron, 1990; Decker and Rotondo, 2001). In their paper, Romero and Pascosolido offer the following definition of organizational humour: '... amusing communications that produce positive emotions and cognitions in the individual, group or organization.' (p. 397). They divide existing theory about humour into three distinct schools. The first, which they call 'incongruity theory', postulates that humour '... functions by establishing an incongruity between bodies of knowledge and the subsequent resolution of the incongruity by the recipient.' (p. 398). The second theoretical stream they identity, which has strong psychoanalytical roots, sees humour and joke telling as a tension relief mechanism. Here, inherent work-related conflicts are played out through joke production and collective consumption. The third and final theoretical school claims that humour is used by organizational actors to try and gain control over the situation and to elevate one's self-image over others at the workplace. An example is ethnic jokes used by one group at the workplace against another. This third approach postulates that workplace humour should be seen as reflecting and even enhancing power relations among groups of workers.

Humour has been briefly mentioned when sales work and sales tactics are discussed. For example, Oakes' (1990) study of insurance sales cites the need to laugh at customers' jokes as a way of flattering and of giving the client a false sense of sovereignty (see Korczynski, 2005 for a discussion of 'the myth of customer sovereignty'). Building on such insights from previous research, in this chapter jokes and humour will take centre stage, in an attempt to better understand the nature of retail work and to expose the main tensions in this line of work.

Research site and methods

This chapter is based on 50 interviews: 41 with salespeople and branch managers of different branches of an Israeli chain store of computers and computer accessories and games, and 9 with suppliers and IT purchasers. An important supplement to the interviews are extensive observations carried out by two research assistants at a branch of a large chain of computer stores in Israel, and the documentation of 122 complete interactions, some short and other lasting over 20 minutes. Most interviews were tape-recorded and transcribed in full, while some of them where summarized in writing and expanded shortly after on a computer. Once a dataset composed of all the interview material had been constructed, ATLAS software was employed to categorize and analyse the data.

What can be said about the broader business culture in Israel? For the past three decades Israel has been slowly integrating into the global economy, shifting from a socialist regime to neoliberalism. With this slow change came the slow but steady adaptation of a service-oriented approach by local retail and service enterprises. After 1977-defeat of the Israeli Labour Party, the reduction of state intervention that followed, the rapid privatization of state-owned and union-owned assets and the liberalization of financial markets proved an economic disaster, and it took a national recovery programme enacted by an emergency coalition government to stabilize the economy (see Warhurst and Darr, 2006). The 1993 Oslo Agreement and the hopes for peace in the region it brought with it, coupled with a mass immigration wave composed largely of highly educated Jews from the former Soviet Union, marked the acceleration of the Israeli economy and its growing globalization (BIPAC Briefing, 1996). As a small indication, McDonald's opened its first Israeli branch in 1993, to be quickly followed in 1994 by Burger King (Ram, 2004: 12). Since then Israel has become a bastion of high-tech and bio-tech industries, and global companies in this sector such as Intel and IBM operate major research laboratories in Israel. The per-capita number of start-up companies in Israel is one of the highest in the world. These facts led Ram (2000) to argue that the level of globalization of Israel ranks high compared with other countries. The integration into the global economy and the penetration of multinational firms into Israeli economy has transformed the retail sector and had made it much more oriented towards quality service.

The retail chain included in the study sells computers as well as computer accessories and games, which are centrally purchased by headquarters and then distributed to the different branches spread nationwide. The company has 56 retail outlets nationwide, and employs about 300 workers. The store where research was carried out was a particularly busy branch, located within a large shopping mall in central Tel Aviv, with customers coming in and out at all working hours. The store is open 10am to 9pm. 12 workers are employed at the store, a number that increases to 15 during summer vacations. Four or five salespeople work on busy shifts, for example in the late afternoon and early evening. A regular work shift of salespeople lasts seven hours, four or five times a week. The branch has one manager, two vice-managers, a stock keeper and floor salespeople. The shop floor workers, as well as the managers, are mostly in their 20s, probably reflecting the transitory nature of sales jobs. Young people, after completing their compulsory military service, tend to work as sales people in the store for a year or two, and then typically move on to other careers or to sales jobs elsewhere. A few become branch managers within the chain. The division of sales labour is as follows: The salespeople attend to the customers, answer the phone and operate the cash register, handle dissatisfied customers who return merchandise, and are also responsible for cleaning the store at the end of the day. They are paid a low hourly rate, close to the minimum wage, and in addition earn a commission on sales. They also receive money vouchers from some of the distributors whose products they sell. The store manager performs administrative tasks and communicates with the corporate headquarters, and, whenever needed, assists the salespeople on the sales floor. In his capacity as manager he also authorizes special deals and gifts that salespeople can offer their clients. The two vice-managers replace the manager on some of the shifts when he is away and work as regular salespeople at other times.

Purchasing in the chain is centralized, and managed by purchasing agents at chain headquarters. While branches can communicate directly with the purchasers through specialized software and ask for specific items and quantities, the final decision is always made by the headquarters. The manager and his deputies are in charge of accepting the merchandise from distributors and taking inventory. The stock keeper is in charge of the storage space and responsible for keeping track of sold items and making the necessary replacements on the shelves. In addition, some distributors of leading brand names have direct ties to the store, when, for example, they visit to present new products and reduction schemes. They also occasionally train the salespeople on the job or in between sales interactions in selling their products. All these activities are done with the approval of the company headquarters. Interestingly, there are no formal training programmes for the salespeople, and the vast majority of learning occurs on-the-job and within the occupational group, when novice salespeople shadow more experienced ones on the shop floor.

In the case of the vast majority of the computers and accessories sold by the store, buyers have considerable knowledge about the products, and they are also protected by counter institutions such as elaborate and global warranty policies and brand names that limit the need for an intensive information search. In addition, buyers can also use specialized internet sites to compare the prices and quality of products across different vendors. Most products on sale are mass produced in the Far East and are distributed by local Israeli firms. While information gaps regarding products' quality and cost between sellers and buyers clearly exist, they are substantially lower than is typical in craft markets. Given these attributes of the product market in which the computer store operates, it is best captured as a type of mass retail market. This type of market dominates the retail sector in advanced economies.

Classifying clients

In the formal interviews the salespeople often expressed satisfaction with the service ideology of their chain store, which specifies, in addition to being patient, polite and attentive to clients, also advising the client as to which product best fits her needs, rather than pushing products with the highest commission. As the chains web site states: 'You can expect the most professional service, as should be expected from one of the largest computer chain's in Israel.' The notion of technical assistance that is part of what management sees as the chain's identity is also reflected in the words of the store's manager, who said in an interview: 'We are not salespeople, we are people with knowledge, we provide clients with what they need and we don't push products.'

It emerges from the salespeople's discussion of their work that providing quality service has even become an occupational value, which at times, and despite management's statement, conflicts with management's preferences. For example, on some occasions corporate management at headquarters has reached a deal with one of the large distributors for purchasing a large quantity of a certain brand. In order to encourage the sales of these products in the stores, the sales division at headquarters offers salespersons gift certificates that can be exchanged at a number of other retailers for a variety of products ranging from food to home appliances. One salesperson explained:

> Let's say we received a large quantity of Brand X; so they [management] want to push it. So they tell us 'who ever sells brand X gets 10 NIS worth of gift certificates', and for us this means clothes, food for those who live on their own ... and this it is not only 10 NIS, since you don't sell one product a month. It can easily come to 400 NIS [about 100 US Dollars – A.D.].

This is a substantial sum for the salespeople given their low basic pay, which typically comes to about 10% of their gross basic salary. Other incentive plans could raise their salary even further. It is important to note, and this was stressed by the informants, that the store did not require them to sell these products rather than others, but did provide an incentive for them to focus their efforts on the former through these material incentives. However, some of the salespeople refused to adhere to the incentive plans or to the more formal directives and used an explicitly moral argumentation to explain their stand. When tension exists between the incentive plan and the need to serve clients, the salespeople who resist the organizational recommendations cite occupational rather that personal norms in explaining their behaviour. In fact, shared perceptions among sales personnel of what constitutes good sales practice was centred on the notion of quality service. For example, when asked about the qualities of a good salesperson one of the interviewees replied: '...look, for me it's not only about selling as much as you can. It is also about not lying to customers, your integrity... to provide assistance.' As we shall see, these qualities proved an important factor in the local moral economy on the retail floor.

In the interviews, the salespeople described their service-orientation and their ability to provide fair and balanced technical assistance, as a feature which distinguishes their chain from its competitors. Yet, jokes about different types of clients that the salespeople quoted during the same interviews revealed the function of humour as a form of resistance to the client-centred culture promoted by the chain, and as a manifestation of a counterculture. However, this counterculture was not opposed to the directives of management, but was rather directed at some of the clients who violated what the salespeople perceived as their moral obligation to buy. The source of the tension was a violation of the local moral economy. Jokes can be seen here as a tension relief mechanism, and as a means of creating a sense of moral superiority over clients who failed to buy. Such superiority over clients was also expressed in jokes that were directed at clients who had little, if any, technical knowledge. The tension between the dictum 'the customer is always right' and the content of the jokes is manifested in an answer provided by a salesperson to a direct question about the jokes they tell about clients:

Funny clients, strange clients, sexy clients, I don't know, we have all sorts. I don't push products on clients, but some workers say 'I pushed her this product and that product'. Or 'It was easy selling to her, all she wanted was a shiny thing.' Or 'This moron, what does' he know?' Listen, someone who works as a salesperson can sometimes get really angry, he expresses lots of emotion, he invests in the client and then at the end the client doesn't buy or just walks away. Sometimes there are clients who make you enthusiastic and you're sure they are about to buy, but at the end they say something like 'good, so I'll buy it at a different branch.' Or 'I'll think about it for a week or two.'

As this excerpt demonstrates, the reason for the anger expressed by the salesperson is the client's failure to buy despite the great efforts, both emotional and technical, invested by the salesperson. The emotional outlet is making fun of the clients' technical illiteracy. This excerpt also indicates a gap between the ideological presentation of quality service and the practice of sometimes pushing products to make a higher commission.

A different salesperson provided the following answer when asked about jokes salespeople tell:

> Sometimes we tell jokes about technical terms that clients mis-pronounce. In a previous store I worked for, there was this salesperson who when, let's say two old people would come into the store wanting to buy a 200 IS worth printer, would convince them to leave the store after spending 1000 IS on a printer. He did it in order to make the highest commission he could, about 3–4%. And we would laugh, we would imitate someone coming to buy... not in front of the client, obviously.

Another example, which clearly demonstrates how jokes are used to gain a sense of superiority over clients, was given by another salesperson:

> Some people come in and buy a computer for 6,000 IS, the best ones, and you sit down with them and explain to them about the computer, and they have no idea. They can tell you: What is this large bar? Well, this is the space bar [Laughs]....a person has just spent a large sum, and he has no idea what he's just purchased. It's just a waste; he purchased it for no reason. So later you make fun of him with your friends: 'What a fool!, How was that deal closed?' We really have a lot of strange customers.

One can argue based on these interview excerpts that the salespeople were proud of their technical knowledge, and that they also expected, as part of the moral economy, clients buying sophisticated equipment to demonstrate high levels of technical skills. Note that the 'real economy' of this sales encounter, that is the incentive to sell, and not the moral economy, influenced the outcome of this specific interaction. Yet, moral perceptions were expressed by the salespeople after the deal was sealed, and at other times these moral perceptions, and not the incentive plans, directed the outcomes of other sales encounters. Those who purchased expensive equipment but had little if any technical skills became the objects of jokes, since the salespeople's expectations from these clients to demonstrate technical know-how were clearly violated.

The salespeople were aware of the role joke telling had in their professional life. This was clearly articulated in the following excerpt from an interview:

> Some [jokes] are more insulting... there was this client who came up to me and asked: 'do you have this product.' So I told him: 'No, we don't

work with this company.' So he said: 'So how much does it cost?' So this is something that makes us [the salespeople] laugh. So, sure, we do speak about this, since also you can't tell these stories to others. I think these are the moments that release some of what happens at work.

This salesperson relates to the fact that joking about clients occurs within the occupational community, and serves to create a sense of social cohesiveness. The store manager and his deputies are part of this joking activity, and the clients are the butt of the jokes. Salespeople shared some stories about easy clients, but mostly about difficult ones, and stories especially about sales encounters with unexpected results. Humorous names for a client who end up not buying, such as 'a stiff', have been also documented in relation to car sales workers (see Korczynski, 2005: 82 for a short review).

One of the most basic activities salespeople engaged in was trying to classify different types of clients. Humour and jokes were often manifested in these attempts. For new salespeople, the classification system was an important part of occupational knowledge. Some of the knowledge was general, some specific. For example, nagging clients were regarded as a major nuisance, since they consumed a lot of time with little or no reward. The clients who repeatedly visited the store, demanded the salespeople's attention and ended up not buying anything were nicknamed 'dust' or 'SATA', which is a type of a computer connector. Both terms refer to things that stick to you and don't let go, just like those nagging clients. They were also nicknamed 'oil drillers', referring to their endless talk drilled into the brains of the salespeople.

Information about nagging clients who fail to buy was transferred to other members of the occupational community through gossip networks and on-the-job training. Some notorious clients had even become part of the occupational socialization of salespeople in the store and in the entire chain, as the next interview excerpt with an experienced salesperson illustrates:

You have these nagging clients who pick your brain with questions. Like this grandmother called Ruth. All the salespeople in the chain know her. She doesn't buy a thing. She just comes in and asks endless questions. One day I sat with her for over 45 minutes trying to explain how to burn a CD, and every 10 minutes when she sees how frustrated I am, so she says 'I buy everything here, I always buy here [*bursts into laughter*]' ... One day, when I couldn't take it anymore, I went into the storage room and asked a new salesperson, she was really nice, I asked her if she could sit with Ruth since I couldn't do it anymore, and she said 'fine'. I told her 'listen, she [*the client*] will drive you crazy, really! She will! and she will ask unrelated questions. And she [*the salesperson*] said 'no problem, I like these kinds of things'. So afterwards I went out [*from the storage room to the sales floor*] with a sign [*directed to the young salesperson*] saying 'will you marry me?' [*Written originally in English*]. She really saved me [*laughs*].

On the sales floor, the salespeople try, although in this extreme case not always successfully, to adhere to the customer-centred culture by playing the role of the patient service provider. But, being on the markets' front line, they can easily be the victims of what they see as forms of abuse. In the case described above it got to the point where the salesperson could no longer control his frustration and sense of moral abuse and had to retreat to the storage room, a classic 'back stage'. There, he sought the help of a fellow salesperson by redefining the sales encounter with Ruth as a form of abuse. The description of the client's behaviour is meant to prepare the new salesperson for what awaits her, and, more generally, to the types of challenges she will face in her daily work. Here, we can see a restoring of the sales situation, this time as a form of training for the novice salesperson. To express his gratitude the salesperson puts on a humorous show by holding up the sign asking the younger, less experienced salesperson to marry him. Publicly holding a sign on the retail floor seems to blur the spatial separation between back and front stage. But by using English rather than Hebrew and by the obscure content ('Will you marry me?') the salesperson actually strengthens this separation, which no longer requires physical boundaries. Although displayed in the public arena, this humorous performance is clearly meant to be observed by members of the occupational community, and as a public expression of resistance to the customers' tyranny. Importantly, the justification for this line of resistance is not wrong or abusive management policy or practice, but rather the perceived unfairness of client behaviour.

Another documented, yet extreme, example of the salespeople being the object of clients' abuse is taken from the observations at the store. Here, a client entered the store and started walking around, briefly talking to the salespeople on the sales floor. He was well dressed, wearing glasses, and seemed full of life. At first his behaviour seemed normal, but after a while he started interfering with other sales interactions. Then, he sat down in the computer game section and requested a cup of coffee in a loud voice. No one reacted to his request. He tried to attract the salespeople's attention, but they avoided him. The client then started loudly singing a song. After some time he simply left the store. In answer to the question of who this person was, one of the salesperson replied: 'a client', and then turned a finger around his ear, indicating that he thought one of the client's screws was loose. Then the salesperson said that this person never buys anything, and that the salespeople nicknamed him 'Kramer', after the character on the American TV comedy show 'Seinfeld'. He went on to say that there were 'some clients who behave in strange ways'. He mentioned, for example, a person called David, who reportedly 'comes into the store and walks around for hours'. If he is approached by a salesperson he does not answer and simply leaves the store. The salespeople took his picture, edited it as a 'Wanted' person, and hung it on a board in the storage room, the only 'private' space in the store. A third client was nicknamed 'Michael Jackson', since he used to dance on the sales floor and do the 'moon walk', never purchasing anything.

Discussion and conclusions

Labour process theory has been sensitive to the current shift from a production-based to a service-based economy. Turning the attention away from the production line to the service and sales floors demands the inclusion of the customer within the traditional management-worker framework, and the constitution of the service triangle (Bolton, 2005; Lopez, 1996). With its strong empirical emphasis, LPT has exposed emerging patterns of control and resistance in a variety of service and sales organizations. Critical studies of service and sales work have yielded a flurry of findings ranging from the routinization of interactive service work to forms of resistance by service workers (Leidner, 1993, 1996). This resistance can take the form of workarounds and unionization (Bain and Taylor, 2000), role distancing (Hochschild, 1983), and the creation of an oral data bank outside of management's reach (Orr, 1996). Without denying the centrality of the management – worker cleavage, this chapter attempts to expose some of the social foundations of the encounters between customers and retail workers. Specifically, this study explores the moral economy that emerges on the retail floor in the computer store between the salespeople and their clients from the salespeople's point of view. This moral economy is a regulating mechanism within the service triangle, and is essential for understanding the nature of retail work. The local moral economy should be understood independently of the authority relations between the salespeople and their managers. The jokes salespeople tell about their customers serve as a diagnostic tool to investigate some of the foundations of this local moral economy. Importantly, the vast majority of jokes are directed at clients and not at management, suggesting that customers rather than managers are a major source of tension in retail work.

The jokes told by salespeople about their clients resolve different types of work-related contradictions, provide a tension relief mechanism, enhance solidarity within the occupational community, and also reveal a clear set of moral expectations from clients. The salespeople in the computer store expect their clients to show a serious attitude and a basic sense of obligation to buy, rather than wasting the salespeople's time by engaging in what they perceive as a fruitless information search. Once these expectations are violated, the clients become the butt of jokes, a means of achieving a sense of superiority over them and restoring the balance in the moral economy.

The salespeople's jokes can be seen as a form of resistance to the client-centred culture. However, this counterculture is not opposed to the directives of management, which are inscribed in formal rules and incentive programmes. A closer and a more fine-tuned analysis places these jokes within a wider normative framework that accepts the dictum 'the customer is always right', but at the same time ascribes to the clients a clear role and a set of social and moral obligations. The moral economy on the sales floor and the micro-negotiations over what constitutes moral or fair exchange is an important area of study for those interested in a critical examination of service and sales encounters, and more generally the changing nature of retail work.

Acknowledgements

This study was supported by a two year grant from the Israel Science Foundation (grant No. 934/07). I would like to thank my research assistants Sharon Rosenthal and Elinor Shmorek.

REFERENCES

Bain, P. and Taylor, P. (2000) 'Entrapped by the "electronic Panopticon"? Worker resistance in the call centre', *New Technology, Work and Employment*, 15(1): 2–18.

BIPAC Briefing (1996) 'Israeli economy has joined the tigers', 3(13): 3.

Bolton, S. C. and Houlihan, M. (2005) 'The (mis)representation of customer service', *Work, Employment and Society*, 19(4): 685–703.

Bourdieu, P. (2005) *The Social Structure of the Economy.* Cambridge, UK: Polity Press.

Callaghan, G. and Thompson, P. (2002) 'we recruit attitude: the selection and shaping of routine call centre labour', *Journal of Management Studies*, 39(2): 233–253.

Caudron, S. (1990) 'Humor is healthy in the workplace', *Personnel Journal*, 71: 63–68.

Coser, L. (1956) *The Functions of Social Conflict.* Toronto: The Free Press.

Darr, A. (2003) 'Control and autonomy among knowledge workers in sales: an employee perspective', *Employee Relations*, 25(1): 31–141.

Darr, A. (2006) *Selling Technology: The Changing Shape of Sales in an Information Economy.* Ithaca and London: Cornell University Press.

▶

▶

Decker, W.H. and D.M. Rotondo (2001) 'Relationships among gender, type of humor, and perceived leader effectiveness', *Journal of Managerial Issues*, 13: 450–466.

Duncan, W. Jack (1985) 'The superiority theory of humor at work: joking relationships as indicators of formal and informal status patterns in small, task-oriented groups', *Small Group Behavior*, 16(4): 556–564.

Dupuy, F. (1999) *The Customer's Victory: From Corporation to Co-operation*. Bloomington and Indianapolis: Indiana University Press.

Fernie, S. and Metcalf, D. (1998) '(not) Hanging on the Telephone: Payment systems in the New Sweatshops', Centre for Economic Performance, London School of Economics.

Fuller, L. and Smith, V. (1996) 'consumers' reports: management by customers in a changing economy', in C. Macdonald and C. Sirianni (eds) *Working in the Service Society*. Philadelphia, PA: Temple University Press, 74–91.

Gambetta, D. (1990) *Trust: Making and Breaking Cooperative Relations*. Oxford: Blackwell.

Geertz, C. (1978) 'The bazaar economy: information and search in peasant marketing', *The American Economic Review*, 68(2): 28–37.

Goffman, E. (1963) *Behavior in Public Places*. New York: Free Press

Goffman, E. (1969) *The Presentation of Self in Everyday Life*. London: Allen Lane.

Grint, K. (1998) *The Sociology of Work*. Cambridge, UK: Polity Press.

Herrmann, G. (1997) 'Gift or commodity: what changes hand in the u.s. Garage sale?' *American Ethnologist*, 24: 910–930.

Korczynski, M. (2005) 'The point of selling: capitalism, consumption and contradictions', *Organization*, 12(1): 68–88.

Leidner, R. (1993) *Fast Food, Fast Talk: Service Work and the Routinization of Everyday Life*. Berkeley, CA: University of California Press.

Leidner, R. (1996) 'rethinking questions of control: lessons from McDonald's', in C. Macdonald and C. Sirianni (eds) *Working in the Service Society*. Philadelphia, PA: Temple University Press, 29–50.

Lopez, Steven H. (1996) 'The politics of service production: route sales work in the potato-chip industry', in L.C. Macdonald and C. Sirianni (eds) *Working in the Service Society*. Philadelphia: Temple University Press, 50–74.

Mechling, E.W. and Mechling, J. (1985) 'Shock talk: from consensual to contractual joking relationships in the bureaucratic workplace', *Human Organization*, 44(4): 339–343.

Oakes, G. (1990) *The Soul of the Salesman: The Moral Ethos of Personal Sales*. London: Humanities Press International.

Orr, J.E. (1996) *Talking about Machines: An Ethnography of a Modern Job*. Ithaca and London: Cornell University Press.

Ram, U. (2000) 'The promised land of business opportunities: Liberal post-zionism in the global age', in G. Shafir and Y. Peled (eds) *The New Israel*, 217–240 boulder, Co: Westview Press.

Ram, U. (2004) 'Glocommodification: how the global consumes the local – McDonald's in Israel', *Current Sociology*, 52(1): 11–31.

Romero, E. and A. Pescosolido (2008) 'Humor and Group Effectiveness', *Human Relations*, 61(3): 395–418.

▶

▶

Sherry, J.F. (1983) 'Gift giving in anthropological perspective', *Journal of Consumer Research*, 10: 157–168.

Sherry, J.F. Jr. and McGrath, M.A. (1989) 'Unpacking the holiday presence: a comparative ethnography of two gift stores', in E. Hirschman (ed.) *Interpretive Consumer Research*. Provo, UT: Association for Consumer Research.

Smith, C. (1990) *Auctions: The Social Construction of Value*. Cambridge: Polity Press.

Smeltzer, Larry R. and Leap, Terry L. (1988) 'An analysis of individual reactions to potentially offensive jokes in work settings', *Human Relations*, 41(4): 295–304.

Sturdy, A., Grugulis, I. and Willmott, H. (eds) (2001) *Customer Service: Empowerment and Entrapment*. New York: Palgrave.

Warhurst, C. and Darr, A. (2006) 'From welfare to profit: The transformation of a trade union-owned firm', *Economic and Industrial Democracy*, 27(2): 285–309.

Watts, Jacqueline (2007) 'Can't take a joke? Humour as resistance, refuge and exclusion in a highly gendered workplace', *Feminism & Psychology*, 17(2): 259–266.

Not the Inevitable Bleak House? The Positive Experiences of Workers and Managers in Retail Employment in Sweden

13

Thomas Andersson, Ali Kazemi, Stefan Tengblad and Mikael Wickelgren

Introduction

This chapter aims to demonstrate that retail work is shaped not only by technological and sector-specific conditions, but also by nation-specific influences. It does so by drawing on the findings of a survey study involving workers and managers in 113 retail outlets from a range of different retail sub-segments in Sweden. The results of the survey are instructive for a comparative discussion of the nature of retail employment in an international context as they highlight the way that retail work can be perceived and experienced as socially rewarding where workers are offered decent working conditions, development opportunities and favourable compensation and benefits. While the overall nature of retail work may not be fully described as 'high road', our findings nevertheless show that in the Swedish context retail employment cannot be accurately characterized as 'low road' either. The study thereby underscores the fact that the retail sector is not inevitably a 'bleak house' for workers.

Since the sample of stores included in the survey includes a wide range of retail businesses ranging from large to small retailers in consumables, clothing, electronics, building materials, etc, the results cannot be attributed to some idiosyncratic conditions offered by exceptionally proactive employers or as the result of a bias that might have been generated by a sample of retailers concentrated in the high skill segment of the sector. A more tenable explanation, we argue, derives from the country-specific institutional arrangements of retail employment, which in the Swedish case discourage exploitative employer strategies. These arrangements include a strong position for labour unions, a cooperative climate between unions and employers as well as between employers, and the institutionalized proactive leadership practices in retail workplaces.

The overall results from the survey show that the sector is actively engaged in the general tenets of Swedish working-life, characterized by cooperation, distributed responsibility and fair treatment. Almost all of the surveyed store managers held the belief that employee satisfaction and commitment were crucial for their store's success and financial performance, and manager – personnel relations were remarkably positive from both parties' perspectives. At the beginning of the project the research team expected to find that the retail sector would have relatively traditional employment practices accompanied by low levels of work satisfaction stemming from high labour turnover, the prevalent use of temporary employment contracts and an inferior status on the labour market. Yet while the sector may not be at the vanguard of exemplary personnel practices in general, the findings contradicted such initial expectations by underscoring the close and constructive relations between retail workers and managers, a possible source of optimism and perhaps even inspiration for employers in retail and various segments of the service sector in different countries.

The chapter is structured as follows. First we present previous studies about retail work and the role of national business systems in influencing work conditions. We then outline the characteristics of the Swedish business system, with reference to which we present and make sense of our survey results. We conclude by discussing the implications of our study for future research.

Low road strategies in retail employment practices

The diversity of the retail industry is such that it is problematic to make sweeping statements about it as *one* industry. There are small shops where the owner is the only worker and there are mass merchandisers like Wal-Mart that are among the biggest employers in the world. Likewise, there is a wide range of products and services on offer, utilizing technology from the simple to the highly sophisticated. Given this variability in the sector, retail *work* also takes on diverse forms (Hernant et al., 2007). Retail work can be designed to be skilled (Gamble, 2006) or unskilled (Kirsch et al., 2000), knowledge-intensive or Taylorized, provide career opportunities or a stop gap job. Research on retail employment has mainly been preoccupied with investigating low road strategies. The main focus has been the hard conditions for low-paid, unskilled workers (e.g., Appelbaum and Schmitt, 2009; Bair and Bernstein, 2006; Ehrenreich, 2001; Kirsch et al., 2000). Various reported problems in retail work include job insecurity, short- and split-shifts, the unpredictability of work hours, low wages in part-time and casual jobs, and the need to juggle multiple jobs to earn a living wage which in turn contribute to workplace problems of stress, absenteeism, high turnover and workplace conflicts (Zeytinoglu et al., 2004).

Retail is and remains a low-wage sector in most countries. According to Grugulis (2007), the pressure for hyperflexibility has resulted in a personnel strategy – based upon zero competence, zero qualifications, zero training and zero career – which explains why retail work is dominated by poorly paid part-time workers. Despite the described general pattern there are some national differences (Gadrey and Lehndorff, 2000). In Germany, the difference is that retail companies have a small number of highly skilled anchor workers, while the majority are low-paid staff (Kirsch et al., 2000; Van Klaveren and Voss, this volume). Furthermore, in France, employers expect their workers to be product experts. This is mirrored in customers' requests of advice (McGauran, 2001). However, in both France and Germany, a strategy based on price discounting has become increasingly common, which seems to influence personnel strategies (Baret, 2000).

Despite recognizing considerable national variability in retail employment, much research in the area highlights the sector's unpleasant features, whereby exploitation of workers is more intense than in other industries (Lynch et al., 1999). High levels of subordination and poorly developed work relations are a central theme in such investigations. Many global retail organizations are very centralized (Dawson et al., 1996; Marchington, 1996; Sparks, 2000a, 2000b; Gereffi and Christian, 2009), and this centralization is played through highly standardized work practices at the operational level as well as low qualified and badly paid workers. According to Rhoads et al. (2002) retail managers and workers on store level are less well paid, experience less variety and autonomy, and are less satisfied and committed to their work compared to managers and workers in other industries. Centralization is also visible in an unwillingness to let workers at store level have sufficient job information (Ramaseshan, 1997). Furthermore, retail work is presumed to be feminized and entails a complex gendering of work tasks, the structure of the occupation and the retail environment (Pettinger, 2005). Gendered work environments and work-personal life conflicts contribute to stressful work conditions (Zeytinogly et al., 2004), especially for women (Backett-Milburn et al., 2008).

Another problematic aspect of retail employment that has received recent attention is the demand that retail workers display 'aesthetic' capacities (Nickson et al., 2001, 2005; Pettinger, 2004; Warhurst and Nickson, 2007). Language, dress codes, manner, style, shape and size of the body are deliberately used to appeal to senses of customers (Thompson et al., 2000). This enhances the view of workers in retail as an aesthetic production resource rather than as people with knowledge and competences who can and want to develop.

Davison et al. (1998) claim that it is characteristic for the retail sector that competence development initiatives do not emanate from companies within the industry, but from government initiatives to improve skills in a typical low-skill sector. Retail employers do not seem to see worker competence as a competitive advantage and retail careers are consequently not very promising (Broadbridge, 2003). In fact, deskilling in forms of rationalizing and simplifying the work progress has been a notable characteristic of the changes that have occurred in the retail sector (Akehurst and Alexander, 1996; Sparks, 1996; Grugulis et al., 2004).

Alternatives to low road strategies in retailing

It is not clear whether the low road conditions reflect the overall quality of retail employment, or if particularly depressing work conditions attract more research interest than relatively less problematic work conditions. The answer may be a combination of both.

Some recent research suggests that the currently prevalent personnel strategies in retailing may not be as unassailable as they appear. For example, the findings of Kim et al. (2009) indicate that job characteristics is of importance for Generation Y (individuals born around 1990) employees, proposing a paradigm shift from passive to active workers and employees who craft their jobs, roles and selves may be imminent within a retail organizational context. Despite this argument there seems to be a general belief that high competitiveness in combination with relatively low-skill requirements discourage anything but low cost strategies in the sector (Harvey and Turnbull, 2010). If this is indeed the case, given the heavy pressure of price discounting strategies, retail employment should almost inevitably be characterized by low road strategies (Baret, 2000). However, even in the context of the most 'lean strategy'-defined sectors there remain possibilities for high road employment strategies, so we argue that the adoption of the low road is not a foregone conclusion (see also Wright and Lund, 2006). Harvey and Turnbull (2010) support this argument by presenting evidence from the airline industry, which has been subject of heavy price discounting during recent years. They claim that there is a risk that the 'low road' of employee relations create dissatisfied workers, which may have negative impact on competitive conditions in any 'customer facing' industry. Consequently, there is clearly scope for 'low frills', not only 'no frills'. In their example, the company was able to forge a distinctive management style that combined low-cost operations with high road employment relations. The airline's flight crew appreciated the management style and supported the company's business strategy.

There are several examples of retail firms choosing to adopt a less low road strategy. For example, Bailey and Bernhardt (1997) describe retail firms implementing a variety of production and workplace reforms, such as 'empowering' the employees and institutionalizing teamwork. In their findings, such reforms did help make workers more motivated and satisfied, although the low-skilled and low-paid jobs remained. Bailey and Bernhardt reached the rather negative conclusion that high road strategies seem to have no place in retailing, while our interpretation of their results is more positive, noting their clear findings that the job satisfaction of workers was increased through the implementation of certain workplace reforms. We argue that the conclusion that there was no 'skill upgrade' is unfortunate, as their study also illustrated that employees were able to engage in a greater variety of tasks and enjoyed greater discretion on their jobs, and in general developed a more complex customer interaction. We argue that task-specific skills may not be the sole or even most important criteria for assessment, and that organization-specific skills such as cooperation, which have been neglected in previous studies, also deserve attention. Even if low-skill service jobs cannot be significantly upgraded, organizational commitment, responsibilities and cooperation can. This is supported by Thompson et al. (2001), who claim that the one-sided focus on technical skills is misleading in defining high- and low-skill work, especially in the context of service work where social skills and competencies are critical even if technical skills requirements remain low. Furthermore, we agree with Lafer (2004), who argues that social skills is perhaps not the most appropriate term, since for example commitment is not a skill that someone possesses or not, but something one chooses to 'give' based on present conditions. Thus, social skills cannot be studied as an individual or separate phenomenon, but as a context contingent one.

One problem regarding high road strategies in retailing that Bailey and Bernhardt (1997) identified is that the good examples never spread. They claimed that the main reason was the lack of sectoral and governmental policies that supported such diffusion. In this chapter we devote some attention to this issue and claim that a national institutional context that contrasts with that of the US, where their study was performed, might be more supportive of the spread of high road strategies.

One established way to describe and analyze country-specific institutional patterns is provided by the literature of national business systems (Haake, 2002; Morgan et al., 2005; Whitley, 1992a, 1992b, 1999). This literature is sensitive to the historical tradition and the interdependence of different actors within a country, for example, the political sector, governmental institutions, labour unions, financial institutions, private business, etc. In order to characterize the Swedish case, we use Haake's (2002) differentiation between individualistic and communitarian business systems. Haake (2002: 720) defines individualistic business systems as systems 'in which actors safeguard their individual autonomy through loose interfaces' and communitarian business systems as systems 'in which actors share tight interfaces that turn these parties into interconnected communities'. It is typical of individualistic business systems that relationships between employees, firms and sector associations are looser since these actors strive for self-reliance. Communitarian business systems, on the other hand, are based on close and stable relationships between actors who act more interdependently. These close relationships and interdependencies often create trust among actors because such relationships create opportunities for the actors to monitor and counteract opportunism, but also a danger of rigidity if the actors lock each other into a well established but rather dysfunctional role pattern.

On Haake's scale of individualism – communitarianism, the US scores the highest on individualism followed by the UK, while Germany and Japan are traditionally more communitarian economies (Haake, 2002: 727). Sweden also traditionally has a communitarian business system with interdependent actors expected to cooperate and negotiate on economic relationships, rights and obligations. Whether this context of relatively close cooperation between employers and workers – and likewise rather low competitive pressures – allow for mutually satisfactory employment relations in retailing is an empirical question that we address in this chapter.

The Swedish working-life – Combining good working conditions and competitiveness

Sweden often stands out in positive terms in international comparisons. The country has one of the most egalitarian income distributions among industrialized economies and jobs in the Swedish labour market have relatively high task variety and job content. This is not achieved at the expense of competitiveness; thriving societal institutions and infrastructural arrangements contribute to Sweden's top position among the EU-member States in this respect (IMD, 2010; WEF, 2010). An important reason for this positive picture is the institutional arrangements in the post-war period where national labour unions accepted rationalizations and downsizings as long as the workers received a fair share of the economic value added and the state maintained efforts to retrain and financially support laid-off workers.

In the 1980s and 1990s a reformed Swedish model evolved gradually, which was less centralized and subject to fewer direct state interventions. Instead, cooperative relations between employers and unions were established on industry and company levels. Managers across different ranks were given greater responsibilities for their staff, for instance in terms of recruitment, competence development and work environment issues. Operational managers were largely given a more general management role while supervisory tasks such as everyday work planning and distribution of work tasks were typically delegated to semi-autonomous work groups. Swedish employees were to a high degree expected to be able to perform their work in a responsible way and in absence of close supervision.

The tendency to reduce or abolish the supervisory function in favour of more general management positions, including responsibilities for many HR-activities and meeting financial targets, has led to a transformation of the role of employees, who are now generally referred to as 'co-workers'. In contrast to research from the UK that reports a reluctance among line managers to take larger responsibilities in HRM-issues (Kirkpatrick et al., 1992; Lowe 1992), Swedish research suggests that HRM has become a major feature for operative managers (Tengblad 2003; Andersson et al., 2010). As a consequence of these changes, a strong tradition of collaboration between management and workers has developed over the years (Jönsson, 1996). In fact, some empowerment critics (e.g., Jönsson and Macintosh, 1997) argue that the only 'true' empowerment they have seen is in Scandinavia, but not under the label of empowerment per se. Even if the word empowerment is seldom used, the idea of empowerment – in the meaning of distributing power from managers to co-workers – has had a much larger practical impact in Scandinavia than in the rest of the world. This Scandinavian pattern deviates from the pattern in Anglo-Saxon countries, where research shows empowerment reforms to largely fail because managers seldom sincerely want to give up their power to supervise (Quinn, 1999; Hales, 2002). Purported empowerment initiatives therefore often degenerate into what Ciulla (2000) refers to as 'bogus empowerment', where employees respond to managers' mixed and incoherent behaviour with cynicism and resistance.

The key factor in the successful implementation of ideas of empowerment in Sweden is the strong institutional support from both the unions and the Swedish Employers' Confederation (for privately owned companies) who were active in the development of a work organization based on production groups with extended responsibilities for planning, preparation and conduct of work (Gustavsen et al., 1996). The strong impact of unions and employers' confederations has to do with the fact that about 80 per cent of the total Swedish work force is unionized and a majority of the employees work for employers belonging to an employer confederation. Delegating greater responsibility to workers was seen by employers' confederations as very beneficial for work satisfaction, commitment, and consequently, productivity.[1]

For several decades the proportion of workers who belong to unions have been in the range 70–80 per cent in Sweden. There is currently a total of around 60 unions belonging to one of the three main federations; one for blue-collar workers, one for white-collar workers, and one for professional employees with higher education degrees.[2] Most conditions concerned work-time, compensation and employment rights and benefits are neither legislated nor decided by the companies, but subject to employer–union negotiation. This is also the case in the retail sector, with a significant impact on the nature of the employment relationship in this context, as we describe in further detail below.

Retail employment in Sweden

In 2008 there were about 563,000 people working in the Swedish retail – and wholesale sector, of whom 43 per cent were female and 57 per cent male. The sector employs around 13 per cent of the total Swedish labour force. A significant segment of the country's economy, it accounts for 10 per cent of the gross national product (GNP) (Statistics Sweden, 2009), with grocery retailing accounting for 44 per cent and durable goods retailing for 56 per cent of the total Swedish purchases amounting to 581.6 billion SEK in 2008 (HUI, 2009). Adjusting for total work hours these figures imply that the value added per hour is just below the national average. The average working hours for retail workers in 2008 were 36 hours per week in total, 33 for women and 39 for men (Arbetskraftsundersökningen, SCB, 2009).

Workers in the retail and wholesale industry are paid less in total than workers in manufacturing, but they earn more than those in the hospitality, agriculture, forestry, hunting and fishery sectors (Statistics Sweden, 2009). However, wages and salaries in Sweden are rather narrow in range by tradition (Ekonomifakta, 2009). This means that, in comparison with many other countries, employees in the lowest paid jobs in Sweden earn more than in most other countries. The retail industry can be seen as an example of this. For instance, in 2008 retail workers in Sweden on average earned 39 per cent more than retail workers in the US, 12.34 versus 8.88 EUR per hour (Bureau of Labor Statistics, US, and Statistics Sweden, 2009).[3] In fact, there are no sectors in Sweden that fall into the common definition of low-wage work – where earnings are below two-thirds of the national gross median hourly earnings (Appelbaum and Schmitt, 2009). Figures for 2007 show that retail employment paid 83 per cent of the Swedish gross national earnings average (Statistics Sweden, 2009). This means that full-time retail workers in Sweden, with few exceptions, can earn incomes that afford a 'normal' living and that do not condemn individuals to a life on the poverty line.

The recent transformation of the Swedish retail sector follows four international trends (Fölster and Bergström, 2005). The first concerns the consolidation of retailing into fewer and larger chains, which are typically growing not only domestically but also internationally. The financial turnover in retail companies varies considerably by size: For Swedish retail companies (on average, regardless of line of business) with 1 – 4 employees the average turnover per employee was 1.2 million SEK in 2005, while the same figure for retail companies (local stores) with more than 20 employees was 2.5 million SEK (HUI, 2008). Obviously, there are economies of scale in retailing, which is the likely driving force behind this trend. Sweden is the country of origin of some of the world's most successful retailers such as IKEA in furniture and H&M in apparel. These companies are an important source of inspiration to the rest of the retail industry with their combination of international expansion, global sourcing, competitive pricing and cooperative labour relations. The second trend concerns the rise of shopping malls in Sweden. This trend is informed by consumers' perceived sense of lack of time for shopping, nurturing the growth of facilities offering 'one-stop-shopping' for a wide variety of merchandise in the same location. A third trend is the expanding number of shops and shopping chains in the lower price segment. Interestingly enough, both IKEA and H&M are also good examples of the growth potential in lower price segments. A fourth trend is the technological development in retail. More shops and shopping chains are utilizing computerized price scanning systems, often connected to personalized customer loyalty pro grammes including electronic customer shopping cards.

All of these major trends have consequences for how retail work is organized at the store level. In the fewer but larger stores, normally belonging to a retail chain, the tangible work can be more or less controlled by the company headquarters. That is, the work is centralized and managers and workers at store level experience different levels of autonomy in different retail chains. Head offices make extensive use of the recent developments in retail technologies, which provide the capability to closely monitor and/or manage a large number of local stores regardless of distance (physical or imaginary). This, however, does not necessarily mean that the work at the local retail stores is subject to total remote control management at the micro level, such as 'McDonaldisation' (Ritzer, 1993), even if this does sometimes occur. The local store manager generally retains considerable discretion regarding local decisions, particularly when it comes to personnel issues. The task of hiring and managing the employees at the local store is normally the sole responsibility of the store manager. The task of developing the employees is also normally the responsibility of the store manager, though usually done with the support of central HR units. When it comes to discharging retail workers, the local store manager usually has to perform such tasks in close cooperation with headquarters and/or regional chain managers, but crucially also with the involvement of Union representatives. This is due to the rigorous Swedish legislation on formalities for giving notice of termination of employment. Any layoffs in Sweden of a non-temporary worker need to be grounded on repeated misbehaviour when the worker has first been notified that continued violations will render termination. Only in cases of serious breaches of the employment contract, such as theft and other criminal behaviour, a worker can be fired directly. In cases of redundancies it is the last employed employees who normally have to go first and the Unions need to be consulted in such cases.

In line with the changes instigated by the aforementioned trends, the skills demands and levels in Swedish retail are currently in rapid transformation. Traditionally, competence development at the store level has been rather low. In 2000, the average number of training days for retail workers in Sweden was 0.8 days per year, which placed the retail industry among the five industries with the lowest provision of training. However in recent years, the average length of training in the sector has doubled, and this increase has rapidly gained momentum (Surtevall, 2010). To meet the new demand for trained staff in the retail industry, four different university/college degree programmes specifically focused on retailing are currently on offer by four different higher education institutions in Sweden, mainly directed to store managers. However, there is no evidence of a general technical skill upgrading for shop floor workers specifically related to the tasks, rather training initiatives seem to be aimed at more generic skills.

The Swedish case in retail employment is also exceptional in terms of the very high rates of union membership among both shop floor workers and store management. About 70 per cent of retail workers in non-temporary employment are unionized and most managers belong to a union. Both the unions and the employers belong to central organizations, whose principal officials know each other well and meet often in their offices in central Stockholm. The Unions and the employer organization Svensk Handel (The Swedish Trade) have also started a joint research and development board, Handelns Utvecklingsråd (HUR) with an annual budget of about 1.5 million EUR. The research reported herein is for example financed by HUR.

To conclude, the retail sector is integrated in the overall institutional pattern of the Swedish labour market, with unionized workers and employees, small wage differences and relatively high employment security. Next, we present results from a questionnaire study that investigated the perceptions of work relations among durable goods and grocery retail store managers and employees.

The study

In the present study we depart from the model Service-Profit-Chain (Heskett et al., 1997) in an attempt to investigate the way in which retail employers organize work in order to evoke employee commitment, which is presumed to lead to enhanced employee satisfaction which in turn renders increased profitability. We have also inquired about the nature of the relations between managers and workers in retail stores, drawing upon Leader–Member Exchange theory (LMX) (e.g., Graen and Uhl-Bien, 1995; Gerstner and Day, 1997) which examines relations from the perspective of both sides. LMX theory assumes that leaders and managers develop unique relationships with their subordinates, not least dependent on the quality and amount of exchanges between these (for instance recognition, loyalty, economic rewards, support, etc). The outcomes of well-established and positive relations can be of many different kinds, such as work satisfaction, commitment, creativity, etc. Five of the items in the survey addressed at managers (see items 5–10 in Table 13.2) and five at employees/workers (see items 15–19 in Table 13.3) come from the LMX-MDM-scale as presented in Liden and Maslyn (1998).

After the collection of responses from managers, workers and customers, we created a database with data from local retail stores in various lines of business in several different areas in Sweden (see Table 13.1 for a description of the research sample). As Table 13.1 illustrates, the number of durable goods retailing stores exceeded the number of grocery retailing stores in both samples from 2008 and 2009. Correspondingly, we have more responses from durable goods retailing stores than in grocery retailing stores. In both samples, there are more responses from female than male retail workers.

Table 13.1 Description of our samples from 2008 and 2009 in terms of absolute frequencies

	2008		2009	
	Grocery Retailing	Durable Goods Retailing	Grocery Retailing	Durable Goods Retailing
Stores (and no of managers)	15	32	22	44
Retail workers	108	141	134	172
Gender				
female	44	63	107	122
male	28	40	25	50

Note: $2008_{workers}$ =74 (29.7%) and $2009_{workers}$ =2 (0.7%) missing for the gender variable.

Survey results

As already mentioned, data were collected in two rounds, in 2008 and 2009. Descriptive statistics are presented in Table 13.1 for each data collection period. This was done to compare the results obtained in each year and to explore the stability of the survey results. Different retail stores were questioned in 2009. Except for some minor refinements survey questions in 2009 were the same as those asked in 2008.

Table 13.2 displays descriptive data regarding retail *managers'* perceptions of work satisfaction, retail worker engagement and leader–member exchanges. Descriptive data concerning retail *workers'* perceptions of work relations and characteristics (i.e., work satisfaction, engagement, leader–member

Table 13.2 Means (M) and Standard Deviations (SD) for selected survey items pertaining to perceptions of work relations and characteristics among retail managers (1–7 scale)

	2008		2009	
Item	M	SD	M	SD
Work stress and satisfaction				
1. To what extent do you feel stressed in your work?	4.31	1.51	3.88	1.46
2. How do you perceive your total job satisfaction?	5.64	0.97	5.88	1.00
Perception of retail worker engagement				
3. What is your perception of your employees' commitment regarding contributing to the store's results?	5.26	1.07	5.34	1.19
4. To what extent do you think that your employees in average make an effort to make satisfied customers?	5.70	0.90	5.92	0.76
Leader–Member Exchange (LMX)				
5. To what extent do you think that your employees are self-propelled and feel responsible?	5.55	1.03	5.72	0.92
6. I like my co-workers a lot as individuals.	6.13	0.72	6.19	0.96
7. I very much enjoy working together with my co-workers.	6.25	0.78	6.13	1.00
8. I defend my co-workers if they are harassed by others.	6.38	0.71	6.65	0.68
9. My co-workers are willing to make an effort, beyond what usually is required, to live up to my work objectives.	5.51	0.94	5.53	1.08
10. I respect the work knowledge and competence of my co-workers.	6.09	0.80	6.33	0.86

exchanges, goal clarity, managerial capacities, co-worker climate, the store's physical attributes and personal development opportunities) are depicted in Table 13.3.

As is shown in Tables 13.2 and 13.3, responses to all questions fall above the midpoint of the scale (a 7-point scale with 1 indicating the 'worst case scenario' and 7 indicating the 'best case scenario'), and in most cases near the positive endpoint of the scale. Taken as a whole these results indicate the largely positive experiences and perceptions of co-workers, with several additional indicators likewise underscoring their favourable assessments of working conditions among both managers and workers. Another interesting observation is that the mean responses did not differ considerably between the two measurement periods, which highlights the consistency and replicability of the results, even though different stores and respondents participated in the two phases of the study.

Describing responses to some specific survey items help illustrate the overall positive tendency in the data. Managers report that they are convinced that the retail workers have a good sense of responsibility for their own work and that they try to satisfy customers. They also report that they like and respect the retail workers in their stores and enjoy working with them.

Eight questions were used to assess various respects of job satisfaction among the retail workforce. The results reveal that the retail workers are most satisfied with their work tasks and how they have improved in their job. The results also show that the retail workers in general have a great interest in further improvement/growth in their job. The responses to questions about satisfaction with work benefits, reward system, salary and chances of promotion fall above the midpoint of the scale. The only satisfaction item that evoked less positive responses was the extent to which the retail workers perceived their chances of influencing their salary. Correspondent with these responses, the respondents report that they are not considering quitting their job for some other place of work with the same salary and that they consider it as very important to contribute to the success of the store. Interestingly, the retail workers display the same positive attitudes towards managers in that they state that they like and respect their manager and enjoy working with him/her. This positive attitude is further confirmed with the observation that the retail workers have a positive evaluation of their managers' managerial capacities and communication skills. The results also show that retail workers have favourable views not only of their manager but also of their colleagues and the work that they do.

At this point, it is of interest to look at the interrelationships between some of the variables in the study. Table 13.4 displays the means, standard deviations, Cronbach alpha reliability coefficients, and Pearson intercorrelations for all study composite variables. In interpreting the findings, we depart

Table 13.3 Means (M) and Standard Deviations (SD) for selected survey items pertaining to perceptions of work relations and characteristics among retail workers (1–7 scale)

	2008		2009	
Item	M	SD	M	SD
Work satisfaction				
1. How satisfied are you with your job?	6.01	1.06	6.17	1.11
2. How satisfied are you with your work tasks?	5.81	1.20	6.05	1.08
3. How satisfied are you with your chances of promotion?	4.04	1.65	4.54	1.86
4. How satisfied are you with your improvement/ growth in your job?	5.13	1.40	5.24	1.47
5. How great is your interest in further improvement/ growth in your job?	5.71	1.32	5.87	1.43
6. How satisfied are you with your salary?	4.02	1.63	4.38	1.71
7. How satisfied are you with your chances of influencing you salary?	3.20	1.77	3.65	1.87
8. How satisfied are you with your other work benefits as an employee?	4.64	1.77	5.01	1.69
9. How satisfied are you with how your employer rewards actions that increase customer satisfaction?	4.53	1.70	4.67	1.71
Loyalty and engagement				
10. Would you quit your job here if you were offered the same salary some other place of work? (reversed)	5.01	1.66	5.14	1.60
11. How important is it for you to contribute to the store's success?	6.29	0.96	6.38	0.94
12. How often do you attend the staff meetings in your store?	4.07	1.67	3.81	1.67
Goal clarity				
13. To what extent do you perceive that there are reasonable goals for how well you are to do your job?	5.49	1.14	5.66	1.26
14. To what extent do you perceive that there are reasonable goals for how much you are expected to work?	5.33	1.25	5.54	1.24
Leader–Member Exchange (LMX)				
15. I like my store manager a lot.	5.89	1.19	6.06	1.28
16. I very much enjoy working together with my store manager.	5.70	1.30	5.77	1.45
17. My store manager defends me if I am harassed by others.	5.86	1.38	6.01	1.41
18. I am willing to make an effort, beyond what usually is required, to live up to the work objectives of my store manager	5.55	1.19	5.74	1.38
19. I respect the work knowledge and competence of my store manager.	5.94	1.20	6.17	1.24

Continued

Table 13.3   Continued

Item	2008		2009	
	M	SD	M	SD
Grading the manager				
20. How do you perceive the communication between you and your manager?	5.95	1.30	5.99	1.26
21. What grade do you give to your manager's managerial capacities?	5.56	1.45	5.39	1.51
22. How good is your manager in listening to employees' suggestions?	5.68	1.37	5.49	1.57
Co-worker climate				
23. How do you perceive the communication between those of you working in the store, except for the manager?	5.69	1.13	5.92	1.11
24. Do your colleagues, those who have an impact on your job, a good job?	5.75	1.02	5.96	1.04
25. Are your colleagues, those who have an impact on your job, cooperative?	5.76	1.06	5.91	1.14
26. What is your perception of working together in this store?	5.80	1.09	6.03	1.07
Attitude towards the store				
27. To what extent do you have the prerequisites to make satisfied customers?	5.78	0.89	6.09	1.01
28. What grade do you give to your store as compared to other stores you have worked at or that you know of?	5.88	1.13	5.97	1.21
Opportunity for personal development				
29. What is your perception of training efforts in your store?	4.80	1.32	5.07	1.44
30. What are your chances of improvement/growth in your job?	4.78	1.51	4.84	1.74

from the four variables (i.e., work satisfaction, co-worker climate, loyalty and engagement, and attitude towards the store) and study the correlations between these and the other study variables.

Work satisfaction is positively and significantly correlated with all variables. It is most strongly associated with the opportunity for personal development (in terms of on-the-job training and its quality) indicating that giving employees the opportunities to improve and grow with regard to their work tasks is associated with the way they judge their work satisfaction in a more general sense. Furthermore, work satisfaction shows the lowest correlation with managerial work satisfaction which may suggest that there is a 'satisfaction mirror', but judging from the magnitude of the correlation they do not reflect each other strongly. Expressed differently, a manager's perceived work satisfaction

Table 13.4 Means (M), Standard Deviations (SD), Reliabilities and Correlations of the study variables

Variable	M	SD	Correlations										
			1	2	3	4	5	6	7	8	9	10	11
1. Worker satisfaction	4.87	0.75	.89										
2. Co-worker climate	5.89	0.650	.47**	.91									
3. Worker loyalty and engagement	5.79	0.67	.65**	.46**	.43								
4. Attitude towards store	5.82	0.63	.58**	.51**	.49**	.64							
5. Manager's work satisfaction	5.76	0.99	.30**	.21*	.19	.27**	.70						
6. Manag. percept. emp. engag.	5.56	0.84	.51**	.34**	.36**	.36**	.34**	.61					
7. LMX (managers)	5.83	0.65	.43**	.36**	.39**	.31**	.30**	.88**	.79				
8. LMX (employees)	5.96	0.71	.63**	.51**	.80**	.58**	.17	.34**	.33**	.93			
9. Goal clarity	5.56	0.66	.54**	.47**	.54**	.64**	.34**	.43**	.41**	.59**	.77		
10. Grading the manager	5.76	0.92	.54**	.48**	.71**	.58**	.17	.31**	.28**	.94**	.58**	.93	
11. Opp. for pers. develop.	4.96	0.95	.71**	.43**	.52**	.52**	.29**	.37**	.31**	.52**	.43**	.49**	.78

Note: Alpha reliability coefficients for composite measures are in boldface along the diagonal.
*p<0.05. **p <0.001.

is related to co-worker satisfaction, but this relationship is not a strong one as the common variance reaches only to 9 per cent. Another interesting but somewhat puzzling observation in this context is, as our data demonstrate, that managerial work satisfaction is associated with neither retail workers' leader–member exchange ratings nor how they grade their manager and his/her managerial capacities and qualities. Thus, how managers perceive their overall work satisfaction is not related to how retail workers perceive their relationships with them or how they perceive their capacities as managers. This finding suggests that in order to be perceived as a good and a capable manager who succeeds in creating and maintaining positive relationships with the co-workers, individual satisfaction may not be that crucial. A tenable explanation is that managers do not let their own work satisfaction influence how they behave towards their co-workers and perform their managerial work.

Co-worker climate is also positively and significantly correlated with all variables, but the mean correlations here are lower than the mean correlations in the case of work satisfaction. Most interestingly, co-worker climate in terms of how retail workers perceive their relationships to their colleagues is most strongly associated with how retail workers perceive their relationships to their manager (employee LMX). That is, the more positive their attitude is towards their manager, the more they tend to perceive their colleagual relationships in a positive way. Co-worker climate is also associated with how retail workers rate the store that they work in and the extent to which they are provided a good work environment. Here also, managerial work satisfaction is the variable that shows the lowest correlation with co-worker climate.

Retail worker loyalty and engagement is positively and significantly correlated with all variables, except for managerial work satisfaction. There are surprisingly strong positive correlations between employee loyalty and engagement on the one hand and employee LMX and how retail workers judge managerial capacities on the other hand, indicating that leader–member exchanges are of importance for the level of engagement and loyalty among retail workers. Employee loyalty and engagement is also positively related to goal clarity. Thus, the more retail workers know about the quantity and quality of work they are expected to accomplish, the more they feel engaged and behave loyally. Furthermore, data show that employee engagement is enhanced by employee development practices, i.e., the more retail stores invest in training efforts, the more the employees tend to feel engaged.

Attitude towards the store is positively and significantly correlated with all variables. It is most strongly associated with goal clarity, indicating that the more retail workers are informed about the quantity and quality of work they are expected to perform, the more positive they are towards the store and the higher grade they tend to give to their employer. Retail workers' attitudes towards the store are also related to employee leader member exchange ratings and judgements about managerial qualities and capacities.

There are some remarkable differences in our empirical data compared with the international research that we have discussed earlier. If low cost strategies should require corresponding low cost employment systems (Harvey and Turnbull, 2010), retailing should almost inevitably become a bleak house. However, our empirical data illustrates the opposite, that is, workers highly satisfied with their tasks, their managers and colleagues. Furthermore, workers are highly committed to the success of their stores. They are even relatively satisfied with their pay, training efforts and opportunities for improvement/growth in their jobs – even though international research describes personnel strategies based upon zero competence, zero qualifications, zero training and zero career (Grugulis, 2007) and that the retail sector is internationally characterized by low-paid jobs (e.g., Appelbaum and Schmitt, 2009; Bair and Bernstein, 2006; Ehrenreich, 2001; Kirsch et al., 2000).

Our empirical data cannot describe any significant upgrade in the technical skills of the tasks, but it illustrates both high levels of organizational commitment and perceptions of the relationship between managers and workers as well as between colleagues as largely cooperative. Relationship competencies (social skills that are individual approaches rather than skills, and goes beyond what Lafer (2004) calls 'whatever employers want'), commitment to the organization and organizational goals, and worker responsibility both for organizational goals and relationship qualities represent another upgrade that can be made within retailing, although the tasks in a technical sense still are rather simple.

Overall, the results from the study reveal a highly positive picture of the experience of retail employment, to an extent that they may be regarded as 'surprising'. In many respects the pattern of responses resemble what might be expected from High Performance Work Systems, in stark contrast to the poor and depressing work conditions described in much of the international literature on retail. The results furthermore illustrate that the retail sector within given national contexts can have satisfying workplace relations and work conditions. In the next section we discuss some tenable explanations of these positive results.

Discussion: National business systems and their influence on high/low road strategies

Where previous research has presented similar positive examples from retailing (e.g., Bailey and Bernhardt, 1997), these were also shown to neither persevere nor spread because of the lack of a supportive sectoral environment and work–life policies. Our research illustrates that national business systems can have greater influence than sector-specific influences in helping sustain favourable employment relations in retail around high-road, rather than low-road, strategies. The Swedish working-life is, in general, characterized by managerial commitment to retail workers and a cooperative orientation towards unions. Gittell and Bamber (2010) describe these factors as significant for high-road strategies. This study supports their claim. Furthermore, it adds that national business systems seem to be able to influence a sector that is internationally described as almost inevitably confined to low-road strategies, to on a broad front choose high- or middle-road strategies. The general values in Swedish working-life seem to have greater influence than international sectoral influence on Swedish retailing.

While retail work can involve skilled tasks and high levels of distributed responsibilities there are limits to how varied and high-skilled it can be. The majority of work consists of routine tasks like exchanging money, answering customer requests, cleaning and moving goods. While these work tasks may appear as only marginally rewarding, a majority of the sampled retail workers in the study reported liking their work. Well-functioning work-place relations deserve to be seen as the main reason for this. It is remarkable that this has been achieved on a systemic scale in a large number of stores in many different sub-segments of the retail sector. Clearly the results of our study cannot be explained by the existence of some enlightened retail companies, store managers or the chance factor. Instead we need to find explanations on the institutional level and to the extent that the Swedish retail sector is a participant in the norms for employee relations in the national labour market. These institutional patterns include a cooperative climate between the involved employer federations and national unions, the high acceptance of working-life regulations for compensation, working time, employment security and work environment. The institutional explanations also include the widespread belief that leader behaviour impacts employee commitment, which in turn is crucial not merely for worker satisfaction, but for customer satisfaction and store performance at the same time as well.

We also think that the relatively small size of a store as a working place (even if the organization as a whole might be very big) as compared with a general hospital, or any other larger production or administrative unit with many different occupations, departments and functions, is beneficial for creating good work relations, commitment and a sense of responsibility for store performance. In a store the manager and the workers can work closely with one another, solve problems informally, provide mutual help, socialize and develop a common understanding about what is going on in the store. This leads us to an interesting question that awaits future research. If it is possible to create high work satisfaction, employee commitment and good work place relations at national and industry levels, what kinds of institutional dysfunctions hinder this development in most other countries? But one might also turn the question around and wonder what impact the globalization of retail and retailers will have on the sustainability of the Swedish 'good examples'.

Conclusions

The results of our study show that the retail workers in Sweden are generally satisfied with their working conditions and the way they are treated by their colleagues as well their employers/managers. That the workforce at large should attest to holding such positive views about their employment experiences and that the store-level management should hold such favourable views of the workers in their stores came as a surprise to the research team.

Moreover, the retail workers demonstrated organizational commitment, a cooperative attitude and high levels of interest in their personal development, that we, forewarned by the findings of previous retail research, had not expected from this rather low-status occupation. While the sector is not without problems, it can by no means be deterministically seen as a low road sector with impoverishing working conditions and no viable alternative arrangements. Rather our results show that it is possible to instutionalize a high-road strategy in a low-skill sector with strong market pressures.

The main conclusion of the present study is therefore that it is possible to organize retail work in a way that creates stimulating tasks, good collaboration with unions and customer-friendly opening hours. The key factor in realizing this aim seems to be a strengthening of the relationship between store managers and workers, and an emphasis on the store manager as a leader with personnel responsibilities. The difference to for example American retailing (Walmart) where store managers also are very much 'responsible' for personnel matters is the shared nature of responsibilities. The Swedish example is that of an 'enabling' leader. Shared and decentralized responsibilities should not be seen as something that have to lead to a marginalization of unions and facilitating activities on the national level, rather they are a means of implementing central agreements on work environment and employee relations matters. A further important implication from our study is that objective measurements of pay, access to formal training, task discretion and variety do not alone determine work satisfaction but that good leadership, delegated responsibilities and a socially well-functioning work environment also have a profound impact.

Still there is need for further inquiry into the possible explanations of the results we have reported here, such as our subsequent effort around a number of case studies of retail companies that are seen as 'exemplary' in their employment practices in the Swedish context. This, and other research, can hopefully provide a better understanding of how high road strategies can be pursued in the retail sector and what their consequences might be.

Notes

1 The former CEO of the airline carrier SAS, Jan Carlzon, developed these thoughts in the best selling management book in Sweden ever – *Moments of Truth* (Carlzon 1988) – where he suggested that every employee should be regarded as a manager with responsibilities to perform their own work, while the managers instead should become leaders. The book was originally published in Swedish in 1985 with the more telling title 'Tear down the pyramids'.

2   There is also a small Syndicalism Union organizing only 0.2% of the total workforce.

3   US in 2007 made an average of USD 12.76 an hour (equals SEK 90,50 or EUR 8,88 at exchange-rates of January 4, 2010), while retail employees in Sweden were paid SEK 125,70 an hour (equals USD 17,72 or EUR 12,34).

REFERENCES

Akehurst, G. and Alexander, N. (1996) 'Introduction', in Akehurst, G. and Alexander, N. (eds.) *Retail Employment*. London: Frank Cass.

Andersson, T.; Hällsten, F.; Rovio-Johansson, A. and Tengblad, S. (2010) *Coworkership and employability*, forthcoming.

Appelbaum, E. and Schmitt, J. (2009) 'Low-wage work in high-income countries: Labor-market institutions and business strategy in the US and Europe', *Human Relations*, 62(12): 1907–1934.

Babin, B. and Boles, J. (1996) 'The perceived co-worker involvement and supervisor support on service provider role, stress, performance and job satisfaction', *Journal of Retailing*, 72(1): 57–75.

Backett-Milburn, K., Airey, L., McKie, L. and Hogg, G. (2008) 'Family comes first or open all hours?: How low paid women in food retailing manage webs of obligation at home and at work', *Sociological Review*, 56(3): 474–496.

Bailey, T. and Bernhardt, A. (1997) 'In search of the high road in a low-wage industry', *Politics Society*, 25: 179–200.

Bair, J. and Bernstein, S. (2006) 'Labour and the Wal-Mart Effect,' in S.D. Brunn (ed.) *Wal-Mart World: The World's Biggest Corporation in the Global Economy*. London: Routledge.

Baret, C. (2000) 'Societal constraints and strategic room for manoeuvre: what options do firms have for improving employee satisfaction?', in C. Baret, S. Lehndorff and L. Sparks (eds) *Flexible Working in Food Retailing – A comparison between France, Germany, the United Kingdom and Japan*. London: Routledge, 167–187.

Broadbridge, A. (2003) 'The appeal of retailing as a career 20 years on', *Journal of Retailing and Consumer Services*, 10(5): 287–296.

Carlzon, J. (1988) *Moments of Truth*. New York: Perennial Library.

Ciulla, J.B. (2000) *The Working Life: the Promise and Betrayal of Modern Work*, New York: Three Rivers Press.

Davison, J., Messenger, S. and Williams, C. (1998) 'Developing competence in retailing: strategic advantages', *Journal of Retailing and Consumer Services*, 5(4): 235–244.

Dawson, J., Findlay, A. and Sparks, L. (1996) 'The importance of store operator on superstore employment levels', in G. Akehurst and N. Alexander (eds) *Retail Employment*. London: Frank Cass, 54–66.

Ehrenreich, B. (2001) *Nickle and Dimed: on Not Getting by in America*. New York: Henry Holt & Co.

▶

▶

Ekonomifakta (2009) http://www.ekonomifakta.se (accessed 15 May 2009).

Fölster, S. and Bergström, F. (2005) *Kampen om köpkraften*. Västerås: Forma Publishing.

Gadrey, J. and Lehndorff, S. (2000) 'A societal interpretation of the differences and similarities in working time practices', in C. Baret, S. Lehndorff and L. Sparks (eds) *Flexible Working in Food Retailing – A Comparison between France, Germany, the United Kingdom and Japan*. London: Routledge, 143–166.

Gereffi, G. and Christian, M. (2009) 'The impacts of Wal-Mart: The rise and consequences of the world's dominant retailer', *Annual Review of Sociology*, 35(1): 573–591.

Gerstner, C.R. and Day, D.V. (1997) 'Meta-analytic review of Leader-Member Exchange Theory', *Journal of Applied Phsychology*, 82(6): 827–844.

Gittell, J.H. and Bamber, G. (2010) 'High- and low-road strategies for competing on costs and their implications for employment relations: international studies in the airline industry', *The International Journal of Human Resource Management*, 21(2): 165–179.

Graen, G.B. and Uhl-Bien, M. (1995) 'The Relationship-based approach to leadership: Development of LMX theory of leadership over 25 years – Applying a multi-level, multi-domain perspective, *Leadership Quarterly*, 6(2): 219–247.

Grugulis, I. (2007) *Skills, Training and Human Resource Development – A Critical Text*. Hampshire: Palgrave Macmillan.

Grugulis, I., Warhurst, C. and Keep, E. (2004) 'What's happening to 'skill'?', in C. Warhurst, E. Keep and I. Grugulis (eds) *The Skills That Matter*. Hampshire: Palgrave Macmillan, 1–18.

Gustavsen, B., Hofmaier, B., Ekman Philips, M. and Wikman, A. (1996) *Concept-Driven Development and the Organization of the Process of Change*. Amsterdam: John Benjamin.

Haake, S. (2002) 'National business systems and industry-specific competitiveness', *Organization Studies*, 23(5): 711–736.

Hales, C. (2002) '"Bureaucracy-lite" and continuities in managerial work', *British Journal of Management*, 13(2): 51–66.

Harvey, G. and Turnbull, P. (2010) 'On the go: walking the high road at a low cost airline', *The International Journal of Human Resource Management*, 21(2): 230–241.

Hernant, M., Andersson, T. and Hilmola, O-P. (2007) 'Managing retail chain profitability based on local competitive conditions – Preliminary analysis', *International Journal of Retail and Distribution Management*, 35(11): 912–935.

Heskett, J., Sasser, E. and Schlesinger, L. (1997) *The Service Profit Chain: How Leading Companies Link Profit and Growth to Loyalty, Satisfaction, and Value*. New York: Free Press.

HUI (2009) *Handelsdata 2009*. Stockholm: The Swedish Retail Institute.

IMD (2010) *IMD World Competitiveness Yearbook*, Lausanne: IMD.

Jönsson, S. and Macintosh, N. (1997) 'CATS, RATS and EARS – making the case for ethnographic accounting research', *Accounting, Organizations and Society*, 22(3): 367–386.

▶

►

Kim, H.J., Knight, D. and Crutsinger, C. (2009) 'Generation Y employees' retail work experience: the mediating effect of job characteristics', *Journal of Business Research*, 62(5): 548–556.

Kirkpatrick, I., Davies, A. and Oliver, N. (1992) 'Decentralization: friend or foe of HRM', in P. Blyton and P. Turnbull (eds) *Reassessing Human Resource Management*. London: Sage.

Kirsch, J., Klein, M., Lehndorff, S. and Voss-Dahm, S. (2000) 'The organisation of working time in large German food retail firms', in C. Baret, S. Lehndorff and L. Sparks (eds.) *Flexible Working in Food Retailing: a comparison between France, Germany, the UK and Japan*. London: Routledge.

Lafer, G. (2004) 'What is skill?', in C. Warhurst, E. Keep and I. Grugulis (eds.) *The Skills That Matter*. Basingstoke: Palgrave Macmillan.

Liden, R. and Maslyn, J. (1998) 'Multidimensionality of leader-member exchange: An empirical assessment through scale development', *Journal of Management*, 24: 43–72.

Lillrank, P. (1996) *T-50 ett svenskt svar på lean production?* [T-50 a Swedish response to lean production?]. Stockholm: Arbetslivsinstitutet.

Lloyd, C., Mason, G. and Mayhew, K. (2008) *Low Wage Work in the United Kingdom*. New York: Russell Sage Foundation.

Lowe, J. (1992) 'Locating the Line', in P. Blyton and P. Turnbull (eds) *Reassessing Human Resource Management*. London: Sage.

Lynch, P.D., Eisenberger, R. and Armeli, S. (1999) 'Perceived organizational support: Inferior versus superior performance by wary employees', *Journal of Applied Psychology*, 84(4): 467–483.

Marchington, M. (1996) 'Shopping down different aisles: a review of the literature on human resource management in food retailing', *Journal of Retailing and Consumer Services*, 3(1): 21–32.

McGauran, A-M. (2001) 'Retail is detail: cross-national variation in the character of retail selling in Paris and Dublin', *International Journal of Retail, Distribution & Consumer Research*, 11(4): 437–458.

Morgan, G., Whitley, R. and E. Moen (eds) (2005) *Changing Capitalisms?* Oxford: Oxford University Press.

Nickson, D., Warhurst, C. and Dutton, E. (2005) 'The importance of attitude and appearance in the service encounter in retail and hospitality', *Managing Service Quality*, 15(2): 195–208.

Nickson, D., Warhurst, C., Witz, A. and Cullen, A-M. (2001) 'The importance of being aesthetic: work, employment and service organisation', in A. Sturdy, I. Grugulis and H. Willmott (eds) *Customer Service: Empowerment and Entrapment*. Basingstoke: Palgrave.

Pettinger, L. (2004) 'Brand culture and branded workers: service work and aesthetic labour in fashion retail', *Consumption, Markets and Culture*, 7(2): 165–184.

Pettinger, L. (2005) 'Gendered work meets gendered goods: selling and serving in clothing retail', *Gender, Work and Society*, 12(5): 460–478.

Quinn, J. and Davies, P. (1999) *Ethics and Empowerment*. London: MacMillan Business.

►

▶

Rhoads, G., Swinyard, W., Geurts, M. and Price, W. (2002) 'Retailing as a career: a comparative study of marketers', *Journal of Retailing*, 78(1): 71–76.

Ritzer, G. (1993) *The McDonaldization of Society*. Newsbury Park: Pine Forge Press.

Sparks, L. (1996) 'Employment characteristics of superstore retailing', in Akehurst, G. and Alexander, N. (eds) *Retail Employment*. London: Frank Cass, 38–53.

Sparks, L. (2000a) 'Employment in food retailing', in Baret, C., Lehndorff, S. and Sparks, L. (eds) *Flexible Working in Food Retailing – A comparison between France, Germany, the United Kingdom and Japan*. London: Routledge, 12–20.

Sparks, L. (2000b) 'The rise of the large format food store', in Baret, C., Lehndorff, S. and Sparks, L. (eds) *Flexible Working in Food Retailing – A comparison between France, Germany, the United Kingdom and Japan*. London: Routledge, 1–11.

Statistics Sweden (2009) *Statistical Yearbook of Sweden 2009*. Örebro: Statistics Sweden.

Tengblad, S. (2003) *Den myndige medarbetaren – Strategier för ett konstruktivt medarbetarskap* [The authoritative co-worker – Strategies for a constructive co-workership]. Malmö: Liber ekonomi.

Thompson, P., Warhurst, C. and Callaghan, G. (2000) 'Human capital or capitalising on humanity? Knowledge, skills and competencies in interactive service work', in C. Prichard, R. Hull, M. Chumer and H. Willmott (eds) *Managing Knowledge – Critical Investigations of Work and Learning*. London: Macmillan, 122–140.

Thompson, P., Warhurst, C. and Callaghan, G. (2001) 'Ignorant theory and knowledgeable workers: Interrogating the connections between knowledge, skills and services', *Journal of Management Studies*, 38(7): 923–942.

Warhurst, C. and Nickson, D. (2007) 'Employee experience of aesthetic labour in retail and hospitality', *Work, Employment and Society*, 21(1): 103–120.

WEF (2010). *The Global Competitiveness Report*. Davos: World Economic Forum.

Whitley, R. (1992a) *Business Systems in East Asia*. London: SAGE.

Whitley, R. (ed.) (1992b) *European Business Systems: Firms and Markets in National Context*. London: SAGE.

Whitley, R. (1999) *Divergent Capitalisms: The Social Structuring and Change of Business Systems*. Oxford: Oxford University Press.

Wright, C. and Lund, J. (2006) 'Variations on a lean theme: work restructuring in retail distribution', *New Technology, Work and Employment*, 21(1): 59–74.

Zeytinoglu, I.U., Lillevik, W., Seaton, M.B. and Moruz, J. (2004) 'Part-time and casual work in retail trade – Stress and other factors affecting the workplace', *Relations Industrielles [Industrial Relations]*, 59(3): 516–544.

Expert Interviews

Dr Mikael Hernant, retail industry scholar, University of Skövde, May 13, 2009.

Gunnar Surtevall, Svenska Handel Kunskap, Responsible for the competence development organisation of Swedish Retail Employer's Federation, Stockholm November 5, 2009.

Representing and Organizing Retail Workers: A Comparative Study of the UK and Australia

14

Samantha Lynch, Robin Price, Amanda Pyman and Janis Bailey

Introduction

As unions are a significant voice for low-paid and otherwise vulnerable workers, it is important to understand how they operate in the retail sector. Unions in this industry face a three pronged challenge. First, atypical employment arrangements are 'typical' in retailing. Second, and relatedly, disadvantaged labour market groups such as low paid[1] women and young people are the norm. Third, and again related to the previous two points, in order to simply maintain aggregate membership levels in a high labour turnover industry, retail unions in both the United Kingdom (UK) and Australia need to sign up 70,000 members a year. This figure represents 20 per cent and 30 per cent respectively, of the unions' memberships – an enormous task by any standards.

Given unions' longevity as industrial relations (IR) institutions, it is surprising that there is little research on retail unions. In Australia, there are only a few studies of retail union operation (Mortimer, 2001a, 2001b; McCann, 1994; Game and Pringle, 1983), and not one within a theoretical model that highlights union action and agency. Similarly, there are few UK studies (for rare examples, see Upchurch and Donnelly, 1992; Conley, 2005). Studies in other countries are also not common (for an exception, see Dribbusch, 2005). The limited extant literature characterizes retail union strategy in the UK and Australia as conservative 'business unionism' defined, pejoratively, by Taplin (1990: 252), as 'a narrowly economistic and bureaucratized, contractual-based system of collective bargaining that systematically denies rank and file workers rights to participate directly in the organization and control of work'. This UK–Australia comparative study of retail unionism utilizing The Union of Shop, Distributive and Allied Workers (USDAW) and the Shop Distributive and Allied Employees' Association (SDA)[2] responds to the dearth of literature on retail unionism. The study also responds to Hyman (2001) and Frege and Kelly's (2003) observations that there are few international comparative studies of union strategy, despite the value of such research.

Accordingly, this chapter provides a wide ranging, qualitative comparison of retail union strategy relating to recruitment and organizing in the UK and Australia, using the union revitalization and renewal literature. The chapter moves beyond a simplistic 'business unionism' descriptor, to comprehensively analyse what retail unions are doing in contemporary workplaces. The chapter firstly considers the literature on union renewal and revitalization and in particular, the 'organizing model'. Second, it examines the context of the retail industry in each country as it affects trade union strategy, highlighting similarities and differences. Third, we describe and analyse the strategies of the respective retail unions as advocated by Hyman (2001) and Frege and Kelly (2003). We argue that the unions' strategies are significantly shaped by retail labour market factors and employers' strategies, resulting in similar approaches to recruiting, servicing and organizing in the two countries. Differences in the institutional framework of IR in the two countries result in some differences in tactics, but they are not particularly significant. Overall, the unions' emphasis in both the UK and Australia is on creating legitimacy with employers via personal relationships between union officials and company representatives, particularly in larger retailers and, in the case of the UK, via formal partnership agreements. Both unions also focus intensively on 'infill' recruiting as opposed to external recruiting in non-unionized workplaces. For reasons that will be discussed, there is much less emphasis on the 'organizing model' that many unions have adopted over the past ten years. In sum, the retail industry provides unique challenges for employee voice and representation, mainly because of high turnover and worker vulnerability. This chapter adds to our understanding of employee voice in retail, and adds to a growing body of literature on the organizing model.

Union renewal and revitalization

Trade unions in most advanced market economies, including the UK and Australia, face increasingly challenging conditions in representing and mobilizing their members, and a related crisis in membership, density and the effectiveness of representation structures (Frege and Kelly, 2003). As Lucas (2009) notes, various scholars (e.g., Oxenbridge, 1997; Heery, 2002) have suggested that unions need to target new or previously neglected categories of workers and extend organization and representation downwards to low wage workers. Such strategic imperatives have been reflected in the aspirations of peak union bodies in both countries. For example, the Trades Union Congress (TUC) in the UK and the Australian Council of Trade Unions (ACTU) both identify a need to target unorganized or poorly organized groups of employees (Lucas, 2009; Barton et al., 2008). Thus, union revitalization, in the face of globalization, neoliberal politics and increased capital mobility, has become a seminal issue (Barton et al., 2008; McIlroy, 2008). Trade union revitalization is however, a contested concept (McIlroy, 2008; Frege and Kelly, 2003). Various renewal strategies have been identified, such as the servicing, organizing and partnership approaches (Heery, 2002), with some scholars seeing these as competing and contradictory, and others viewing them as compatible and/or complementary (McIlroy, 2008). Both union practice and the academic literature, therefore, are preoccupied with 'crisis' discourses on the one hand, and revitalization and new strategies on the other, although there is by no means consensus on how union renewal should occur.

There has been a particular emphasis on the 'organizing model', a new set of techniques for recruiting and mobilizing based on the United States (US) Service Employees International Union's (SEIU) strategic model that has been transplanted to, and adapted in, other countries including the UK and Australia (Heery, 2002). The organizing model contrasts with the servicing model, with the former placing emphasis on increasing membership involvement and issue-based campaigning, whereas the servicing approach places responsibility for action on union staff (Fiorito, 2004). An organizing approach is often seen as requiring 'social' (or 'social movement') organizing, to link workplace strategies with the actions of community groups other than unions: the US 'Justice for Janitors' campaign being a paradigmatic example (Williams, 1999). Organizing, it is argued, emphasizes active membership engagement with unionism at the workplace, whereas servicing is a passive approach. Unions themselves are advocates of the organizing model, evidenced in both discourse and behaviour (Burchielli and Bartram, 2009). The organizing model has not been immune to academic criticism, but such critique is 'largely related to the practicalities of implementation... rather than to its underlying merits' (Bowden, 2009: 139). Difficulties with operationalizing the model include: 'top down' as opposed to the 'bottom up' implementation implicit in the concept; disagreements within unions about how the model should be applied; the need for a 'cultural shift' amongst union officials and the related difficulty of disturbing their vested interests; and the emphasis on gaining new members rather than supporting existing members, with some officials asserting that this represents a misallocation of resources (Griffin and Moors, 2004; Peetz, Pocock and Houghton, 2007;

Carter and Cooper, 2002; Fletcher and Hurd, 1998; Dolvik and Waddington, 2004). Going beyond these criticisms, Bowden (2009: 139, 140) argues that there is no evidence to show that the organizing model has in fact had any real impact on union membership or effectiveness, and that a focus on workplace strategies ignores the need for centralized and coordinated approaches that go 'back to basics' in terms of regulating occupational labour markets. More broadly, the philosophy and objectives of organizing have recently been challenged, with the focus on organizing as 'a toolbox of practices' obscuring the political dynamics of unionism (Simms and Holgate, 2010). Thus both the philosophy behind the organizing model, and its application in particular settings, is subject to ongoing contest. Given the amount of description and analysis devoted to union strategy since the 1990s, when the organizing model came to prominence, it is therefore timely to examine strategy in large service sector unions of low-paid workers, such as retail unions.

Unions do not organize in a vacuum. The literature on service sector unionism points to the importance of *context* in shaping union strategy. It has recently been argued, for example, that low unionization in the hospitality sector is largely due to employer and employment characteristics; as a result, unions need to gain a foothold with managers and obtain legitimacy, but that cannot be achieved without evidence of appreciable membership (Lucas, 2009). Heery and Simms's (2010) research into union organizing supports this: where a union has a presence in a workplace, management responses to union organizing attempts are less antagonistic and the number of issues around which unions organize expands. Such a presence can be formalized by a 'partnership' arrangement. There is however, controversy about this issue: Fairbrother and Stewart (2003) and Fichter and Greer (2004) characterize employer acceptance of unions as 'incorporation'. They argue that this approach constrains union activities, resulting in a narrow 'business unionism' model that disempowers workers and reduces their 'voice'. Thus, labour market characteristics and the nature and functions of union management relationships shape union strategy in the service sector.

The context and contours of retail trade unionism

Retailing is one of the largest sectors in the UK and Australian economies, both in terms of financial size and employment. It provides jobs for around 3 million people in the UK and around 1.2 million people in Australia (Burt and Sparks, 2003; ABS, 2009a); that is, around 10 per cent of the labour market. The retail labour force is both feminized and youthful: women make up

65 per cent of the labour force in the UK and 56 per cent in Australia (Burt and Sparks, 2003; ABS, 2009b). In the past two decades, however, young full-time workers have been largely replaced by part-time student workers. In both countries, the industry is heavily concentrated, and is dominated by a handful of large multiple retailers, especially in food retailing (Mead, 2003; Burt and Sparks, 2003), with such employers' accounting for around half of both employment and market share (Burt and Sparks, 2003; ABS, 2007). Upchurch and Donnelly (1992: 63) argue that retail concentration has 'created a more favourable climate for union expansion', as industry concentration assists union recruitment. However, in other respects unions are challenged by an industry environment marked by increasing price competition, falling gross margins and returns, extended operating hours, and acquisitions and mergers (Burt and Sparks, 2003; Mead, 2003). These factors affect union strategy, as labour is a major cost component for retailers and profit margins are low. Not surprisingly, employers' labour use strategies centre on cost reduction, especially numerical flexibility. Part-time employment, for instance, accounts for 58 per cent of all employment in UK retailing (Burt and Sparks, 2003) and 50 per cent in Australia (ABS, 2009b), a much higher percentage than in the wider labour force. This has implications for retail unions, as part-time employees are much less likely to become members (Grainger, 2006). In the UK, labour turnover in retailing is around 30 per cent (Chartered Institute of Personnel and Development, 2008) while in Australia it is 15 per cent overall, but more than 34 per cent in some firms (Price et al., 2010). Again, this has implications for retail unions, as ongoing recruitment must be a priority.

A major difference in employment practices between the two countries is in the use of temporary employment contracts. The incidence of temporary working in the UK retail industry remains low and although more acute forms of flexible employment have been introduced, including zero or minimum hour contracts, the use of such casualized labour is lower than in Australia (Purcell and Purcell, 1998). In Australia, the longstanding use of casual contracts – employment on an hourly basis with no guarantee of ongoing employment – is widespread, with over 40 per cent of the retail workforce on such contracts, as opposed to 25 per cent of the wider workforce (ABS, 2009c). In effect, this means that a casual employee can be required for three hours work in one week and none the next. Casualization inhibits union recruitment as permanent employees are more than three times as likely to be trade union members than casual employees (ABS, 2008).

For retail unions, employers' predominant use of numerically flexible labour with its associated high levels of staff turnover creates major challenges. Simply to maintain existing aggregate membership numbers, leaving aside the task of expanding their reach and density, unions must recruit intensively. Not surprisingly, given the nature of the labour market, USDAW and the SDA have low density: 12 per cent in the UK (Barratt, 2009) and 15 per cent in Australia (ABS, 2009a). This is comparable with overall private sector density, which is 15.5 per cent in the UK (Barratt, 2009), and 14 per cent in Australia (ABS, 2008). Given the difficulties of organizing in the retail labour market, the two unions are thus holding their own in comparison with other private sector unions. Nevertheless, there is significant potential to further increase union membership numbers.

Union management relationships in retail have particular features that are shaped by the service-based, low-waged nature of the work. The UK retail industry is well known for its management union partnerships (Bacon and Samuel, 2009; Teague and Hann, 2009; Cassell and Lee, 2009; Fichter and Greer, 2004; Fairbrother and Stewart, 2003), although the term partnership is itself contested (de Turberville, 2007). As we outline below, the SDA uses de facto partnership strategies. Other factors related to the nature of management may advantage unions. For example, employers cannot use the threat of geographical relocation as they might in manufacturing or call centre operation. Further, retail employers need to compromise between the logic of profit creation and creating social order within the firm, meaning that unions can use the 'communities of coping' that are widespread in service workplaces (Korczynski, 2002: 177). Hence, there are factors inherent in the organization of work and the labour process that unions could utilize to enhance solidarity among workers.

A final issue that should be noted is the coverage of both unions. USDAW recruits general retail workers in a range of occupations and industries, including shops, factories and warehouses, drivers, call centres, clerical, insurance, dairy, butchers and meat packers, catering, laundries, chemical processing, home shopping and pharmaceutical. The SDA has similar coverage, with a significant difference being that it has a large number of members in the fast food industry. In both cases, store departmental managers may be, and often are, union members. Both unions have coverage of store managers, but in practice it is uncommon for them to be members.

Overall, the retail industry context between the two countries is very similar. However, the institutional arrangements for IR differ in the two countries, which in turn affects union strategy. Recognition procedures differ considerably. The UK has a statutory recognition process while Australia has de facto recognition that requires neither a formal vote by members nor recognition by the employer. Wage setting structures also differ considerably between the two countries. In the UK, if a union is successful in gaining recognition via the statutory route, the employer must recognize the union in the negotiation of pay, hours and holidays. Australia has a broader 'safety net' for workers via awards (industry-wide documents that set wages and

conditions), but at the same time legislation has decreased awards' significance and degree of protection, and has emphasized collective bargaining,
so that union density and other measures of union strength at the workplace
are as important in Australia, as they are in the UK. Finally, in Australia, overlapping union membership is discouraged and thus the SDA has no competing unions. In the UK, however, USDAW competes with UNITE, the largest
union in Britain with over two million members. Sectors covered by UNITE
that overlap with USDAW include food, drink and tobacco and servicing
industries (i.e., servicing companies associated with retailers or manufacturers of white and brown goods).

Research methods

This chapter presents the preliminary findings from a comparative, explora-
tory study of the strategies used by USDAW and the SDA to recruit and
represent members. The research design is qualitative, using multiple data
gathering methods to address the weaknesses of the existing literature on
comparative union strategy which, as Frege and Kelly (2003:8) note, is usually focused on quantitative analyses. The case studies are based upon semi-
structured interviews with union officers and branch representatives across
different regions in the UK and in Australia. Preliminary findings are presented here as the research is ongoing. Interviews were conducted with three
senior officials in three Australian states, one senior national official, and
five organizers in two states. In the UK, interviews were conducted with two
organizers in two regions. Interviews, each in excess of one hour in duration,
were digitally recorded, transcribed and thematically coded.

Trade union strategy in the UK and Australia

The extant research on retail trade unionism does not explore recent
developments in union strategy, whether in response to the spread of the
'organizing model' in the union movement, or other factors. This section,
therefore, describes and analyses recent recruiting, organizing and servicing approaches in the two unions, to determine their continuities and
discontinuities with the past. Utilizing Heery, Simms, Delbridge, Salmon
and Simpson's (2003) framework of union recruitment policy, we examine
the extent to which the two unions have adopted formal policies regarding
recruitment and organizing, the recruitment methods deployed, the nature
of recruitment and organizing roles and, finally, the outcomes of recruitment
and organizing policies.

Policy commitment and direction

Previous research has characterized the approach of both USDAW and the SDA as moderate 'business unionism' (Game and Pringle, 1983; Upchurch and Donnelly, 1992; McCann, 1994; Simms and Holgate, 2010). Cooperative relations with employers are central to a business unionism approach, as is a focus on 'bread and butter' industrial issues. USDAW and the SDA are both politically conservative, aligned to the right wing of the respective labour parties (Upchurch and Donnelly, 1992; McCann, 1994; Warhurst, 2008). USDAW portrays itself as a campaigning union, evidenced by current efforts to support working parents and carers in the workplace, campaigns to raise awareness of violence against retail workers, attempts to secure the full minimum wage for young workers and to gain a ban on New Year's Day trading in Scotland. The SDA also campaigns, with current initiatives including workplace health and safety representatives, and an additional holiday when Christmas Day falls on a Saturday (SDA state branch secretary 1, 2009).

Both unions claim that they are organizing unions, with an emphasis on recruitment. The two unions have a similar set of commitments and directions regarding recruiting and organizing. Given the challenge of simply replacing members who leave, recruiting is a priority for both unions. Recruitment strategy and targets are set nationally, and cascaded to the regional (divisional) level in the case of the UK, and state/territory level in Australia, where specific plans are devised for reaching these targets. Targets are reviewed in both unions at six monthly intervals (SDA national official, 2009; USDAW area organizer, 2009). Some state SDA branches consider the nationally set targets unachievable in the short term and therefore set their own performance targets (SDA state branch secretary 2, 2009).

The two unions' general approach to workplace organizing is similar. USDAW's strategy is largely centred on growing membership in organizations where they are already recognized, while using union recognition legislation to broaden their presence in the industry. The core of the SDA's organizing approach is a union legitimation strategy involving the gradual pursuit of collective agreements with large retailers, in return for assistance with recruiting new members and ease of access to workplaces. A second focus of the SDA's strategy is the development of relationships with retailers which do not have a collective agreement, often in the absence of any sizeable union membership. The union then attempts to negotiate an agreement. In short, the SDA bargains, and then recruits. Once ratified, the agreement is then 'rolled out' by union officials via information sessions for potential members. The signed agreement gives legitimacy to the union, as it delivers above award pay and conditions and demonstrates union achievements. The

SDA avoids confrontation with employers, waiting for the right time to move. For instance, by developing relationships with key Aldi management, the SDA hopes to sign a union collective agreement with the company in 2011 when Aldi's current (non-union) collective agreement expires (SDA national official, 2009). Both unions pursue union membership agreements with employers, particularly the deduction of union fees from employees' wages – with the written agreement of the employee.

As institutional arrangements for IR differ in the UK and Australia, union tactics take different pathways in the two countries. While USDAW has the option to use the UK's statutory recognition legislation, to date this has not been particularly successful in widening the union's access to non-union retailers. The SDA's 'bargain first, recruit later' strategy is predicated on Australia's lack of any legislative requirement for unions to establish recognition. However, both unions' strategic focus is on infill (or 'internal') recruiting in large retailers with existing collective agreements (SDA national official, 2009; USDAW area organizer, 2009). Some branches of the SDA have had recruitment successes in areas where they do not have a collective agreement (SDA state branch secretary 2, 2009). However, it is not a union priority to undertake 'external' recruiting in small retailers (SDA national official, 2009) that do not have a collective agreement or arrangements for payroll deductions of union fees.

Overall, union strategy is similar in the two countries, with institutional differences shaping particular tactics. But do the two unions intensively organize in the way suggested by the 'organizing model'? The next section evaluates the recruitment methods used by USDAW and the SDA.

Recruiting and organizing methods

Recruitment methods have been identified in the literature as a key determinant of organizing success, yet there is no widespread agreement on which methods yield superior results (Heery et al., 2003). There are three commonly identified 'union building' methods: individual servicing; partnership with employers and organizing (Heery et al., 2003). Unions commonly use a combination of methods, but with an emphasis on one (or more). Increasingly both union discourse generally, and the academic literature, has been emphasizing 'organizing' over 'servicing'.

Individual service provision is very important for both unions. Examples include legal advice and consumer discounts. While other Australian unions are consciously moving away from the 'free set of steak knives with union membership' approach, the SDA still continues to emphasize the value of its consumer services. In particular, it offers textbook vouchers to young, part-time, low-waged student members, emphasizing that they are an important income component for such workers (Bailey et al., 2010).

Partnership with employers is a key component of both unions' recruitment strategies. USDAW and the SDA both stress the importance of building and maintaining cooperative relationships with retail store managers, particularly in the large retailers, since being able to attend staff induction sessions is a key recruiting strategy. Retail unions, in the words of Heery et al., (2003) 'organize employers' to facilitate management sponsored access to potential recruits. Such an approach is vital for retail unions in both countries due to the dominance of large multiple operators in the industry, particularly food retailers. As one area organizer (2009) in USDAW explained:

> retail is a funny environment... [you] need relationships with senior managers to get things done.... Building relationships with store managers is important... if you've got that kind of support from the management team with regard to what you are trying to achieve you are going to get a better outcome.... We have good relationships with most store managers... if [the union] went in with an anti company program it would not work .... Visibility is important... we're good at ensuring that we are not seen as the enemy.

Similarly, an Australian official emphasized that 'it is important to keep going back [to non members]... they build up that trust in you. ... We may not be a militant organization but we are very determined, and we keep going back and back' (SDA area organizer, 2009). Relationships with employers depend on organizers' active engagement with store managers. The nature of such relationships is however ambiguous, being heavily dependent upon managers' personalities, and their attitudes towards, and personal views of, the union.

As previously noted, attending formal store inductions is central to the SDA's recruiting strategy. The union contacts store delegates and managers to capture information on new recruits (SDA state secretary 2, 2009). 'We email, fax or phone hundreds of stores each week to check if they've got any new starters' (SDA lead organizer, 2009). The SDA then 'use a bouncy four minute recruitment video, followed by a short talk from either an organizer or an experienced delegate', with a success rate estimated at around 60 to 70 per cent (SDA national official, 2009). As more of the larger retailers are using pre-employment online induction of new employees, SDA organizers have adapted their recruitment tactics, still using their relationship with store managers to ensure delegates or organizers know when new employees have started. Individualistic recruitment is more time consuming than group inductions. It draws on the SDA's traditionally strong relationships with store managers and ultimately with senior HR staff, but also relies on having well trained and knowledgeable delegates versed in one-on-one recruiting.

A key difference between the two countries is that in the UK, USDAW uses the Statutory Trade Union Recognition provisions, part of the Employment Relations Act 1999, to gain recognition for the purposes of collective bargaining with an employer, voluntarily or via statute, on the issues of pay, hours and holidays. For example, USDAW is currently attempting to gain recognition at Marks and Spencer using the recognition legislation. USDAW have existing union recognition agreements with retailers including Tesco, Bargain Booze, Ladbrokes (betting shop), Sainsbury's, Poundland and Northern Foods. With no such legislation in Australia, the SDA finds it more useful to simply follow the 'bargain first, recruit later' method, described previously.

While both unions focus on recruitment during inductions, both group and individual, USDAW supplements this approach with formal partnership agreements with employers, particularly food retailers such as Tesco, Morrisons and The Cooperative, improving the union's access to inductions. While partnership has been actively supported by the Labour government as a means of achieving 'better' employment relations (Bacon and Samuel, 2009), it has been the subject of much debate within UK unions. However, for USDAW there have been benefits; its partnership agreement with Tesco is credited with increasing union membership and density, and enhancing union input into Tesco's organizational policy. As part of the agreement, Tesco commits resources to train union representatives, who also benefit from 'time off' for union duties. However, while the benefits of formal partnership are acknowledged, some organizers maintain that adversarialism persists largely unchanged: 'to us it's still "them and us" – it's just a word' (USDAW area organizer, 2009). While the term 'partnership' is rarely used in the Australian context, the SDA nevertheless pursues union management cooperation. Whilst there are no formal memoranda between the SDA and employers, the SDA emphasizes person to person contacts between senior union officials and human resource managers in the major companies (SDA national official, 2009). The SDA's non militant approach at the workplace level and its orderly rounds of collective bargaining mimic 'partnership', but without a formal agreement. Therefore, despite the differences in the institutional context of IR in the UK and Australia, both unions recognize that partnership with employers, formal or informal, assists in recruitment.

Both unions make use of a similar 'bundle' of organizing or 'union building' activities, namely strategic workplace mapping techniques, one to one recruitment, and like with like recruiters. Workplace mapping has become a more formalized process over time in USDAW (USDAW area organizer, 2009). After a year of using the TUC's Organizing Academy, USDAW established its own Organizing Academy, based on the belief that the TUC trainees were not sufficiently adept at organizing in the retail industry: 'we were getting people from a totally different background.... [T]o come into retail is totally different...they were a bit lost [and could not cope] with how difficult it was' (USDAW area organizer, 2009). The SDA also conducts its own training.

In sum, the two unions place a heavy emphasis on recruiting, particularly via in-store inductions; a tactic that relies on good relationships with managers. Individual service provision continues to be important.

Recruitment roles

The nature of recruitment and organizing roles within unions can improve recruitment success (Heery et al., 2003). Clearly, organizers are a key component of successful recruiting. In some unions, however, there has been a trend towards specialist recruitment roles. This section will examine the types of recruitment roles used in USDAW and the SDA.

Driven by high labour turnover in retail, both USDAW and the SDA have developed methods to support their recruitment policy (as discussed in the previous section). Recruitment roles however differ between USDAW and the SDA. Some state branches of the SDA employ specialist 'recruitment' organizers, some of whom may be university students working part time for the union. Under a lead or 'project' organizer, these specialist organizers work in teams with a focus on 'building the union'. Specialist recruiters are cheaper; for instance, they do not require a union car since their focus is on direct recruitment in one or a few locations and, as they do not need significant industrial experience, they can be paid less than organizers. In addition, they can more easily do weekend work, thus improving the work–life balance of full-time union staff (SDA state branch secretary, 2009). According to SDA interviewees, employing 'recruitment only' organizers also helps address the heavy workload of union officials and the problem of organizer 'burn out', which has led to problems with the retention of union organizers. SDA organizers with 'generalist' roles therefore focus much less on direct recruiting, and more on planning and organizing campaigns, identifying and training workplace representatives, and representing individual employees with problems.

In contrast, USDAW have no specialist recruitment only roles. Recruitment activities are divided between full-time union officers and workplace representatives with recruitment being 'mainstreamed' (Heery et al., 2003: 67) in contrast to the approach in some SDA state branches. Forty per cent of USDAW organizers' time is intended to be spent on recruitment, including encouraging and supporting workplace representatives, promoting workplace organization, setting targets and planning recruitment campaigns, and directly recruiting new members (USDAW area organizer, 2009). In addition to these recruitment responsibilities, an organizer's role involves servicing individual member issues, negotiating partnership agreements with employers on a local basis, planning relevant local campaigns, and providing support for workplace representatives. The heavy workload of union officials and the strategy of 'mainstreaming' recruitment meant that workplace representatives have been critical to USDAW's recruitment strategy. Recognition of the importance of workplace representatives to the union is illustrated by USDAW establishing its own Organizing Academy. USDAW also has divisional-based training officers to develop the recruitment and organizing skills of workplace representatives. USDAW sees officials' and representatives' recruitment roles as complementary. Full-time officers develop relevant recruitment strategies, in terms of setting recruitment targets and methods, in conjunction with undertaking direct recruitment, when their union representatives are not at work: 'representatives recruit while they are there, but not while they are not there ...' (USDAW area organizer, 2009).

Development of delegates is a key priority. USDAW's full-time officers aim to 'organize the membership so that it looks after itself' (USDAW area organizer, 2009), enabling officials to devote more time to growing, rather than sustaining the membership. The importance of workplace representatives in recruiting is emphasized by officials, and full-time officers see their role as one of supporting representatives in the main task of recruitment: 'my job is to empower reps, whose job it is to empower members' (USDAW area organizer, 2009). This again reinforces the key role of workplace representatives in achieving the union's demanding recruitment targets. It also emphasizes the importance of ensuring the right people are selected to act as representatives, since their commitment, effectiveness and confidence are vital to the recruitment success of the union. In the SDA, there is also a significant priority placed on improving delegates' capabilities for recruitment, and on growing the number of delegates. The union aims to have one or two delegates on every floor in a large retailer, plus people who work on weekends, plus night fillers, so that a retail supermarket may have four or five delegates (SDA national official, 2009) and a large department store many more. Delegates tend to be permanent employees with long job incumbency, perhaps ten or twenty years, whereas store managers tend to have high mobility, so 'in many ways they [delegates] run the store more than the store manager' (SDA national official, 2009).

As can be seen, both unions place a strong emphasis on recruitment as a strategic priority, but use their paid staff in somewhat different ways, with specialist recruitment organizers being employed in some union branches in Australia, but not in the UK. The direct recruitment of new members is vital to the activity of both USDAW and the SDA as the nature of their membership makes it challenging to maintain workplace organization.

Recruitment outcomes

USDAW has been particularly successful in their strategy of 'growing' membership, recruiting 90,000 new members in 2008; that is, 20,000 more than required to maintain aggregate membership. SDA membership has been more static, with a net fall of 4,000 members between 2000 and 2009 (SDA 2000, 2009). Density remains around 12 to 15 per cent in both countries. There is thus a significant gap between current and potential membership levels, especially since almost half of all retail workers are employed by large multiples where ease of access is not difficult and the unions already have a presence via collective bargaining, servicing and in most cases, delegate structures.

Collective bargaining coverage is lower in the UK than in Australia. In the UK, 26.6 per cent of workplaces have a union presence (a least one union member), yet only 16.1 per cent of employees have their wages set by a collective agreement (collective bargaining arrangements involving a union in negotiations) (Barratt, 2009). The majority of the UK retail workforce is therefore paid under individual contracts, with a proportion being reliant on the National Minimum Wage. In Australia, union collective agreements cover 37.4 per cent of retail employees; individual agreements 31.8 per cent; and awards 30.8 per cent (Peetz and Price, 2007). The disparity between union presence and collective bargaining coverage in the UK suggests that retail unions have the potential to be more effective in securing collective bargaining agreements. The figures also suggest that the SDA has been more successful in obtaining collective bargaining coverage than USDAW, despite similar membership density levels. However, while the SDA appears to be the more successful bargainer, it would seem to have a large number of free riders, judging by the difference between its density (15 per cent) and its collective bargaining coverage (well over a third of employees). The much higher collective bargaining coverage in Australia reflects differences in the institutional context and industry structure. First, as previously mentioned, Australian unions do not have to be formally recognized by the employer in order to bargain. Second, the industry is even more concentrated than the UK's in that a smaller number of major retailers dominate the sector in Australia, so bargaining takes place with fewer retailers and more resources can be devoted to each employer.

For both unions therefore, there is a large 'recruitment gap', and much energy must be devoted to replacing members as a result of high turnover levels. In short, retail unions have significant opportunities to grow, and to improve wages and working conditions for a large number of low-wage workers.

Discussion and conclusion

In sum, union strategy in both countries shows considerable continuities with the past in terms of an emphasis on recruiting and building representative structures in areas of existing bargaining strength. The strategies used by both unions revolve around maintaining membership in the context of high 'leakage', and the gradual pursuit of moderate collective agreements, with an underlying focus on positive relationships with both store managers and more senior managers. Both the SDA and USDAW have developed greater sophistication in their recruitment techniques over the past few years, but a striking feature is the overall continuity of strategies with the past (see Upchurch and Donnelly, 1992, with respect to USDAW, and Mortimer 2001a, 2001b, with respect to the SDA).

Using Danford, Richardson and Upchurch's (2003:16) suggestion that key elements of the organizing process are 'organizing for recruitment' and 'organizing *against* the employer', both the SDA and USDAW intensively 'organize for recruitment' by 'organizing the employer'. This is not to suggest they do not organize *against* the employer, but simply that the latter is not their primary focus. High labour turnover in the retail industry plays a key role in dictating this approach. The challenge of replacing members simply to sustain membership levels leaves both unions with little alternative but to focus primarily on 'organizing for recruitment'. As a result, they adhere to mapping and target setting in order to consolidate and expand membership (Heery and Adler, 2004) with an emphasis on consolidation rather than expansion. There are some signs of limited engagement with both the rhetoric and the realities of 'the organizing model' in both unions, in terms of workplace activism and worker self-organization. Both unions pursue campaigns and place an emphasis on workplace delegate/representative structures. USDAW and the SDA thus 'organize against the employer', but in a more limited way than many other unions, who have more wholeheartedly adopted 'the organizing model'.

A key focus for both unions is on building relationships with both store and senior retail management which is in direct contrast to 'organizing against the employer'. USDAW has pursued formal partnership approaches where possible. In Australia, where there is no institutional support for such practices, the SDA's strategies mimic 'partnership', resulting in access to staff inductions, which is a critical means of maintaining membership levels in the context of high retail labour turnover. Both unions thus rely heavily on relationships with managers, whether through the development of informal, local level relationships, as is apparent in both countries, or through formal partnership approaches, as in the UK. A 'relationship building' approach is consistent with the centrality of social relationships in the industry (Korczynski, 2003).

It is clear that both unions have very similar approaches in terms of their policy direction and commitment, methods of recruitment and to some extent the recruitment roles, particularly in terms of their reliance on workplace representatives for recruitment purposes. Where differences are noted these are largely due to institutional differences, such as the use of union recognition legislation and partnership agreements in the UK. In Australia, the SDA bargaining strategy has shifted in response to changing labour laws. Traditionally an 'arbitral' union (Gardner and Ronfeldt, 1996), the SDA has in the past used Australia's compulsory conciliation and arbitration system to improve awards. With the legislative shift towards enterprise bargaining from the 1990s, the SDA has had to pursue collective bargaining, particularly with large employers, with the result that a third of retail workers – a relatively high percentage compared to USDAW's figure – are now covered by collective bargaining agreements. Provisions in Australia's new Fair Work Act create a 'low waged bargaining stream' (Cooper and Ellem, 2009), but it is too early to ascertain whether this creates a significant opportunity for the SDA to increase members' wages.

There appears to be little desire by either union to change their current strategies in any significant way. In any case, due to their sheer size, neither union is at risk of institutional obliteration. Both unions' revitalization strategies appear to be based on refining and updating strategies that have had demonstrable success in the past. The kinds of innovative, radical approaches to organizing that have been used by other unions in the UK, Australia and the USA have largely been eschewed by USDAW and the SDA. It appears that USDAW and the SDA, in line with Bowden (2009) and Lucas' (2009) arguments progress their organizing agenda by attempting to regulate their (difficult) labour markets, and by establishing legitimacy with employers (a related objective), to maintain and attempt to improve membership. The characteristics of the retail industry, with high levels of labour turnover and significant use of atypical labour, prioritize recruitment as a key strategy, and shape the nature of the recruitment roles in both unions. The characteristics of the labour process may also encourage the relationship-building activities evident between unions and managers. As a result, continuity with past strategies appears to be more important than experimentation with new approaches.

Notes

1   Average weekly earnings in retail in the UK were £340 in 2008, with retail being the second lowest paid sector behind agriculture and fishing (£310). Average weekly earnings for all sectors in 2008 were £436; hence retail

workers in the UK earn 78 per cent of average earnings (Office for National Statistics, 2009). Retail is the lowest paid industry in Australia, with average weekly earnings in May 2006 of $684 (£385) per week, around 71 per cent of Australian average weekly earnings (Peetz and Price, 2007).

2   In 2008, USDAW was the fourth largest union in the UK with 386,000 members (USDAW, 2009), and the SDA was the largest union in Australia with 217,000 members (SDA, 2009).

REFERENCES

ABS (2007) *Retail and Wholesale Industries 2005–06*, August 2007, catalogue 8622.0.

ABS (2008) *Australian Social Trends 2008, Article: Trade Union Members* July 2008, catalogue 4102.0.

ABS (2009a) *Employee Earnings, Benefits and Trade Union Membership*, April 2009, catalogue 6310.0.

ABS (2009b) *Labour Force, Australia, Detailed Quarterly*, February 2009, catalogue 6291.0.55.003, Table 5.

ABS (2009c) *Australian Labour Market Statistics*, April 2009, catalogue 6105.0

Bacon, N. and Samuel, P. (2009) 'Partnership agreement adoption and survival in the British private and public sectors', *Work, Employment and Society,* 23(2): 231–248.

Bailey, J., Price, R., Esders, L. and McDonald, P. (2010) 'Daggy shirts, daggy slogans? Marketing unions to young people', *Journal of Industrial Relations*, 52(1): 43–60.

Barratt, C. (2009) 'Trade Union Membership 2008', A National Statistics Publication, Department for Business, Enterprise and Regulatory Reform, Employment Market Analysis and Research, April, Department for Business, Enterprise and Regulatory Reform, London, UK.

Barton, R., Snell, D. and Fairbrother, P. (2008) 'The state of unions and union research', Refereed proceedings 22nd AIRAANZ conference, Feb 6–8, Melbourne, Australia.

Bowden, B. (2009) 'The organizing model in Australia: a reassessment', *Labour & Industry*, 20(2): 138–158.

Burchielli, R. and Bartram, T. (2009) 'What helps organizing work? The indicators and facilitators of organizing', *Journal of Industrial Relations*, 51(5): 687–708.

Burt, S. and Sparks, L. (2003) *Competitive Analysis of the Retail Sector in the UK*, Stirling, Institute for Retail Studies, University of Stirling.

Carter, B. and Cooper, R. (2002) 'The organizing model and the management of change: a comparative study of unions in Australia and Britain', *Relations Industrielles*, 57(4): 712–742.

Cassell, C. and Lee, B. (2009) 'Trade union learning representatives: progressing partnership?' *Work, Employment and Society*, 23(2): 213–230.

▶

▶

Chartered Institute of Personnel and Development (2008) *Recruitment, Retention and Turnover*, Chartered Institute of Personnel and Development Annual Survey Report: London.

Conley, H. (2005) 'Front line or all fronts? Women's trade union activism in retail services', *Gender, Work and Organization*, 12(5): 479–496.

Cooper, R. and Ellem, B. (2009) 'Fair Work and the re-regulation of collective bargaining', *Australian Journal of Labour Law*, 22(3): np.

Danford, A., Richardson, M. and Upchurch, M. (2003) *New Unions, New Workplaces: A Study of Union Resilience in a Restructured Workplace*. London, Routledge.

De Turberville, S. (2007) 'Union organizing: a response to Carter', *Work, Employment and Society*, 21(3): 565–576.

Dolvik, J. and Waddington, J. (2004) 'Organizing marketized services: are trade unions up to the job?', *Economic and Industrial Democracy*, 25(1): 9–39.

Dribbusch, H. (2005) *Trade Union Organizing in Private Sector Services: Findings from the British, Dutch and German Retail Industry*, WSI Discussion paper No. 136, April, http://opus.zbw-kiel.de/volltexte/2008/6904/ (accessed 1 May 2009).

Fairbrother, P. and Stewart, P. (2003) 'The dilemmas of social partnership and union organization: questions for British unions', in P. Fairbrother and C. Yates (eds) *Trade Unions in Renewal: A Comparative Study*. London: Continuum, 158–179.

Fichter, M. and Greer, I. (2004) 'Analysing social partnership: a tool of union revitalization?' in C. Frege and J. Kelly (eds) *Union Revitalization Strategies in Comparative Perspective*. Oxford: Oxford University Press, 71–92.

Fiorito, J. (2004) 'Union renewal and the organizing model in the United Kingdom', *Labor Studies Journal*, 29(2): 21–53.

Fletcher, B. and Hurd, R. (1998), 'Beyond the organizing model: the transformation process in local unions', in K. Bronfenbrenner, S. Friedman, R. Hurd, R. Oswald and R. Seeber (eds) *Organizing to Win: New Research on Union Strategies*. Ithaca (NY), ILR Press: 37–53.

Frege, C. and Kelly, J. (2003) 'Union revitalization strategies in comparative perspective', *European Journal of Industrial Relations*, 9(1): 7–24.

Game, A. and Pringle, R. (1983) *Gender at Work*. Sydney: Allen and Unwin.

Gardner, M. and Ronfeldt, P. (1996) 'The arbitral model: what remains?' in R. Fells and T. Todd (eds) *Current Research in Industrial Relations: Proceedings of the 10th AIRAANZ Conference*. Perth: Association of Industrial Relations Academics of Australia and New Zealand, 157–166.

Grainger, H. (2006) *Trade Union Membership 2005,*. London, Department of Trade and Industry.

Griffin, G. and Moors, R. (2004) 'The fall and rise of organizing in a blue-collar union', *Journal of Industrial Relations*, 46(1): 39–52.

Heery, E. (2002) 'Partnership versus organizing: alternative futures for British trade unionism', *Industrial Relations Journal*, 33: 20–35.

Heery, E. and Adler, L. (2004) 'Organizing the unorganized', in C. Frege and J. Kelly (eds) *Varieties of Unionism: Strategies for Union Revitalization in a Globalizing Economy*. Oxford: Oxford University Press, 45–69.

▶

▶

Heery, E. and Simms, M. (2010) 'Employer responses to union organizing: patterns and effects', *Human Resource Management Journal*, 20(1): 3–22.

Heery, E., Simms, M., Delbridge, R., Salmons, J. and Simpson, D. (2003) 'Trade union recruitment policy in Britain: form and effects', in G. Gall (ed.) *Union Organizing: Campaigning for Trade Union Recognition*. London: Routledge, 56–78.

Hyman, R. (2001) 'Trade union research and cross-national comparison', *European Journal of Industrial Relations*, 7(2): 203–232.

Korczynski, M. (2002) *Human Resource Management in Service Work*. Basingstoke: Palgrave Macmillan.

Lucas, R. (2009) 'Is low unionization in the British hospitality industry due to industry characteristics?', *International Journal of Hospitality Management*, 28: 42–52.

McCann, R. (1994) 'Shop till you drop', *Refractory Girl*, 47/48: 63–65.

McIlroy, J. (2008) 'Ten years of New Labour: workplace learning, social partnership and union revitalization in Britain', *British Journal of Industrial Relations*, 46(2): 283–313.

Mead, J. (2003) 'The retail revolution', *Business Review Weekly*, 23 January: 54–55.

Mortimer, D. (2001a) 'Trade union and management strategy: a case study of compulsory unionism', *Employment Relations Record*, 1(2): 81–97.

Mortimer, D. (2001b) 'Management employee relations strategy: the case of retailing', *International Employment Relations Review*, 7(1): 81–93.

Office for National Statistics (2009) *Average Earnings Index August–September 2009*. London: ONS.

Oxenbridge, S. (1997) 'Organizing strategies and organizing reform in New Zealand service sector unions', *Labor Studies Journal*, 22: 3–27.

Peetz, D. and Price, R. (2007) 'Profile of the retail and hospitality industries,' report prepared for the Office of the Victorian Workplace Rights Advocate, August.

Peetz, D., Pocock, B. and Houghton, C. (2007) 'Organizers' roles transformed? Australian union organizers and changing union strategies', *Journal of Industrial Relations*, 39(2): 151–167.

Price, R., Bailey, J. and Oliver, D. (2010) 'Managing young workers: the privileged generation?' in G. Strachan, E. French and J. Burgess (eds) *Managing Diversity in Australia: Theory and Practice*. North Ryde (NSW): McGraw-Hill.

Purcell, K. and Purcell, J. (1998) 'In-sourcing, outsourcing and the growth of Contingent labour as evidence of flexible employment strategies', *European Journal of Work and Organizational Psychology*, 7(1): 38–59

Shop, Distributive and Allied Employees' Association (SDA) (2000) 'Annual financial report 30 June 2000', *The Link*, 23(4): 29–36.

Shop, Distributive and Allied Employees' Association (SDA) (2009) 'Annual financial report 30 June 2009', *The Link*, 32(3): 32–43.

Simms, M. and Holgate, J. (2010) 'Organizing for what? Where is the debate on the politics of organizing?', *Work, Employment and Society*, 24(1): 157–168.

▶

▶

Taplin, I. (1990) 'The contradictions of business unionism and the decline of organized labour', *Economic and Industrial Democracy*, 11(2): 249–278.

Teague, P. and Hann, D. (2009) 'Problems with partnership at work: lessons from an Irish case study', *Human Resource Management Journal*, 20(1): 100–114.

Upchurch, M. and Donnelly, E. (1992) 'Membership patterns in USDAW 1980–1990: survival or success?', *Industrial Relations Journal*, 23(1): 60–68.

Union of Shop Distributive and Allied Workers (USDAW) (2009) *About Us*, http://www.usdaw.org.uk/aboutus.aspx (accessed 8 July 2010).

Warhurst, J. (2008) 'The Catholic lobby: structures, policy styles and religious networks', *Australian Journal of Public Administration*, 67(2): 213–230.

Williams, J. (1999) 'Restructuring labor's identity: the justice for janitors campaign in Washington, D.C.', in R. Tillman and M. Cummings (eds) *The Transformation of U.S. Unions*. Boulder (CO): Lynne Reinner Publishers, 203–217.

Endnote: Retail Work – Perceptions and Reality

15

Chris Tilly and Françoise Carré

Most people reading this final chapter will fall into two groups: those who have worked in retail (or similar jobs, such as food service), and those who are glad they never had to do so. At the risk of egregious over-generalization, we would argue that both experiences have helped to feed certain widespread views of retail work. Let us suggest seven such views:

1. Retailers will hire anybody without regard to skill; due to labour supply differences, they end up with large numbers of women and students.
2. Retail jobs involve low skill and little discretion; automation has intensified this.
3. Part-time jobs predominate in retail, further undermining job quality.
4. Career possibilities in retail are minimal.
5. Overall, retail businesses exploit their workers.
6. Unions are weak in the retail sector.
7. These patterns are pretty much the same all over the world.

Do these widely held perceptions of retail jobs match up with reality? The chapters in this volume, along with our own research (much of it carried out with co-authors), suggest that the answer is a resounding 'Yes and no!' In this Endnote, we consider each of these propositions in turn. Subsequently, we offer some observations on the connections between the seven phenomena in question, and – given that chapters cover a variety of countries – raise issues of cross national comparison. We then close with a brief discussion of possible policy responses.

Retailers will hire anybody without regard to skill; due to labour supply differences, they end up with large numbers of women and students

Though managers we have interviewed sometimes laughingly refer to the 'pulse test' (does the candidate have a pulse?) or the 'mirror test' (does his/her breath fog a mirror?), the research presented in this volume by Mary Gatta (looking at the US) and by Dennis Nickson et al. (with a British sample) makes it clear that, at least for some jobs, retailers will *not* hire just anybody. The authors emphasize the centrality of screening based on soft skills, defined quite broadly to include appearance and physical self-presentation and 'aesthetic skills' or cultural capital. Gatta summarizes the process as 'blink' screening, a manager's intuitive evaluation based on a brief interview, and is wary of its likely discriminatory impact. Of course, both chapters focus on fashion-driven retail, especially apparel, where one might expect image to matter more.

There is no question that women and young people (especially students) are overrepresented in retail. We and co-authors Maarten van Klaveren and Dorothea Voss-Dahm have summarized the demographics from the US and five European countries, including the UK (Carré et al., 2010). Gatta's description of being hired as a teen-aged 'Betsy's girl' exemplifies the gender-typing of much retail work, but this in itself does not fully explain the gender mix, since retail also includes stereotypically male jobs (hardware and appliance sales, stock handling). We would argue that indeed, labour supply factors linked to the heavy use of part-time employment are key determinants of retail's employment profile. Notably, women with family responsibilities and students seeking limited work hours staff short part-time shifts. But Steven Roberts, in his chapter, reminds us that retail also employs substantial numbers of young men who are not students, many of whom are part-time but would prefer to be working full-time. These 'lost boys' do not fit tidily with the dominant images of retail workers.

Retail jobs involve low skill and little discretion; automation has intensified this

It's not surprising that a volume growing out of the Labour Process tradition has much to say about skill and worker discretion. And many of the findings conform with the conception of retail jobs as allowing little room for skill development and discretion. As the papers by Gatta and Nickson and company point out, retail employers *screen at the initial hire* for soft skills, including aesthetic skills. Particularly in what Nickson et al. call 'style jobs', they argue that 'middle classness is being recast as a skill.' Similarly, Gatta postulates that her qualifications for being a 'Betsy's girl' consisted of 'being a young, white, middle class woman who was friendly and energetic; would look good in the clothing sold in the boutique; and with whom customers would be comfortable soliciting fashion advice.' These descriptions do not seem to leave much room for skill development – though it is important to bear in mind that the nature of product sold colours the potential degree of skill and autonomy of jobs.

Congruent with the stress on soft skills are accounts of deskilling on the hard skill front. Robin Price describes the relentless squeezing out of virtually all skill and discretion in Australian large-scale food retailing, to the point where 'simple remembering knowledge' is the only knowledge required. Kate Mulholland deconstructs the shift to 'teamworking' at a British supermarket, discovering that the 'team' is an ideological construct, not a framework for worker autonomy or even input. She further finds that the concurrent shift to defining each department as a cost centre responsible for localized profit and loss has *impeded* cross-training by making departments reluctant to let go of staff.

But despite this rather bleak skill landscape, there is a bit more going on. First, there is evidence for learning on the job. Nickson et al.'s Mancunian retailers *hire* for soft skills, but then *train and appraise* workers for both hard and soft skills. The long list of training items employers checked off in Nickson et al.'s survey indicate their belief in the possibility and need for continued learning, including 25 per cent who train on 'makeup and personal grooming' and even 8 per cent providing 'voice and accent coaching'. Perhaps middle classness *can* be taught, Pygmalion-style! Roberts's Kentish 'lost boys' evince a somewhat cynical view of management training processes (and Prue Huddleston, in her contribution, agrees that management-provided training is uneven at best), but nonetheless describe a tacit learning process developed by 'picking it up as you go along, talking to customers' in the case of soft skills, and more formal training in the case of hard skills. Though the degree of learning doubtless differs by sector, Roberts' sample includes supermarkets, the sub-sector in which Price and Mulholland describe pervasive deskilling.

Second, a number of the studies in the volume discover islands of skill and initiative amidst the deskilled landscape. Though Irena Grugulis and co-authors conclude that British supermarket managers retain little discretion, they also find that these managers revel in their limited areas of discretion, such as motivating the workforce and breaking the rules by deviating from mandated store layouts. Similarly, Alan Felstead and company describe a highly automated ordering process, but then note that local managers still have room for discretion and negotiation with the head office. Even in Price's deskilled Australian supermarket, bakers and meat-cutters retain some skill.

Felstead et al. also spotlight an understudied dimension of retail deskilling: the diminution of discretion within *suppliers* in retail-led supply chains. They describe how prepared-sandwich manufacturers under the domination of retailers exercise a highly constrained form of new product development, in contrast with large manufacturers selling to small retailers, in which R&D has much wider ambit.

Finally, evidence summarized in Carré et al. (2010) indicates that Germany diverges significantly from this low-skill model. In Germany, 81 percent of retail employees have completed a retail-specific two- or three-year apprenticeship training, providing a highly skilled workforce at low cost (apprentices work for reduced wages during training). As a consequence, German retailers can base work organization on *vertical* functional flexibility (Voss-Dahm, 2009). In contrast with the horizontal functional flexibility common in the UK and US, in which clerks and shelf-stackers float between various areas of the store including the cash registers, vertical flexibility involves specialization in one type of merchandise, but with the ability to take on any task up to and including ordering and display configuration, the province of managers, supervisors, and a select few full-timers in the Anglo-American countries.

Part-time jobs predominate in retail, further undermining job quality

This volume contains surprisingly little on work schedules. Laura Jordan, in her chapter, does describe how 'Hometown,' a big-box chain in the US Midwest, shifted from a full-time to a part-time workforce, with attendant speed-up of the pace of work. However, her concern is not with the stresses of a part-time schedule, but rather with how the thinning of full-time ranks forecloses career avenues for the workers, a pattern our own field work has also surfaced.

But more broadly, in our work on retail jobs in the US (Carré et al., 2007) and in research comparing the US with European countries (Carré et al., 2010), we and co-authors identify fragmented and unpredictable schedules as a major issue in retail job quality. Accordingly, Maarten van Klaveren and Dorothea Voss-Dahm (our co-authors in the US–European comparison) point out that in Germany and the Netherlands, scheduling software designed to closely match head count with customer flows has intensified such schedule fragmentation and unpredictability. This is a classic case of management-driven technological change reducing workers' control over their jobs, and one might have expected more attention to it among researchers working within the Labour Process tradition. We would add that although the scheduling situation of German and Dutch retail workers is dire, they actually have more collective leverage points over schedules than do their US counterparts. Dutch and German laws and collective bargaining contracts require months of advance notice for schedule changes (a requirement often honoured in the breach, but a lever nonetheless), and European works councils are empowered to negotiate over schedules at the enterprise level. The US has no such mandate.

Career possibilities in retail are minimal

The research compiled here in general agrees with the proposition of very limited retail career possibilities. Moreover, the low pay so prevalent in retail also drives high employee turnover (Ahmed and Wilder, 1995). However, the researchers add texture to this tale of stunted trajectories by exploring how varied groups of workers make sense of their options. Prue Huddleston, in interviews with student retail employees from a single British city, confirms that 'the majority of the young people in this sample had no intention of making a full-time career in this sector.' But of her small sample of eight respondents, a significant subgroup of three were staying on, due to fit with their degree qualification, opportunities to progress and/or lack of alterna-tives. Roberts draws an interesting distinction between the 'blue sky' aspirations of part-time workers in his sample ('I'd like to be spotted by a scout and end up doing music'), and the more grounded plans of full-timers. Roberts's full-timers *do* speak in terms of a career in retail, though in many cases the plan requires leaving the current employer.

Perhaps the most interesting take on retail careers comes from Jordan's analysis of work at Hometown. She describes in arresting detail how jobs at this US chain, which once provided decent pay and career opportunities, have been degraded. Nonetheless, some workers continue to make a career out of these jobs, principally in order to access health insurance, which remains in short supply in US jobs accessible to those with limited educational credentials (though the recently passed health reform, when fully implemented, will increase employer incentives to provide this benefit). However, these *de facto* permanent, career workers *view* themselves as temporary. Jordan shows that this stance is a practical one, reflecting a continuing search for other options, but also an act of psychic self-defence.

In our own case studies of US food and electronics retailers (Carré et al., 2007), we have found that internal labour markets are increasingly being externalized. That is, management jobs that were once filled from within are more and more being filled by external candidates judged on the basis of educational credentials, predominantly management degrees. Nonetheless, particularly in food retail, a surprisingly large share of managers comes from internal promotion, relative to other service sectors. None of the papers in this collection touch on such changes in internal labour markets, and it would be fascinating to learn if this process is emerging in other countries as well.

Overall, retail businesses exploit their workers

Most of the papers in this volume sing a tune of low wages, though Thomas Andersson and colleagues sound a dissonantly positive note by observing that Swedish retail workers are relatively well paid and satisfied with their jobs. The papers that make the most convincing case for exploitation are those that trace how retail jobs have gotten worse over time. Thus, van Klaveren and Voss-Dahm show how price wars and nationally-specific 'exit options' (the short-term 'mini-job' in Germany, the youth sub-minimum wage in the Netherlands) have conspired to drive down pay and other elements of retail job quality. In similar fashion, Jordan describes how cost-cutting tied to escalating price competition turned good jobs into bad ones at her Hometown big-box chain, trapping workers in dead-end jobs. If retailers are driving workers harder and paying them less, that is *prima facie* evidence for exploitation.

But Asaf Darr and Robin Price remind us of the importance of the third person in the retail triangle: the customer (see also Korczynski, 2009). This third party complicates notions of exploitation premised on an employer–worker dyad. Price argues that the restructuring of retail work shifts control to customers, especially at the checkout, where client expectations enforce the pace of work. Darr's study of employee humour at an Israeli electronics store uncovers a strongly held moral expectation that customers will be serious about buying – so that employee jokes lampoon clients who don't conform to this norm. One could also argue that deep discounters have cut labour costs largely in order to pass savings on to customers (and thus to expand market share), meaning that even in a conventional economic sense shoppers may be exploiting retail workers. Interestingly, the young men in Roberts's sample do *not* see deference to customers as incompatible with masculinity; instead, their complaints focus on the Taylorization of checkout work.

Unions are weak in the retail sector

Unions do not crop up much in these descriptions of retail work, which may in itself be an indicator of their weakness. Van Klaveren and Voss-Dahm note the limited degree to which unions have been able to halt the slide of retail job quality in Germany and the Netherlands. The union at Jordan's Hometown chain, likewise, has had little success in defending career jobs, though it has managed to hold onto the key fringe benefit, health insurance.

Janis Bailey and collaborators offer a more thorough look at the principal UK and Australian retail unions, USDAW and SDA respectively. They do not paint a picture of powerful labour organizations, but they do identify some strengths and assets as well as weaknesses. Though these unions conduct few campaigns against retail employers, they do organize in the sense of recruiting members and seeking to extend collective bargaining. USDAW and SDA tend to be partnership oriented rather than confrontational in their relations with employers. They do engage in politics (especially in the case of USDAW's link to the Labour Party), but rarely participate in action coalitions.

However, Sweden is a contrasting case. Andersson et al., do not provide much detail on Swedish retail unions, but they do note that Swedish retail union density is 70 per cent (of non-temporary workers), and that most managers are also unionized. The post-World War II social bargain gave unions considerable strength and a centralized bargaining system, and despite some subsequent loss of union power, a continuing consequence is the wage compression that keeps Swedish retail wages higher relative to other countries. We found parallel outcomes in Denmark, another Nordic country with a muscular unions and centralized bargaining (Carré et al., 2010).

These patterns are pretty much the same all over the world

The Swedish exception (and the Danish one) point out that there *are* significant cross-national differences in retail jobs. Most of this volume limits its attention to an Anglo-American world, with occasional glimpses into retail settings in Germany, the Netherlands, Israel and Sweden. Even within the Anglosphere, however, some differences emerge. Bailey et al. highlight UK–Australian differences – more formal employer–union partnerships and more concerted union political action in the United Kingdom – tied to differences in national labour relations systems. Though Grugulis et al. describe thorough-going deskilling, the British and Australian cases do not show the same kind of sweeping degradation of job conditions as Jordan's Hometown case from the US. Instead, it is van Klaveren and Voss-Dahm's analysis of Germany and the Netherlands that shows similar declines in job quality. Of course, a difficulty in drawing comparative conclusions is that the cases differ widely in terms of retail sub-sector and thematic focus.

Conclusions: Connections, future research, public policy

This far-ranging odyssey through the many dimensions of jobs in commerce teaches us a great deal. In these brief concluding remarks, we seek to draw some connections across the themes we have traversed, suggest useful future directions for labour process research and comment on public policy options to improve retail jobs.

Two main connections cut across the varied themes. One, a fairly self-evident one, is the link between skill and hiring. Retailers' emphasis on soft skills leads to an attempt to screen on these skills at the hiring stage. This implies, more than in many industries, an attempt to 'buy' rather than 'make' these skills. Retailers count on reproductive processes such as the socialization of women to generate the necessary customer service skills. This focus on skills that are financially undervalued in the labour market, in turn, predisposes the industry to a low-wage path. But as we have seen, retail businesses *do* also provide training for both hard and soft skills, and in cases like Germany workers may enter the industry with a far broader and 'harder' set of skills (though due to the mini-job 'exit option', retail jobs in Germany are nonetheless low-paid).

A second, related connection is that part-time employment, low pay, low skill, high employee turnover, and scarce career opportunities are all linked into a self-reinforcing employment regime. Each part of this regime supports the other, so attempts to make an isolated change in one aspect – say, skill or labour turnover – are likely to fail. Jordan makes this point most clearly in her case study of declining job quality. But to some extent most of the chapters in this volume affirm some part or parts of this model. Still, there is a spectrum of variation within this model: drawing on our work with van Klaveren and Voss-Dahm (Carré et al., 2010), we can say that labour turnover is much higher in the US than in major European countries, even after controlling for some of the determinants of turnover, and, as noted above, Germany deviates from the low-skill aspect of the regime though it hews to other aspects. And there are countries that stand outside of this regime altogether: Sweden as described by Andersson et al., Denmark and, as it turns out, France as reported in Carré and co-authors (2010).

Suggestions for future research largely grow out of our discussion thus far. More research on retail work schedules from a labour process perspective would be extremely valuable. Similarly, examination of the implications of schedules for household life and for worker trajectories would be useful. Also, following job transformations along the supply chain, as Felstead and company do, is an important supplement to analyzing the labour process within retail itself. We have only mentioned job satisfaction in passing, as the Andersson et al. chapter is the only one that addresses it explicitly and measures it. But dissatisfaction rings from the employee quotes in many of these chapters, and added research focused on this topic would be quite useful. It would be even more useful to the extent that retail workers' satisfaction is compared to a meaningful reference group; unfortunately Andersson and co-authors do not do so, leaving us to wonder if the satisfied workers in their study reflect the Swedish workforce overall, or whether there is something distinctive about retail workers' cheer.

Two other suggestions point to more ambitious comparisons. One need is for more systematic comparisons across retail sub-sectors and formats. The samples in this volume include electronics retailing, supermarkets, big-box stores (or hypermarkets), clothing stores and heterogeneous retail samples. Our own work comparing food and electronics retailing (Carré et al., 2010, Carré et al., 2007) convinces us that there are important differences across sub-sectors. Fielding cross-sectoral comparative studies will be important in filling out the picture on retail. The other crying need is for more cross-national comparison. Though the chapters straddle a variety of countries, only two of the chapters conduct cross-national comparisons (each for a pair of countries). Absent altogether are the global South, the emerging markets of Central and Eastern Europe, even the rich counties of East Asia, such as Japan and South Korea. Though national case studies have unquestionable value, in a world where international retailers such as Wal-Mart, Carrefour and Tesco increasingly girdle the globe, cross-national comparisons become ever more relevant.

What of policy implications? This volume does not include a great deal of policy discussion. Nonetheless, we want to pick up on two policy themes that do surface in the articles. The first is the question of access to retail jobs, and in particular the better retail jobs. Gatta laments that 'blink' screening is likely to be discriminatory, and Nickson et al.'s comments on 'middle classness' point in the same direction. We and our co-authors (Carré et al., 2010) find that in most of the six countries in our sample, people of colour and immigrants are under-represented in retail jobs, even entry-level ones – though our analysis does not look into the reasons for this under-representation. In earlier work, Tilly and co-author Philip Moss have described discriminatory processes at work in the informal hiring so prevalent in retail (Moss and Tilly, 2001). As Gatta suggests, there are two main ways that public policy could attempt to mitigate such discriminatory impacts. One is to mobilize the public and non-profit training systems to help provide more broadly distributed training in the soft skills for which employers screen. A second is to regulate hiring, through various types of anti-discrimination regulations and monitoring, to push employers away from 'blink' screening. We would add that the development of apprenticeship and credentialing systems (of which the German vocational education programme is an outstanding example) would help.

A second policy theme, and a crucial one, is how to make retail jobs better. Most of the retail jobs described in this volume are bad in the multiple dimensions we described above as a linked regime. Unions can certainly make a difference, but do not necessarily do so, as Bailey et al. and van Klaveren and Voss-Dahm point out. What really seems to make a difference, as Andersson and company indicate, is a full labor relations and employment regulation system that pushes retailers away from a low-wage, low-skill regime. In Sweden, this system is built on high union density, centralized bargaining and efforts by organized labour to compress wage differences. But our own work with van Klaveren and Voss-Dahm (Carré et al., 2010) shows that this is not the only route to better retail jobs. In France, with low union density and little union strength in the retail sector, a high economy-wide minimum wage has 'raised the floor' under employees in retail and other low-paid sectors. If the rich and varied research in this volume can help contribute to new thinking about how to improve retail jobs around the world, that would be a very positive outcome indeed.

REFERENCES

Ahmed, Z.Z. and Wilder, P.S. (1995) 'Productivity in retail miscellaneous shopping goods stores', *Monthly Labor Review*, October.

Carré, F. and Tilly, C. with Holgate, B. (2007) 'The changing world of work in retail trade', report to the Russell Sage Foundation, December, Washington, D.C.

Carré, F., Tilly, C., Van Klaveren, M. and Voss-Dahm, D. (2010) 'Retail jobs in comparative perspective', in J. Gautié and J. Schmitt (eds) *Low-Wage Work in The Wealthy World*. New York: Russell Sage Foundation, 211–268.

Korczynski, M. (2009) 'Understanding the contradictory lived experience of service work: the customer-oriented bureaucracy', in M. Korczynski and C.L. Macdonald (eds) *Service Work: Critical Perspectives*. New York: Routledge, 73–90.

Moss, P. and Tilly, C. (2001) *Stories Employers Tell: Race, Skill, and Hiring in America*. New York: Russell Sage Foundation.

Voss-Dahm, D. (2009) Low-paid but committed to the industry: salespeople in the retail sector', in G. Bosch and C. Weinkopf (eds) *Low Wage Work in Germany*. New York: Russell Sage Foundation, 253–287.

Index

Note: Page numbers followed by "*f*" and "*t*" denote figures and tables, respectively.